Romani Chronicles of COVID-19

New Directions in Romani Studies
Edited by:
Huub van Baar, Leuven University
Angéla Kóczé, Central European University

Romani Studies has emerged as an interdisciplinary field that offers perspectives derived from the humanities and social sciences in the context of state and transnational institutions. One of the series' aims is to remove the stigma surrounding Roma scholarship, to engage with the controversies regarding Roma identity and, in this way, counter anti-Roma racism. This series publishes innovative, critical, and interdisciplinary scholarship, both in monographs and in edited collections. *New Directions in Romani Studies* includes within its scope migration and border studies, ethnicity studies, anthropology, cultural studies, postcolonial and decolonial studies, and gender and queer studies.

Volume 6
ROMANI CHRONICLES OF COVID-19: TESTIMONIES OF HARM AND RESILIENCE
Edited by Paloma Gay y Blasco and Martin Fotta

Volume 5
CONTESTING MORALITIES: ROMA IDENTITIES, STATE AND KINSHIP
Iliana Sarafian

Volume 4
TEXTURES OF BELONGING: SENSES, OBJECTS AND SPACES OF ROMANIAN ROMA
Andreea Racleş

Volume 3
THE ROMA AND THEIR STRUGGLE FOR IDENTITY IN CONTEMPORARY EUROPE
Edited by Huub van Baar and Angéla Kóczé

Volume 2
INWARD LOOKING: THE IMPACT OF MIGRATION ON ROMANIPE FROM THE ROMANI PERSPECTIVE
Aleksandar G. Marinov

Volume 1
ROMA ACTIVISM: REIMAGINING POWER AND KNOWLEDGE
Edited by Sam Beck and Ana Ivasiuc

Romani Chronicles of COVID-19
Testimonies of Harm and Resilience

Edited by
Paloma Gay y Blasco and Martin Fotta

berghahn
NEW YORK · OXFORD
www.berghahnbooks.com

First published in 2023 by
Berghahn Books
www.berghahnbooks.com

© 2023 Paloma Gay y Blasco and the Institute of Ethnology Czech Academy of Sciences

All rights reserved. Except for the quotation of short passages for the purposes of criticism and review, no part of this book may be reproduced in any form or by any means, electronic or mechanical, including photocopying, recording, or any information storage and retrieval system now known or to be invented, without written permission of the publisher.

Library of Congress Cataloging-in-Publication Data

Names: Gay y Blasco, Paloma, editor. | Fotta, Martin, editor.
Title: Romani chronicles of COVID-19 : testimonies of harm and resilience / edited by Paloma Gay y Blasco, and Martin Fotta.
Description: First edition. | New York : Berghahn Books, 2023. | Series: New directions in romani studies; 6 | Includes bibliographical references and index.
Identifiers: LCCN 2023000748 (print) | LCCN 2023000749 (ebook) | ISBN 9781800738911 (hardback) | ISBN 9781800738935 (paperback) | ISBN 9781800738928 (ebook)
Subjects: LCSH: Romanies—Social conditions—21st century. | COVID-19 Pandemic, 2020—Social aspects. | Romanies—Health and hygiene. | Romanies—Medical care.
Classification: LCC DX145 .R66154 2023 (print) | LCC DX145 (ebook) | DDC 305.89149704—dc23/eng/20230411
LC record available at https://lccn.loc.gov/2023000748
LC ebook record available at https://lccn.loc.gov/2023000749

British Library Cataloguing in Publication Data

A catalogue record for this book is available from the British Library

ISBN 978-1-80073-891-1 hardback
ISBN 978-1-80073-893-5 paperback
ISBN 978-1-80073-892-8 ebook

https://doi.org/10.3167/9781800738911

Contents

✻ ✻ ✻

Foreword. Words and Waves — viii
   Iliana Sarafian

Introduction. Chronicles of a Tragedy Foretold — 1
   Paloma Gay y Blasco and Martin Fotta

PART I. SPANISH CHRONICLES

Chapter 1. Introduction to the Spanish Chronicles: From Ordinary Crisis to Pandemic Emergency — 33
   Paloma Gay y Blasco

Chapter 2. Gitana Intercultural Mediators in the Space between Despair and Hope — 44
   Dulce Flores Torres, Pilar García Bizárraga, Estrella Iglesias Pérez, Francisca Mayoral Silva, Manuela Mayoral Silva, Fernanda Montaño García, and Paloma Gay y Blasco

Chapter 3. "Who Cares . . . ? Hunger Will Kill Us If the Virus Does Not": The COVID-19 Pandemic in an Informal Settlement in Madrid — 59
   Beatriz Aragón Martín

Chapter 4. Researching and Mitigating the Impact of Lockdown on Gitano Families in Spain: An NGO Worker Speaks — 69
   María Félix Rodriguez Camacho

Chapter 5. Illness and Death Are So Much Worse When You Are Alone — 77
   Liria Hernández

Chapter 6. "COVID-19 Is a Trial from God": Gitanos, Pentecostal Imaginaries, and Compliance — 80
   Antonio Montañés Jiménez with Gory Carmona

PART II. BRAZILIAN CHRONICLES

Chapter 7. Introduction to the Brazilian Chronicles: How Systemic Racism and Government Neglect Led to Increased Harm Suffered by Vulnerable Groups — 93
 Juliana Miranda Soares Campos, Martin Fotta, Gabriela Marques Gonçalves, and Aline Miklos

Chapter 8. "Get Out of Here!": Discrimination and Prejudice against Ciganos in the Context of the Pandemic — 104
 Igor Shimura

Chapter 9. "Everything Is on Hold": The Pandemic and the Ciganos in Minas Gerais — 110
 Valdinalva Barbosa dos Santos Caldas and Juliana Miranda Soares Campos

Chapter 10. The Creation of the #*OrgulhoRomani* Collective amid the Pandemic — 117
 Gabriela Marques Gonçalves, Aluízio de Azevedo Silva Júnior, and Aline Miklos

Chapter 11. Interlacing Black and Romani Experiences during the Coronavirus Pandemic in Paraíba, Northeast Brazil: A Personal Reflection — 127
 Edilma do Nascimento Souza

Chapter 12. Romanies in Brazil and the Escalation of Necropolitics during the Pandemic — 135
 Aluízio de Azevedo Silva Júnior

PART III. SLOVAK CHRONICLES

Chapter 13. Introduction to the Slovak Chronicles: Indifference, Securitization, and Antigypsyism — 147
 Andrej Belák and Tomáš Hrustič

Chapter 14. Quarantine, Segregation, and Resistance: The Case of Žehra — 159
 Alžbeta "Haľka" Mižigárová

Chapter 15. Coffee and Cigarettes in State Quarantine: Stuck on the Way Home — 165
 Albín Peter and Tomáš Hrustič

Chapter 16. "In Difficult Times We Should Stick Together": Roma Self-Help Initiatives and Awareness Raising Activities as an Immediate Reaction to the Spread of COVID-19 in Early March 2020 — 173
 Tomáš Hrustič

Chapter 17. The Hoaxes and Incorrect Information Related to
COVID-19 Showed a Lack of Trust between the Majority and
the Roma, and a Lack of Knowledge   183
Jurina Rusnáková and Zuzana Kumanová

Chapter 18. Oh, My Antiracist Friends, Where Are You?
A Health Expert's Diary of Hopes and Disappointments Regarding
Pandemic Prevention and Control across Segregated Roma Enclaves   192
Andrej Belák

PART IV. POLISH CHRONICLES

Chapter 19. Introduction to the Polish Chronicles: Digital Kinning
and Care   205
*Kamila Fiałkowska, Michał P. Garapich, Ignacy Jóźwiak,
Elżbieta Mirga-Wójtowicz, Sonia Styrkacz, and Monika Szewczyk*

Chapter 20. Pandemic (Im)Mobilities of Polish Roma   215
Sonia Styrkacz, Michał P. Garapich, and Kamila Fiałkowska

Chapter 21. The Internet and Transnational Polish Roma Families
in a Time of Pandemic   229
Monika Szewczyk, Elżbieta Mirga-Wójtowicz, and Ignacy Jóźwiak

PART V. CZECH CHRONICLES

Chapter 22. Introduction to the Czech Chronicles: Of Loss
and Silence   247
Yasar Abu Ghosh

Chapter 23. The Impact of the Pandemic on Activism and
the Activist: Conversations with Jozef Miker   259
Yasar Abu Ghosh

Chapter 24. Denial of Danger: COVID-19, Disinformation,
and When to Burst Our Bubbles   270
Gwendolyn Albert

Chapter 25. Locked Down in Our Own Personal Quarantine:
How Nothing Can Be Taken for Granted   277
Iveta Kokyová

Concluding Reflections   285
Paloma Gay y Blasco and Martin Fotta

Index   289

Foreword
Words and Waves
Iliana Sarafian

Experience. Feel. Protect. Grieve. Isolate. Speak. Cry. Worry. Need. Survive. Remember. Forget. Hope. These are not mere words. They have multiple meanings and yet fail to fully convey the ebbs and flows, the changing impacts and contradictions of the COVID-19 pandemic. The synoptic power of words is unquestionable, but no single word or book can capture the complexity of the impact of COVID-19 on Romani groups. Thus, and inevitably, this collection of chronicles only skims Romani lifeworlds. Yet in doing so, it also, unpretentiously, opens new ground within Romani studies and beyond in several ways.

With its multiplicity of stories, methods, approaches, voices and accounts of witnessing and knowing, *Romani Chronicles of COVID-19* is a call, a cry even, to pay attention to the suffering, need, survival, hope, and advancement of a people and individuals yet to be understood, heard, seen, and fully acknowledged as part of society. The entanglements of situations, choices made, words uttered, and lives lived captured by this collection underscore a deep, heart-wrenching plea, both of desperation and hope, to see the ocean of inequality concealed and caused by the pandemic waves; to acknowledge Romani potentiality; and to support Romani survival. Indeed, the means of representation and writing employed by the authors are an acknowledgment of the varied and limited forms of articulation, of words we use to voice, to accommodate, to avoid speaking *for* Roma. Instead, this book predicates the idea that "to give voice" is a limiting concept, and its thesis goes beyond the politics of voice—of who writes and who reads. Naturally, the writing style is polyvocal, and not necessarily obscured by theoretical considerations, yet astutely critical.

Historically, Romani experiences of calamities, pain, inequality, discrimination as well as joys, celebration of life and kin, have been written about mostly by non-Roma. What this work does differently is to engage both Roma and non-Roma from various walks of life, working together or individually to present a fairer, more responsible, and reflexive storytelling. What this entails is the presentation of illuminating, persuasive, provoking, and non-reductionist narratives of Roma realities. Given the auspices, spectrum, and reach of the chronicles, they are not merely reflexive exercises but go beyond the politics of authorship. It seems to me this work is about candor and taking care, about reciprocity, friendship, solidarity, and social impact, similar to the propositions of Paloma Gay y Blasco and Liria Hernández.[1] The collection is people-centered, knowledge-situated, and socially responsible.

Candor is a summative key word underlying the stories of this collection. Candor is what we humans owe each other in the face of an inhuman reality, and where historical amnesia has seemingly erased the pain of "before." The pandemic stories narrated here are not the starting point, or written on a clean slate, a *tabula rasa* of sorts. Each of the narrations is drenched in previous painful histories. As it happened, the pandemic did not abolish the past—on the contrary, in the manner of ocean waves, it concealed the past of persecutions, tragedies, and stigma under the sea of assumptions that "we are all in the same boat." The COVID-19 crisis intermeshed with an ocean of past histories, consisting of destructive chronic and acute accumulations of social and viral waves formed together in people's lives to divide and exclude further. These very waves then washed the painful histories ashore, leaving only the debris of precariousness and the yearning for survival. For some, the pandemic has been a rocky boat ride; but for others it has been a shipwreck, beyond repair and beyond life itself. The strain of the pandemic has made the latent structures of societal life even more visible, indeed it has led us to question what we value and whose words matter the most—those of close kin, of governments, of unknown social media actors, or simply the voices within ourselves. In a similar vein, this collection questions the values of society and it is a proponent of the idea that at a time of social upheaval, candor and care for the underprivileged and most affected is of utmost importance for justice and equality.

Running through this collection is the interaction between Roma and the state, with its multiple faces and intangible margins. Jumping from the pages is an intense proclivity of the chroniclers to ask questions about the centers of power. The inference is that the pandemic policies have either been oblivious to social inequality or have been prolifically designed to generical solutions without considering the lived realities of those already predisposed to entrenched poverty and discrimination. The chronicles provide ample examples of the missteps taken by state and regional authorities holding power and fueling social conflict. The cases reflect on the limits of public health interventions while challenging the logic behind large-scale policies designed to simultaneously protect and punish. Therefore, the chroniclers rightly question such oxymoronic approaches and moral calculus to conclude that people's everyday struggles can elude state responses.

As I read the stories of this collection, I am reminded of the contradictions of state responses in my own experience. In the summer of 2020, I happened to be in quarantine with my family in a Bulgarian Roma neighborhood. This, however, was not my individual quarantine; it was a securitized action towards an entire neighborhood of approximately one thousand people, whereby police circulated the exits of the neighborhood, and restricted all forms of movement outside its borders. This restriction happened because the first case of COVID-19 in my hometown was that of a Roma man. As a result, the outrage and resentment towards the local Roma population became palpable. The mayor took to social media and the regional news to address his constituency by distinctly pointing to the Roma as culprits causing havoc in the otherwise peaceful and prosperous town. The contagiousness, it seemed, was not only viral, but it was also moral. The historical regimes of division and public violence came to the surface yet again to scapegoat, to shame, to exclude, to assign responsibility.

At the time I could not make complete sense of the experiences around me, as I was part of the COVID-19 storm happening to the people whom I grew up with. I was enraged by the way my community was treated only to be reminded by my childhood friend that "we have always been powerless," that this was nothing novel for the people in the neighborhood. The local Roma had experienced "territorial stigmatization"[2] long before the onset of the pandemic, and they had dealt with the stigma as and however best they could. Inside the neighborhood, access to food, medication, and employment were a challenge, as most people relied on both formal and informal work outside its borders. Paradoxically, the mundaneness of everyday life continued in the face of the extraordinary shocks of the pandemic. Acts of solidarity abounded. The Roma of my hometown, the subjects of the local authorities' health and protection plans, provided the key to survival solutions themselves. The display of care ranged from exchanges of food, to the sewing and delivery of masks for the protection of the elderly and chronically ill. The state had long withdrawn from protecting the margins, and the local Roma knew this well. In fact, the long histories of division and shaming had made them somewhat immune to the resentment coming with each COVID-19 wave. It was not that people did not care about the public weaponizing of words with each subsequent COVID-19 wave; it was because they focused on their immediate and private survival—to provide for their livelihoods.

These are chronicles of "the inside," of Roma communities and relationships embedded in kin, home, and community—all connections that require the understanding of trust, hope, mutuality, and Roma perceptions of the pandemic and its manifold impacts. The strength and fragility of these "inside" networks compose socioeconomic life; they are the lifeline of existence for many Roma. The texts presented in this collection speak of the inequality and destruction in the air that people breathe, literally and symbolically; of individual and communal ways of expressing grief, fear, frustration, and doubt, as well as love and solidarity. In the face of adversity, the chronicles record the tragedy of people who continue to swim against each COVID-19 wave despite the continuous depletion of resources, livelihoods, and health. Importantly, it is this "inside" that is the crucible of engagement, understanding, voicing, and experiencing Romani lives.

Romani Chronicles of COVID-19 does all this whilst challenging the unilateral, straightjacketed, and universally accepted norms of academic writing. The multiplicity of styles, methods, disciplines, and representations in this work points to the many phases of life, the abundance and the limitations of words to capture the multiple public and private ways of Roma living, coping, and striving. Life as it evolves is represented in every single chronicle as a stage, a step towards a level of understanding of the various meanings and purposes behind the events of the pandemic. Notably, the underpinning idea is not to comprehend and privilege one theoretical way of seeing and interacting with Roma. Instead, the stories laid here provide positions, sometimes at odds with each other, of the tenuous dispositions of life's precariousness, and how these affect the writers' positionality. Moreover, the real-time disruptions caused by COVID-19 transpire through the authors' thinking and writing, varying from singular encounters to cosmological understandings of viral experiences, containment and state biopower. The complex social realities presented ask for innovative analyses that put informants in the center, engaging with the unfixed social worlds and acknowledging the unfinished nature of research. This has relevance for both academic and non-academic circles when they consider and imagine the possibilities of science and methods to come.[3]

The word "chronicles" (derived from the Greek word *chronos* for linear and chronological time) in the book's title suggests that each of the contributions in this collection is complicated and limited by the concept of time and space. Addressing how the ensuing COVID-19 waves have been dealt with in various geographical localities and temporalities provides a different yet ubiquitous overview of the heterogeneity and similarities of Romani lives. Arguably, however, the chronicles are written neither for the purpose of archiving Roma experiences, nor for contributing to Roma histories only. Indeed, I would urge that the individuals and communities captured in these pages are not seen and read only as "chronotopes," as "ready-made and pre-determined,"[4] but as people with a future—as people who may be at odds with the past and the present, yet who still have horizons.

Writing of horizons, *Romani Chronicles of COVID-19* precisely depicts the moments we need to remember to be able to imagine Roma trajectories in the future. The people of the chronicles lose loved ones, relationships, livelihoods; they grieve, suffer, and recover; they hope and fight for normalcy. Nonetheless normalcy, as the editors of this volume insightfully explain in the Introduction, is not about going back to the suffering and inequalities of the past. It is about a future life and well-being yet to materialize; a future seen in the potentialities of Romani children, a breakthrough of social justice through the communal practices of solidarity, and a changed perception of Roma not as victims and needy subjects but as agents of change. Importantly, the chronicles are also there to suggest, to provide lessons to be learnt, and to show that Roma are people like everyone else. They are humans living life and its uniqueness, routineness, and unpredictability. Prosaically, this is the very meaning of the endonym word *Roma*—being human.

Finally, it is the centrality of knowledge and the experiences of Romani people that are fundamental in social and public interventions. The hidden message in the pages of this collection is that in the face of utter disaster, there are little rays of sunshine, of hope, of yearning to be and to live; of a people striving "to become."[5] In a way, beyond the foreshadowing semantics of words and descriptions of pandemic waves, this for me is the most important contribution of *Romani Chronicles of COVID-19*. And so I request the reader to see that between the lines of desperation, disheartening prejudice and stigma also rests the hope for a better future.

Iliana Sarafian is a postdoctoral researcher at the Centre for Public Authority and International Development at the London School of Economics and Political Science, and the author of *Contesting Moralities: Roma Identities, State and Kinship* (Berghahn, 2023). She received her doctoral degree in Social Anthropology from Goldsmiths College, University of London, where her studies focused on the reproduction of social inequalities among Bulgarian Roma in gender, kinship, and state relationships. She is currently conducting research on minority and migrant health and well-being in Italy and the United Kingdom.

Notes

1. Gay y Blasco and Hernández, *Writing Friendship*.
2. Wacquant, "Territorial Stigmatization."
3. Pandian, *A Possible Anthropology*.
4. Bakhtin, *The Dialogic Imagination*.
5. Biehl and Locke, *Unfinished*.

Bibliography

Bakhtin, Mikhail M. *The Dialogic Imagination: Four Essays*. Austin: University of Texas Press, 1981.

Biehl, João, and Peter Locke (eds). *Unfinished: The Anthropology of Becoming*. Durham, NC: Duke University Press, 2017.

Gay y Blasco, Paloma, and Liria Hernández. *Writing Friendship: A Reciprocal Ethnography*. Cham: Palgrave Macmillan, 2020.

Pandian, Anand. *A Possible Anthropology: Methods for Uneasy Times*. Durham, NC: Duke University Press, 2019.

Sarafian, Iliana. *Contesting Moralities: Roma Identities, State and Kinship*. Oxford: Berghahn, 2023.

Wacquant, Loïc. "Territorial Stigmatization in the Age of Advanced Marginality." In *Symbolic Power in Cultural Contexts*, ed. Jarmo Houtsonen and Ari Antikainen, 43–52. Leiden: Brill, 2008.

INTRODUCTION

CHRONICLES OF A TRAGEDY FORETOLD

Paloma Gay y Blasco and Martin Fotta

Under COVID I have noticed a horrible neglect of these people in this neighborhood. This neighborhood is excluded from society, it is always under lockdown because it is isolated; even in normal times, if you don't have a car, there is no way to get in or out. Ambulances don't go in, or firefighters—nothing. And to this situation of isolation in which they always live, now is added the experience of the pandemic, lockdown, fear, dread, ignorance. *If I get sick, what will happen to my dear ones? How can my family support themselves?*

They called me with anguish, with fear, fears, crying, *I can't, I don't have anything in the fridge, I don't have food*. Because in normal times, you go calling for scrap, you go to sell some socks, you make ends meet as we say, and you bring the daily bread to your house. But all this was no longer possible during lockdown. They reach such desperation that, as they don't have enough, within families they blame each other.

—Dulce Flores Torres, Chapter 2, this volume

This book brings together the voices of thirty-seven chroniclers who narrate the ongoing impact of the first year of the COVID-19 pandemic on Romanies in five countries: Spain, Brazil, Slovakia, Poland, and Czechia. Twenty-four of these chroniclers are Romani, and thirteen non-Romani, and they speak from a wide diversity of positions: as affected individuals, NGO workers, health practitioners, policy makers, community mediators, activists and academics living and working among or alongside Romani communities. Often, they occupy more than one of these roles at once. Out of this multiplicity of voices emerges the conversational character of this book, with each chronicler addressing each other and the readers in ways that foreground their individual story, experience, and perspective. Whilst the chroniclers from Brazil, Poland, Spain, and Slovakia write primarily about the spring and summer of 2020 (now commonly referred to as the first wave), the Czech contributors tend to focus on the winter of 2020/21 (the second wave).

The project emerged in April 2020, when it became obvious to us that the incipient pandemic was already having devastating effects on Romani groups in many countries, and that, because of their extreme marginalization and historical demonization, these effects risked being disregarded by decision makers. While in the first months there was a glut of online activity by pro-Romani actors, with webinars, newspaper articles and reports on the impact of the pandemic appearing almost daily, during the second half of 2020 their number decreased significantly. To start with, we shared the same sense of urgency and hoped to publish these chronicles rapidly, possibly even within 2020. But bringing such a complex project together took much longer than we anticipated, and we came to appreciate that the slowness of traditional academic publishing can be a boon.

As the pandemic went on, the book became a task of testimony, not just to the initial shock and confusion, but also to how individuals, families and communities have been affected by consecutive waves and lulls, and by successive governmental directives. Whilst working on the book, we have seen policies emerge and harden into established practices and infrastructure (relating to public health, security, borders, data), as well as into taken-for-granted worldviews and dispositions (to do with threat, bodies, citizenship, choice). The chroniclers evidence how, as a result of these processes, the vulnerability of Romani communities has increased in ways that will shape Romani lives for many years to come. This book documents and analyses this increase, and so labors against its normalization.

From the start, we conceived the book as a vehicle for witnessing as well as analysis, reflection, and debate. Chronicles are firsthand accounts, and chroniclers are witnesses who document what happens around them. Chronicles are written from within the entanglements of life, not from outside. Unlike ethnographers or journalists, for whom participation is a choice, a strategy to make observation possible, chroniclers are enmeshed in the situations they describe, and they cannot but take part. They are guides who take the reader down the singular paths that they necessarily traverse in their everyday lives. Chroniclers record those details of existence that impose themselves forcefully, that cannot be shrugged off or avoided. Their authority and strength come not from neutrality or detachment but from involvement, partiality, and experience. We value them precisely because they are individual, situated, and partisan.[1] It is important to emphasize that the chroniclers present contrasting viewpoints on policy, practice and public discussion. They engage in debates around the pandemic with each other, but also with actors outside this volume. These debates overflow the boundaries of this book, and in fact, as editors, we sometimes cannot grasp their nuances or implications fully.

It is from within the crisis that these *Romani Chronicles of COVID-19* explore the interplay between the one-off, concrete and singular, on the one hand, and the larger dynamics that give it shape, on the other. The chroniclers address questions of crucial social and scholarly relevance: How is the enormity of the global pandemic crystallizing within Romani communities at local level? And how is it unfolding individually, within the singularity of changing and diverse Romani lives? How has the crisis intersected with pre-existing inequalities, health disparities and antigypsyism? And what new inequalities and forms of marginalization is the pandemic seeding? What do the different ways in which Romani individuals are living the pandemic tell us about the nature of oppression and exclusion in the contemporary world, and about how they are and could be challenged? Finally, what does the post-pandemic future look like for Romanies?

In the *Chronicles*, these multiple levels and arenas are important. The focus on the crisis—unprecedented, traumatic, demanding immediate attention—does not distract us from the long-term, routinary, ongoing inequalities and power disparities. Crucially, the personal is not erased or subordinated to the general, and individuals and their stories are never just examples or illustrations of wider trends. In fact, by foregrounding such diverse ways of being and knowing, we hope that the *Chronicles* will help challenge the stereotyping, homogenizing depictions of Romanies under which Romani individuals labor.

We take as our starting point the awareness that experience can be at once forceful and elusive, that it cannot always be adequately captured or analyzed, and that academic concepts and approaches are not always adequate or sufficient for this task. This is why we have encouraged the chroniclers to write in a plurality of styles and registers: you will find memoir, fiction, and diary extracts alongside single- and multi-authored scholarly accounts. This diversity is important: it has enabled authors to convey their complex knowledge, identities, and experiences in nuanced ways; and it reveals the critical and analytical strength of ways of knowing that are often disregarded as non-academic, non-analytical, or non-rigorous. This diversity also reflects the distinctive position that each chronicler, whether Romani or non-Romani, occupies vis-à-vis the Romani communities they write about—as family member, activist, or engaged professional. These different ways of knowing and writing are offered as contrasting avenues through which to approach the multifaceted and shifting realities of the pandemic. Gathering these voices and outputs in one single volume makes it evident that academia, still very much the preserve of non-Romani scholars such as the two of us, provides one set of questions and methods whose role and value need to be contextualized and evidenced.

Although all the contributors are witnesses in one way or another, their witnessing is far from uniform or monolithic. Some contributors write about their daily lives during the pandemic, often looking back on harrowing experiences and events. Other writers, particularly professionals and activists who have been attempting to ameliorate the impact of the crisis on local communities, blend descriptions of personal experience with different kinds of critical social analysis. For instance, the team who have written the Polish chronicles, have taken a similar approach. Lastly, there are academic contributors, such as the two of us, whose role has primarily been that of facilitators, coordinators, editors, and analysts. If we are witnesses at all, it is to the hardships of others.

Each contributor occupies a different position vis-à-vis the multiple frameworks of hierarchy and inequality that shape Romani lives, and these positions are foregrounded in the chronicles. For many of our authors, official indifference, racism, deprivation, structural violence, necropolitics and slow harm are not just concepts but immediate, embodied, relentless experiences. By contrast, the two of us are non-Romani academics who have spent the last two years far away from our field sites in Brazil and Spain. Throughout our careers we have attempted to bring to light the mechanisms through which our Romani interlocutors build meaningful lives in the context of continued social marginalization. Increasingly, we are becoming aware of some of the ways in which our work itself may strengthen the very inequalities that we hope to uncover. While we value university-based research for the space and time it allows us to learn deeply, through prolonged listening, documentation, and analysis, we believe that these resources should help facilitate social transformation.[2] On the one hand, the material infrastructure of academia has enabled us to steer the common effort of chronicling in this book. On the other hand, we cannot ignore the fact that, want it or not, we risk being complicit in the reproduction of Romani disempowerment. As middle-class, non-Romani editors of a book about the impact of the pandemic on Romani communities, we know that our task now is to help facilitate the inclusion of as wide a variety of critical Romani voices as possible into academic and public debate.

We hope that this book, in which we have gathered texts by people from many walks of life—not just intellectuals or those with formal education—, will stimulate discussion about the kinds of voices that academia should open to, and about how best to achieve this opening in practice. Romani-related scholarship, most visibly through the work loosely described as "critical Romani studies," has witnessed a growing demand to decolonize academic knowledge. Our aim is to help create arenas where traditionally marginalized speakers will be listened to attentively. This is always urgent, but particularly so at a time of global upheaval. It is also, at its core, a practical process that involves working with authors, publishers, and audiences to shift taken-for-granted understandings of what a text of academic value should look like.

So, whilst in content this book deals with COVID-19, in approach and form it raises questions about how knowledge about Romani lives is and can be produced and deployed, and about the future of research on Romani issues. Key concerns underlying this book are: Who benefits from this kind of volume, written as it is in English? What do we hope to achieve with this work? Who are our audiences? Once again, the responses of the chroniclers are not monolithic, and each writer addresses these questions differently in their texts.

Lastly, we are very aware of the effects of time on our work. When we started planning and writing this book, back in the spring of 2020, it seemed to us that the pandemic would soon be over. Our book proposals were all written in the past tense: we took it for granted that, by the time of publication, COVID-19 would be a thing of the past. In fact, almost two years on, the effects of the pandemic continue to proliferate. These *Romani Chronicles of COVID-19*, then, are presented also as a historical document, a glimpse of a moment in the constantly evolving production of knowledge. If anything has become obvious to us working on this book it is that, as scholars and as humans too, we only ever really know provisionally. Individually and as a collection, the chronicles make this provisionality visible.

This book thus offers to the shifting field of research on Romani issues, and to the growing field of research on COVID-19, the proposal of chronicles as method. Chronicles as we conceive them, in the plural, are multiple, positioned, and partisan. They are collaborative and conversational, yet also singular and irreducible. They are timely but also time bound. In the pages of this book, readers will find examples of collaborative recording, writing, editing, debating, and co-theorizing, developed jointly by contributors with contrasting competences and backgrounds. Many of the contributions strive the boundary between the testimonial and the analytic, and between the personal and the deliberately detached. They demonstrate that authors with widely diverse skills can address scholarly audiences and, crucially, choose the terms on which to do so.

Segregation, Containment, and Control

Folk antigypsyism is characteristic for its focus on the body: Romani bodies are commonly viewed as dirty, smelly, unruly, diseased, and contaminating, indexing the environment to which they are assumed to belong. This has justified, for example, the ongoing segregation of Gitano children in special schools and classrooms in Spain,[3] and of Romani women in the maternity wards of some hospitals in Slovakia.[4] The history of modern European antigypsyism is also a history of continued isolation, exclusion, and confinement of Romanies within specific places—slums, state-built ghettos, designated rural settlements, *mahalas*, orphanages, special schools—often through deliberate planning and forceful relocation.[5] These spaces are consistently presented by planners and policy makers as exceptional and temporary, and they are frequently refused the same services and legal standing as comparable neighborhoods and institutions. They are often sites of punitive intervention, and they confirm in the popular imagination the status of the Romanies who live there—and by extension, all Romanies—as outsiders and non-citizens who must eventually disappear.

These places are imagined as best for "them," the abject, who have been evicted from other locales or are seen as inherently incapable of adapting to societal norms. They are also feared as spaces of resistance to the social order, areas from which contamination, deprivation and anomie will spread. Alongside the Romani people who occupy them, they are conceptualized as stickily delinquent and transgressive. Although described as provisional, like other marginal spaces such as inner-city ghettoes or refugee camps, they have become a permanent and constitutive feature of our societies.[6] These spaces point us to the pre-existing geographies of racialization that have directed the course of the pandemic and exacerbated its effects.[7]

Under COVID-19, long-established forms of punitive containment of Romanies across areas as diverse as housing, health management, education, and employment have combined with new measures aimed at controlling the virus, some targeted at the whole of society but others at Romani groups specifically. Even before European states started to impose lockdown measures during the spring of 2020, in many areas Romanies as a collective were singled out as potential vectors of infection.[8] There, public authorities resorted to the policing of Romani neighborhoods, arguing the need to protect the health and safety of all citizens from Romani irresponsibility: checkpoints were established around Romani neighborhoods, camps were quarantined or cordoned off to prevent the spread of the virus, and nomadic groups were expelled or not allowed to stop. In March 2020 in the north of Spain, for example, the regional government dispatched the militarized police to the town of Haro, arguing that Gitanos who had contracted COVID-19 might not respect the compulsory quarantine. Towards the end of the same month, Bulgarian mayors contained tens of thousands of Roma in urban neighborhoods, imposing police controls of access and exit, as well as bans on group gatherings, even though no cases of infection had yet been reported.⁹ Whilst these actions were not universal, and not all Romanies across the five countries in this book experienced them directly, similar steps were not taken against non-Romani groups. It is through these processes—often small-scale and local—that the distinctiveness of Romanies as racialized, disruptive collectives is routinely produced, even during such an exceptional and globalized event as the COVID-19 pandemic. And, as chroniclers Jurina Rusnáková and Zuzana Kumanová explain, these processes harden and perpetuate interethnic distrust and fear.

These actions were neither accidental nor isolated: they emerged from widespread antigypsyist assumptions and reveal taken-for-granted forms of everyday harm. In the spring of 2020, fake news, hoaxes, and false accusations proliferated on social media, framing Romanies as responsible for spreading the virus or suggesting that they refused to follow guidelines that should apply to all. It was often asserted that Romanies were inherently asocial and inadaptable, and so had to be forcefully controlled or, better still, expelled. Entrenched stereotypes depicting Romanies as unable to self-regulate were once again deployed to argue their unfitness for citizenship. Meanwhile, mainstream media offered analyses of how Romani "culture," poor living conditions or movement patterns (for example, as migrants within the European Union) would make it impossible for them to follow social distancing guidelines or would increase the likelihood that they would import the virus from abroad, implicitly or explicitly justifying securitization and scapegoating.[10]

Crucially, throughout the pandemic it has been Romanies' assumed inability to behave properly *as a group* that has been stressed—particularly but not only by the right-wing media. Whereas non-Romanies who crowd parks and beaches or who attend clandestine parties are portrayed as selfish individualists, Romanies have been described as collectively primitive or animal-like, "non-human,"[11] and therefore as collectively threatening. When the Spanish broadsheet *ABC* reported that Gitano Evangelicals had gathered to pray in the streets of one of the poorest neighborhoods of Seville, it also characterized them as belonging to "unstructured clans unused to public order and discipline," and described their songs as "healing chants."[12] Without naming Romanies directly, but singling them out in terms familiar to his audience, one Romanian mayor referred to "a group of people with kinship ties" who neglected the rules by organizing "kinship gatherings"— with kinship marking Romani "culture" and standing in for antisocial gregariousness.[13] Similarly, media reports claimed that nomadic Ciganos, being led from Spain into Portugal by a police escort, had not known about the pandemic because they did not have phones or computers—that is, because they were backward and primitive, existing outside of time.

Portrayed as an anonymous, undifferentiated, threatening mass "living outside the rule of law,"[14] Romanies are denied the individuality that is considered the hallmark of modernity—even when this individuality is depicted as dysfunctional as under COVID-19. Instead, their "culture," "traditional behaviors" and "customs" are foregrounded as potential relay points for infection, with these terms used to refer to supposed shared, unchanging, Romani-specific behaviors such as nomadism, overintensive sociability, or lack of personal hygiene. And, as was already common before the pandemic, under COVID-19 these depictions of Romanies as a threat to others have intertwined in complex ways with narratives and actions that emphasize their vulnerabilities and their need for additional protection.

Official discourse frequently recognized the likelihood that the pandemic would have a disproportionate impact on Romani groups—whether because of their poorer health, poverty and overcrowding, their cultural specificities, or their assumed reluctance to adhere to emergency regulations. As a consequence, during the pandemic as before, care and restraint have gone hand in hand. Disciplinary measures aimed at Romanies were presented as benevolent and as emerging from the protective actions taken by state authorities.

These coercive dimensions of state care are discussed in particularly revealing ways by the Slovak chroniclers: they scrutinize the decision taken by the Slovak authorities in March 2020 to forcefully quarantine five Roma settlements before any other lockdown measures were established, and to test their inhabitants for COVID-19. This was justified by arguing that COVID-19 would decimate Romani communities, whose health was considerably poorer than that of non-Romanies, and also that Romanies would act as vectors of contagion into the wider society, overwhelming the fragile local healthcare system. The Slovak contributors—some of whom were themselves involved in the design and implementation of this policy—unpack the various strands of debate around this action and its outcomes. Reflecting with candor on their own complex positions, these chroniclers demonstrate how state interventions regarding Romanies are often molded by paternalism, racism, and bureaucratic indifference.

Gypsyness and Its Effects

The belief that during the pandemic Romanies will resist shared standards of adequate behavior goes hand in hand with a second entrenched expectation: that they will unavoidably and naturally suffer and die more, just as they do in non-pandemic times. Because policy makers, state representatives at all levels, and the media often approach Romanies through the master symbol of "Gypsyness"—as disorderly, primitive, willfully transgressive—Romani suffering is often constructed as unfortunate but predictable, rather than as intolerable and avoidable. Whilst factors such as poverty, antigypsyism, and underemployment appear in popular and governmental narratives as likely to increase the vulnerability of Romanies to COVID-19, it is also generally accepted and expected that Romanies will inevitably be poor and underemployed, that their lives are simply more vulnerable and precarious, and that this is bound to become more visible during this most globalized and unprecedented crisis.[15] Structural inequalities are then downplayed because, so the story often goes, Romanies are ultimately responsible for their own predicament. As Beatriz Aragón Martín explains for the Gitano families who live in the slum of Cañada Real in Madrid, "it is as if living in an informal settlement was the Gitanos' cultural choice," their preference.

The chroniclers describe how, in the context of the pandemic in the five countries studied, Romanies struggle under the impact of ideologies that naturalize their marginality. The trope of Gypsyness legitimates the punitive treatment of Romanies across multiple arenas, from routine and apparently unremarkable encounters—such as at a Madrid hospital in Dulce Flores Torres' piece—to exceptional events, like the quarantining of Romani settlements in the Slovak chronicles. Through visceral accounts of firsthand experience, the chroniclers challenge abstract proclamations of the universal and extraordinary character of the pandemic, which asserted that "we are all in it together", that "the virus doesn't discriminate" and that "this is an unprecedented crisis." Instead, the contributors reveal how the pandemic has generated a magnification of ongoing Romani experiences of marginalization, separation, and slow harm.

In the eyes of non-Romanies, the arrival of COVID-19 was remarkable precisely because it was unprecedented; it was unlike anything they had ever experienced before. People struggled to find words and frameworks of comparison, and spoke of sci-fi films and dystopic novels to convey their disorientation. For Romanies, on the other hand, the novelty was entangled with an awareness of earlier harms, with a deeply embodied history of harassment and tribulation. The collective remembrance of past events, and the resulting distrust towards state actions, give meaning to the present crisis. So Jurina Rusnáková and Zuzana Kumanová explain how rumors spread among Slovak Romanies that a planned quarantine center at a military airport would serve as a concentration camp, and that the large-scale testing of Romani communities for COVID-19 in Slovakia was in fact a hidden attempt at experimenting on Roma. We argue that these interpretations were not misguided or ignorant, but perceptive, experience-driven commentaries on the relationship between Romanies and the state, and between Romanies and the dominant society.

In the five countries discussed in this book, Romanies have been expected to comply with the very measures that proclaim their incapacity to behave as responsible citizens, or indeed as proper humans. In places such as Žehra in Slovakia and Cañada Real in Spain, Romanies were asked to accept and cooperate with the additional invigilation and testing for their own good and that of others, understanding that this differential treatment was for the benefit of society as a whole. As captured by Tomáš Hrustič, this has demanded very specific kinds of labor from Romani professionals. He explains how, when police and the army were called upon to prevent the spread of the virus in Slovakia by enforcing social distancing measures, Roma community health workers and social fieldworkers prevented the escalation of tensions between the inhabitants of the segregated settlements and the police.

Romani segregated neighborhoods, settlements, and slums across Europe are most often the result of evictions or relocations from areas considered to be more civilized—materializing expulsion and reminding Romanies that they are not welcome elsewhere. It is therefore not surprising that, as the chroniclers document, their inhabitants sometimes experience state biomedical policies as dangerous and punitive, even when they are presented as caring and protective. Those subjected to these policies see through these claims, apprehending the measures as indifferent to their needs and even threatening to their individual and family lives. For Brazil, Aluízio Silva Júnior is adamant: the mismanagement of the pandemic by the Bolsonaro government, which has put Ciganos and other ethnic minoriities in Brazil disproportionately into harm's way, "does not represent the appearance of some accidental event, but instead [is] an uninterrupted continuation of power relations that have existed since colonial times."

At an individual, subjective level, this intertwining of past and present harm involves the routinary awareness that distrust will most likely frame one's behavior: time and again the Romani chroniclers describe having to anticipate the effects of prejudice. Tellingly, many contributors to this book have felt the need to stress that Romanies have indeed complied with pandemic rules, that they have behaved as responsible citizens. "The Romani population endured the lockdown like the rest of society," states Manuela Mayoral Silva in her contribution, but adds "I would say maybe with even more fear and more caution." Her statement is a complex affirmation of belonging and a rejection of widespread racist suggestions of Romani incompetence and disregard for their own and others' health. Likewise Gory Carmona, writing with Antonio Montañés Jiménez, emphasizes that "contrary to what people think, Gitanos take great care and try not to catch COVID." And he goes on to point out how "almost no Gitano family" celebrated on 31 December 2020, but that in a bar next to his house "dozens of Payos (non-Gitanos) celebrated the new year by drinking alcohol, and they were not wearing masks." These statements have a double edge: by asserting Romani compliance, these chroniclers object to antigypsyism but help reinforce the notion that to be a citizen one should not behave as a "Gypsy," and in so doing, they put their own behavior under additional scrutiny.

Like Manuela and Gory, other chroniclers strive to claim a space for Romanies within the nation-state as proactive, responsible, and responsive citizens on a par with others. Yet they also describe a multitude of catch-22 situations whereby their attempts at compliance with citizenship ideals have simultaneously worked to reinforce their marginality. As Dulce Flores Torres reveals in her account of her repeated attempts to get schools to send learning materials to Gitano children during lockdown, Romani lives are shadowed by the specter of Gypsyness with state representatives at all levels acting on the basis that Romanies will simply suffer more, and that this suffering is unpreventable because Romanies will unavoidably behave as "Gypsies." During the crisis, just as before, the majority have "known" that Romanies are bound to fail and have expected nothing less: after all, knowledge is not only a question of discipline but of desire.[16] The result is the perceived need for containment and control both in one-to-one encounters—for example, between social workers and Romani mothers struggling to feed their families—and at larger scales—as with the enclosing of Romani areas even before infections were confirmed. The *Chronicles* evidence that, for Romanies, this interplay between compliance and exclusion unfolds as recurring, deeply felt, embodied experiences of individual and collective trauma. In the context of generalized vulnerability and fear created by COVID-19, these experiences gain additional force.

Violence and Vulnerability

For the Romani people whose lives are discussed in the *Chronicles*, there is no pandemic without the experience of pre-existing routinised crisis—an experience that the contributors document with care. Whilst shared in many aspects, this experience is molded also by specific national and transnational trajectories. In Brazil, for example, Romanies are inserted into a long history of colonial oppression of Indigenous and racialized minorities. As the Brazilian chroniclers emphasize in their joint introduction, analyzing the unfolding of the pandemic among Brazilian Romanies demands that we examine the proliferation of unashamedly explicit state violence against minorities under Bolsonaro. They draw on Achille Mbembe's concept of necropolitics[17] to demonstrate that the relationship between Romanies and the Brazilian state is not just one of punitive regulation à la Foucault, but one of deliberate (or deliberately neglectful) exposure to death, with the state dictating through action and inaction which groups deserve to live and which must die under the pandemic.

In the Spanish chronicles, on the other hand, the emphasis lies on the effects of austerity policies in the wake of the 2008 financial crisis. By the time the pandemic erupted in early 2020, Spanish Romanies had been battered by twelve years of relentless cuts to all kinds of essential services, affecting in particular the working classes and the urban poor. At the core of the Spanish chronicles is the statement by UN Special Rapporteur Philip Alston, issued in February 2020 just before the outbreak, that an entrenched "lack of urgency and resignation"[18] directed the responses of state representatives to the deep crisis that already engulfed the Gitano community. As the chroniclers describe, this lack of urgency has been magnified under COVID-19 by the expectation that, during the pandemic, services and support will unavoidably be reduced or stopped. We read the acceptance that Romanies will suffer and even die more than non-Romanies—for example, because they are unable to earn the most basic living under lockdown—as complicit. As the people of Cañada Real told Beatriz Aragón Martín, "If the virus doesn't kill us, hunger will." Just like the Brazilian chroniclers, the inhabitants of Cañada know that by forcing poor people, including Romanies, to choose between hunger or infection in the name of protecting society at large, state representatives decide who should pay for the pandemic.

The chroniclers identify a key problem in documenting these processes in all the countries covered in the book: the normalized, taken-for-granted character of structural harm, and the effects of its invisibility on the course of the pandemic. Debates around data and its uses are particularly relevant here. It may seem obvious that numerical information about the impact of the pandemic on Romani communities is a basic precondition for an objective assessment, yet legislation in many countries prohibits the collection of ethnically disaggregated data.[19] This absence is interpreted differently by different chroniclers. Edilma Souza, speaking from her position as a Black Brazilian anthropologist working with Romanies, emphasizes how important it is to acknowledge that the pandemic does not affect all groups in the same way. She calls for statistics to be disaggregated according to race/ethnicity as a first step towards the development of much-needed targeted protective measures for ethnic minorities. By contrast, in Slovakia, where policies aimed at shielding the segregated Romani settlements were put in place at the start of the crisis, Romani activists worried that the collection of ethnic data and the development of targeted measures would unavoidably be shaped by and lead to stigmatization. Andrej Belák, who was involved in the planning and implementation of these policies throughout 2020 and 2021, describes his growing unease as he saw measures such as community quarantines and tests come to be permeated by institutional racism, bureaucratic inertia, and populism.

As chroniclers rather than statisticians, the authors in this book provide qualitative, ethnographic, and deeply personal accounts. They unpack the meanings and effects of pandemic vulnerability, and demonstrate that it is not equally distributed. Their accounts of pre-pandemic life evidence that the environments in which Romanies subsisted before February 2020 were not conducive to the flourishing of individuals or communities, and that Romani vulnerability was bound to be exacerbated by the pandemic, and in turn to exacerbate its effects. Their descriptions can be read through the lens of social science concepts such as "structural violence,"[20] "necropolitics,"[21] "slow death,"[22] "structural vulnerability,"[23] or even "syndemics,"[24] as in Yasar Abu Ghosh's text. Yet their chronicles also ask us to step beyond these theoretical frameworks and to confront the irreducible texture of singular encounters and individual lives.

Acts and Spaces of Care

The contributors document the complex understandings about affect and responsibility that have guided the actions of Romani individuals and groups as they have attempted to avoid the virus, support themselves and others, and make ends meet. They reveal acts and spaces of care—some well-established, others new or improvised, which have often been disregarded by the non-Romani majority, treated as irrelevant or misguided. So, for example, in Spain in March 2020, Gitano Evangelical leaders, keenly aware of the health and economic vulnerability of their congregants, ordered all churches to close their doors several days before the government prohibited large gatherings. Across Brazil throughout the first months of the pandemic, nomadic Calon Romanies abandoned larger towns and began avoiding urban centers. They moved into the interior, fearing variously contagion, the crumbling healthcare infrastructure, and limited possibilities for economic survival after street commerce had been shut down. "This is no time for us to be far from our people, from our family," Maria José "Zeza" Silva told chronicler Edilma Souza as the latter was trying to make her way across Brazil, still at the beginning of the tragedy that would engulf the country in the months to come. Meanwhile, Polish and Slovak Roma living in the UK undertook complex journeys to return to their countries of origin.

Seeing that social distancing and mask wearing were being adopted earlier at home than in Britain, a Polish Roma man summarized for Sonia Styrkacz, Michał Garapich and Kamila Fiałkowska the skepticism that many in his community felt about Boris Johnson's policies: "Half of the people are going to die here." As these chroniclers argue, this distrust was magnified by the uncertainties surrounding Brexit, and it propelled many Central and East European Roma to abandon the UK. One of these returnees was chronicler Albín Peter, who drove together with his extended family across Europe in March 2020, and who recorded in his diary the journey and days spent in a state quarantine facility upon arrival in Slovakia. He narrates the good humor, ingenuity, and resilience with which relatives cared for each other through weeks of uncertainty and powerlessness.

Across the five countries, extended families have been the center of the response to the crisis, with relatives attempting to help each other emotionally, practically, and economically. The strong reliance on the support of kin was already essential to Romani survival and mutual protection before the pandemic, as a response to generalized marginalization and to institutional strategies of indifference and deliberate harm. As Liria Hernández explains, "We are taught to be together as much as possible, and above all to support each other with our presence when there is some misfortune." Coming together to care for the sick and their families, she says, takes precedence "above any problem, any difficulty; even jobs are abandoned if necessary, even if that means that no money will come into the house that day, or that the family will have serious financial difficulties."

The chroniclers describe two key processes shaping family and community bonds during the pandemic. On the one hand, they identify an intensification of caregiving, an active reinforcing of kinship attachments, and they interpret it as a continuation of pre-pandemic efforts to make a good life for oneself with others amidst adverse circumstances.[25] The Polish chroniclers in particular document the inventiveness and ingenuity with which Roma migrants, dispersed across Europe, have used social media to share information about the pandemic, reassure each other, and reinforce shared expectations of individual and collective behavior around Romanipen, the Romani way. The physical separation first caused by migration and then by the pandemic has been a challenge to the intensive endosociability that is essential to Polish Roma life. Yet it has also been a motor for the intensification of care and the renewal of waning ties. Monika Szewczyk, Elżbieta Mirga-Wójtowicz, and Ignacy Jóźwiak speak about the "digitalization of everyday life," and describe their Romani interlocutors as "pioneers in digital kinning." Social media has provided Polish Roma with a safe arena where they can strengthen their kinship ties, use their own language, and preserve and transform traditions. These chroniclers interpret social media as an opportunity for self-creation, at individual and collective levels, in the midst of the tremendous challenges for everyday survival posed by the pandemic.

On the other hand, the centrality of kinship bonds to Romani survival, both individual and communal, means that the impossibility of physically coming together to care for each other has created enormous practical difficulties and emotional anguish. Liria Hernández, who was very ill as a result of COVID-19 throughout 2020, explains that "what hurt me the most was not that I was alone and sick, but that in the midst of the pandemic I could not accompany my relatives in their illnesses and needs... This virus stole this right from us, which is our law." For Liria this was an onslaught on ties of love and also on the essence of Gitano life, family unity, and on her sense of herself as a Gitana woman.

Like not being able physically to care for each other, not being able to mourn together has been lived as an assault on the essential link between persons and their communities. For Romanies across the five countries, accompanying the dying and mourning jointly confirms the continuation of shared life in the context of dispersal among a hostile majority. Elaborate mourning rituals embed a person within their family and community, enabling their continuation and reconstruction in the face of adversity. Thus, while across the world countless people have been unable to mourn properly and bury their dead, this inability has been felt in very specific ways by Romanies. For them, the dismantling of social relations generated by the biopolitics of pandemic management carried a very real threat to both individual and collective survival. It was lived through the awareness of necropolitics—through the embodied knowledge that dominant majorities and governments would rather Romanies did not exist, or at least not nearby.

At the same time, families and communities are not homogeneous wholes. Pre-existing patterns of gendered division of labor, including affective labor, as well as gendered hierarchies and inequalities, have also shaped how the pandemic has been lived. Our contributors emphasize how, from the start of the pandemic, women's affective and practical work has become even more central to family and community protection and survival: women have carried the burden of keeping households fed and clean at a time when basic subsistence has become extremely challenging for so many Romanies. With everybody around the world being instructed to be extra-vigilant with regards handwashing, air circulation, and the disinfection of surfaces, these requirements demand much additional effort from those living in poorer conditions, and often without running water.

In Spain, Gitana women tend to be the ones who act as mediators with the institutions of the state, from social workers to teachers. Manuela Mayoral Silva explains how, when the first lockdown started in March 2020, women were expected and expected themselves to manage to obtain help, and they struggled deeply against the slowness and indifference of the state response, as mentioned earlier. She says, "I do not want this book to leave no record of those women, brave women, who have done everything possible to overcome their challenges, who have had to call a mediator twenty times to ask for help, searching everywhere, queueing at the Red Cross or Cáritas." The compelling account of Fernanda Montaño García, also in the Spanish chronicles, reveals her distress about her inability to provide for her children whilst going through the illness and self-isolating in a small flat. For

Fernanda, fear of the virus and of death carried with it a dread that her children would be left destitute. This intertwined with the deep anxiety generated by the knowledge that there was very little food in the house, and that her husband had no means to earn a living under lockdown.

María Félix Rodriguez Camacho describes how Gitana women in Alicante used social media to express their dismay at the paucity of Red Cross relief packages, but also to attempt to set up swaps and share advice about how to feed large families "on milk and biscuits." Indeed, the support of extended families could only go so far among the poor who, throughout the national lockdowns at the start of the pandemic, lost their income and had no savings to fall back on, who were confined to small apartments and to neighborhoods without the most basic amenities, and whose children had no access to computers for online education. Like the Spanish Gitana women, many other Romanies were rightly anxious about physical survival, looking for solutions and not knowing to whom to turn.

When the pandemic hit, Romanies were repeatedly told that everybody was in the same situation and that it was difficult for all. As the chroniclers explain, Romani grassroot organizations saw through these assertions, acutely aware of the devastating impact that lockdown and social distancing measures would have on the ability of large numbers of Romani families to survive. They knew also that state support processes are, even in the most favorable of normal circumstances, slowed down by bureaucracy and by entrenched expectations about the unruliness, anomie, and childishness of Romanies. And, indeed, once the pandemic hit, authorities across the five countries were often inattentive or slow to recognize the very specific challenges that Romanies faced. Several chroniclers, such as Juliana Campos and Valdinalva dos Santos Caldas, describe how Romani NGOs and associations worked to compensate for the lack of official assistance. Initially, their pleas and their denunciations of racism were often treated as exaggerated—as if Romanies had not noticed that the whole world was facing an unprecedented public health and economic crisis—or as evidence of a Romani tendency to want to hog resources or jump the queue. In their contributions, both Estrella Iglesias Pérez and Manuela Mayoral Silva document the slowness and ineffectiveness of the institutions, and the enormous emotional toll that attempting to obtain help for desperate families took on Romani grassroots workers.

Return to Normal

Only a few weeks into the COVID-19 crisis, pundits, academics, and public intellectuals began reflecting on the post-pandemic future. Many portrayed the pandemic as a moment of undoing, one that could go two ways: it could radically worsen existing social inequalities, environmental degradation, and the authoritarian leanings of governments; or it could usher in a new era in which the opposite tendencies would prevail. They described the pandemic as a game changer for humanity, one way or another: "We will always be marking time with respect to our lives BC (Before COVID) and AC (After COVID)," wrote sociologist David Fasenfest.[26] As we finish this introduction at the end of 2021, all we know for certain is that the pandemic has not yet delivered a beautiful, better world.

These time-bound imaginaries also underly *Romani Chronicles of COVID-19*. When we set out on this project in the early summer of 2020, like many around the world we wondered whether we would ever return to normal, and what "the new normal" would look like. As ethnographers, we thought that our task was to document how this momentous event was transforming Romani communities, and to communicate whatever we learnt. During the prolonged process of preparing this volume—while writers dropped out of or joined the project, public concerns and debates shifted, and the countries in which we live had their diverse experiences with the virus and its management—we became increasingly aware of the undesirability of attempting to provide a comprehensive account that would fix the meaning of the pandemic for Romanies. We realized that, as a global event that sediments into institutions and shapes our positions as writers, the pandemic is not just inescapable but elusive: in the words of Maurice Blanchot, "[t]here is no reaching the disaster."[27]

This tension pervades this book. There are continuities but also many differences in how the chroniclers have lived through and depicted the crisis, and this diversity itself challenges the homogenizing depictions of Romanies whose marginalizing effects we have outlined above. Moreover, the knowledge of the contributors has evolved throughout the process of writing and rewriting, as their own experiences, understandings, and concerns have shifted. As a result, the chronicles are permeated as much by certainty as by ambiguity and inner conflict. Both individually and as a collection, the essays in this volume embody multiple, changing, and even contradictory meanings, the traces of previous meanings, and the seeds of future ones.

From this perspective, the pandemic cannot be conceptualized as a problem that will be overcome if only we deploy the proper scientific, technological, social, or digital fixes.[28] And yet, this is precisely how in the modern world we are encouraged to think about any crisis (economic, ecological, public health), and hence the logic of all the deferrals we have been offered—until the curve is flattened, until the summer, just until Christmas (so we can all enjoy it), until March... Currently, we are being asked to imagine what the world will be like after vaccinations have been successfully rolled out, as governments present the public with their own versions of the return to normal, of our future lives "AC."

But future speculation is not only never-ending: it also does not address everybody in the same way. Being invited to participate in these imagined futures is dependent on being seen as part of both society and the state. This future participation requires inclusion in national narratives, in hegemonic stories of the pandemic, and in History itself: it is meant for those who partake in modern citizenship, who are considered rational and must be offered sympathy for their suffering. Romanies are not seen in this light; they are not portrayed as recipients of promises of return to normal, because they were not perceived as existing within the norm to start with. This is why authorities did not think it necessary to tell inhabitants of segregated Romani settlements in Slovakia when their quarantines would be over.

We emphasized above how Romanies are, physically and/or metaphorically, confined to those exceptional spaces that are also routinized as constitutive of our societies—ghettos, "segregated enclaves," "socially excluded localities," and so on. This is where their pre-pandemic normality unfolded and where, as the chroniclers explain, the exceptionality of the pandemic also took place as a routinary crisis, a continuation of ongoing struggles. So, if "normal" here refers to the normalization of everyday structural violence, poverty, and neglect, and to the broad societal acceptance of this fact, is this also the normal to which Romanies will return? What, if anything, has COVID-19 changed for them?

Children, Education, and Romani Futures

As the pandemic continues to evolve, and as public debates and policy priorities shift, predictions about how the crisis will shape Romani lives in the coming years inevitably change too, making it unwise for us to define the new Romani normal. Nevertheless, the experiences and events captured by the chroniclers do point to processes already in motion: they show how pre-existing vulnerabilities and racism have amplified the social, economic, mental, and physical health reverberations of the pandemic for individual Romanies, making their lives even more precarious.

Growing numbers of studies are documenting housing insecurity and indebtedness as a result of the pandemic globally, among poor and vulnerable populations.[29] And while there are as yet no large quantitative analyses specifically on Romanies, other evidence, including from our chroniclers, suggests severe economic impacts: the pandemic has already led to the further exclusion of marginalized Romanies and to the impoverishment of members of the Romani lower-middle class.[30] As Jozef Miker recollected for Yasar Abu

Ghosh, "That was the worst crisis for me. My wife couldn't go to work, so we went into a lot of debt... Like everyone who worked in the hospitality industry, she lost everything from one day to the next... We were threatened with living on the street, with having our child taken away... Every month that we were locked up at home, our debt grew, and I had to borrow from decent friends." Here COVID-19 does not work alone: for East European Romanies in particular, it intertwines with Brexit to make transnational circulation harder if not impossible, closing off not just a key survival strategy but one of the very few paths for upward economic mobility available to them.

We are particularly alarmed by the chroniclers' descriptions of the widening educational gap between Romani children and their non-Romani peers.[31] The racial segregation of Romani children in schools was widespread across Europe before the pandemic but, unlike the racial segregation of other marginalized children in other areas and periods, it attracted little or no public outrage. Chronicler Yasar Abu Ghosh explains how the education system was a key location for the production of Roma marginalization, and that any efforts in place to challenge these processes were interrupted by the pandemic. The majority of European Romani children were educated in racially segregated classrooms and in classrooms where they followed adapted curriculums that took their intellectual and cultural incapacity for granted.[32] For many months in 2020, school closures and the shift to online learning left thousands of Romani children with no or greatly reduced access to their already limited education.[33] The chroniclers document how local education authorities and schools were often slow to react to the lockdowns, or refused to take the specific needs of Romani children into account and to address them:[34] decisions were guided by stereotypes that depict Romani children as more likely to fail and as less committed to education than their non-Romani peers.

The Spanish and Slovak chroniclers explain that the education that Romani children have been able to access throughout the pandemic has tended to depend on the inclinations and initiative of individual teachers or on the determination of local community mediators and social workers. Pilar García Bizárraga is scathing in her account of the first lockdown in Cañada Real in Madrid:

> The teachers thought it was not worth it, sending homework to children who were not going to do it: *I am not going to bother to send homework to this boy*. The same happened with the distribution of tablets to children so that they could do homework: there wasn't a single Gitano child on the list to receive a tablet. But these are the children who need it the most because they have the least; maybe in a family of ten they only have one mobile phone and the children cannot download their homework there.

Even when children were offered tablets or computers, the new system of online learning worldwide relied on access to Wi-Fi and on parental educational competence and literacy (digital and otherwise), two additional factors that placed many Romani children at a distinct disadvantage.[35]

The result is that the pandemic has disrupted early educational support for younger children and has increased rates of educational failure and dropout among older children.[36] Francisca Mayoral Silva describes the work that Romani mediators are already doing to try to mitigate this trend. What this educational loss will mean for each individual Romani child will depend on their age, the determination of their parents and teachers, and their ongoing access to digital and other resources. Overall, it is likely that, in combination with growing automation, restrictions on migration, and the precarization of employment, the educational impact of the pandemic will lead to high future income losses within Romani communities at large. As María Félix Rodríguez Camacho puts it, Romani children "now face added challenges that, once again and even more forcefully, push them towards poverty."

Governance and Leadership

Under the pandemic we have witnessed an unprecedented transformation of democratic governance. During the months captured in the *Chronicles*, from March 2020 to the summer of 2021, democratic governments worldwide invoked states of emergency and ruled by decree in the name of public health and the communal good. Just as has happened within the larger arena of public debate, the contributors too experienced and evaluate these developments differently. For some, such as Gwen Albert, the imposition of countrywide restrictions in Czechia and Slovakia provided reassurance, whilst others, such as Jurina Rusnáková and Zuzana Kumanová, criticized the additional measures aimed at Romanies as racialized and marginalizing. For their part, the Brazilian chroniclers were deeply worried about the lack of action taken by the federal government, which neglected or deliberately harmed vulnerable groups such as Romanies, Indigenous people, and the elderly.

As editors, we believe it is necessary to inquire about the long-term implications of these forms of governance for future Romani lives. We know that Romanies have historically been excluded from the nation and the body politic because they have been perceived as a threat to the health of others; and we also know that the punitive control of Romanies has often taken health-related forms. The chroniclers were witnesses to the instinctual intensification of these approaches in the early months of the pandemic as panic engulfed the world, revelatory of antigypsyism. As Carlo Caduff warned, the pandemic "risks teaching people to love power and call for its meticulous application."[37] We need to ask what this application of power, with its use of metaphors of war and sacrifice, may mean over the next years for racialized minorities traditionally treated as abject outsiders, and as people whose bodily closeness is to be feared.[38]

Although now, in late 2021, many restrictions have been lifted, and although economic activity and much-needed mobility have resumed for many Romani groups, we must remain alert to how biosecurity preoccupations might combine with antigypsyism to shape emergent political debate and policy design. We need to question how the vulnerability of particular groups is established and politicized. We need to pay attention to how calling upon worst-case scenarios—which justified the closing off or patrolling of Romani communities in Bulgaria, Slovakia, Romania, and elsewhere—strengthens the racialization of Romanies and dismisses resulting harm as mere externality. And not least, we need to keep investigating what "social distancing" as an organizing principle of social life might mean for Romanies. For instance, as we write, vaccination passes are being introduced across several countries, assuming that citizens are contagious unless proven otherwise. How does the generalized institutionalized suspicion of another's closeness, with its accompanying forms of surveillance and control, mold lives that are already indelibly marked by segregation and "social distance"?

Whilst the pandemic has led to the emergence of novel kinds of governance, or at the very least to the realization and proliferation of governance potentialities already present in pre-pandemic times, it has also been the ground where new forms of resistance, communal organization and leadership have emerged. In particular, the chronicles document the important roles that committed individuals working locally have played in mitigating the impact of the crisis within their immediate environments. We are speaking here of cultural mediators, health practitioners, school support workers and so on—roles occupied by many of the chroniclers who work either within Romani associations and NGOs, or on their fringes. Mobilizing quickly, and often making huge personal sacrifices, these professionals did their best to step into the void left by social services, and in the process they often emerged as local leaders, to whom others looked for help and guidance during a terrifying time.

These chroniclers take us back to moments when they were confronted with the overwhelming needs of others. Health worker Alžbeta "Hal'ka" Mižigárová, for example, powerfully describes being fully dressed in protective clothing when meeting family and acquaintances who had suddenly found themselves confined in community quarantine:

I don't know how it's possible, because I was as much covered as I could be, but still they recognized me. "Hal'ka, will everything be all right? All will be well, won't it? When will they let us go?" they were calling at me. That's when I realized that it's not about the outer appearance but about the people who look at you. They recognize you despite that protective wear. You are one of them. And they keep asking you, they keep telling you how sad they are, how afraid they are.

Several chroniclers tell of their attempts to challenge state directives that deliberately or not slowed down the provision of emergency support during the first lockdowns, as well as to counter the indifference of both central and local government officials. Their carefully documented experiences encourage us to ask about the forms that leadership takes at times of profound disruption, in particular within minority communities. During the pandemic, in the neighborhoods and settlements that the chroniclers write about, leadership has often been ephemeral, and leaders have been individuals whose capacities and positions tend to be disregarded by those in roles of greater power. Leadership has emerged out of despair, and out of the urgent needs of their families and immediate communities. This is leadership as care, by community mediators, school assistants, and health workers, often women. These informal gendered forms of leadership are susceptible of being overlooked and even disavowed, not just by non-Romanies but by established leaders. Although their efforts are crucial at the times of greatest need, they risk being soon forgotten.

In the five countries, the tremendous pressure of the pandemic is also driving a reinvigoration of Romani political activism. For Brazil, Igor Shimura argues that the need to respond to new challenges and hardships has "served to empower Cigano leaders, who have been learning to access public arenas and defend themselves more effectively than before." Activists Gabriela Marques, Aluízio Silva Júnior and Aline Miklos recount how they have developed novel forms of engagement through social media which, crucially, entail the creation of new links among different Romani groups within Brazil and with other social movements, such as Indigenous or Afro-descendant. These emerging connections are transforming Romani politics in the country, and will continue to do so in coming years. They evidence the fact that the period captured in this book has been also characterized by the global awakening to systemic racism in the wake of Black Lives Matter—a fact that is most clearly visible in the accounts of Edilma Souza and Jozef Miker.

In her piece, Souza, a Black anthropologist, thinks through her own embodied experience of racism, interlacing her experiences of the pandemic in Bolsonaro's Brazil with those of her Calon interlocutors. Jozef Miker, a Roma grassroot activist, reflects on his involvement with the family of Stanislav Tomáš, whose death by asphyxiation in police custody on 19 June 2021 drew comparisons with George Floyd's in the United States a year before, and which sparked "Roma Lives Matter" protests across Europe.[39] In his conversation with Yasar Abu Ghosh, Miker's attempts to help individuals in poverty and debt, the threat of police violence, and a vaccination campaign blend into one another. For both Souza and Miker, the physical incapacity to breathe when infected by COVID-19 becomes inflected—and is magnified—by the suffocation generated by poverty and racism.

How This Book Was Written

The chapters in this book narrate the impact of the COVID-19 pandemic on Romani individuals, families, and communities by foregrounding singular voices, experiences, and perspectives. Although the narratives are very diverse in format, style, and content, and although many do not fit standard models of scholarly writing, they all provide critical perspectives on the complexity of the pandemic. They present contrasting or even opposing standpoints, beliefs, and conclusions, and it is through this multiplicity that they constitute an effort at dialogue and co-theorizing.

We draw inspiration from a long tradition of collaborative research in anthropology, stretching back to the 1970s if not earlier, that seeks to create conversations between local and academic forms of knowledge and analysis. Western scholarship has most often separated data from analysis, treating the perspectives and lives of non-academic interlocutors as material to be dissected.[40] These chronicles, by contrast, ask readers to engage with the critical insights of people who are living through the pandemic, and reflecting on it from both scholarly and non-scholarly standpoints. In all these accounts, whether more or less academic, analysis and critique emerge out of experience—sometimes forceful, relentlessly difficult experience—rather than being separated from it. Both experience and analysis are laid out for evaluation.

It is important to emphasize that the texts do not constitute a representative sample of Romani experiences in the five countries, let alone worldwide. When looking for contributions, we did not set out to find exemplars, individuals who would fit our preconceived ideas about whose life, role, or perspective would be most relevant or generalizable. Instead, we invited friends, collaborators, and colleagues to consider taking part in the project, and also encouraged them to invite others who might be interested in participating. As anthropologists we took it for granted that any life, no matter how distinct or how generic, is worth paying attention to. There are also some conclusions and interpretations that we, as editors, have found ourselves disagreeing with.

For each country, one or two people took on the role of coordinators: Kamila Fiałkowska and Elżbieta Mirga-Wójtowicz for Poland, Yasar Abu Ghosh for Czechia, Tomáš Hrustič and Andrej Belák for Slovakia, Martin Fotta for Brazil, and Paloma Gay y Blasco for Spain. The two of us, Martin and Paloma, oversaw and coordinated the whole project, providing also in-depth editorial guidance and advice, as well as English-language help. Each part starts with an introductory chapter where salient features of the Romani experience in that particular country are discussed, before and during the pandemic, and where the method, focus, and contribution of that part of the book is outlined.

Each of the five parts is the result of different collaborative techniques and relationships. Four of them include texts written in several different genres, and there are texts that do not fit into any ready-made, easily recognizable category. Some of the chroniclers have written single-authored texts, whilst others have co-authored their chapters. Some chapters have been produced by teams of collaborators who have jointly planned, carried out, and written up their research. Other texts are the result of dialogues between individual scholars and local interlocutors whose work showcases a wide variety of collaborative methods.

The contributions include memoirs, opinion essays, transcriptions of conversations or interviews, ethnographic analyses and a compelling short story by Romani writer Iveta Kokyová, as well as pieces that stride the boundaries between one or more of these genres, or that fit into none. This diversity testifies to the willingness of the chroniclers to adapt methods and approach, and creatively to develop ways of working and writing that suit each specific combination of skills as well as each relationship and situation. We gather these texts together as "chronicles" in an attempt to flatten established hierarchies of knowledge.

This book makes a double contribution. It documents and analyses the pandemic and its reverberations, showing how it is molding the lives of Romanies who, even before March 2020, were struggling under the burden of normalized marginalization and oppression. Crucially, it does so by foregrounding voices that do not usually address academic audiences, and by paying attention to analytical and critical insights embodied in non-normative ways of knowing and writing. As editors, we hope that the examples of methodological experimentation, dialogue, and cooperation collected in this book will inspire others, whether working within or outside the field of Romani studies, to develop their own collaborations.

Paloma Gay y Blasco teaches social anthropology at the University of St Andrews in Scotland. She has authored books and articles on ethnographic methods, collaborative anthropology, and Romani issues, including, with

Liria Hernández, *Writing Friendship: A Reciprocal Ethnography* (Palgrave Macmillan, 2020).

Martin Fotta is a researcher at the Institute of Ethnology, Czech Academy of Sciences. He is the author of *From Itinerant Trade to Moneylending in the Era of Financial Inclusion* (Palgrave Macmillan, 2018). His current work explores transformations across the Romani diaspora of the Lusophone South Atlantic region.

Notes

This book was prepared with support of the Lumina Quaeruntur Award of the Czech Academy of Sciences (LQ300582201).
1. We acknowledge that chronicles are viewed differently in different literary and scholarly traditions. We have found the following texts helpful when developing our own approach to the concepts of chronicle, witness, and testimony: Angel-Ajani, "Expert Witness;" Marcus, "The Anthropologist as Witness;" Mahieux, *Urban Chroniclers*; Stephen, "Bearing Witness;" Thomas, "Witnessing."
2. See Welcome, "After the Ash."
3. Gay y Blasco, "The Best Place."
4. Center for Reproductive Rights, *Vakeras Zorales*.
5. Picker, "That Neighbourhood." Picker, *Racial Cities*.
6. Brooks, "Camp."
7. Whitacre et al., "COVID-19 and the Political Geography."
8. A report by the European Roma Rights Centre (Rorke and Lee, "Roma Rights") provides the most systematic overview of human rights violation against Romanies across Europe during the first half of 2020.
9. Nikolov, "Bulgarian Authorities."
10. Costache, "'Able to Gas Them;'" Rorke and Lee, "Roma Rights;" Matache, Leaning, and Bhabha, "The Shameful Resurgence."
11. Brooks, "Camp."
12. Tubio, "Así incumplen la orden;" Tubio, "El confinamiento."
13. Berta, "Ethnicizing a Pandemic," 14–15.
14. ABC España, "El barrio de las Tres Mil Viviendas."
15. Sandset, "The Necropolitics of COVID-19."
16. Stoler, *Race*.
17. Mbembe, "Necropolitics."
18. Alston, "Statement."
19. The only such data were collected for the *Healthy Regions* organisation in Slovakia through a network of community health mediators, including the chronicler Alžbeta "Haľka" Mižigárová, discussed in the introduction to Slovak Chronicles. These data confirmed higher levels of infection rates in the second wave (winter 2021). While, given the young age profile of inhabitants, infection rates did not lead to high levels of hospitalizations in absolute terms, in relative terms the picture was different: the

rate of mortality within each age groups was higher. than among non-Romanies. This discrepancy has at least two causes: higher prevalence of pre-existing conditions (comorbidities), and delayedhospital admissions when compared to the majority population.

20. Farmer, "On Suffering."
21. Mbembe, "Necropolitics."
22. Berlant, "Slow Death."
23. Quesada, Kain Hart, and Bourgois, "Structural Vulnerability."
24. Singer et al., "Syndemics."
25. Howarth, "A Life Without Flowers."
26. Fasenfest, "On the Threshold," 961.
27. Blanchot, *The Writing of the Disaster*, 19.
28. Savransky, "Problems."
29. World Bank, *Poverty*.
30. Willis, "Economic Effects."
31. AECGIT, "Impacto del Covid-19;" Fundación Secretariado Gitano, "Impacto de la Crisis." There is growing evidence that what the chroniclers have observed firsthand in the five countries also happened elsewhere: Hackl and Müller, "Online Teaching;" REF, "Statement on COVID-19;" Friends, Families and Travellers, "Written Evidence."
32. Farkas "Report on Discrimination;" Gay y Blasco, "The Best Place."
33. Fox, "EU Faces Challenge;" Hackl and Müller, "Online Teaching."
34. Tammi, "The Great Divide."
35. Bešter, and Pirc, "Remote Learning."
36. Krumova and Kolev, "The Distance Learning."
37. Caduff, "What Went Wrong," 480.
38. Roy, "Fear of Others."
39. Ryšavý, "Roma Lives Matter Demo;" Benstead, "Europe's Romani population;" BIRN, "Roma Lives Matter."
40. For a recent experiment in collaboration, see the book by Gay y Blasco and Hernández, *Writing Friendship*. For other reflections on collaborative ethnography in Romani studies, see Hrustič and Poduška, *Romano Džaniben*; and Fotta, "Review Article." For a comprehensive review of the development of collaborative methods in anthropology see Lassiter, *Chicago Guide*.

Bibliography

ABC España. "El barrio de las Tres Mil Viviendas en el punto de mira para volver a la fase 1" [The neighbourhood of Tres Mil Viviendas comes under scrutiny to return to Phase 1]. Atlas España, *ABC España*, last modified 8 September 2020. Retrieved 22 November 2021 from https://www.abc.es/espana/abci-barrio-tres-viviendas-punto-de-mira-para-volver-fase-1-202009082136_video.html.

AECGIT. "Impacto del Covid-19 en los centros educativos con alumnado Gitano" [Impact of COVID-19 on the education centres with Gitano students]. Asociación de Enseñantes con Gitanos, published in December 2020. Retrieved 22 November

2021 from https://www.aecgit.org/impacto-del-covid-19-en-los-centros-educativos-con-alumnado-gitano.html.

Alston, Philip. "Statement by Professor Philip Alston, United Nations Special Rapporteur on extreme poverty and human rights, on his visit to Spain, 27 January." United Nations Office of the High Commissioner for Human Rights, published on 7 February 2020. Retrieved 14 September 2022 from https://www.ohchr.org/en/statements/2020/02/statement-professor-philip-alston-united-nations-special-rapporteur-extreme.

Angel-Ajani, Asale. "Expert Witness: Notes Toward Revisiting the Politics of Listening." *Anthropology and Humanism* 29(2) (2004): 133–44. https://doi.org/10.1525/ahu.2004.29.2.133.

Benstead, Sean. "Europe's Romani Population Can't Breathe." *Jacobin*, 18 July 2021. Retrieved 22 November 2021 from https://jacobinmag.com/2021/07/europe-roma-czech-republic-stanislav-tomas-police-killing-world-romani-congress-movement.

Berlant, Laurent. "Slow Death (Sovereignty, Obesity, Lateral Agency)." *Critical Inquiry* 33(4) (2007): 754–80. https://doi.org/10.1086/521568.

Berta, Péter. "Ethnicizing a Pandemic: COVID-19, Culture Blaming and Romanian Roma." *Society for Romanian Studies Newsletter* 42(1) (Spring 2020): 14–15.

Bešter, Romana, and Janez Pirc. "Impact of Remote Learning during the Covid-19 Lockdown on Roma Pupils in Slovenia." *Razprave in Gradivo: Revija za Narodnostna Vprasanja* 85 (2020): 139–64. https://doi.org/10.36144/RiG85.dec20.139-164.

BIRN. "'Roma Lives Matter' Protests Erupt in Teplice." *Balkan Insight*, In Pictures, 28 June 2021. Retrieved 22 November 2021 from https://balkaninsight.com/2021/06/28/roma-lives-matter-protests-erupt-in-teplice/.

Blanchot, Maurice. *The Writing of the Disaster*. Lincoln: University of Nebraska Press, 1995.

Brooks, Ethel. "Camp." In *Posthuman Glossary*, ed. Rosi Braidotti and Maria Hlavajova, 77–79. London: Bloomsbury, 2018.

Caduff, Carlo. "What Went Wrong: Corona and the World after the Full Stop." *Medical Anthropology Quarterly* 34(4) (2020): 467–87. https://doi.org/10.1111/maq.12599.

Center for Reproductive Rights (Poradňa pre Občianske a Ľudské Práva). *Vakeras Zorales—Speaking Out: Roma Women's Experiences in Reproductive Health Care in Slovakia*. 2017. Retrieved 22 November 2021 from https://www.poradna-prava.sk/en/documents/vakeras-zorales-speaking-out-roma-womens-experiences-in-reproductive-health-care-in-slovakia/.

Costache, Ioanida. "'Until We Are Able to Gas Them Like the Nazi's, the Roma Will Infect the Nation': Roma and the Ethnicization of COVID-19 in Romania." *DOR*, 22 April 2020. Retrieved 22 November 2021 from https://www.dor.ro/roma-and-the-ethnicization-of-covid-19-in-romania/.

Farkas, Lillia. "Report on Discrimination of Roma Children in Education." European Network of Legal Experts in the Field of Non-discrimination. Brussels: Directorate-General for Justice, 2014. https://ec.europa.eu/research-roma-children/?publications/48/.

Farmer, Paul. "On Suffering and Structural Violence: A View from Below." *Daedalus* 125(1) (Winter 1996): 261–83. http://www.jstor.org/stable/20027362.

Fasenfest David. "On the Threshold of a New Era." *Critical Sociology* 46(7–8) (2020): 961–64. https://doi.org/10.1177/0896920520960699.

Fotta, Martin. "Review Article of *Staging Strife: Lessons from Performing Ethnography with Polish Roma Women*. Magdalena Kazubowski-Houston. Montreal: McGill-

Queen's University Press. 2010." *Romani Studies* 27(1) (2017): 95–102. https://doi.org/10.3828/rs.2017.5

Fox, Benjamin. "EU Faces Challenge of Closing Roma Education Divide." *Euractiv*, 28 June 2021. Retrieved 22 November 2021 from https://www.euractiv.com/section/non-discrimination/news/eu-faces-challenge-of-closing-roma-education-divide/.

Friends, Families and Travellers. "Written Evidence Submitted by Friends, Families and Travellers (CVB0048)." July 2020. Retrieved 22 November 2021 from https://committees.parliament.uk/writtenevidence/8641/pdf/.

Fundación Secretariado Gitano. "Impacto de la crisis del COVID-19 sobre la Población Gitana en España" [Impact of the COVID-19 crisis on the Gitano population of Madrid]. Madrid: Fundación Secretariado Gitano, 2020. Retrieved 22 November 2021 from https://www.gitanos.org/upload/15/60/Resultados_Encuesta_a_Participantes_FSG_-_Covid-19__1_.pdf.

Gay y Blasco, Paloma. "'It's the Best Place for Them': Normalising Roma Segregation in Madrid." *Social Anthropology* 24(4) (2016): 446–61. https://doi.org/10.1111/1469-8676.12333.

Gay y Blasco, Paloma, and Liria Hernández. *Writing Friendship: A Reciprocal Ethnography*. Cham: Palgrave Macmillan, 2020.

Hackl, Thomas, and Stephan Müller. "Without Access to Online Teaching, Roma Children's Education Has Been Put on Hold by COVID-19." *euronews*, updated 27 October 2020. Retrieved 22 November 2021 from https://www.euronews.com/2020/10/27/without-access-to-online-teaching-roma-children-s-education-has-been-put-on-hold-by-covid-.

Howarth, Anthony. "A Life Without Flowers: Toxic Attachments, Travellers' Ways, and Pessimistic Scholarship." Unpublished Manuscript.

Hrustič, and Ondřej Poduška (eds). *Romano Džaniben* 25(2), Special issue Participácia a Kolaborácia v Akadémii a Verejnej Politike [Participation and Collaboration in the Academy and Public Policy], 2018.

Krumova, Teodora, and Deyan Kolev. "The Distance Learning in Bulgaria over the Past School Year: What Has Happened during the COVID-19 Pandemic." *International Journal of Roma Studies* 3(3) (2021): 322–34.

Lassiter, Luke Eric. *The Chicago Guide to Collaborative Ethnography*. Chicago: The University of Chicago Press, 2005.

Mahieux, Viviane. *Urban Chroniclers in Modern Latin America: The Shared Intimacy of Everyday Life*. Austin: University of Texas Press, 2011.

Marcus, George A. "The Anthropologist as Witness in Contemporary Regimes of Intervention." *Cultural Politics* 1(1) (2005): 31–49.

Matache, Margareta, Jennifer Leaning, and Jaqueline Bhabha. "The Shameful Resurgence of Violent Scapegoating in a Time of Crisis," *OpenDemocracy*, 5 May 2020. Retrieved 22 November 2021 from https://www.opendemocracy.net/en/can-europe-make-it/shameful-resurgence-violent-scapegoating-time-crisis/.

Mbembe, Achille. "Necropolitics." *Public Culture* 15(1) (2003): 11–40. https://doi.org/10.1215/08992363-15-1-11.

Nikolov, Krassen. "Bulgarian Authorities Struggle to Enforce Containment with Roma Population." *EURACTIV*, 20 March 2020. Retrieved 22 November 2021 from https://www.euractiv.com/section/languages-culture/news/bulgarian-authorities-struggle-to-enforce-containment-with-roma-population/.

Picker, Giovanni. *Racial Cities: Governance and the Segregation of Romani People in Urban Europe.* London: Routledge, 2017.

———. "'That Neighbourhood is an Ethnic Bomb!' The Emergence of an Urban Governance Apparatus in Western Europe." *European Urban and Regional Studies* 23(2) (2016): 136–48. https://doi.org/10.1177/0969776413502659.

Quesada, James, Laurie Kain Hart, and Philippe Bourgois. "Structural Vulnerability and Health: Latino Migrant Laborers in the United States." *Medical Anthropology* 30(4) (2011): 339–62. https://doi.org/10.1080/01459740.2011.576725.

REF. "Roma Education Fund's Statement on COVID-19 Effecting [*sic*] Roma Communities and Access to Education." Roma Education Fund, 2020. Retrieved 22 November 2021 from https://www.romaeducationfund.org/wp-content/uploads/2020/04/Roma-Education-Fund-Statement-on-COVID-19-pandemic.pdf.

Rorke, Bernard, and Jonathan Lee. "Roma Rights in the Time of Covid." ERRC (European Roma Rights Centre), 9 September 2020. Retrieved 22 November 2021 from http://www.errc.org/uploads/upload_en/file/5265_file1_roma-rights-in-the-time-of-covid..pdf.

Roy, Arpan. "Fear of Others: Thinking Biopolitics." *Social Anthropology* 28(2) (2020): 343–44. https://doi.org/10.1111/1469-8676.12876.

Ryšavý, Zdeněk. "Roma Lives Matter Demo in Czech Capital Hears Eyewitness Testimony." *Romea*, 2 June 2021. Retrieved 22 November 2021 from http://www.romea.cz/en/news/czech/roma-lives-matter-demo-in-czech-capital-hears-eyewitness-testimony-that-stanislav-tomas-was-carried-motionless-on-a.

Sandset, Tony. "The Necropolitics of COVID-19: Race, Class and Slow Death in an Ongoing Pandemic." *Global Public Health* 16(8–9) (2021): 1411–23. https://doi.org/10.1080/17441692.2021.1906927.

Savransky, Martin. "Problems All the Way Down." *Theory, Culture & Society* 38(2) (2021): 3–23. https://doi.org/10.1177/0263276420966389.

Singer, Merrill, Nicola Bulled, Bayla Ostrach, and Shir Lerman Ginzburg. "Syndemics: A Cross-Disciplinary Approach to Complex Epidemic Events Like COVID-19." *Annual Review of Anthropology* 50(1) (2021): 41–58. https://doi.org/10.1146/annurev-anthro-100919-121009.

Stephen, Lynn. "Bearing Witness: Testimony in Latin American Anthropology and Related Fields." *The Journal of Latin American and Caribbean Anthropology* 22(1) (2017): 85–109. https://doi.org/10.1111/jlca.12262.

Stoler, Ann Laura. *Race and the Education of Desire: Foucault's History of Sexuality and the Colonial Order of Things.* Durham, NC: Duke University Press, 1995.

Tammi, Lynne. "Across the Great Divide: The Impact of Digital Inequality on Scotland's Gypsy/Traveller Children and Young People during the COVID-19 Emergency." *International Journal of Roma Studies* 2(2) (2020): 52–65. https://doi.org/10.17583/ijrs.2020.6301.

Thomas, Deborah A. "Witnessing." *American Anthropologist* 22(4) (2020): 717–20. https://doi.org/10.1111/aman.13487.

Tubio, Silvia. "Así incumplen la orden de confinamiento en las Tres Mil Viviendas [This is how they fail to comply with the lockdown order in Tres Mil Viviendas]." *ABC de Sevilla*, 19 March 2020. Retrieved 22 November 2021 from https://sevilla.abc.es/sevilla/sevi-incumplen-orden-confinamiento-tres-viviendas-202003181826_noticia.html.

———. "El confinamiento para frenar el coronavirus fracasa en los barrios marginales de Sevilla" [The lockdown to slow down coronavirus fails in the marginal neighborhoods of Seville]. *ABC de Sevilla*, 20 March 2020. Retrieved 22 November 2021 from https://sevilla.abc.es/sevilla/sevi-coronavirus-sevilla-confinamiento-para-frenar-coronavirus-fracasa-barrios-marginales-sevilla-202003192257_noticia.html.

Welcome, Leniqueca A. "After the Ash and Rubble Are Cleared: Anthropological Work for a Future." *American Anthropologist: Commentaries on "The Case for Letting Anthropology Burn,"* 28 May 2020. Retrieved 22 November 2021 from https://www.americananthropologist.org/commentaries/welcome-after-the-ash.

Whitacre, Ryan, Adeola Oni-Orisan, Nadia Gaber, Carlos Martinez, Liza Buchbinder, Denise Herd, and Seth M. Holmes. "COVID-19 and the Political Geography of Racialisation: Ethnographic Cases in San Francisco, Los Angeles and Detroit." *Global Public Health* 16(8–9) (Aug–Sep 2021): 1396–410. https://doi.org/10.1080/17441692.2021.1908395.

Willis, Craig. "Economic Effects of the COVID-19 Pandemic on Roma Communities in Albania, Bosnia and Herzegovina, Moldova, Montenegro, North Macedonia, Serbia and Ukraine," *ECMI Research Paper* #122. European Centre for Minority Issues (ECMI), October 2020. https://www.ecmi.de/publications/ecmi-research-papers/122-economic-effects-of-the-covid-19-pandemic-on-roma-communities-in-albania-bosnia-herzegovina-moldova-montenegro-north-macedonia-serbia-and-ukraine.

World Bank. *Poverty and Shared Prosperity 2020: Reversals of Fortune*. Washington, DC, 2020. https://www.worldbank.org/en/publication/poverty-and-shared-prosperity.

PART I

SPANISH CHRONICLES

CHAPTER 1

Introduction to the Spanish Chronicles
From Ordinary Crisis to Pandemic Emergency

Paloma Gay y Blasco

GENEVA (22 December 2020) – A two-month power outage in a vast informal settlement near Madrid is endangering the health of some 1,800 children, UN human rights experts said today, calling on the Government of Spain to immediately restore electricity as temperatures fall to freezing.

"Children in Cañada Real Galiana are truly suffering, and their health is at risk," the experts warned. "Now that winter is closing in – and especially during the COVID-19 pandemic – electricity must be restored." . . . The settlement is home to some 8,000 people who live in a 16 km-long, 75 m-wide strip established more than 40 years ago. Many residents are migrants or Roma.

"Madrid is notoriously cold and now that temperatures are plunging at least one baby had already been taken to hospital with symptoms of hypothermia," the experts said.

"Without electricity, there is no heat in homes and no hot water, meaning children cannot shower or wash properly. During the COVID-19 pandemic, when hygiene is more important than ever, this is especially troubling."[1]

The text above, from a press release issued at the end of 2020 by the United Nations Office of the High Commissioner for Human Rights, describes one of the harshest instances of deprivation to have faced Romanies in Spain during the COVID-19 pandemic. Three months earlier, when the electricity company cut supply to the slum—claiming that power was used to run cannabis farms—the authorities refused to intervene and argued that families had turned down offers of housing elsewhere. Negotiations between Gitano associations, government representatives, the energy provider and international NGOs yielded no result. Then, between 6 and 11 January 2021, storm Filomena brought the heaviest snows to Spain since the 1970s, and 50 cm fell on the unheated shacks and unpaved streets of the slum, isolating it for two weeks. The eight thousand inhabitants of Cañada did their best to survive the severe winter without electricity and, as I write in mid-October 2021, the impasse continues. Approximately half of them are Romanies, and the rest North African migrants. Throughout, the media have debated whether or not the people of the settlement have brought the situation upon themselves: some have argued that they deserve or even desire their hardships, that the problem is of their own making, and others that as Romanies and migrants they are victims of institutional racism and discrimination.

Here, the unimaginable, the one-off (COVID-19, Filomena) and the everyday (extreme poverty and marginality) overlap and blend into each other. This intertwining of extraordinary and routine forms of crisis is the focus of the Spanish chronicles: through their detailed descriptions, the chroniclers demonstrate that this is a fundamental and enduring dimension of Romani experience.

The Spanish chroniclers provide compelling depictions of the multiple forms of marginalization that pre-dated, shaped and magnified the impact of the pandemic on the Gitano population. These accounts of everyday crisis are well supported by statistical data: the evidence I briefly summarize below shows how, in the twenty years since the start of the century but particularly in the wake of the 2008 economic crisis, the Gitano population has undergone a progressive impoverishment and deterioration of their already poor quality of life. Paradoxically, this deterioration has gone hand in hand with a proliferation of initiatives, programs and assessments purportedly aimed at improving the so-called integration of Gitanos within Spanish society.

The chroniclers speak of the human suffering that ensues when an unprecedented global emergency settles on top of ongoing forms of structural violence. They describe meeting the entrenched expectation by the state and its representatives that Gitanos will be intractable and resistant, rebellious, irresponsible and childlike, that they will need less than non-Gitanos, and that they will regrettably but unavoidably suffer more. Their accounts explain how "the politics of indifference"[2] fed on and reinforced popular discourses about Gitanos to set the scene for COVID-19. They critique governmental meanings and actions, attempting also to document and analyze Gitano responses and forms of agency.

Pre-pandemic Crisis: Spanish Romanies at the Start of 2020

The Spanish Romani community is very diverse. Regional origin, class, language, and religious affiliation all contribute to this heterogeneity. There are approximately three-quarters of a million Spanish Gitanos, living mostly in the poorer districts of the larger cities, and since 2002 the country has received at least fifty thousand Romani migrants from other EU countries—Romania and Bulgaria in particular.[3] Spanish legislation does not allow the collection of ethnic origin data by government agencies, and so analyses and policies draw on large-scale surveys by Gitano associations and academic institutions. These tend to amalgamate Romanies of local and migrant origin under the category "Gitano," obscuring the complex relationships between Spanish Gitanos, Romani migrants, and the institutions of the state.[4] The chapters in the Spanish chronicles focus primarily, though not exclusively, on the stories of local Gitanos rather than those of Romanies of East European origin.

In spite of their diversity, Gitanos as a population suffer much higher poverty, deprivation, and marginalization than non-Gitano Spaniards. Remarkably, although Gitano standards of living rose in the decades after the end of the Franco dictatorship in 1976, they began to decline again at the start of the twenty-first century. This deterioration was worsened by the economic crisis of 2008, which affected Gitanos severely and disproportionately:[5] street sellers were hit by the overall decrease in spending throughout the country; those working in the collapsed construction industry lost their employment; and new environmental legislation devastated the precarious subsistence strategies of families who lived off recycling and scrap collection.[6]

The trend is well documented, with figures across all arenas telling the same story. The social exclusion index, which integrates statistics on employment, consumption, political participation, housing, education, health, conflict, and social isolation shows a clear overall deterioration trajectory for Gitanos.[7] Between 2009 and 2014 the proportion of Gitanos living in a situation of severe exclusion grew from 18 to 54 percent.[8] In 2018, 70 percent of Spanish Gitanos lived in moderate or severe social exclusion, in contrast to 38.1 percent of immigrants from within and outside the EU, and 15.8 percent of non-Gitano Spaniards.[9] The Gitano population is very young, with 40 percent of Gitanos being under twenty years of age. Almost 90 percent of Gitano children live in poverty, compared to 31 percent of Spanish children as a whole.[10]

The deterioration evidenced by the data belies the progressive depictions put forward by government discourse,[11] as well as the overall expectation that things can only get better for Gitanos, or that Gitano history since the end of the Franco dictatorship has been characterized by a steady improvement of life conditions and ever greater integration. Crucially, it means that the Gitano community, already battered through fifteen years of cuts and austerity, entered the pandemic from an exceptionally fragile position.

The education figures are particularly worrying because they reveal how inaccessible upward social mobility will continue to be for Gitanos in the future. From the end of the dictatorship, the number of Gitano children in education grew steadily even though the model was primarily one of educational segregation of Gitanos. Although the vast majority of Gitano children of primary age are nowadays enrolled in school, the overall proportion of Gitanos who have not completed their compulsory secondary education has been rising since the 2008 crisis. This grew by a whopping 14.2 percent in five years, from 43.3 in 2013 to 57.5 percent in 2018: worryingly, this means that the number of Gitano children leaving school early increased very significantly in the years leading to the pandemic.[12] Paradoxically, the Spanish model of inclusion of the Gitano population is regularly described as the gold standard against which other national programs should be measured.[13]

This overall deterioration did not happen by itself, nor was it just the result of the general shrinking of the economy that followed the economic crisis of 2008. The detailed analysis produced by the NGO Secretariado Gitano demonstrates that the austerity policies implemented at national level through the 2010s had a "very direct effect on an important part of the Spanish Gitano community, reducing their income levels and their quality of life, and raising poverty levels for many families."[14] Key support programs—such as textbook grants and free school meals for the poorest children—were severely reduced or altogether cancelled, with education being particularly affected. New hurdles to basic entitlements in health, employment, education, and housing intersected to generate a cascade of disenfranchisement experiences for Gitano families. The result was the overall regression to deprivation and exclusion levels not seen since the 1990s.[15]

The panorama for Spanish Gitanos at the start of 2020 was so dire that in February UN Special Rapporteur Philip Alston argued that it demanded a "crisis-level response."[16] He spoke not just of "years of plans and benchmarks that have left Roma poverty indicators at deplorable levels" in Spain, but of the "lack of urgency and resignation" with which politicians and government officials approach the inequalities that give shape to Gitano lives.[17] His interpretation is consistent with that of scholars who have analyzed the micropolitics of encounters between Gitanos and state representatives who gatekeep access to welfare benefits. As Ariadna Ayala Rubio has meticulously documented, these officials tend to draw on widely shared conceptualizations of citizens as responsible for their own fate, able to overcome hardships through discipline, effort, self-motivation, and asceticism. They tend to perceive Gitanos as deliberately unwilling to adopt these attitudes, and therefore as undeserving of the public help that, in popular discourse, should be available only to those who genuinely cannot help themselves.[18] Encounters between poor, dispossessed Gitanos and state institutions, including health services, are often occasions of punitive control.[19] From housing to health and education, both policy design and policy implementation have revolved around conceptualizations of Gitanos as disruptive, problematic, uncivilized, and undesirable.

It is also clear that Gitanos are not the only ones who have suffered as a result of the austerity policies that followed the 2008 crisis. They share key aspects of this experience of growing impoverishment and marginalization with a significant number of non-Gitano Spaniards. As Alston put it just as the pandemic was hatching across Europe, "Spain is thriving economically; half of its population is not... [T]he post-recession recovery that has been so good for some has left many people behind, and... all too little has been done for most members of that large group."[20] Official poverty thresholds have fallen consistently since 2008, and there has been an important impoverishment of working-class people in employment, which has gone hand in hand with an ongoing reduction in salaries and a deterioration of life quality for a large section of the Spanish population.[21]

Spanish Gitanos are therefore part of a highly divided and unequal society, one where both wealth and poverty keep rising. This is a society characterized by deep economic, political, and social fragmentation, and in which, unsurprisingly, political extremism is gaining ground. It is also ethnically very diverse, particularly in the peripheries of the great cities where most Gitanos live. The poorer districts of cities like Madrid and Barcelona are home not just to Gitanos and working-class Payos but to large numbers of migrants from Latin America, the Caribbean, and North Africa, who survive precariously on small incomes.

Growing deprivation and fragmentation frame the ways the Gitano community is perceived and represented by non-Gitanos, as well as how policies regarding Gitanos are devised, implemented and resisted. In the district of Villaverde in Madrid, for example, where I have carried out long-term research, working-class non-Gitanos described their struggles against impoverishment and saw having to live and be educated alongside Gitanos as evidence of the indifference of middle-class politicians towards their own plight. Some campaigned vigorously against the relocation of Gitanos in the district.[22] State representatives sanctioned their fears of contagion as legitimate bases for the segregation of Gitano children in local schools, and the practice continues to the present day. Gitanos continue to be perceived in Spain primarily as delinquent scroungers, resistant to accepting civic norms and to integrating into the dominant society. It is significant that since the 1980s many policies aimed at Gitanos, particularly in housing and education, have revolved around the concept of "inclusive exclusion"—the notion that Gitanos need to be separated from non-Gitanos as a key step towards their re-education and eventual integration into the larger society.[23]

Gitanos since March 2020

At the end of March 2020, *Chronicles* contributor María Félix Rodriguez Camacho and I published a piece on the website *Somatosphere* in which we described factors that we believed put the Gitano community at particular risk during the pandemic.[24] The state of emergency in Spain had been declared only two weeks earlier, and the country had just entered one of the longest and harshest lockdowns in Europe. In the article we talked about the reliance of Gitano families on street-based economic activities such as market selling, vending, and scrap collecting, all of which had suddenly become impossible under quarantine. We spoke of the poor housing conditions under which many Gitanos live, and the difficulties that many were already facing with regards to self-isolation. And we emphasized the worse health that Gitanos suffer compared to non-Gitanos, their lower life expectancy, and the fact that they are much more likely to experience key chronic conditions associated with poverty, such as obesity, COPD and diabetes, all of which affect COVID-19 survival rates.[25]

Ethnic origin is not recorded on death certificates in Spain so there are no data regarding the impact of COVID-19 on the death rates of underprivileged ethnic minorities such as Gitanos. However, all the Gitano contributors to this volume have lost family members to the virus. In the large cities such as Madrid and Barcelona, during the spring of 2020, COVID-19 spread much faster in disadvantaged neighborhoods than in other areas. Once the national lockdown finished and the government of Madrid started imposing district-specific restrictions, the zones of the city where most Gitanos live were the ones that spent the longest periods under the most severe restrictions. This has had important knock-on effects on the capacity of Gitano families to earn a living.

Back in March 2020, the Spanish chroniclers witnessed the devastating impact of the sudden lockdown on Gitano subsistence strategies, which were already very precarious. The majority of Gitanos survive on very small incomes. Almost 44 percent of Gitano men and 27 percent of Gitano women earn a living through street vending, either in open-air markets or on foot. Others depend on scrap collecting or seasonal agriculture. As the chroniclers describe in detail, both under full lockdown and later under "softer" restrictions, many families have undergone severe hardship. As I write in October 2021, the impact of social-distancing regulations on street- and market-vending is compounded by the difficulties that many Gitano families are experiencing when they try to access the welfare aid developed in response to the pandemic. Once again, the health crisis feeds on the vulnerability of the Gitano community.

What María Félix and I did not anticipate a year ago was the impact the pandemic would have on the education of Gitano children. This theme is prominent in the accounts of some of the chroniclers, and its significance is underscored by two large-scale surveys carried out by Gitano NGOs in the spring of 2020.[26] Lack of access to technology and Wi-Fi, together with crowded or sub-standard living conditions, severely limited the extent to which many Gitano children were able to access online learning under the first 2020 lockdown, and this continues today. But the chroniclers emphasize as well that these recent problems are exacerbated by older ones, in particular by the very low expectations that non-Gitano teachers and education officials have of Gitano children, by their slowness in responding to crises, and by their lack of understanding of the practical challenges that the children face. All of these are well documented in the literature, and together they combine to make the hurdles generated by the pandemic so much harder to overcome.

Speaking from Within the Crisis

The Spanish chronicles have been written using a diversity of collaborative strategies. They include three pieces written in the first person, and two that were produced in conversation between anthropologists and local interlocutors. They do not aim to provide a comprehensive overview of the effects of the pandemic. Instead, they foreground experiences that, although partial and located, are suggestive of larger trends and dynamics.

María Félix Rodriguez Camacho, a Gitana NGO worker based in Alicante on the east coast, describes how Gitano associations tried to mitigate the devastating effects of the first lockdown on Gitano families who suddenly found themselves with very few resources to survive, and no means to earn a living. She describes the slowness of welfare institutions in responding to the emergency, but her account points also to what Alston denounced in his biting critique: the entrenched acceptance by the Spanish state and its representatives of the inevitability of Gitano deprivation. In the words of Ruth Gilmore, this deprivation is most often regarded as an "unfortunate given" rather than an "intolerable failure."[27]

Like Rodriguez Camacho, the six Gitana community mediators of the Artemisa Network (Dulce Flores Torres, Pilar García Bizárraga, Estrella Iglesias Pérez, Francisca Mayoral Silva, Manuela Mayoral Silva, and Fernanda

Montaño García) stress the precariousness and marginalization that already shaped Gitano lives before the pandemic. Narrating their work in Vallecas, one of the poorest areas of Madrid, they detail pre-existing inequalities in education, employment, social support, and housing. Their stories also evidence the punitive dimension of encounters between Gitanos and state representatives during the crisis, and the consequences for individuals of all ages, from children to the elderly.

The perceived failure of Gitanos to be responsible citizens underlies many state policies and initiatives. Gitanos are often assumed to be unable to behave as demanded by the rules of urban coexistence and, particularly at the start of the pandemic, the Spanish press often depicted them as unruly spreaders of the virus. Beatriz Aragón Martín, an anthropologist and doctor working as a general practitioner in Cañada Real in the spring of 2020, discusses the securitarian measures put in place by the Madrid authorities because of their fear that the Gitanos of the slum would not respect the lockdown. Concerned primarily with the supposed threat posed by Gitanos, they disregarded the vulnerability of the inhabitants of the slum to the pandemic. Whilst non-Gitanos who break the rules are depicted as extreme individualists, it is the collective irresponsibility of Gitanos as an ethnic group that is emphasized both in the media and in state responses.

Yet, as Antonio Montañés Jiménez and Gory Carmona explain in their joint contribution, Evangelical Gitanos living in Villaverde Alto in Madrid saw through and challenged these representations. They attempted to reclaim and rephrase the meaning of civic responsibility, going beyond government requirements in adhering to lockdown and social distancing rules—for example, closing churches throughout the pandemic and keeping services online, even when religious gatherings are allowed by the authorities.

Indeed, all the Spanish chroniclers document the many active, creative strategies that Gitano individuals and groups have put in place to attempt to limit contagion and to mitigate the effects of the pandemic. They describe the ingenious attempts of the Gitanos of Cañada to self-isolate even when basic hygiene and social distancing were so difficult to achieve in the slum; the activities of NGOs who distributed food and basic supplies in the first days of lockdown; and the efforts of families who mobilized to share their resources with their most vulnerable members. Since March 2020, these strategies have provided Gitanos with a network of support that critiques and attempts to replace the absent or reluctant welfare state.

Yet most of these forms of care have limits and, most often, do not overcome the difficulties that they attempt to address. Instead, they provide partial relief only. As Liria Hernández explains, although it is true that Gitanos have made extensive use of online technologies to strengthen support networks, the fact is that the pandemic has devastated their deep reliance on face-to-face contact. Familial solidarity, being physically together, particularly at times of illness and hardship, has been one of the core mechanisms through which Gitanos have historically managed to survive as a distinct community. Hernández describes the huge practical and emotional cost of being forbidden to gather together in these times of death and sickness.

Finally, all the accounts provided by the Spanish chroniclers are unapologetically personal, deeply experiential, and committed. They take as their starting point firsthand experience, speaking from within the entanglements of the crisis. The authors foreground the emotional dimensions of situated knowledge, speaking openly about their anger, distress, doubt, fear or relief. Emotions here are essential components of the events under analysis, but they are also instruments for observation and evaluation: the chroniclers speak of their forceful reactions to the pandemic's effects on Gitanos as tools through which the readers can come to understand the crisis better.

Paloma Gay y Blasco teaches social anthropology at the University of St Andrews in Scotland. She has authored books and articles on ethnographic methods, collaborative anthropology, and Romani issues, including, with Liria Hernández, *Writing Friendship: A Reciprocal Ethnography* (Palgrave Macmillan, 2020).

Notes

1. UN Special Rapporteurs, "Spain: Power Outages."
2. Davies, "Slow Violence," 13.
3. MSSSI, *Estrategia Nacional*, 12.
4. Magazzini and Piamontese, "'Roma' Migration."
5. Fundación Secretariado Gitano, *El impacto de la crisis*; Fundación Secretariado Gitano, *Estudio Comparado*, 212; Hernández-Pedraño, Luque, and Gehrig, *Situación social*, 3.
6. Fundación Secretariado Gitano, *El impacto de la crisis*, 10–11.
7. Hernández-Pedraño, Luque, and Gehrig, *Situación social*, 1–2, 10.
8. Rodriguez, "Los Desafíos," 54.
9. Hernández-Pedraño, Luque, and Gehrig, *Situación social*, 10–11.
10. Fundación Secretariado Gitano, *Estudio comparado*, 125.
11. Hernández-Pedraño, Luque, and Gehrig, *Situación social*.
12. Hernández-Pedraño, Luque, and Gehrig, *Situación social*, 20. By 2018, 65.5 percent of Gitanos aged 16 to 24 had not completed the compulsory education, in comparison with only 7.2 percent of non-Gitano youths (ibid.).
13. cf. CNIIE, *La escolarización*, 1; Magazzini and Piamontese, "'Roma' Migration," 235.

14. Fundación Secretariado Gitano, *El impacto de la crisis*, 13.
15. Ibid.
16. Alston, "Statement."
17. Ibid.
18. Ayala Rubio, "Las Políticas Sociales," 337ff.
19. Ayala Rubio, "Las Políticas Sociales;" Gay y Blasco, "The Best Place."
20. Alston, "Statement."
21. Aragón, et al., "Trabajadores pobres," 120; MSCBS, *Evolución de la pobreza*, 4. The result is that it is no longer possible to take formal employment as an unproblematic sign of upward mobility or integration for Gitanos.
22. Gay y Blasco, "The Best Place."
23. Gay y Blasco, "Place for Civilised People."
24. Gay y Blasco and Camacho, "COVID-19 and its Impact."
25. MSSSI, *Segunda Encuesta*.
26. Arza Porras et al., "COVID-19 Crisis;" Fundación Secretariado Gitano, *Impacto de la crisis*.
27. Gilmore, "Fatal Couplings," 17.

Bibliography

Alston, Philip. "Statement by Professor Philip Alston, United Nations Special Rapporteur on Extreme Poverty and Human Rights, on his Visit to Spain, 27 January." United Nations Office of the High Commissioner for Human Rights, published on 7 February 2020. Retrieved 21 October 2021 from https://www.ohchr.org/EN/NewsEvents/Pages/DisplayNews.aspx?NewsID=25524.

Aragón, Jorge, Jesús Cruces, Luis de la Fuente, Alicia Martínez and Amaia Olategui. "Trabajadores pobres y empobrecimiento en España" [Poor workers and impoverishment in Spain]. *Gizarte Zerbitzuetako Aldizkaria, Revista de Servicios Sociales* 52 (2012): 119–28.

Arza Porras, Javier, Diana Gil-González, Lluís Català-Oltra, Francisco Francés García, María Eugenia González Angulo, Maria Félix Rodríguez Camacho, María José Sanchís Ramón, Belén Sanz-Barbero, Carmen Vives-Cases, and Daniel La Parra Casado. "COVID-19 Crisis: Impact on Households of the Roma Community." *International Journal of Roma Studies* 2(2) (2020): 28–51. http://doi.org/10.17583/ijrs.2020.6242.

Ayala Rubio, Ariadna. "Las políticas sociales en perspectiva socio-antropológica: estudio de la gestión y aplicación de la renta mínima de inserción de la Comunidad de Madrid con el colectivo gitano" [Social policies from a socio-anthropological perspective: A study of the management and implementtion of the minimum integration income among the Gitano collective within the Madrid Region]. PhD diss., Universidad Complutense De Madrid, 2012.

CNIIE (Centro Nacional de Innovación e Investigación Educativa). *La escolarización de la población gitana en España* [Schooling of the Gitano population in Spain]. Madrid: Ministerio de Educación, Cultura y Deporte, 2014.

Davies, Thom. "Slow Violence and Toxic Geographies: 'Out of Sight' to Whom?" *Environment and Planning C: Politics and Space* 40(2) (2022): 409–27. https://doi.org/10.1177/2399654419841063.

Fundación Secretariado Gitano. *El impacto de la crisis en la comunidad gitana* [The impact of the crisis on the Gitano community]. Madrid, 2013.

———. *Estudio comparado sobre la situación de la población gitana en España en relación al empleo y la pobreza 2018* [Comparative study on the situation of the Gitano population in Spain with regards to employment and poverty, 2018]. Madrid, 2018.

———. *Impacto de la crisis del COVID-19 sobre la población gitana en España* [Impact of the COVID-19 crisis on the Gitano population in Spain]. Madrid, 2020.

Gay y Blasco, Paloma. "'It's the Best Place for Them:' Normalising Roma Segregation in Madrid." *Social Anthropology* 24(4) (2016): 446–61. https://doi.org/10.1111/1469-8676.12333.

———. "'This is not a Place for Civilized People:' Isolation, Enforced Education and Resistance among Spanish Gypsies." In *Isolation: Places and Practices of Exclusion*, ed. Alison Bashford and Carolyn Strange, 197–209. London: Routledge.

Gay y Blasco, Paloma, and Maria Félix Rodriguez Camacho. "COVID-19 and its Impact on the Roma Community: The Case of Spain." *Somatosphere*, 31 March 2020. Retrieved 21 October 2021 from http://somatosphere.net/forumpost/covid-19-roma-community-spain/.

Gilmore, Ruth Wilson. "Fatal Couplings of Power and Difference: Notes on Racism and Geography." *The Professional Geographer* 54(1) (2002): 15–24. https://doi.org/10.1111/0033-0124.00310.

Hernández-Pedraño, Manuel, Olga García Luque, and Rainer Bernhard Gehrig. *Situación social de la población gitana en España: balance tras la crisis* [Social situation of the Gitano population in Spain: Evaluation after the crisis]. Murcia: Observatorio de la Exclusión Social de la Universidad de Murcia, 2019.

Magazzini, Tina, and Stephano Piamontese. "'Roma' Migration in the EU: The Case of Spain between 'New' and 'Old' Minorities." *Migration Letters* 13(2) (2016): 228–41. https://doi.org/10.33182/ml.v13i2.304.

MSCBS (Ministerio de Sanidad, Consumo y Bienestar Social). *Evolución de la Pobreza en España 2009–2018: Principales Indicadores* [Evolution of poverty in Spain 2009–2018: Key indicators]. Madrid, 2019.

MSSSI (Ministerio de Sanidad, Servicios Sociales e Igualdad). *Estrategia Nacional para la Inclusión de la Población Gitana en España, 2012–2020* [National strategy for the inclusion of the Gitano population in Spain, 2012–2020]. Madrid, 2014.

———. *Segunda Encuesta Nacional de Salud a Población Gitana 2014* [Second national health survey on the Gitano population, 2014]. Madrid, 2014.

Rodriguez, Isidro. "Los desafíos de la intervención social con la comunidad gitana" [Challenges of social intervention with the Gitano community]. *Rediteia* 49 (2017): 47–60.

UN Special Rapporteurs. "Spain: Power Outages Put Children's Lives at Risk in Informal Settlement." United Nations Office of the High Commissioner for Human Rights, published 22 December 2020. Retrieved 21 October 2021 from https://www.ohchr.org/EN/NewsEvents/Pages/DisplayNews.aspx?NewsID=26624.

CHAPTER 2

Gitana Intercultural Mediators in the Space between Despair and Hope

Dulce Flores Torres, Pilar García Bizárraga,
Estrella Iglesias Pérez, Manuela Mayoral Silva,
Francisca Mayoral Silva, Fernanda Montaño García,
and Paloma Gay y Blasco

Introduction
Paloma Gay y Blasco

The sudden lockdown in mid-March 2020 took public service agencies in Madrid by surprise. From schools to unemployment agencies and social work centers, key institutions became paralyzed as government workers attempted to determine whether and how to continue providing their basic services. Yet at that very moment the needs of individuals and families became, in many cases, even more urgent and extreme. Into that vacuum stepped local organizations, including Gitano associations and NGOs that had already been working in the most deprived and marginalized areas of the city before the pandemic. One of them is the Artemisa Network, which brings together several Gitano NGOs, including Asociación Barró, to coordinate programs in areas such as education (for children and adults), gender equality, cultural mediation, and social assistance.

On 3 June 2020, I met on Zoom with a group of five community mediators from Barró and one from Artemisa who work in Vallecas, one of the districts of Madrid with the largest and most vulnerable Gitano population, and also in Cañada Real, the largest informal settlement in Europe. When we met, Spain was under the state of emergency imposed in response to the first wave of the pandemic, and the new coronavirus world we were living in still felt new.

Before the pandemic, the six mediators had worked on a wide variety of projects supporting Gitano children and parents in their relations with schools, running adult education classes, or setting up workshops on domestic violence. Once the pandemic hit, working from home through mobile phones and tablets, they focused on supporting Gitano families who relied on street vending and whose income had, overnight, been drastically reduced. They also attempted to communicate to schoolteachers the enormous challenges that many Gitano children had to overcome in order to access the most basic forms of online learning. Vallecas was one of the areas of Madrid where COVID-19 spread earliest and fastest, and by the time of our Zoom meeting, five of the women had themselves already had and recovered from the illness.

The mediators described to me their experiences of the lockdown, both as affected individuals and as professionals struggling to bridge the many gaps between Gitano families and the institutions of the Spanish state. Our conversation lasted three long hours, with each mediator presenting her own experiences and perspectives to the group, and everybody commenting on, adding to, and clarifying points made by others. Over the next few days, I transcribed our conversation and constructed each contribution out of the statements made by each of the women. I then sent it to them to review and amend. I acted as facilitator, translator, and editor, attempting to identify and foreground each of the mediator's concerns whilst transforming a chat into a series of coherent written texts. The mediators spoke very much spontaneously, without a script. Each then made some changes to the transcription I presented to them, and they take final responsibility for their own words, as conveyed below.

Their accounts narrate and analyze a series of key themes that run through this book. They describe and critique the marginalization and dehumanization of Gitanos by the institutions of the state and their representatives, before and during the pandemic. In particular, they document the punitive dimensions of encounters between Gitanos and welfare agencies, and their impact on the capacity of Gitano families to survive the severe first lockdown. They also outline the local, grassroots responses put in place by a variety of Gitano institutions, from local associations to Evangelical churches. They discuss the effects of popular and governmental discourses regarding Gitanos on Gitano children, and on their ability to learn on a par with their non-Gitano peers, again both before and during the health emergency. Crucially, they movingly convey how the new experiences of trauma born from the crisis feed on and build upon an earlier, deeply embodied awareness of vulnerability and marginalization.

Positive Actions against the Pandemic
Manuela Mayoral Silva

The Romani population has been greatly affected by the pandemic, especially in Madrid. Back in March 2020, the Gitano associations got to work right away. Within the first week of lockdown, they were all organizing direct actions, working with the most disadvantaged families affected by the situation. However, the official institutions only launched their own responses sometime later. The state institutions took a month or more to show signs of life. They were slowed down by their structures, their systems. They took a long time to decide what was the responsibility of one, what was the competence of another. For example, schools took a long time to decide how to get learning materials to children, and how children were going to access the online platform to carry out the tasks. Schools weren't taking into account that some children do not have internet access or the tools necessary for studying in this situation. By contrast, the associative movement within neighborhoods got up to speed much faster, whichever way they could, without the help of anyone else.

We responded quickly, not only in terms of help but prevention. In Madrid in early March 2020, schools closed, but the state of emergency had not yet been declared by the government. The Artemisa Network has a team of health mediators who, analyzing the situation, realized that Evangelical churches could be important areas of contagion for our population, much like schools. Services take place almost daily, and many elderly people attend as well as many vulnerable people aged over forty-five. We were concerned that there might be infections in the churches, and also that the virus could be more aggressive towards these people because many of them were in poor health.

We analyzed our own population and contacted the public health officials to explain that we were going to inform those responsible for the Evangelical churches, so that they could take action. At the beginning we talked about measures such as reducing the number of days of worship, from five to three, or proposing that the oldest people should not go to church because they are in a risk group. But four or five days before the state of emergency was declared, the president of the Evangelical Church of Filadelfia at the national level, with the elders of the Church, decided to close all the churches in the country, starting with the ones in Madrid and ending with the regions that at that time did not have any recorded cases. In other words, there was an immediate act of prevention in the churches as soon as we realized the challenges of this situation.

For the Gitano population, some of the rules of lockdown were particularly harsh, due to the characteristics of our culture, of our cultural codes. We know that in the Gitano culture it is very important for families to accompany the sick, to be close to the person who suffers and their family—for example, by being present at the hospital. Or when there is a death, it is important and necessary to go to the funeral home and be there all night, while in the majority society when someone dies they do not have the same custom; many of them go home to sleep and come back the following day. And despite this, the Gitano community complied with these lockdown norms; for example, by not holding wakes or by having only three relatives attending funerals. We have endorsed the established norms like the whole society without any conflict.

The Romani population endured the lockdown like the rest of society, I would say maybe with even more fear and more caution. When at long last the rules were eased, and children were allowed to go out for a walk, the Gitano population had so much fear that they said, *It makes little difference, fifteen days earlier or fifteen days later; let's not let the children go out just yet.* And on WhatsApp they said to each other, *Do not take your children out.* And yet this caution has not been recognized by the dominant society—quite the contrary. The press has treated the Gitano population as a whole as irresponsible, particularly at the beginning of the pandemic. When there has been news of groups of other denominations who have not respected the norms, the interpretation has been very different from when Gitanos have been involved, and the issue hasn't received the same elaboration. For me, this is an example of antigypsyism.

It is very important to talk about the situation of Gitano women during lockdown. Gitano women have been the ones who have had to look for resources to support their homes, to find food, to be the caretakers of everyone, even though they may also have been ill themselves. I do not want this book to leave no record of those women, brave women, who have done everything possible to overcome their challenges, who have had to call a mediator twenty times to ask for help, searching everywhere, queueing at the Red Cross or Cáritas. They have been the ones who have gone to find resources to keep their families afloat. And they have done all this despite the fact that they were exposed to the virus, that they were defenseless. They have been the ones who have been proactive when it comes to searching for help and coping with everything.

In the Artemisa Network and the Asociación Barró, when doing our work, we too have had to mobilize and develop new ways of doing things, overcoming barriers and difficulties ourselves as professionals. For example, there has been talk of the digital divide with regard to children and schooling, but it is necessary to also talk about the digital divide that we, as Romani professionals, have faced. Mediation is a very down-to-earth profession; we become very close to our clients, and this has not been possible during lockdown. We have had to change the way we work, and begin to learn to use computers, learn to do things differently, and become familiar with technology that we were not very used to. We have had to catch up. And we have encountered barriers and discrimination even here, because there are some of us mediators who find this new work easier, and others for whom it is much harder. Some can do it and do it quickly, whilst others have more difficulty. We have to face the need to be fair and to help that person who is not so agile working through these platforms. Even in these places, in these circumstances, we have also had to break stereotypes and prejudices.

Mediators between a Stone and a Hard Place
Estrella Iglesias Pérez

I work as a mediator in a social services center. Before COVID, social workers used to refer to me some of those cases that needed more specific attention from the figure of the mediator. These are cases in which social workers have made a previous intervention but with few results. I followed up with them through visits, calls, and meetings. My job was a bit like providing support for social workers.

With the pandemic, my work changed radically because the phone would not stop ringing. Many families contacted me, even those who were not in my caseload. The biggest problem was that, before COVID, many of the families survived thanks to the informal economy; they lived in part from unregulated street vending. And they needed that income along with the help they received from social services. Gitano people do not have many avenues open to obtain regular employment, but neither can they support themselves with only what they receive from state aid, what with the cost of food, rent, and bills. And the reality is that surviving just on state aid is impossible. You live as you can. Families could not declare this additional income from street vending because it would have been deducted from their Minimum Income,[1] leaving them unable to survive.

With lockdown they could not continue doing their kind of work. But social services thought that these families did not need additional help in the face of the pandemic, because in their eyes their situation was the same as before, given that they continued to receive the same aid. *You don't need help. You subsisted with this money, so you will continue to have that money and we will not be able to help you with more.* So the situation for many families became very desperate.

When a Gitano family needs urgent help, they have to call 010, and from there they are passed on to the social workers, and it takes a long time until they communicate with the workers, and until the help is approved and received. So, of course, what do they do? They contact me, because they know that I work directly with the social workers, so that I can call them and expedite it. I always take forward their request, and I explain to the families that it's a slow process, and that the social workers are dealing with emergencies, and so it is difficult to get hold of them. You feel so bad seeing the families that are in need, you put yourself in their skin; what they are asking for is help. I tell myself, *Calm down, this is not my fault. I have requested this, everything takes its time, I cannot do anything.* But sometimes families become impatient.

The processes are very slow and inflexible. For example, a family had the Minimum Income withdrawn due to the child's absence from school in March, and in June they still hadn't had the Income reinstated. The Asociación Barró has helped them for two months, but with just 200 euros per month, which is very little money for a family to survive on. And then the social services, seeing that Barró had already given that help, decided to give aid instead to other people in need. Sometimes the social services do not seem aware that 200 euros per month is not enough for a family to support themselves... It's very frustrating.

During the lockdown, I was overwhelmed, very anguished and feeling very helpless. I belong to the same ethnic group as the people who are requesting aid, and I know firsthand the situation of each one. The families contacted me at all hours, and of all the cases that came to me and that I transmitted to social services, they did not receive a single positive response, despite the very bad situations that they found themselves in.

We the mediators are an important and useful resource that the social workers are often not fully aware of. I pass on information and at all times I tell them, *You can count on me for whatever you want.* But during the pandemic they only contacted me a few times. The social services professionals do not know about the roles and the benefits of mediation. Because our profession is so unusual, and because we belong to the Gitano community, it is difficult for them to see us fully as experts or professionals. They do not have the same attitude towards us that we have towards them. There is a clear power differential. The actions and decisions that we want to undertake have to be assessed and approved by various people. This means that our self-esteem goes down because we realize that it is the established professions that are valued. They are professionals, and we... I don't know what we are.

My opinion is that this situation arises because there is mistrust towards mediation as a profession and because we belong to same community as the clients; and so it seems to the social services that we are going to try to take advantage, so that the families will be given aid. And it seems to some professionals that, if they call on us mediators, they are going to be even more overwhelmed, and that it will make more people apply for aid. Because it is true that when there is a demand from families, social services deal with it but processes are slow. And they know that our role is seen by the Gitano families as closer to them, more empathetic, and that we know well the real situation of the people who come to us. This means that we deal with issues faster if we can, and according to the various needs.

So during the pandemic, working within social services, I have not always felt fully included or fully legitimized by some people or professionals. More recently, with the pandemic easing off, the situation has become normalized, and I feel much more like just another colleague or professional.

No Means to Earn a Living
Fernanda Montaño García

I was infected, and I was isolated in my room for thirty-five days, inside the family apartment, away from my husband and my children. During this time, I went to the hospital, I went to the health center, and they always told me the same thing, *Go home and take paracetamol.* They told me that my pneumonia was not severe, and to isolate myself at home. The last time, at the hospital, they told me that if I can't isolate myself at home, to stay in the waiting room all night until eight in the morning, and then they will send me to the field hospital. I didn't think I had the strength to spend the night in a waiting room that was bursting with people with the same symptoms, and so I went home to isolate myself.

I came home and I was very worried, I was very frightened, because I had seen around me so many people that I knew were dying, they were very gravely ill. At home I wouldn't leave the bedroom because I have my husband and three children, so as not to infect them. And I felt tremendous helplessness and fear, for myself and for my family.

I receive the Minimum Income. My husband sells fruit in the streets, and during the entire time of lockdown, three months that went by, my husband could not go out to sell. It is a home with five people and there are many bills, and of course locked in the room I felt all the worry, all the fear, and I said, *My God, and if I die, what are my husband and my children going to do?* Because I thought I was going to die, truly, I was terribly afraid. And of course, I also felt a lot of helplessness, because we didn't have enough money, it just couldn't be stretched. What do we do?

After thirty-five days like this, they repeated the test for the virus at the health center and now it was negative, so they told me that now I can leave my room. So of course, I felt a lot of anxiety. I couldn't stand up, I came out very weak, I had lost ten kilos, I felt like everything was collapsing on top of me. It was something emotional that I haven't told anyone until now. I've had a very bad time, very bad. I'm better now, thank God.

When I left, and as we were in a very difficult financial situation, I called the emergency number to ask for help, because we needed food. My social worker called me and said, *Look, you can't have anything else because you are collecting Minimum Income, so you can't be helped in any way.* Then I explained, *We need food.* She said no, it couldn't be done because I received the Minimum Income, and they didn't help me. And she didn't call me again.

I use the Minimum Income to pay the house bills, and we use the income from street vending for our food and other needs. And that money from vending we need it to survive, it is essential. But that is not seen by social services or any institution. Gitano people are not listened to, even if they try to communicate. Even if they hear us, they don't listen to us because they don't take us seriously, they don't believe us.

I remember that in 2012 I was working in Plata y Castañar at the pool, and I also had the Minimum Income and was earning 500 euros at that time. And because of having worked three summer months, they suspended my Income for sixteen months. It was something tremendous—we got behind with all the bills, the apartment, the rates, well, it was something awful. And I remember that I had a meeting with the social worker and she told me that they don't take us seriously because they know that there is always a black economy, and that Gitanos do not have the need that we always say we have. And I remember on another occasion that I said, *I want to get out of the Minimum Income, I want a job, I want to work.* And the social worker told me, *But are you a Gitana?* And I tell him, *Yes.* He says, *Well, how weird that you want to get out of the Minimum Income.*

So of course, they don't listen to us, they don't hear us, and they never take seriously what a Gitana woman tells them, never, if it is not through another person. Very few Payo people believe the truth of what we say, very few.

When you have a real need, it really hurts a lot, being treated like this. You say, *Why do they have to treat me like this if I am going to do something that is a humiliation, to beg? Why do they have to mistreat me over the need that I am going through, or the process that I am going through?* But it happens to us so often, that you take it as a norm. You don't even stop to think about it anymore. If they give it to you, good. If they don't give it to you, then you hold on.

New Forms of Discrimination
Dulce Flores Torres

Well, I've been working in the association for a little while. But I've had contact with our people, as I say, with my people, our people, well, my whole life. I am working as a social mediator supporting women in a neighborhood a little more complicated than others in Madrid, a more vulnerable population. I work with a group of Gitana women and another of Moroccan women to empower them, give them knowledge, convey to them a little of what there is outside their environment. Help them get to know themselves. I am also working in the high school, with the teenagers of this population, of this neighborhood.

These are children with more difficulties than other children: they are Gitanos and with the added bonus of living in this neighborhood. They are doubly disadvantaged. *Not only am I a Gitano or Gitana, a boy or a girl, a teenager, but I also live in this neighborhood.*

With COVID I have noticed a horrible abandonment towards these people in this neighborhood. This neighborhood is excluded from society, it is always under lockdown because it is isolated; even in normal times, if you don't have a car, there is no way to get in or out. Ambulances don't go in, or firefighters—nothing. And to this situation of isolation in which they always live, now is added the experience of the pandemic, lockdown, fear, dread, ignorance. *If I get sick, what will happen to my dear ones? How can my family support themselves?*

They called me with anguish, with fear, fears, crying, *I can't, I don't have anything in the fridge, I don't have food.* Because in normal times, you go calling for scrap, you go to sell some socks, you make ends meet as we say, and you bring the daily bread to your house. But all this was no longer possible during lockdown. They reach such desperation that, as they don't have enough, within families they blame each other. And they call me, *Look, because of my mother-in-law's fault I can't get the Minimum Income, let's see if you can help me.* More fears.

And me, *What path do I take? What do we do?* I find myself between a rock and a hard place. Because as a mediator if you ask me for help and I tell you, *There isn't enough to help you*, I am giving the feeling of failure, not as Dulce the Gitana person but as Dulce the person who works in this organization, like I am not reliable, I fail, I am even making my role look bad, saying that it is not worth it.

In my own life, I have also seen how the crisis has worsened the discrimination that already existed. In the high school, on the day when we went to close everything down to begin the lockdown, it was crazy; we met to see how we were going to carry on working during lockdown, and I noticed that the teachers looked at each other to see who dared to ask me something. And one of them dared and said to me, *Dulce, because you are Gitana you go to the Evangelical church, right?* And I say, *Yes, I am a Gitana, but these days I am not going to church. Why? What do you want to know? What do you want to ask me?* And she tells me, *Nothing, I don't know if you have found out, I imagine you may have found out from your family, that the Gitano population has infected several people because things have got a bit out of control.* I didn't know what she was talking about, until later I found out that there was a church where there were some infections. Just as there were care homes, schools, and other places where there were so many infections.

And the most curious thing is that one of them had been on a trip to Italy where at that time the situation was extremely difficult with the pandemic. And they didn't ask her anything. But they, they asked me if I went to church. But you cannot say anything because afterwards you have to go on working there, you have to gain their trust, you cannot be defensive. But you always have to be justifying yourself, pretending that you have as much human value and as many human qualities as them, that you and I are the same. But there is always that barrier. And it's something that you already adapt to yourself, to your being, to your chromosome; it's like you must accept it gradually.

And you notice the rejection even within your neighborhood, with neighbors that you have known all your life but who refuse to greet you during the coronavirus; they close the door in your face when you're going to go in or out through the staircase of the building. Before, they asked you if your son could help them with a shopping bag, and now they won't even speak to you. And at the shop, in the queue to enter, the shop employees react differently because you are a Gitana, *Please don't lower your mask, use the hand gel*, ordering you around. And it is true that it's not a big deal, but they are details that you notice gradually.

It even happens at the hospital. I took my boy to the emergency room because he had a very, very hard time breathing and he had a very high fever. I got scared, *This is not a cold, it is not pharyngitis, there is something else, he has developed pneumonia*. And they told me no, that Gitanos are always going on the same. *You all* (there wasn't anybody else there, my son and I were alone), *you all are always the same, you want us to treat you very quickly*. I insisted so much they took an X-ray and he had pneumonia. The answer was that we always come with the same attitude, demanding, and wanting to be the first to be served.

As for the adolescents and the high school, with the lockdown it has taken a lot of effort for the teachers to realize that they cannot do the work, as they don't have the resources or the financial means to do their homework online as demanded. In Cañada there is no internet, not everyone has a laptop, a computer, a very good mobile phone. They don't even get regular mail. How did the teachers want the children to do their homework? The teachers even said, *They have mobiles and can do their homework with the mobile.* The children said, *I can't download documents or upload homework because I don't have a computer, I don't have a tablet, I don't have enough money to get credit for my phone.* There were documents that were very large and they could not download them, or work on them, or upload the homework.

I insisted a lot that the children couldn't work like that, that they, the teachers, had to take their homework to them printed out, in folders. It took a lot of effort before the teachers finally got it, you had to force them to chew it. And it took a long time, but finally the high schools sorted things out very well so that it could be done that way. And that was the work that I did. Then I did see that I had something to contribute. It was a good feeling. I felt very happy because, of course, the homework arrived late, because in the schools they came to understand things late, but eventually it did arrive. And in the neighborhood they knew me and said, *She's my teacher and she's bringing me the materials.* The bad thing is that the children missed almost the entire year.

Advocating for Gitano Children
Pilar García Bizárraga

I work on absenteeism issues at a high school. The children already faced a lot of challenges there before the COVID crisis. Gitano children are segregated at the high school, and there are classes only for Gitano children. It is true that they don't say it like that; clearly, the teachers say that the classes are separated according to the level of the children. But, what a coincidence that all the children on the same level are Gitanos! A first-year class only with Gitano children, another second-year class only with Gitano children. And then there are the SSG, which is the acronym for Singular Specific Group, which is where children who have very low grades go, and are usually all Gitanos, although sometimes there is also a child of Moroccan origin.

Most of the students I work with are from a marginal neighborhood here in Madrid, a neighborhood with many difficulties, where there are no buses; they cannot go out and they cannot go in, and the children don't have internet. These children have the right to an education, and during the COVID crisis I have had to argue or fight for them to have access to what other children were getting.

It was decided in Madrid that schools were going to send homework to children online. But in reality, in the high school where I work, homework was not sent to all children, but only to those that the teachers chose, the ones the teachers thought were going to do the homework. Because the teachers thought it was not worth it, sending homework to children who were not going to do it: *I am not going to bother to send homework to this boy.* The same happened with the distribution of tablets to children so that they could do homework: there wasn't a single Gitano child on the list to receive a tablet. But these are the children who need it the most because they have the least; maybe in a family of ten they only have one mobile phone and the children cannot download their homework on there. These children have to fight twice as hard to get the easiest things done.

These are families who face very serious difficulties, who sometimes do not even have a plate of food, who are isolated, and in which the fathers and mothers do not know how to defend the rights of their children. The teachers think, *Well, since these mothers are not going to give me trouble, I'm not going to concern myself with those children.*

Already in normal life, outside the lockdown, children and families face much misunderstanding. The teachers think that Gitano children have no interest in going to secondary school. The head of studies at the high school told me when I myself went to enroll in the third year of secondary, *What do you want to study for if you are Gitana?* So, sure, it's demoralizing. If they tell you, *You are not worth it, you are not worth it, you are not worth it, why do you bother studying*... children take on that message and it creates a trauma for them. When they enter high school they are 11 or 12 years old, and from the beginning they are told, *You go here, to the class where the children misbehave, here you don't have to work, you only listen to music, and you can just fall sleep if you want to.* Well, of course they assume that role and they think that is what they have to do. And all of this has been greatly aggravated by the coronavirus.

The same thing happens in primary schools. It has happened to me, with my son. Now with the crisis, I went to school to pick up the child's homework so that he could do it at home. But then his tutor wouldn't answer me when I sent him emails to ask how we should hand in the homework, or for the child to participate in online activities. And I was wondering, *Why is the child going to do homework here if there is no teacher to send it to.* I felt a horrible unease, I spent a terrible week; even at night I had trouble sleeping. I felt helpless, I couldn't understand it. Then I was very angry and just had to send an email to the director of the school. The next day she called me apologizing. And from then on, communication has been fluid.

But there are families that don't have those resources that I had, they don't have the ability to say *I'm going to send an email to the headteacher*, or *Who do I have to complain to?* They don't even know how to send an email; they don't know where to go. They are people who have never used a computer, so it's impossible for them to get online and download something, even if they try. The digital divide that Gitano boys and girls face has affected them very much in this crisis, and of course they are not going to advance but to regress now. When the children go back to school they will be very delayed, because they have not had access to digital platforms during lockdown, and because many parents do not have the educational level to be able to help their children. *I don't know how I can help my child, I don't even know how to do it myself.*

Looking to the Future
Francisca Mayoral Silva

There is an article that I was reading recently that said, *How beautiful and how difficult it is to be Gitano*. Well yes, how beautiful, and how difficult.

We are experiencing very strong racism. Before the pandemic there was already racism but with COVID I think it has tripled. Because some Evangelical people in Seville skipped the lockdown, it has been said that all the Gitanos have skipped it, that no Evangelical church respected the rules. This led to the armed forces being sent there and also to comments such as *Shitty Gypsies, you are giving us coronavirus*. Gitanos have been said to have spread the virus, for example at the beginning, at a funeral. We have heard it said that all Gitanos are infected and that we are spreading it.

The media has not paid attention to the positive things that many Roma people have done during the crisis. For example, they do not talk about the food banks that the Gitano associations have organized, and that have helped both Gitanos and non-Gitanos. And when the lockdown is over and we go back to work, we are going to have to work hard on this whole issue of racism, both with our people, who are very hurt (*Payos always say the same things about us*), and with Payo people, to make them aware that Gitanos have not acted the way they think.

I also want to tell you that many Gitano families have experienced great difficulties during lockdown. It is very easy to say that a person who becomes ill must self-isolate in a room. But if an extended family lives in a small apartment, with grandparents, parents, grandchildren, how can a person self-isolate? With the schools we have also had many difficulties, and I have realized that the role of the cultural mediator is increasingly important. We have had to help families with homework over the phone, constantly. There are many families that cannot access technology and they have said to me, *Teachers send me the children's homework with an app, but I don't know how to use it, it's very difficult*; or *My mobile phone is very old and it's not good for this, they have to send it to me by email and I do not have email*. And we have had to mediate between the two parties, explaining the situation to the teachers, *Let's see if you can send it through WhatsApp, in an easier format for the family who are having a very hard time. It's not that they don't want to try, it's that they can't.*

And we have also encouraged women a lot, because in most families it is women who have borne the most. They tell me, *I get up, I've got so much to do that I can't stop... My mother has fallen ill, I have to take care of my father-in-law, I have to take care of my family, I don't have time to sit down to do homework.* And we have encouraged the mothers to help the children with their homework, *Yes, I understand, but you have to give it a bit of your time.* We have facilitated and encouraged.

And now that the lockdown is over, we are trying to make the young girls see how important it is to study, which is something that has become very clear to us during lockdown, seeing so many people who have lost their jobs or cannot go out to sell in the streets. I contribute to a project where, before the pandemic, girls were trained, empowered, listened to, encouraged to talk about their needs. We were working with them on very beautiful things such as the importance of getting an education and how they saw the significance of school. And now with the pandemic we are working with them, reflecting with them, so that they realize that studying is increasingly important, with so many people they have been left without work and everything that this entails.

Dulce Flores Torres is an intercultural mediator working at the Asociación Barró in Madrid, focusing in particular on the district of Villa de Vallecas. Her work centers on the needs of the Gitano and Moroccan populations in the informal settlement of Cañada Real Galiana.

Pilar García Bizárraga is an intercultural mediator working at the Asociación Barró in Madrid, working on education and school absenteeism. She also works within the program Leadership Against Gender Violence, also organized by the Asociación Barró.

Estrella Iglesias Pérez is an intercultural mediator working at the Asociación Barró and a social services centre, both in Madrid. She works on mediation issues in connection with the Gitano population in the district of Puente de Vallecas.

Francisca Mayoral Silva works as intercultural mediator at the Asociación Barró in Madrid. She has worked for many years in mediation projects in schools, health contexts, and communities, contributing also to European mediation projects. She currently works within social services in the Puente de Vallecas district of the city, focusing specifically on the Gitano community.

Manuela Mayoral Silva works as intercultural mediator and coordinates the mediation projects of Asociación Barró in Puente de Vallecas and Villa de Vallecas in the south of Madrid. She is also the president of the Federación Red Artemisa, which gathers together a number of NGOs working on issues of social exclusion and marginality in Spain.

Fernanda Montaño García is an intercultural mediator at the Red Artemisa in Madrid. She works in the field of education, in both primary and secondary schools. She also works at local health centers on issues to do with the health of Gitana women.

Paloma Gay y Blasco teaches social anthropology at the University of St Andrews in Scotland. She has authored books and articles on ethnographic methods, collaborative anthropology, and Romani issues, including, with Liria Hernández, *Writing Friendship: A Reciprocal Ethnography* (2020 Palgrave Macmillan).

Note

1. The Minimum Income for Integration, or Renta Mínima de Inserción, is a governmental economic support for people considered to be at risk of social exclusion in the region of Madrid. To receive it, recipients must enter into a tailor-made so-called integration contract. Receiving the money is dependent on the beneficiary undertaking a series of agreed activities, such as attending re-education classes or taking children to school regularly. Since compliance needs to be monitored on an ongoing basis, the Minimum Income is one of the key tools of Gitano control and invigilation.

CHAPTER 3

"Who Cares...? Hunger Will Kill Us If the Virus Does Not"

The COVID-19 Pandemic in an Informal Settlement in Madrid

Beatriz Aragón Martín

In March 2020, the COVID-19 pandemic, the global event in a globalized world, stopped the world for a while. In the era of hypermobility, airports were empty, highways were transited by just a few trucks carrying "essential goods," and there were no more traffic jams on the main roads of the big cities of the Global North. Images of deserted tourist destinations circulated on social media to illustrate that the world had come to a standstill. However, while the public health recommendations to "stay home" and "keep socially distant" were feasible for those who had a home in which to stay, for those who had enough space and enough savings to live on, there were other lifeworlds where not being outside presented unsurmountable challenges. For those who made a living from informal economies, who relied on daily income to survive and who were unable to afford a dwelling that would include the most basic facilities, the pandemic was not an interruption. Instead, it involved not just the continuation but the intensification of their daily struggles.

Gautman Bahn, Teresa Caldeira, Kelly Gillespie, and AbdouMaliq Simone reflect on this continuity in the everyday lives of the southern majority, despite the global pandemic crisis: in the contexts they describe, crisis is already part of the everyday.[1] They urge us to look at what they call *collective life* as "it keeps the focus where it must be: on the ways in which the urban majority is trying to survive and cope with structures of inequality that now bear both the new imprint of COVID-19 while equally holding the continuities of older forms of distancing and exclusion."[2]

Focusing on *collective life* as these authors urge us to do, in this chapter I reflect on my experience as a general medical practitioner in an informal settlement on the southern outskirts of Madrid during the months of the severe lockdown between mid-March and mid-June 2020. I look back on a very specific moment when the impact of the virus itself and the number of infections was proportionally lower in the settlement than in the rest of the city (Madrid was one of the most affected cities in Spain during the first wave). Nevertheless, while I am writing this article in November 2020 the number of cases is rapidly increasing both in Madrid and in the settlement, and I wonder what is going to happen this time around. Moreover, since last month, a power outage in the settlement means the inhabitants have no electricity and, despite the pandemic, neither the national nor the regional governments have restored it. The reflections I present here are not universal public health mandates applicable to any settlement, but a description of how the Gitano inhabitants of Cañada Real have translated unfeasible public health dictates into creative ways of protecting and caring for each other.

The Settlement

Located on the south-east periphery of Madrid, Cañada Real is a de facto slum, an informal lineal settlement built on the sides of an old cattle track (thus its name, *cañadas reales* were paths used for transhumance up to the mid-twentieth century). Around three thousand people, of whom twelve hundred are children, live in the most populated sector of Cañada Real (Sector 6). Single-story houses made of recycled scrap materials connected illegally to the electric grid and water supplies are scattered along the 7 kilometers that make up this sector.[3] Usually, an extended family live on one plot where three or four rickety houses share a common yard. Since migrants from Spanish rural areas claimed their allotments here in the aftermath of the Spanish Civil War (1950s), the physiognomy of the settlement has evolved. Nowadays, North African migrants who arrived during the 2000s "construction boom" occupy shacks next to the rudimentary houses of elderly non-Romani Spaniards. Among them live Romanian Romanies, and also Gitanos who had been displaced from settlements demolished by the council during the many "slum eradication plans" of the 1990s and early 2000s, or who were evicted from their homes for other reasons. The sporadic pass of cattle has been replaced by the continuous circulation of garbage trucks that go to the nearby dumpsite, and the traffic of drug users who hang around the area.

Isolated between busy highways, Cañada Real lacks basic public services (such as schools, a primary healthcare center, and public transport) but it does have a highly negative image in the public sphere. The Spanish media depict Cañada Real as the "biggest drug supermarket in Europe",[4] and emphasize how close this place of unruliness and backwardness is to the city center, implicitly showing the threat that its existence poses to the ideal of modern citizenship. In a similar fashion, the negative stereotypes linked to the settlement are also connected to its dwellers, particularly and more intensively with the Gitano inhabitants who make up half the population of the settlement.

In Spain, and specifically in Madrid, Gitanos are overrepresented in the lower social strata and in informal settlements. In a city where housing is becoming more and more unaffordable for vast segments of the population, Gitanos have a long history of segregation and poor access to housing, which have been explained in political and media debate as a cultural phenomenon.[5] As I have explained elsewhere, it is as if living in an informal settlement was the Gitanos' cultural choice: the argument goes that it is their unruliness and backwardness that keep them in settlements that are "out of place" and "out of time."[6]

Low Incidence

Before the first lockdown started in Madrid, many of my patients in Cañada asked me about that new virus coming from China, making jokes about the possibility of being infected when someone had a fever. I tended to answer those questions with another one: "Have you recently been to China? Me neither, so do not worry."[7] When infections in Italy started to grow, I began to worry, but could not imagine what was to come. On 15 March 2020, the national government declared the state of emergency, implementing a three-month national lockdown that only permitted people to go outside to walk their dogs or shop for groceries, and essential workers to go to their jobs. Over the following weeks, as an essential worker I needed a special pass (to show at the mobile checking points) to go to work every day, and every day I drove almost alone along the empty highway that leads to the settlement. There were very few cars, few people in the street, just the odd queue—spread out through distancing—indicating an open supermarket. Streets were empty. People followed the official mandate and stayed home.

Yet, arriving at the settlement, life seemed to keep going as if there was no lockdown. People were outside their houses, just sitting by the door or doing their domestic chores in the yards. At first glance, it seemed that the pandemic was not affecting these people's lives, or else that they did not care about the virus. In fact, the Gitanos of Cañada were highly concerned and worried about the spread of the virus, and they incessantly demanded information from the healthcare workers about new cases of local transmission of COVID-19 at the settlement, and about ways to protect themselves from getting infected. As healthcare workers, we shared the inhabitants' preoccupation with the possibility of a quick spread of the virus within the slum. We were very concerned about the limited options available at the settlement for self-isolation in cases of infection.

But the cases did not increase and, by contrast with what happened in the surrounding neighborhoods, during the first wave (March–May 2020) COVID-19 incidence remained low at Cañada Real. How can we explain that in a deprived area, where most inhabitants live in substandard crowded houses and shacks, sometimes using communal toilets and having limited access to clean water, the virus did not spread as much as it did in more affluent areas? There are multiple factors that could partially illuminate this. First, and maybe most saliently, is the fact that the settlement is isolated from the rest of the city, which may have helped stop the spread of the virus. In this sense, the pandemic highlighted the pre-existing segregation of those who live in the settlement from the rest of the city, with all the implications that this has in terms of accessing public services. The settlement embodies the truest meaning of what we have wrongly come to call "social distance:"[8] there are scarce social relations between its inhabitants and the rest of Madrid. The people of Cañada were in very real terms already confined to their slum before the pandemic: surrounded by motorways and wastelands, and serviced by just one public bus line, Cañada Real is close to the city center yet also very clearly segregated from it. Most of the Gitano people living in Cañada only leave the slum to collect scrap, buy food, or visit relatives from time to time.

Nevertheless, there were some cases of people who became infected (mostly at their workplaces) and aggregated cases from families, but the chains of contagion stopped within the immediate kin group. And, while the governmental demand that infected people must isolate came late, I saw, even before it was announced, very creative methods of isolation in the settlement, albeit ones that would not fit the ideals of public health officials. For example, one elderly couple who live with their children and grandchildren managed to isolate themselves in one room and put a ladder to get out through a small window to go to an external toilet that they did not share with the rest of the family.

Indeed, the second factor that could have influenced the limited spread of the virus is the settlement's architecture. Although the houses are usually extremely small, crowded, and poorly ventilated, most of them are located within a bigger plot shared with other members of the extended family, and most of the communal familial life takes place outdoors. Furthermore, the lineal disposition of the houses, spreading alongside the track, creates a distance between neighbors too. In fact, there were two levels of isolation: firstly, the settlement was isolated from the rest of the city; and secondly, families isolated themselves in kin clusters from the rest of the settlement inhabitants.

Control versus Care

Despite the low incidence of COVID-19 in the slum, the local authority (the Regional Commissioner for Cañada Real) required from the national government the deployment of the army to the slum "to assure that all the inhabitants of Cañada comply with the confinement measures and to supervise movements from the settlement and avoid those that are not allowed."[9] This request was made several times and was echoed by the media, even though forcing people in Cañada to stay inside their houses with minimum ventilation and extremely limited space would carry considerably more risk than allowing them to be outside.

The demand for an authoritarian response was not an isolated phenomenon in Cañada but happened in other neighborhoods throughout Spain with a majority Gitano population.[10] The emphasis on the social control of Gitanos is rooted in the commonly shared idea that they are unable to comply with social norms and that, even if they try, they will fail. Therefore, special measures are required to ensure compliance. This idea is not new and has not arisen from the COVID-19 crisis management: it is deeply embedded in the history of state management of Gitanos through so-called "inclusion strategies."[11]

In the end, the army has not been deployed in Cañada and people have continued their adapted routines to the pandemic. During the first week of lockdown, the primary healthcare unit in the settlement (a mobile healthcare van where I work as a GP)[12] visited those families that had members with chronic health conditions, and who were therefore more vulnerable to the virus. The primary healthcare unit consists of a nurse and a general practitioner who have been working at the settlement for more than ten years now, and so know who the most vulnerable inhabitants are. The healthcare team provides care at people's houses on a regular basis, and we profited from that knowledge and from the trust gained during all the time working at the settlement, evaluating the risks of contagion, and planning strategies to avoid it. The healthcare team aimed to assess and consider together with families' different ways of protecting themselves—ways that were feasible, and acceptable for the families. The preventive strategy devised was twofold: first, by identifying those people who were physically more vulnerable to the infection (because of age and chronic conditions) and, secondly, by assessing together with them the different situations that would entail more risk of contagion, and advising how to avoid them.

One of the prevention strategies that worked better was to keep children outdoors and prevent them from being near those who were more vulnerable to the virus (people with chronic conditions, grandparents). Gitanos in Spain, and especially in Cañada, have a below-average health status: the proportion of chronic conditions such as diabetes, COPD, and high blood pressure is greater than in better off populations, with younger onsets and higher morbidity.[13] Having lunch together tended to be the riskiest activity: it is usual for several related nuclear families to come together for lunch, elders included. In the conversations, one of the ideas that came up was to share the food but not the table. For example, if the grandmother is the one who cooks for their children and grandchildren, she could continue doing so, but instead of eating at the grandmother's house, the rest of the family could gather in another house to protect the grandmother in case any of them was infected. The healthcare team advised the people of Cañada to have social interactions outdoors as much as possible and to limit them to those who shared the same yard; this was feasible and it would reduce the risk of contagion. These guidelines were not planned in advance by the healthcare team and just transmitted to the population: families and the healthcare team together discussed and thought through the biomedical information they had about the virus at that time, and about the possibilities, constraints, and preferences of the families. Still, sometimes it was impossible to implement all these strategies: for example, grandparents had to take care of their grandchildren if their parents became sick and were admitted to the hospital.

Besides the proactive initiative of the healthcare workers visiting Gitano families with vulnerable patients to discuss the best ways to care for and protect each other, many other slum inhabitants directly asked the healthcare workers for help. Some people asked for face masks, others wanted guidance to keep the house clean, and yet others were worried about symptoms. Gitanos in Cañada, as most of the Spanish population elsewhere, were worried by the pandemic and made rearrangements in their lives to avoid contagion. For example, one family that was going through a very difficult economic moment because of the lockdown restrictions decided not to go to the social center (where some NGOs are located) to ask for emergency aid, fearing that meeting a lot of people there would entail a high risk of contagion. Other extended families organized themselves to send just one person to the supermarket (another risky place) to buy food for everyone. At a time when wearing face masks was yet not compulsory or widespread, Gitanos in Cañada were already improvising, handcrafting them from pieces of cloth.

Meanwhile, the regional commissioner repeatedly called for the deployment of the army to the settlement, arguing the need to control movements from the settlement to the city, and wanting to restrict these movements to those authorized. There were mobile check points on the main roads where police attempted to identify those who did not have a permit to move, and where, if stopped, you had to prove that you were less than one kilometer from your residence. As previously mentioned, during the national three-month lockdown, being outside was limited to essential activities such as buying food, medicines, and going to the hospital. Nevertheless, this national regulation had particular consequences for the settlement's inhabitants. Because of the total lack of facilities such as shops and pharmacies at the settlement, it was harder for the inhabitants to fulfil basic needs than it was for people living in regular neighborhoods with facilities close at hand. For example, to get out of the settlement you need a car as the exits lead to a highway where pedestrians are not allowed. There is one public bus stop at one of the entrances to the settlement, but during the lockdown there was no service. Only one person per car was permitted to go out, and non-residents were not allowed into the settlement. So, it was impossible for adult children living elsewhere to deliver food to their elderly parents. On one occasion an elderly couple who have no car and no children living in the settlement asked their neighbor to give the wife a lift to withdraw money from a cash point: they were stopped at the exit of the settlement by the police and not allowed to get out. These kinds of situations were not specific to the settlement; they also happened in other neighborhoods as the regulation that triggered them was national. However, the lack of basic public infrastructure and amenities, the total dependence on private transport, and the perception that Gitanos and immigrants were unruly and uncompliant all added extra layers of difficulty. For the people of the settlement, the mobility restrictions entailed further limitations with regards to how to communicate with others (not being able to top up your phone), how to feed yourself adequately, and how to access basic facilities such as health centers and cash points.

Not Earning a Living

Moreover, one of the main problems that the mobility restrictions posed was the impossibility for most of the people of the settlement to earn a living during lockdown. Most of the Gitanos in Cañada work in the informal economy collecting scrap. During the lockdown, due to the precarious and irregular character of their work, they had no way to prove that their displacements were lawful. Thus, the choices they had were either to stay at the settlement and try to find some means of earning a living, or to venture out of the settlement to collect scrap but with the risk of getting fined (and of not even finding an open scrapyard). As the council emergency aid was not delivered during the first weeks of the lockdown, several families struggled to obtain sufficient food, and worried intensely about their inability to make a living. Following the fear in the first weeks of pandemic of getting sick, another fear emerged and remained: how to subsist economically in "the new normality," and more urgently how to feed one's family. "Hunger will kill us if the virus does not" was uttered several times in those days, accompanied by complaints about what was seen as institutional abandonment.

Conclusions

The inhabitants of the settlements took all the precautions they could to avoid contagion. This was very far from the catastrophic image presented by the media, which echoed the institutional discourses of the regional commissioner and other authorities, that Cañada was a place where people "did not understand quarantines."[14] Looking at *collective lives*[15] of Cañada inhabitants we discover multiple mechanisms of resistance, protection, and adaptation to cope with the difficulties of the lockdown measures and to safeguard themselves from the virus. Nevertheless, the economic and social effect of the pandemic for the Gitano population in Cañada was and continues to be extremely severe, exacerbating their marginalization and economic precarity. While Gitano families have drawn upon all their survival skills to endure the COVID-19 crisis as well as the ongoing chronic crisis they live in, the institutional responses aimed at mitigating the pandemic's effects have clearly been insufficient, and nuanced by antigypsyism. In the case of Cañada, as well as other "Gitano neighborhoods" in Spain, the institutional and media promotion of securitarian responses are more concerned with the Gitano population as a threat to society than to improving the extreme conditions they have to live in, and which compound the effects of the pandemic.

Beatriz Aragón Martín holds a PhD in anthropology and an MSc in medical anthropology from University College London. Trained as a medical doctor, she works as a general practitioner, and her research focuses on health inequalities in minoritized groups, and on racism and racialization in health care.

Notes

1. Bhan et al., "The Pandemic."
2. Ibid.
3. Cañada Real Galiana is divided into different sectors that depend on different local authorities. In this chapter I refer specifically to Sector 6, as that is where I work.
4. Antena3, "La Cañada Real."
5. Beluschi Fabeni, López, and Piemontese, "Assimilation;" Gay y Blasco, "Place for Civilised People."
6. Aragón Martín, "Ill-Timed Patients."
7. Before 15 March 2020, it was only possible to test people for possible SARV-Cov infection who fulfilled the epidemiological criteria of having visited China or having been with someone who had visited China during the previous fifteen days.
8. See Hodgetts and Stolte, "Social Distance." There is a debate about using "physical distance" instead of "social distance," as the latter term implies breaking social relations with those you distance from and the former just refers to the physical distance without breaking social bonds.
9. Comunidad de Madrid, "Requerimos."
10. Gay y Blasco and Camacho, "COVID-19 and its Impact."
11. Gay y Blasco, "The Best Place"; Bereményi and Mirga, *Lost in Action?*
12. This is a local government initiative aimed solely at Cañada Real. Everywhere else in the city, medical care is delivered in buildings.
13. MSSSI, *Segunda Encuesta.*
14. ABC, "'Cuarentena' por el coronavirus."
15. Bhan et al., "The Pandemic."

Bibliography

ABC. "'Cuarentena' por el coronavirus" en la Cañada Real ['Lockdown' because of coronavirus in Cañada Real]." *ABC*, 20 March 2020. Retrieved 17 September 2021 from https://www.abc.es/espana/madrid/abci-cuarentena-coronavirus-canada-real-40434529526-20200320040016_galeria.html#imagen11.

Antena3. "La Cañada Real, el mayor supermercado de droga de Europa" [Cañada Real, the Largest Drug Supermarket in Europe], *Antena3*, 7 November 2015. Retrieved 17 September 2021 from https://www.antena3.com/noticias/sociedad/canada-real-mayor-supermercado-droga-europa_20151107571ba7ff6584a8abb580a5c1.html.

Aragón Martín, Beatriz. "Ill-Timed Patients: Gitanos, Cultural Difference and Primary Health Care in a Time of Crisis." PhD Diss., University College London, 2017.

Beluschi Fabeni, Giuseppe, Juan de Dios López López, and Stefano Piemontese. "Between Assimilation and Heritagization: The Linguistic Construction of Gitanos in Spanish Housing Policies." In *Wor(l)ds Which Exclude: The Housing Issue of Roma, Gypsies and Travellers in the Language of the Acts and the Administrative Documents in Europe*, ed. Leonardo Piasere, Nicola Solimano, and Sabrina Tosi Cambini, 81–116. Fiesole: Fundazione Michelussi Press, 2014.

Bereményi, Bálint-Ábel, and Anna Mirga. *Lost in Action? Evaluating the 6 Years of the Comprehensive Plan for the Gitano Population in Catalonia*. Barcelona: The Federation of Roma Associations in Catalonia and the EMIGRA Group, Universitat Autònoma de Barcelona, October 2012. https://grupsderecerca.uab.cat/emigra/en/content/reports-and-non-periodical-publications.

Bhan, Gautam, Teresa Caldeira, Kelly Gillespie, and AbdouMaliq Simone. "The Pandemic, Southern Urbanisms and Collective Life." *Society and Space*, 3 August 2020. Retrieved 17 September 2021 from https://www.societyandspace.org/articles/the-pandemic-southern-urbanisms-and-collective-life.

Comunidad de Madrid. "Requerimos nuevamente la presencia de la UME en la Cañada Real Galiana" [We demand again the presence of the UME in the Cañada Real Galiana]. Published 7 April 2020. Retrieved 17 September 2021 from https://www.comunidad.madrid/noticias/2020/04/07/requerimos-nuevamente-presencia-ume-canada-real-galiana.

Gay y Blasco, Paloma. "'It's the Best Place for Them:' Normalising Roma Segregation in Madrid." *Social Anthropology* 24(4) (2016): 446–61. https://doi.org/10.1111/1469-8676.12333.

———. "This Is Not a Place for Civilised People." In *Isolation: Places and Practices of Exclusion*, ed. Alison Bashford and Carolyn Strange, 197–209. New York: Routledge, 2003.

Gay y Blasco, Paloma, and Maria Félix Rodriguez Camacho. "COVID-19 and its Impact on the Roma Community: The Case of Spain." *Somatosphere*, 31 March 2020. Retrieved 17 September 2021 from http://somatosphere.net/forumpost/covid-19-roma-community-spain/.

Hodgetts, Darrin, and Ottilie Stolte. "Social Distance." In *Encyclopedia of Critical Psychology*, ed. Thomas Teo, 1776–78. New York: Springer, 2014. https://doi.org/10.1007/978-1-4614-5583-7_559.

MSSSI (Ministerio de Sanidad, Servicios Sociales e Igualdad). *Segunda Encuesta Nacional de Salud a Población Gitana* [Second national health survey to the Gitano population]. Madrid, 2014. Retrieved 17 September 2021 from https://www.gitanos.org/upload/58/44/Segunda_Encuesta_Nacional_de_Salud_a_Poblacion_Gitana_2014.pdf. .

CHAPTER 4

Researching and Mitigating the Impact of Lockdown on Gitano Families in Spain
An NGO Worker Speaks

María Félix Rodriguez Camacho

My name is María Félix Rodríguez Camacho, and I am a woman of Spanish Gitana origin. Over the last ten years I have been working for an NGO, the Autonomous Federation of Gitano Associations of the Valencian Community (FAGA), which is dedicated to the promotion and defense of the Gitano people located in the Valencian Community, specifically in the province of Alicante. My job at FAGA consists of drawing up work plans that promote education and health, especially in relation to Gitana women and children in this province. In addition, I have worked on the design and implementation of workshops for women in health promotion.

On 14 March 2020, a state of emergency was declared in Spain as a result of the COVID-19 pandemic, leading to a severe lockdown. This was the start of a particularly difficult period for the Gitano community and for other vulnerable groups. The situation soon became critical in the region Comunidad Valenciana, specifically in the north of the city of Alicante where Gitano families live very precariously, what we call "day to day". This is a low-skilled group, with limited resources and with very low levels of formal employment.[1] A good example is one of the families I worked with during the lockdown, comprising two parents and three young children. Both mother and father were formally unemployed, and they lived in a council flat. They received welfare subsidies (which they used to pay for housing, electricity, water, gas, telephone), but they also engaged in street vending and scrap collecting, and they relied on this income for food and similar daily expenses. Because of the reliance of the Gitano families of the north of Alicante on street-based economic activities, the sudden confinement plunged many of them into deep economic crisis.

The State of Emergency and Its Impact on Gitano Households: March to May 2020

Six days into the state of emergency, which officially began on 20 March 2020, the workers at FAGA started to receive requests from families who found themselves in an unprecedented situation of despair and anguish. They suffered from having to spend days without meeting their relatives, without leaving home, without attending church, without school, without being able to generate an income. They had to depend on their kin to survive. Many Gitanos explained to us that they were desperate because they were supporting not just their own nuclear family but those of sisters or brothers, using the very limited welfare benefits that they received, and that they did not know how long they would be able to continue doing this.

Among Gitanos, the family continues to be the greatest source of emotional and practical support, and with COVID-19 it has been put to the test like never before. The people who called us at FAGA for help often described how difficult it was not being able to see their extended kin. To avoid this emotional stress and to save on food and expenses, some families moved in together during the most critical period of the pandemic. Authors such as Javier Arza and José Carrón[2] explain that Gitanos use these strategies in times of crisis as a consequence of the historical exclusion they have suffered in Spain.

At FAGA we began doing our best to attend to the families and collect the necessary information, using our own personal telephones. At the same time, we contacted the municipal authorities to inform them of the critical situation in which the inhabitants of the most vulnerable area of our city found themselves. To start with, and so as to present the most objective data possible, we gathered as much information as we could and we wrote a preliminary report on the crisis,[3] describing the emergency situation of 157 highly vulnerable families and their needs, both in terms of food and of hygiene. They needed food, but also basic supplies in order to be able to clean and disinfect their homes, and wash themselves and their clothes. In fact, being able to feed their families had become their primary preoccupation. I remember how one family called me saying that they were going to breach the lockdown; they did not care even going to jail because at least there they would have food and a bath. I could not believe what I heard, and hardly knew what to answer. Could there really be somebody in such despair that they thought that being in jail was safer than being at home?

Throughout the whole national territory, Gitano associations started developing initiatives to provide emergency services to thousands of families. In FAGA we set up an account number where people could make donations. We gathered all the necessary data about the families in need (personal details, and details of their socioeconomic situation) and provided them with the funds to buy supplies and do a weekly family shop, whilst we waited for the local governments to put their own plans of action in place. Other Gitano individuals and groups also developed similar initiatives. APROIDEG (Association for the integral promotion and economic development of the Gitano people), a non-profit organization, distributed emergency food rations to families in the Community of Andalusia. The Catalan Association of Young Gitanos of Gracia likewise collected and distributed packets of food, not just during the harshest period of the lockdown but later on too. These are examples of how the Gitano community supported other Gitanos (and also non-Gitanos) during the severe economic and food crisis that we suffered during the state of emergency.

In the Comunidad Valenciana, the response of the local governments was far from immediate, and it was different organizations, such as schools and residents' associations, who asked the local government to speed up the procedures for social aid and to address the food emergency. FAGA made a statement that was published in the local press,[4] denouncing the extreme situation experienced by people who depended on street vending and similar street-based trades, and the desperate situation that many Gitano families from Alicante were going through. At a national level, the Gitano social crisis and their vulnerability was also denounced by larger entities, such as the Khetane Platform, which brings together all the Gitano NGOs in Spain.[5]

Those of us working at FAGA were deeply concerned by the problems we were witnessing during the lockdown, and our Zoom meetings became very long and worrying. We felt impotent and powerless. We really wanted to be able to feed all the families who needed it. Our virtual work meetings were also therapeutic for us, because we shared concerns, we cried together, and we thought together about possible solutions. Sleeping at night, knowing that there were families who had struggled to eat that day, was not easy. Furthermore, according to the data we collected, there were 717 children among the families we were caring for at that time.

Having shared our private telephone numbers with the community, our phones never seemed to stop ringing. We found ourselves almost providing therapy to those who called in despair. But... what could we do? That question hit us with force every day, with each call, with each story, with each description of hunger or discrimination that we heard.

In April, we ran a questionnaire using Mentimeter software, and asked the Gitano families we worked with what had been the worst aspect of the lockdown. We received eighty responses in just a few hours, and there were some who used WhatsApp instead because they could not work out how to use Mentimeter. The words and phrases that most participants mentioned were anxiety, overwhelmed, uncertainty, not leading a normal life, not being able to be with one's family, sadness, loss of freedom, having almost no food.

We were in daily contact with the women of these families, and tried to improve their situation. They were the ones who looked for ways to get food at the height of the lockdown. I remember that one WhatsApp group shared the phone telephone numbers of NGOs and similar entities who were handing out emergency food rations. The women described that the rations were not the same for everyone, and one described her frustration because she had only been given milk and cookies to feed her families for a fortnight, asking "How do I make a stew with cookies?" Suddenly, another woman answered saying that she could share what they had given her. Mutual help was frequent during these lowest moments. The women shared recipes to take advantage of their meagre resources, and even encouraged each other by recording themselves doing some exercise, and then sharing the videos with the group.

Women have been the true heroes of their families, and are the ones who have carried the heaviest burden. I remember a mother who was very worried that her children would miss out when the school closed, and who told me about her day: "I get up at six in the morning. I make breakfast, clean the house. At 9 o'clock I review each child's schoolwork. I see the homework of each one and I give it to them so they can do it for a little while. These are cards that I copy from my mobile phone by hand and give to them. When they do it, I take a picture and send it to the teacher. I make food for my family and my sister, then take it to her. In the afternoon I take care of the children, go shopping, wash clothes, disinfect the house..."

Knowing that there was little else that we ourselves could do, at FAGA we offered to collaborate with the local government. Although we appreciated all the efforts of the public administration workers in the face of the emergency, we observed that the official help mechanisms were overwhelmed and were not enough to meet the real needs of citizens, and we knew that aid was not arriving with the speed that was needed in those critical moments.

We struggled to find ways to communicate the situation we were experiencing. We issued press releases, we went to meetings with the managers of the social services, and we set up solidarity campaigns. Our exhaustion was overwhelming, because few of our efforts were producing the results we needed. And we found that the most difficult thing was to fight the underlying intolerance and racism that blinds and dehumanizes.

Assessing the Impact of the Lockdown on the Gitano Population of Spain

As a result of what we were experiencing, we believed it necessary to analyze rigorously the social and health impact of the pandemic on Gitano families, and so at FAGA we proposed this work to our colleagues from the Equi Sastipen Network, Daniel La Parra Casado (University of Alicante) and Javier Arza Porras (Public University of Navarra), and to the Health Group of the State Council of the Gitano People. All the different Gitano associations shared the same concerns about the physical, emotional, and social deterioration that the Gitano population in Spain was suffering as a result of the pandemic. The aim was to ensure we analyzed this impact across all the diverse social, economic, and political contexts within which Gitano people live. And it was agreed to carry out a survey of all the autonomous regions in Spain, even though there was no specific funding for this project. I worked with the questionnaire through all its stages: from preliminary design, to deploying it with families, and then to final analysis.[6] And I helped train the researchers from the various associations to administer the questionnaire together with Daniel La Parra Casado. Through the questionnaire we collected information on the impact of the pandemic on family units, on health, education, employment, and basic household needs.

Our hypothesis when planning the questionnaire was that COVID-19 not only affects health, but the whole social environment. Is it the same to obey the dictate to stay at home for someone who lives in a small flat of 40 sq. m. as it is for someone living in a large house where each person has their own space? Under what conditions do we expect people to stay at home? Is it possible to self-isolate if you share a bedroom with several others? Do you suffer greater anxiety? What does it mean for a Gitano family not to be able to earn money from street vending? Would Gitano boys and girls be able to access their schoolwork online? Together, the answers to these questions provided us with a picture of the impact of this crisis on the Gitano population.

We administered the questionnaire between 12 April and 10 May 2020 among 596 Gitano families who had used one or more of the services of several associations—FAGA (Alicante, Valencia, Castellón, and Murcia), UNGA (Asturias), Federación Gaz Kalo (Navarra), Red Artemisa (Madrid), and Nevipen (Vizcaya). It is an emergency investigation (inspired by the methodological trends included under the title of "Participatory Rapid Appraisal"), designed for application during the start of the state of emergency.

I asked participants whether they had suffered discrimination during the lockdown, and some told me that yes, they had, but no more than what they usually suffered. The idea that people would normalize injustice in this way affected me very deeply; it reminded me of when women go to report abuse and the police tell them that they must have done something to put themselves in that situation. It is unfair and painful for people to feel alone in situations of inequality and oppression.

Some families told me that they had nothing to eat and were accused of taking advantage of the system, even though three months into the lockdown they had still not received any aid. And because I have worked with children, I felt disheartened when they told me that the boys and girls who were in secondary school wanted to abandon their studies, and those who were in primary school had lost many of their literacy skills. This made me realize that the development of children has been delayed by the pandemic, and that their lives may have been affected permanently: they now face added challenges that, once again and even more forcefully, push them towards poverty. I was surprised by the deep helplessness that families felt, but at the same time by their resilience and their capacity to survive with such meagre resources, and in the face of so much adversity.

It is important to keep in mind that the results of the survey cannot be extrapolated to the entire Gitano population of Spain. However, they do represent a useful window onto the situation of the most vulnerable sector of the Gitano community, which of course is the group with which the Gitano associations work most.

The results reflect the significant impact that COVID-19 has had on households that were already affected by multiple processes of social exclusion and inequality. This impact goes beyond health, and affects all areas of life. Thus, the questionnaire reveals a worsening in the self-perception of health during lockdown, and its severe impact on mental health. About 50 percent of the households reported difficulties with the most basic tasks in home schooling, and the same proportion saw their work activity significantly reduced because of the lockdown. Likewise, over half the households suffered a severe reduction in their income, and as a result found it harder to access basic food supplies. In addition, all this occurred in a context in which most households perceived an increase in the discrimination they face as Gitanos. The results across the different geographic areas we studied was generally the same.

I was very surprised by the percentage of families who said they had not noticed any change in their relationship with their children's school or with their teachers (48 percent). I found this very worrying: we are in the middle of an unprecedented pandemic, when for most families it has become harder to have fluid communication with schools, and yet Gitano families do not notice a change? What kind of relationship did they have previously? The employment situation also caught my attention: at FAGA we already knew that few Gitanos are employed by others, but when I realized that not a single Gitano in the sample had been furloughed I wondered about the lack of stable employment and the possible impacts on health. Without a stable job, getting out of poverty or acquiring good health habits is almost impossible — and sadly there are many families in this situation.

Final Thoughts

Participating in the design and analysis of the data of this survey has allowed me to develop new methods to express and capture the day-to-day work in a Gitano association. I have been able to get to know better the families with whom I work, and also to see the situation from a wider point of view. The marginalization and inequality that affect Gitano families were present long before the pandemic, and what the crisis has done is to make them even more extreme. With this study we have shown that as Gitano associations we have great potential to participate in research processes and thus improve our service to our users.

Lastly, the pandemic has shown us that the structural problems that affect Gitanos are long-standing, and they are not being addressed. Resources need to be targeted better, and the various state institutions involved need to improve their cultural competence, and their understanding of the Gitano community. The pandemic has shown that state strategies aimed at the Gitano population must be part of a broader political agenda. For the moment, public policies cannot generate the change that is needed at all levels. The Gitano population continues to be discriminated against with total impunity by the majority, and it is a serious matter that is affecting society as a whole.

There is an anonymous meme on the web that says: "Take care of yourself as if everyone has coronavirus; take care of others as if you have it". What if we all behaved as if we were Gitanos? What if we took care of our policies as if we belonged to a historically criminalized and discriminated minority? What would the outcome be?

María Félix Rodriguez Camacho is a doctoral student in health sciences at the University of Alicante in Spain. She also works on health promotion within an NGO that aims to protect the rights of Roma people (FAGA, Federación Autónoma de Asociaciones Gitanas de la Comunidad Valenciana). She is a member of the network Red Equi Sastipen and of the Health Group of the State Council for the Roma People in Spain.

Notes

1. Ayuntamiento de Alicante, *Estudio Barrios Vulnerables*, 72ff.
2. Arza and Carrón, "Comunidad Gitana."
3. FAGA, *Informe sobre la situación*.
4. Hernández, "FAGA Alerta."
5. Khetane, "Las Organizaciones Gitanas."
6. Arza Porras et al., "Covid-19 Crisis."

Bibliography

Arza Porras, Javier, and José Carrón Sánchez. "Comunidad Gitana: La Persistencia de una Discriminación Histórica" [Gitano community: Persistence of a historical discrimination]. *Revista de Ciencias Sociales* 10(2) (2015): 275–99. http://doi.org/10.14198/OBETS2015.10.2.01.

Arza Porras, Javier, Diana Gil-González, Lluís Català-Oltra, Francisco Francés García, María Eugenia González Angulo, Maria Félix Rodríguez Camacho, María José Sanchís Ramón, Belén Sanz-Barbero, Carmen Vives-Cases, and Daniel La Parra Casado. "COVID-19 Crisis: Impact on Households of the Roma Community." *International Journal of Roma Studies* 2(2) (2020): 28–51. https://doi.org/10.17583/ijrs.2020.6242.

Ayuntamiento de Alicante. *Estudio Barrios Vulnerables Zona Norte Alicante* [Study of the vulnerable neighborhoods of the North Zone of Alicante]. Alicante, 2006.

FAGA, Federación Autonómica de Asociaciones Gitanas de Alicante. *Informe sobre la situación de familias gitanas alicantinas en situación de emergencia alimentaria a causa del estado de alarma por la COVID-19* [Report on the situation of Gitano families in the situation of food emergency because of the COVID-19 State of Emergency]. Alicante, 2020. Retrieved 2 November 2021 from http://www.fagacv.info/FAGAALICANTE/COVID_19/016_09042020/INFORME%20COVID%2019%20FAGA.pdf.

Hernández, J. "FAGA Alerta de la Situación de Vendedores Ambulantes y Personas que Vendían Chatarra" [FAGA warns of the situation of street sellers and scrap dealers]. *Información*, 27 March 2020. Retrieved 2 November 2021 from https://www.diarioinformacion.com/alicante/2020/03/27/faga-alerta-situacion-vendedores-ambulantes/2249946.html.

Khetane. "Las Organizaciones Gitanas Hacen Propuestas para Salvar la Venta Ambulante" [Gitano organizations put forward proposals to save street commerce]. *Plataforma Khetane*, 27 April 2020. Retrieved 2 November 2021 from http://plataformakhetane.org/index.php/2020/04/27/las-organizaciones-gitanas-hacen-propuestas-para-salvar-la-venta-ambulant/?fbclid=IwAR1MhpekD2cdo6pjJxCN9qURkUzWXiFLsTBrn-NjxZinfbOqCj9URQR9kg4.

CHAPTER 5

ILLNESS AND DEATH ARE SO MUCH WORSE WHEN YOU ARE ALONE

Liria Hernández

My name is Liria Hernández. On 16 March 2020, I fell ill with the coronavirus, which caused a severe pneumonia that lasted for almost three months. Afterwards, I continued to be ill with coronavirus symptoms until October 2020, and also with many anxiety attacks because of what I went through during the months of illness. I was so traumatized by my experiences in hospitals, and by how difficult it was to go through the illness completely alone during the months of lockdown, that I can hardly even write about what I saw and went through.

I can't stop crying as I write.

My family and I were among the first to fall ill. My family continues to suffer the consequences of the pandemic, as there have been four deaths. Since then, we have all been sick, some twice, and even today in December 2020 one or other of us are still ill with COVID.

What has been most difficult for us has been all the unknowns of this pandemic, especially because each family was attacked by the virus in different ways, and we go through tremendous uncertainty and fear. Some die in just four days, others endure months with severe pneumonia, others just have a common flu, plus the asymptomatic ones, who at first did not even know that people transmitted it without knowing.

I got sick very early on, and soon I had severe pneumonia, and it was very difficult for me to survive because I live alone, and of course nobody came to help me. Fear invaded everyone and we could not turn to each other. We only kept up with video calls on WhatsApp or Zoom so as not to lose contact.

This has been very hard for the Gitano people because we were not used to being apart for so long—on the contrary, we are taught to be together as much as possible, and above all to support each other with our presence when there is some misfortune.

And it is not that Gitanos love our families more, but that from a very young age we are taught values within our own culture that should endure even above the hardest circumstances. But the pandemic ruined so many years of teaching. Because until then nothing had separated Gitano families, much less illnesses and deaths. But this virus has undone so many years of insistence on the fight for family unity.

This pandemic destroyed one of the most beautiful traditions that Gitano people and families had, and that is that when someone got sick, all of us, relatives and friends, would go to the hospital or to their home, all united so that the sick never felt alone.

I remember as if it were yesterday, before the pandemic, how many times we took my father to the emergency room, for a simple colic, and not only my sisters and I used to go, but all my uncles, cousins, even friends of my father; and until he left the hospital, nobody moved from there. And with my mother, who was ill for five years, we all went, including our babies in their strollers. We went through all the consultations, chemotherapies, or any test, all together. We could spend whole days, the whole family at the hospital. Because if the patient knew that the majority of the family accompanied them, it was a way of knowing the importance that people give you, and the place you occupy within the family.

Because it's not just going to the hospital together when someone gets sick. Unity with the family goes much further; when there are problems with the family from the oldest such as grandparents to the youngest, everyone comes together to solve the problems. For example, in problems with marriages you never go to the police. Gitana women, if they have problems with their husbands, go to the elders for help. And if a patient has a very long illness, relatives never stop supporting them. Consistency in caring for the sick is valued above all else. Any other problems are put aside—jobs are abandoned if necessary, even if that means that no money will come into the house that day, or that the family will have serious financial difficulties.

This virus stole this right from us, which is our law, but we are all aware that it is the only thing that helps us survive: to survive, we have to be separated from each other.

And what hurt me the most was not that I was alone and sick, but that in the midst of the pandemic I could not accompany my relatives in their illnesses and needs. In the midst of the pandemic, doctors operated on one of my brothers-in-law, removing a malignant kidney, and the same day that he was being operated on, I was in an emergency room under observation for pneumonia and possible COVID-19 pericarditis. In the midst of my illness, I felt a lot of guilt for not being able to be close to my brother-in-law and my younger sister, because no visitors were allowed in the hospitals. And I remember that I picked up the phone to ask all the people in my church to pray for my brother-in-law and my sister, because I could not bear the pain within me and the anguish of knowing that they were completely alone. I even lost my fear for myself, and I came to feel guilty for having caught COVID because I felt that I was betraying all those values that my parents taught us.

But the worst was yet to come. In May, in the middle of the pandemic, another of my brothers-in-law fell ill, and as they could not do surgery on him because of the pandemic, he died. And that's when everything finally exploded inside me. I still had many symptoms of coronavirus and could not accompany my widowed sister, or my niece who had just lost her father. I have never felt so much helplessness, pain, anger—a mixture of feelings in the face of a virus that managed to destroy a culture rooted and preserved from generation to generation, a culture that until now had never been broken.

The only thing that saved us was that we learned, even with very little knowledge of technology, how to download applications, and so at least we were constant in seeing each other in the only way we could.

Liria Hernández was granted an Honorary Master of Arts by the University of St Andrews in 2019. With Paloma Gay y Blasco she is the co-author of *Writing Friendship: A Reciprocal Ethnography* (Palgrave Macmillan, 2020) and of several articles on gender issues among Spanish Gitanos.

CHAPTER 6

❊ ❊ ❊

"COVID-19 Is a Trial from God"
Gitanos, Pentecostal Imaginaries, and Compliance

Antonio Montañés Jiménez with Gory Carmona

Early in 2020, the COVID-19 pandemic found me, Antonio, a non-Romani student, at the University of St Andrews (Scotland), finishing a PhD dissertation on the conversion to Pentecostal Christianity of Gitanos in Madrid and Barcelona. My life at St Andrews—a place frequented mainly by tourists, students, and golfers—felt quiet and isolated, as most people left the town following the university's decision to transition to online teaching soon after the first virus outbreak in town. By contrast, and from a distance, life in Spain struck me as eventful. On 14 March 2020, Spain entered an unprecedented national lockdown to contain the rapid spread of the virus. The drastic measures approved by the Spanish government limited freedom of movement and all non-essential economic activities. Spanish news depicted a bleak scenario in which the virus spread rapidly, politicians blamed each other for it, and unemployment became rampant. Online interactions and phone conversations with family and friends from Madrid, who regularly provided me with details about their emotional and practical struggles, only cemented further my feeling that Spain was in a state of turmoil.

As the COVID-19 crisis unfolded, I often thought of my Evangelical Gitano interlocutors, who had helped me during my doctoral fieldwork. It seemed to me that the emerging global health crisis was posing an unparalleled threat to the Evangelical sociality, religious life, and economic survival of my Gitano friends. At the beginning of the crisis, churches and religious centers, including Gitano ones, were closed. Afterwards, and to this day (February 2021), local governments still uphold demanding restrictions regarding the number of believers allowed in churches and at religious meetings. Many Gitano Evangelical churches in the south of Madrid still remain temporarily closed. Since Gitano churches heavily depend on donations and tithing collected at daily religious ceremonies, many congregations face rental and maintenance expenses, as well as debt, all of which threaten their survival. Another cause of concern for Gitano believers is the lack of group ritual interactions. Although many engage in ceremonies online, lockdowns and restrictions prevent Gitano believers from experiencing the emotional connection and sense of togetherness that only face-to-face rituals can provide. Adding to what was an already stark reality for believers, at the start of the pandemic some right-wing Spanish media reported that a small number of Gitano churches had breached the lockdown by gathering for outdoor religious meetings, portraying Evangelical Gitanos as religious fanatics who are unable to comply with basic health guidelines.

One Gitano Evangelical interlocutor I have been regularly speaking with during this ongoing pandemic is my friend Gory Carmona.[1] I met Gory whilst doing fieldwork in Villaverde, a deprived neighborhood in the south of Madrid where I was born and grew up as a non-Gitano. When I met him, he was a member of La Pequeña Villa Church, a Pentecostal congregation affiliated to an autonomous Gitano-led church, the Iglesia Evangélica de Filadelfia (IEF). Gory was born and raised in an Evangelical Gitano family in which six men are IEF pastors, and he converted to the Evangelical faith at the age of nineteen. In Spain, the IEF holds great sway over Gitanos' social and spiritual lives.[2] The IEF has established over sixteen hundred places of worship and more than six thousand ministries,[3] and is one of is the largest Evangelical churches in Spain.

This chapter features my and Gory's joint effort to shed light on Gitanos' experiences during the pandemic in the south of Madrid. Gory's personal experience comes to the forefront as we examine together his autobiographical accounts, feelings, and reflections. We also discuss his interpretation of the origin of the pandemic and his response to the stigmatizing effect of those public discourses that portray Gitanos as super-spreaders of the virus. Given the impossibility of conducting classic face-to-face ethnography amid a global pandemic, we produced our material by recording our phone and online conversations. I, Antonio, wrote the piece and translated Gory's words. Gory engaged and commented during the writing process, and gave feedback on the final version of the chapter.

Pandemic, Hardship, and Faith

Gory is a father of two in his early forties. He makes a living working as a flea market vendor and composing music for flamenco singers. For the last few years, his life has been defined by the pressing health concerns of chronic migraine. Because of his illness, Gory often finds it challenging to make ends meet, and his family relies on the Renta Mínima de Inserción (RMI), an emergency minimum income allowance granted by the Madrid regional government. To make matters worse, in November 2020, Gory's family was hit by the COVID-19 virus. His beloved father died, and some close relatives were hospitalized. Gory himself became ill, and he still suffers from fatigue and respiratory problems. Unable to work or resume any economic activity due to the government's restrictions and his own health problems, Gory feels the Spanish government is failing to aid his family in this time of radical uncertainty and dire need.

Gory's story is not so very different from the experience of many Gitano and some non-Gitano families in Villaverde. In the working-class and impoverished periphery of Madrid, where both of us grew up, residents have fewer opportunities to work from home, are more dependent on public transport for commuting, live in smaller homes, and their access to material protection is more restricted due to economic instability--all of which made them more likely to struggle during the first waves of the virus than other city residents.[4]

Gory's recent memories of the pandemic are shaped by and inseparable from his Christian beliefs. This is how Gory recounted his pandemic experience to me in one of our phone conversations:

> A few months ago, I lost my father to COVID. A few days before he died, he began to feel ill and was hospitalized. When I saw him at the hospital, the doctors told us that he was extremely sick. At that moment, God spoke to me: "You should be happy; I'm going to take him with me." Despite the sadness, I began to feel peace, a great deal of peace, and I still feel that peace to this day. Every day I say this phrase to my father and God: "Dad, I am glad that you are with God because the world is so bad down here, there is a lot of evil, and the pandemic is destroying everything. Tell God on my behalf that I am incredibly grateful that he has welcomed you into his arms."

In the same conversation, Gory reflected on his experience of becoming infected with the virus.

> A few days after my father died, I began to feel very, very tired. And after doing the tests, they diagnosed me with COVID. To top it all off, I get chronic mi-

graines, and the pain of COVID was combined with the migraine, and it drove me crazy; I had no strength at all. I waddled around my home the same way a baby does when they start to walk. I would get out of bed, and it would take hours just to put on a sock! Those days were an odyssey for me. I am now cured of COVID, but I still have some long-term physical consequences. I am drained; my kidneys hurt. However, when I went through COVID, I was not afraid; I had confidence in God because I am a profoundly faithful person. I knew that God would protect me, and even if I did die, everything would be okay because I would be with Him. During my period with COVID, I said to myself, "well, look, if this is the end, I'll go with Him, and that's it because sooner or later we are all going to die, and if it is my time, so be it." Thanks to my faith in God, I was super calm.]

As he explains above, Gory felt that his faith eased the fears and physical and emotional pain he had to cope with when infected with COVID-19. His faith not only helped him to cope with his father's passing, but it was also crucial to mustering the strength to face both his chronic illness and the virus. Both Gory and I believe that religion can be a source of comfort for Gitano believers in times of need; therefore, attending to religious faith is required to begin to understand Gitano communities experience of the pandemic crisis.

Pentecostal Imaginaries: Making Sense of the COVID-19 Global Health Crisis

One day in January 2021, Gory and I talked about the origin of the pandemic over the phone, and he explained his personal views to me. We have different opinions on what caused the pandemic. I believe that unregulated forms of capitalism in economic powerhouses such as China are increasingly generating animal–human encounters under inappropriate hygiene conditions, facilitating contagion. By contrast, Gory believes we need to look to and read the Bible to determine why the COVID-19 pandemic threatens humanity.

Crisis and tribulation are recurrent themes that give shape to Christians' understanding of human history. The Bible includes countless episodes, such as wars, plagues, floods and famines, in which humanity repeatedly faces enormous calamities.[5] Gitano believers recurrently interpret catastrophic events (terrorism, wars, natural disasters, humanitarian and economic crises, etc.) that feature prominently in the news as prophetic signs. In that vein, Gory thinks that the outbreak of COVID-19 is a chastisement from God, signaling the eschatological end of human history and the second coming of Jesus Christ. According to Gory:

Personally, I do believe that COVID-19 is a sign. What's more, the Bible says that signs will come before the world's end, such as diseases and plagues during the apocalypse. Therefore, I believe that COVID is a sign from God. It is not only a pandemic; the other day, there was an earthquake in Granada. These are signs. By not following biblical teachings, the human being is audacious and offends God. I do not want to single out anyone because we are all sinners, and we all are to blame. I believe that God is tired. I believe that God can't stand it anymore.

According to Gory, the pandemic will allow God to test Christians and distinguish genuine believers from those who are not committed to their faith. Gory explained this to me as follows:

COVID-19 is a trial from God, another one. With this crisis, you can see what level of faith and loyalty Christians have with God. Here you can see if you go to Church to meet with your cousin, or with your uncle, with your brother or with your family, or to hang out. God is testing us to see which Christians live close to Him, to see if we follow Him or lose our faith.

One crucial teaching common to all branches of Christianity is that Christians must seek God in times of suffering, stick together, and remain hopeful. Drawing on biblical imageries, Gory sees the pandemic as both a sign to repent and a trial through which real Christians will prove their commitment to God.

"Gitanos Are Not to Blame": Challenging Anti-Gitano Discourses

The stigmatization of particular groups as "the infected Other" often arises in emergency public health situations.[6] In Spain, moral and civility hierarchies have formed as the notion of infectious Others—those who fail to follow basic health guidelines and spread the virus with their actions—has gained prominence in popular media and political discourses. The media disseminated an image of Gitanos as one of the groups who failed to comply with health standards and regulations.[7] Thus, Gitanos, as is often the case within Spanish society, have been on the receiving end of scapegoating discourses during the pandemic.

Like every Gitano person I know, Gory rejects depictions of Gitanos as "infectious Others" and reckless non-citizens who spread the virus. Discussing the issue in one of our conversations, Gory argued:

Once again, Gitanos are singled out. It is clear that a few Gitanos have acted wrongfully, but Gitanos are not guilty of this pandemic, far from it. No one should believe that the Gitanos have brought this about. If you go to a club, 100 percent of the people who do not follow protocols are Payos; there is not a single Gitano person present at the clubs. Because if there is one thing that characterizes Gitanos, it is that our elders take care of us. Even if you are married and are twenty-one or twenty-five or thirty, and your father finds out that you want to go to a place where many people have fun, but where you would put yourself at risk of catching the virus, he will give you a firm reprimand.

Contrary to what people think, Gitanos take great care and try not to catch COVID. To give you an example, on 31 December, my family did not join the festivities, and here in my neighborhood, almost no Gitano family celebrated the new year. However, here in the pub next to my house, dozens of Payos celebrated the new year by drinking alcohol, and they were not wearing masks.

The Spanish media also targeted Evangelical Gitanos as a religious group. Reinforcing well-entrenched stereotypes of Gitanos as an unruly group unable to comply with good citizenship conventions, the Spanish press reported that Evangelical ceremonies held by Gitanos during lockdown were unlawful, breached health and safety guidelines, and acted as spreading channels for the virus. As Gay y Blasco and Rodriguez Camacho note, it is the assumed inability of Gitanos as a group to behave as citizens that the Spanish media, especially right-wing leaning newspapers, elaborate on in their accounts of incidents involving Gitanos.[8] When right-wing newspapers reported that few Gitano Evangelicals gathered to pray in the streets, Gay y Blasco and Rodriguez argue, they characterized Gitanos as belonging to "unstructured clans unused to public order and discipline."[9]

By contrast, out of Gory's narrative emerges an image of Gitano communities as composed of moral beings inserted in a web of authority relations and abiding by high standards of behavior and ethics. As opposed to dominant portrayals of Gitanos as unruly subjects, he constructs a counterimage that emphasizes Gitanos' moral and civic qualities, which, Gory argues, are embodied and enforced by Gitano elders. Gory asserts that the disruptive individuals are not Gitanos but instead those Payos who engage in irresponsible drinking and partying.

When, during one video call, I broke the news to Gory that some Spanish newspapers had reported that a Gitano church had violated the COVID-19 health guidelines and gathered to pray, he made an outraged face. He rapidly reproved these actions and became visibly upset; he was uncomprehending of the few Gitano congregations that had decided against following the Spanish government rules. In so doing, Gory took a stand not only against the few Gitano congregations that ignored health and safety protocols but he also faulted believers who see their Christian faith and their desire to gather as a church as a valid reason *not* to follow public health guidelines or comply with regulations. It is worth noting that his reaction is in line with a public statement issued by the IEF, jointly with other Spanish Evangelical churches, advising believers to follow public health guidelines.[10] Gory insisted that I should emphasize to our readers that the incident above was a rare instance of disobedience. The truth, as he reminded me in that conversation, is that the IEF churches stayed closed, and complied with all regulations during the pandemic.

Gory's words gain full significance within a local political landscape defined by a strong resistance from some conservative political actors to comply with the policies and regulations set out during the pandemic by the Spanish government (led by a coalition between the Spanish socialist party and the left-wing populist party Podemos). In August 2020, right-wing and upper-middle-class anti-mask protesters and COVID-19 deniers rallied in the streets of Madrid, gathering 2,500 people.[11] Also, from the start of the pandemic, conservative Partido Popular leader and Madrid region president Isabel Díaz Ayuso contested the Spanish government decision to limit the free circulation of people between Spanish regions and to restrict opening times for bars and restaurants, choosing instead to introduce more lenient restrictions than other Spanish regions. Díaz Ayuso claimed that her decision to stand against the government was based on her desire to protect the Madrid hospitality industry, people's freedom, and the right of individuals to have a beer in a bar at the end of a long day.[12] In May 2021, she was rewarded for her liberal stance as she was re-elected president of the regional government of Madrid. Gory told me that, against this backdrop, the fact that the IEF had obeyed the advice of health experts and the regulations set out by the Spanish government is a cause for pride for many Gitano believers. Importantly, Gory's praise of the IEF for its commitment to remain closed during the pandemic is also a clear political stand that strikes a chord with other accounts of Christian churches as "compliant actors" who showed attitudes of collaboration, adherence, and support for government directives.[13]

Conclusions

The COVID-19 pandemic demands that we re-conceptualize how Gitanos face existential and social vulnerabilities. Also, it illustrates the critical importance of Evangelical religious organizations to understanding how Gitano communities deal with the experience of suffering and the negative consequences of inhabiting the margins of Spanish society. Faced with a wide variety of dire circumstances—temporal church closures, infections and the risk of virus transmission, lockdowns, lack of income, limitation of movement—Gory has found in Pentecostal Christianity answers to coping with uncertainty, disease, and sorrow.

Gory conceptualizes the pandemic—and this is shared by many Gitano believers—as a trial sent by God to urge them to separate themselves from a world they perceive as decaying and evil. Consequently, he interprets the pandemic as an eschatological sign for them to repent and strengthen their commitment to the church.

Gory contests portrayals of Evangelical Gitanos as religious fanatics, and claims that Pentecostal Christianity has played a positive role in the Spanish political and legal landscape during the COVID-19 global health crisis. Of note, Gory also reflects on the discriminatory representation of Gitanos in the media during the pandemic. He challenges and inverts discriminatory depictions of Gitanos as an unruly and anomic group who contribute to legitimizing and normalizing anti-Gitano discourses by posing positive moral frameworks predicated on Gitanos' self-representations as beings inhabiting a high moral ground. In so doing, Gory takes an explicit political stance vis-à-vis political debates around the pandemic and the tension between the state, the community, and the individual in Madrid. Neither Gitanos nor Gitano Evangelical churches, Gory claims, should be conflated with COVID-19 deniers or unruly subjects. Importantly, these competing representations during the pandemic—Gitanos as a dutiful community, or Gitanos as a threat to Spanish society—engage broader and long-standing ideological discussions regarding Gitanos' compliance with the norms of good citizenship. The outcome of this discussion, Gory and I both think, is vital for the future and well-being of Gitanos in Spain. By engaging in the writing of this piece, Gory hopes to combat the prejudices and stereotypes that negatively shape the social image of Gitanos, and to encourage a more accurate and fairer understanding of how Evangelical Gitanos, and Gitanos at large, behaved during the pandemic.

Antonio Montañés Jiménez is a Margarita Salas postdoctoral fellow affiliated with the School of Anthropology and Museum Ethnography at the University of Oxford (UK), and a member of St Antony's College, Oxford. His research interests include the anthropology of Christianity, the sociology of religion, and the field of Romani studies.

Gregorio "Gory" Carmona is a Gitano artist born and raised in Madrid. He is related to "Los Carmona Habichuela," a celebrated flamenco family. He leads the Christian musical project "Dracma Sounds Music," and collaborates as an interlocutor and co-author in Antonio Montañés Jiménez's research project on Romani Pentecostalism.

Notes

1. Gory's real name is Gregorio. However, acquaintances, Gitano believers, and his family always refer to him by the name of Gory. He asked me to keep the name Gory in the chapter.
2. Cantón Delgado, "Gypsy Pentecostalism;" Gay y Blasco, *Gypsies in Madrid*; Griera, "New Christian Geographies;" Montañés Jimenez, "Etnicidad e Identidad."
3. Cantón-Delgado, "Narrativas," 2.
4. Dore, "COVID-19 in Madrid."
5. Montañés Jimenez, "Pentecostal Christianity."
6. Roy, "Fear of Others."
7. BBC, and Khetane, "El Antigitanismo;" Hedgecoe, "Spain Still Haunted;" Sánchez, "Los Gitanos;" Unión Romaní, "Comunicado de Prensa."
8. Gay y Blasco and Rodriguez Camacho, "COVID-19 and its Impact."
9. Ibid.
10. Saiz and Sánchez, "La Iglesia Evangélica."
11. Franco, "2.500 Personas."
12. Carlin, "Isabel Díaz Ayuso."
13. Picciaredda, "Religions;" Sim, "Singaporean Christians."

Bibliography

BBC, and Khetane. "El antigitanismo en la España del Coronavirus, Crónica de la BBC" [Antigypsyism in Spain during coronavirus]. *Plataforma Kethane*, 20 May 2020. Retrieved 15 November 2021 from https://plataformakhetane.org/index.php/2020/05/20/el-antigitanismo-en-la-espana-del-coronavirus-cronica-de-la-bbc/.

Cantón Delgado, Manuela. "Gypsy Pentecostalism, Ethnopolitical Uses and Construction of Belonging in the South of Spain." *Social Compass* 57(2) (2010): 253–68. https://doi.org/10.1177/0037768610362418.

———. "Narrativas del despertar Gitano: Innovación religiosa, liderazgos Gitanos y políticas de identidad" [Narratives of Gitano awakening: Religious innovations, Gitano leaderships and identity politics]. *Revista Internacional de Sociología* 76(2) (2018). https://doi.org/10.3989/ris.2018.76.2.16.96.

Carlin, John. "Isabel Díaz Ayuso Gave them Beer and Tapas — They Handed Her a Shot at PM." *The Sunday Times*, 9 May 2021. Retrieved 15 November 2021 from https://www.thetimes.co.uk/article/isabel-diaz-ayuso-gave-them-beer-and-tapas-they-handed-her-a-shot-at-pm-03m7g0qc0.

Dore, Mayane. "COVID-19 in Madrid: Vulnerability, Precarity and Essential Work." *City & Society* 3(22) (2021): 1–7. https://doi.org/10.1111/ciso.12358.

Franco, Lucía. "2.500 Personas se concentran en Colón contra el uso obligatorio de las mascarillas" [2,500 people gather in Colón to protest against the compulsory use of face masks]. *El País*, 17 August 2020. Retrieved 15 November 2021 from https://elpais.com/espana/madrid/2020-08-16/2500-personas-se-concentran-en-colon-contra-el-uso-obligatorio-de-las-mascarillas.html.

Gay y Blasco, Paloma. *Gypsies in Madrid: Sex, Gender and the Performance of Identity*. Oxford: Bloomsbury Academic, 1999.

Gay y Blasco, Paloma, and Maria Félix Rodriguez Camacho. "COVID-19 and its Impact on the Roma Community: The Case of Spain." *Somatosphere*, 31 March 2020. Retrieved 15 November 2021 from http://somatosphere.net/forumpost/covid-19-roma-community-spain/.

Griera, Mar. "New Christian Geographies: Pentecostalism and Ethnic Minorities in Barcelona." In *Sites and Politics of Religious Diversity in Southern Europe*, ed. Ruy Llera Blanes and José Maril, 225–49. Leiden: Brill, 2013.

Hedgecoe, Guy. "Spain Still Haunted by Spectre of Poverty Trap." *BBC News*, Seville, 20 May 2020. Retrieved 15 November 2021 from https://www.bbc.com/news/world-europe-51737422.

Montañés Jimenez, Antonio. "Etnicidad e identidad gitana en los cultos pentecostales de la Ciudad de Madrid: El caso de la 'Iglesia Evangélica de Filadelfia' y el 'Centro Cristiano Vino Nuevo el Rey Jesús'" [Gitano ethnicity and identity within Pentecostal services in the City of Madrid: The Case of 'Iglesia Evangélica de Filadelfia' and the 'Centro Cristiano Vino Nuevo el Rey Jesús']. *Papeles del CEIC: International Journal on Collective Identity Research* 2 (2016). https://www.redalyc.org/articulo.oa?id=76547309007.

———. "Pentecostal Christianity, COVID-19 and the Digital World." *The Sociological Review* [Online], 5 May 2021. https://doi.org/10.51428/tsr.wtfg8908.

Picciaredda, Stefano. "Religions, Africa and Covid-19." In *Law, Religion and Covid-19 Emergency*, ed. Pierluigi Consorti, 109–18. Pisa: Diresom, 2020.

Roy, Arpan. "Fear of Others: Thinking Biopolitics." *Social Anthropology* 28(2) (2020): 343–44. https://doi.org/10.1111/1469-8676.12876.

Saiz, Eva, and Nacho Sánchez. "La Iglesia evangélica reprueba el desafío a la cuarentena de algunas de sus congregaciones" [The Evangelical Church criticises the lack of compliance with the lockdown within some of its congregations]. *El País*, 20 March 2020. Retrieved 15 November 2021 from https://elpais.com/sociedad/2020-03-19/la-iglesia-evangelica-reprueba-el-desafio-a-la-cuarentena-de-algunas-de-sus-congregaciones.html.

Sánchez, Gabriela. "Los gitanos, nuevo foco de mensajes racistas que les acusan de extender el coronavirus en España" [Gitanos become the target of racist messages that accuse them of spreading coronavirus in Spain]. *eldiario.es*, 22 April 2020. Retrieved 15 November 2021 from https://www.eldiario.es/desalambre/gitanos-bulos-racistas_1_5894352.html.

Sim, Joshua Dao Wei. "Compliant Singaporean Christians? State-Centred Christian Responses to COVID-19 in a Single-Party Dominant State." *Studies in World Christianity* 26(3) (2020): 239–60. https://doi.org/10.3366/swc.2020.0308.

Unión Romaní. "Comunicado de prensa ante el antigitanismo informativo relacionado con la epidemia del coronavirus COVID-19. Medios que alimentan el racismo" [Press release in view of the antigypsyism in the media related to the epidemic of the coronavirus COVID-19]. Last modified 17 March 2020. Retrieved 15 November 2021 from https://unionromani.org/2020/03/17/comunicado-de-prensa-ante-el-antigitanismo-informativo-relacionado-con-la-epidemia-del-coronavirus-covid-19/.

PART II

✸ ✸ ✸

BRAZILIAN CHRONICLES

CHAPTER 7

INTRODUCTION TO THE BRAZILIAN CHRONICLES
How Systemic Racism and Government Neglect
Led to Increased Harm
Suffered by Vulnerable Groups

*Juliana Miranda Soares Campos, Martin Fotta,
Gabriela Marques Gonçalves, and Aline Miklos*

The Pandemic's Unequal Impact

In 1916, *Gazeta Medica da Bahia*, a leading medical journal of the period, published an article by ophthalmologist Dr Raymundo Ribeiro da Silva about trachoma, a highly contagious eye disease causing blindness, which had then been spreading throughout parts of Brazil. In the article, he discussed his long experience with this infectious disease and the state of knowledge about trachoma. He appealed for the government to establish public health initiatives aimed at fighting it. In a manner typical for the journal, which was concerned with the impact of racial miscegenation on the future of the nation, he associated the infection with hygiene and with race. He also speculated on the origins of trachoma in the state of Bahia, where he worked. As the disease was not native to the country, had not existed among the enslaved blacks during the slavery and could not have been brought by recent European immigrants, of whom there were few in Bahia, he pointed to Ciganos (Romanies)— "the vagabond race, who claim to come from Egypt"[1]—as the vector of the infection. After all, the ophthalmologist reasoned, trachoma was endemic to Egypt and was known as an "Egyptian (eye) disease." It was widespread among the Bahian Ciganos, who, he said, moved often and lived in filth, misery, and in a promiscuous manner that was an affront both to public hygiene and to morality. "Given their habits, their origin and the frequency of the disease, we are led to express the opinion that we owe to them the spread of the disease, in the interior of Bahia, if not in the whole north of Brazil", Dr Ribeiro da Silva summarized.[2]

There is a startling sense of déjà vu when reading this article one century later during the height of the global COVID-19 pandemic. In the first half of 2020, Calon Romanies were expelled from some municipalities in southern Brazil. Local authorities argued that they represented a threat to public health. Allegedly, their mode of life (street vending, mobility, social life in camps composed of tents) made them prone to getting infected and to spreading the virus.

Like then, also today, Brazilian doctors and public health authorities have been appealing to the central government for a more decisive approach to the pandemic. While by the middle of the last century Brazil was successful in suppressing trachoma, the current president Jair Bolsonaro has marginalized the sanitary community, downplayed the coronavirus as a "little flu", accused others (politicians, scientists, media) of "hysteria" and promoted the use of hydroxychloroquine as a drug against COVID-19, despite studies showing it to be ineffective.[3] All this in a country that has been one of the hardest hit by the new virus. Since 26 February 2020, when the first case was diagnosed, until the end of May 2021, when we revised this introduction, Brazil saw 460,000 COVID-19 deaths.

Just like with trachoma, not all segments of the population have been affected by the new coronavirus in the same way. Class, race, and region explain many of the differences in infection and mortality rates, as well as in kinds of policy response or neglect: COVID-19 has been disproportionately deadlier to Black Brazilians.[4] The differential course of the pandemic within Brazilian society must also be seen against the backdrop of the stigmatization of difference and vilification of non-hegemonic modes of relating and being in the world, which has intensified in recent years. Within the juridico-political framework, these modes of life have been figured under the sign of "traditional peoples and communities," a term that includes Indigenous peoples, communities of descendants of *quilombolas* (maroons) and Ciganos, among others.[5] In the context of a continued erosion of protections and provisions for ethnic minorities and traditional populations under the current reactionary government, the comments made by the minister of education Abraham Weintraub during a meeting of the ministers in April 2020—that is, in the middle of the exponential growth of infections with coronavirus—did not surprise us. He was vehement that he "hated" the terms "*povos indígenas*" (Indigenous peoples) and "*o povo cigano*" (Romani people), which according to him were only used to secure unfair privileges, and that, in any case, there was only one "Brazilian people."⁶

The pandemic has brought into plain view the vulnerability of these communities and the fragility of any advances made in the last decades related to the recognition of their rights. Most tellingly and tragically, the deforestation of the Amazon and the ethnocide of Indigenous populations accelerated during the COVID-19 pandemic, while in July 2020 president Bolsonaro vetoed the most important emergency measures to protect Indigenous peoples. When analyzing the impact of COVID-19 on Romanies and other vulnerable populations, it is therefore important to take into account the effects of violence, racism, and dispossession, with their roots in colonialism and slavery. Social position and the space of action ascribed to Romanies must be understood in relation to the ways other communities are racialized. Unlike in Europe—where Romanies are often portrayed as the "largest" minority, a position of uniqueness as there is no "second largest" minority—in Brazil the place of prominence in the social imaginary and in the structuring of social relations has been occupied by Indigenous peoples and people of African descent. These populations are larger than the Romani population, and their experiences in social imagination are tied explicitly to the history of modern Brazil. By contrast, Romani communities have remained invisible to intellectuals pondering Brazil as a nation and to the Brazilian central state. On a local level, however, the persecution of Romanies, linked to folk stereotypes, has been present throughout the centuries, in the form for example of municipal ordinances expelling Romanies from towns during the colonial period, or of police persecutions during the First Republic.

Brazilian Romanies in 2020

Brazil is home to Latin America's largest Romani population. While no official statistics exist, estimates suggest that between half a million and one million Ciganos live in Brazil.⁷ Over centuries, different Romani groups have reached the country at different times, for different reasons and via different routes.⁸ Some settled, some passed through, and for others Brazil became a point within a broader network or circulation. Calon are the most numerous, and have been documented in all Brazilian states; contributors Valdinalva Barbosa dos Santos Caldas and Aluízio de Azevedo Silva Júnior belong to such communities. Ancestors of the Brazilian Calon started settling in Brazil from the earliest days of the Portuguese colonization.⁹ Calon live primarily in peri-urban areas, often comprising distinct settlements and sometimes living in tents. By contrast, ancestors of the Roma, including the family of Aline Miklos, started arriving from Eastern Europe at the end of the nineteenth century, a displacement that many Roma preserve within family memory, even when they do not maintain transcontinental links.[10] Today, Roma live primarily in the major cities of South and Southeast Brazil, dispersed among non-Roma, with households belonging to one extended family commonly located close to each other within the same neighborhood.

We provide this overview in order to give some sense of the Romani population in the country. We also want to highlight the diversity of Romani experiences and identifications, with some of us preferring to speak of "Romani peoples," in the plural. Significant differences exist in socioeconomic situation, in territorial and settlement patterns, in relations to the state or the majority society, as well as in forms of visibility in local social relationships. Our own contributions to the Brazilian chronicles focus on Calon communities, some of them itinerant and most earning a living through trade.[11] In a survey conducted by the central statistical office (IBGE) in 2014, 337 municipalities had identified Romani (primarily Calon) "camps" (*acampamentos*) within their administrations; but this number is sure to be an underestimation, as many Calon settlements are small and ephemeral. Many Calon communities have limited access to drinking water, electricity, and other basic necessities.

Brazil is a federation, and legislation mandates that health policies are to follow a unified national plan determined by the Ministry of Health, rather than each state adopting its own policies. The main legislation for the protection of traditional peoples is also determined by federal legislation, and applies throughout the country. Since 2007, the National Policy of Traditional People and Communities provides a framework within which Romani collective rights should be promoted at all administrative and governmental levels. In addition, within Brazil's publicly funded healthcare system (Sistema Único de Saúde, SUS) the National Comprehensive Health Care Policy for Cigano/Romani People could have, in theory, informed pandemic measures. While individual communities and local authorities have drawn on these frameworks in their attempt to fight the effects of the pandemic, in practice they have proven inadequate.

Besides the lack of resources, the major reason for the failure has been the position the federal government has taken, and its impact. To be precise, president Bolsonaro has refused to mobilize state capacities and has even systematically disrupted responses to the unfolding crisis. Indeed, a comprehensive analysis of federal and state regulations (laws, decrees, guidelines, etc.) concluded that, rather than trying to minimize the negative impacts of the pandemic, the Brazilian government adopted "an institutional strategy to spread the virus . . . with the declared aim of resuming economic activity as soon as possible, and at any cost."[12] Largely as a result of this study, in April 2021 the Brazilian Congress launched an inquiry into the government's mismanagement of the pandemic.[13] Instead, state governors and mayors instituted social distancing measures, the opposition pushed for emergency aid, the Supreme Federal Court mandated measures aimed at Indigenous communities, and the underfinanced SUS took a central role in tackling COVID-19 in this highly unequal society.

Adoption of any state or local measures recognizing the differential impact on individual Romani communities has to be understood against this background—but they were few, isolated, and fragmented.[14] For many Brazilians, hygiene recommendations proved to be difficult to adhere to on a practical level, and COVID-19 measures threatened their economic survival. Population density in the peripheries of cities, overcrowding of houses or, in case those living in tents, the non-existence of separate rooms, made isolation impossible for the poor. Many informal workers, who represent 41 percent of the total Brazilian workforce, needed to continue working in order to survive. Poor people in urban peripheries had difficulty in accessing clean water or could not afford items such as soaps and alcohol gels. Calon were no exception, although at least some communities managed in the early months to isolate and close themselves off, and thus to slow down the spread of the virus. It is also important to mention the problems faced while accessing diagnosis and treatment through SUS, on which those without money depend. Moreover, thousands of families who lost relatives during this pandemic, and communities that faced difficulty with reconstructing their life in the wake of death, had also to live with the president's banalization of deaths: "I'm sorry, some people will die, they will die, [but] that's life."[15]

The Themes of the Brazilian Chronicles

Although only four of us wrote this introduction, ultimately our text emerges from conversations between all contributors to the Brazilian chronicles. We met online in a series of video meetings (which became so common in 2020) to discuss ways in which the experiences and observations captured in individual texts were in conversation with each other, what possible connections existed between them, and what knowledge could be built from these accounts. We did not want to ignore ways we were implicated in our texts and how we produced situated knowledges, to uses Donna Haraway's expression.[16] These knowledges emerged from our specific locations and from interactions and relations that go beyond our meetings and exchanges when preparing these chronicles. As scholars, community leaders, and activists linked variously to the Romani cause in Brazil, we have been caught up in a collective effort to understand the situation Romanies have faced in the context of the pandemic, and to act—from within our different roles in the community, in academia, in state agencies—to mitigate its multiple impacts. The contributions also stem from these other activities in which we have been involved in different ways and to different degrees—with each other, and with other people to whom we are accountable.

Finding connections between the texts was not difficult, because even though they vary in content and style, many common points stand out. All show, in different ways, the dilemma imposed by efforts to manage the pandemic between, on the one hand, the need for social isolation in order to avoid contracting or spreading the coronavirus, and, on the other hand, the importance of living together, of being in a family, which is a crucial condition for the continuation and reproduction of Romani life and community while living dispersed among non-Romanies. This intensive collective life has been used against Ciganos by those public authorities who have accused them of being potential disseminators of the virus. Here the greatest problem becomes the response to the dilemma that the authorities adopted: instead of taking into account the singularities that make up Romani communities and looking for specific policies that would help mitigate contagion, the most convenient option became the same one offered for at least a century by the Brazilian state—namely, to expel the Romanies by using public hygiene arguments.[17]

Brazilian chronicles illustrate how, in various ways, the pandemic has served as a pretext for an upsurge in exclusionary measures. Igor Shimura's chapter describes the expulsions of Calon camps by municipal authorities claiming that they posed a danger of contagion; and Juliana Campos and Valdinalva Caldas speak of the difficulties faced by Calon when accessing emergency aid paid by the federal government. More broadly, the chapters discuss how Romanies and other traditional peoples and communities have been excluded from access to water, basic sanitation, and virus-prevention measures.[18] In all these and other ways, the COVID-19 threat exacerbated the existing social inequalities in Brazilian society, and further divided the country between those who can and those who cannot claim access to fundamental rights—to health, to dignity, and to life itself. These inequalities impact all Brazilian minorities, but are especially acute for traditional peoples, such as Ciganos.

The theme of the exclusion and destruction of minority lives as a state policy runs through the Brazilian chronicles. Not by coincidence, Edilma Souza and Aluízio Silva Júnior, like many Brazilian intellectuals draw on Achille Mbembe's concept of "necropolitics"[19] in their attempts to capture what is happening in Brazil today. Souza's chapter also reflects on acute observations made by Mbembe about the consequences of the articulation between the pandemic and racism on the right to breathe, as even this right is being denied to subaltern bodies.[20]

Yet, in 2020, there have also been exceptional state and municipal initiatives, some based on the demands made by the public prosecutor's office, that aimed at providing for vulnerable individuals and at protecting the rights of traditional peoples, including Romanies.[21] This evinces the importance of the rights and gains won by these populations over the last three decades, starting with the 1988 Federal Constitution, even if these rights are not always respected. The Ministry of Health itself recognized the disproportionate threat of the pandemic on the survival of traditional peoples, when in 2021 it made them one of the priorities in the National Immunization Plan. At the end, however, Ciganos were not included among priority groups of traditional peoples to receive vaccines—only Indigenous people, *quilombolas*, and fisherfolk were specified.[22]

Another thread running through our contributions relates to various creative ways through which Romani groups and their allies attempted to overcome the adversities imposed by the pandemic context, whether these relate to day-to-day community contexts or to the field of activism. Both Edilma Souza and Igor Shimura describe how in early 2020 some Calon communities adopted a strategy of avoidance of, and distance from, urban centers and conglomerates, which were highly susceptible to the spread of coronavirus, and so looked to settle in less populated places. Fewer festivities and encounters between families, the reduction of trading with outsiders and, generally, communities keeping themselves to themselves also emerge as common strategies, and are documented by several chroniclers, including Juliana Campos and Valdinalva Caldas, Igor Shimura, Aluízio Silva Junior, and Edilma Souza.

The chapters also highlight the importance and role of Cigano associations and organizations in promoting actions to guarantee Romani rights, to fight the coronavirus, and to reduce its harm. Gabriela Marques, Aline Miklos, and Aluízio Silva Júnior in their contribution point to their own increased productive use of virtual tools and platforms in the early months of social isolation, to bring together and strengthen relations between Romani leaders, activists, and supporters from various corners of Brazil and beyond. Witnessing the intensification of racism and xenophobia during the pandemic, they established a collective #*OrgulhoRomani* that through campaigning on social media has been challenging antigypsyism.

Other chroniclers speak of their struggles on the ground. The work of Valdinalva Caldas within a Cigano association, which she runs with her husband, to mitigate the impacts of the pandemic on Calon camps in Minas Gerais, and the steps taken by another association, in which Igor Shimura has been involved, to stop the expulsion of a Calon community from a town in Paraná, are some of the examples of resistance by Brazilian Cigano activists against the current state steamroller. As Juliana Campos observes, women in particular have played an important role in this emerging Calon movement for social justice.

In sum, collectively, our chronicles suggest that the vulnerability and struggles of Brazilian Romanies—especially those who maintain a life perceived in some ways as distinct from that of most Brazilians—during the pandemic (and beyond) should be understood in connection with experiences of other racialized and subaltern communities. Individually, the contributions speak of structural racism, naturalization of death and suffering, and the lack of solidarity with Romani and vulnerable groups, which is characteristic of the dominant segments of the Brazilian society, and of the worsening of this situation due to the current health crisis and political climate. As a whole, the Brazilian chronicles capture the sense of urgency we felt as we observed the unfolding consequences of the pandemic among the Brazilian Romanies during the first half of 2020.

Juliana Miranda Soares Campos obtained a PhD in anthropology from the Federal University of Minas Gerais (UFMG). She has been working with Calon Romanies in Minas Gerais since 2013, conducting research and advising several Calon communities on issues related to the struggle for specific rights and for regularization of their territories. Her research among Calon focuses primarily on marriage, territoriality, kinship, and gender.

Martin Fotta is a researcher at the Institute of Ethnology, Czech Academy of Sciences. He is the author of *From Itinerant Trade to Moneylending in the Era of Financial Inclusion* (Palgrave Macmillan, 2018). His current work explores transformations across the Romani diaspora of the Lusophone South Atlantic region.

Gabriela Marques Gonçalves holds a PhD in audiovisual communication and advertising from the Universidad Autónoma de Barcelona (UAB-Spain) and an MA in communication from the Federal University of Juiz de Fora (UFJF-Brazil). She is a journalist, and a collaborating researcher of the UNESCO Chair in Communication at the Instituto de Comunicación (InCom-UAB).

Aline Miklos is an art historian, a cultural producer, composer, singer and PhD candidate at the École des Hautes Études en Sciences Sociales, France. She currently works as a senior fellow at the United Nations (OHCHR / South America). Since 2016 she has been coordinating a project in Argentina entitled "Kalo Chiriklo—Latin American Romani Music" from which she released an album *Pájaro Negro* in 2021.

Notes

1. Ribeiro da Silva, "O trachoma," 77.
2. Ibid., 78.
3. See e.g., Casarões and Magalhães, "The Hydroxychloroquine Alliance;" Domingues, "Brazil in the Face of COVID-19."
4. Peres et al., "Sociodemographic Factors Associated with COVID-19."
5. Dolabela and Fotta, "Ciganos as a Traditional People."
6. G1, "Eu, por mim, botava esses vagabundos."
7. SEPPIR, *Brasil cigano*.
8. Some Sinti, for instance, came at the beginning of the twentieth century when they were expelled by authorities in Italy (Trevisan, "Austrian Gypsies.").
9. Portugueses Ciganos, a distinct Calé community from Portugal, have started migrating to Brazil in recent decades.
10. Budur, "Gypsy Myths."
11. For ethnographies of the Calon communities mentioned in the Brazilian chronicles, see Shimura, *Ser cigano*; Monteiro, "Tempo, redes;" Campos, "O nascimento da esposa."
12. CEPEDISA, "Mapeamento e análise," 6–7.
13. BBC, "Covid."
14. For instance, in April 2020 the state of Rio Grande do Norte adopted an *Emergency Plan for the Prevention and Combating of COVID-19 among the Romani Population*. Several Romani activists, Rom and Calon, including Aluízio de Azevedo Silva Júnior, collaborated on the development of the document (see SESAP, *Plano Emergencial*).
15. Fonseca and Rochabrun, "Brazil's Bolsonaro."
16. Haraway, "Situated Knowledges."
17. Borges, "Portas fechadas."
18. See e.g., Oxfam Brasil, "Entenda."
19. Mbembé, "Necropolitics."
20. Mbembé, "The Universal Right."
21. To give one example, on 17 September 2020 the Public Prosecutor's Office of the State of Bahia (MPB) wrote to the State Secretariats of Health and of Social Justice, Human Rights and Social Development, as well as to the Municipal Secretariats of Health and of Social Assistance of the city of Vitória da Conquista, asking them to provide the MPB with information about the measures they had adopted to ensure the health and social well-being of Ciganos living in the city. It also reminded them that there were guidelines on how to deal with the impact of COVID-19 among Ciganos (from https://mpba.mp.br/noticia/53514, last accessed 15 January 2021).
22. Queiroz, "OAB-CE pede inclusão de ciganos."

Bibliography

BBC. "Covid: Brazil's Bolsonaro Defiant as Congress Launches Inquiry." *BBC News*, 27 April 2021. Retrieved 29 May 2021 from https://www.bbc.com/news/world-latin-america-56899177.

Borges, Isabel Cristina Medeiros Mattos. "Cidades de portas fechadas: A intolerância contra os ciganos na organização urbana na Primeira República" [Cities of closed gates: Intolerance against Gypsies in urban organization in the First Republic]. Master's thesis, Universidade Federal de Juiz de Fora, 2007.

Budur, Diana. "Gypsy Myths and Romani Cosmologies in the New World: The Roma and Calon in Brazil." PhD diss., Princeton University, 2015.

Campos, Juliana Miranda Soares. "O Nascimento da esposa: Movimento, casamento e gênero entre os calons mineiros" [The birth of the wife: Movement, marriage and gender among the Calon in Minas Gerais]. PhD diss., Universidade Federal de Minas Gerais, 2020.

Casarões, Guilherme, and David Magalhães. "The Hydroxychloroquine Alliance: How Far-Right Leaders and Alt-Science Preachers Came Together to Promote a Miracle Drug." *Revista de Administração Pública* 55(1) (2021): 197–214. https://doi.org/10.1590/0034-761220200556.

CEPEDISA & Conectas Direitos Humanos e do Centro de Pesquisas. "Mapeamento e Análise das Normas Jurídicas De Resposta à COVID-19 No Brasil" [Mapping and analyzing the legal norms in the response to COVID-19 in Brazil]. *Bulletin nr. 10 of Direitos na Pandemia*, 20 January 2021, Conectas. Retrieved 29 May 2021 from https://edisciplinas.usp.br/pluginfile.php/6624564/mod_folder/content/0/Normas%20Jurídicas%20de%20Resposta%20à%20Covid-19%20%20no%20Brasil%20.pdf.

Dolabela, Helena, and Martin Fotta. "Ciganos as a Traditional People: Romanies and the Politics of Recognition in Brazil." *Ethnopolitics* 22(2) (2023): 157–76. https://doi.org/10.1080/17449057.2021.2008671.

Domingues, José Maurício. "Brazil in the Face of COVID-19: Tragedy and Political Choices." *Environment: Science and Policy for Sustainable Development* 63(1) (2021): 4–14.

Fonseca, Pedro, and Marcelo Rochabrun. "Brazil's Bolsonaro Questions Coronavirus Deaths, Says 'Sorry, Some Will Die.'" *Reuters*, 27 March 2020. Retrieved 29 May 2021 from https://www.reuters.com/article/us-health-coronavirus-brazil-idUSKBN21E3IZ.

G1. "'Eu, por mim, botava esses vagabundos todos na cadeia, começando no STF', diz ministro da Educação em reunião" ['I, for one, would put all these bums in jail, starting with the STF,' says the education minister at a meeting]. *G1*, 22 May 2020. Retrieved 29 May 2021 from https://g1.globo.com/politica/noticia/2020/05/22/eu-por-mim-botava-esses-vagabundos-todos-na-cadeia-comecando-no-stf-diz-ministro-da-educacao-em-reuniao.ghtml.

Haraway, Donna. "Situated Knowledges: The Science Question in Feminism and the Privilege of Partial Perspective." *Feminist Studies* 14(3) (1988): 575–99. https://doi.org/10.2307/3178066.

Mbembe, Achille. "Necropolitics." *Public Culture* 15(1) (2003): 11–40. https://doi.org/10.1215/08992363-15-1-11.

———. "The Universal Right to Breathe." *Critical Inquiry* 47, S2 (Winter 2021): 58–62. https://doi.org/10.1086/711437.

Monteiro, Edilma do Nascimento Jacinto. "Tempo, redes e relações: Uma etnografia sobre infância e educação entre os calon" [Time, networks and relationships: An ethnography about childhood and education among the Calon]. PhD diss., Universidade Federal de Santa Catarina, 2019.

Oxfam Brasil. "Entenda como a pandemia de coronavírus afeta as comunidades tradicionais" [How the coronavirus pandemic affects traditional communities]. *Oxfam Brasil Blog*, 2 September 2021. Retrieved 2 October 2021 from https://www.oxfam.org.br/blog/entenda-como-a-pandemia-de-coronavirus-afeta-as-comunidades-tradicionais/.

Peres, Igor Tona, L.S.L. Bastos, J.G.M. Gelli, J.F. Marchesi, L.F. Dantas, B.B.P. Antunes, P.M. Maçaira, F.A. Baião, S. Hamacher, and F.A. Bozza. "Sociodemographic Factors Associated with COVID-19 In-hospital Mortality in Brazil." *Public Health* 192 (2021): 15–20. https://doi.org/10.1016/j.puhe.2021.01.005.

Queiroz, Adriano. "OAB-CE pede inclusão de ciganos entre grupos prioritários de plano estadual de vacinação" [OAB-CE asks for inclusion of Romanies among priority groups for the state vaccination plan]. *Eco Nordeste*, 2 February 2021. Retrieved 29 May 2021 from https://agenciaeconordeste.com.br/oab-ce-contesta-diretrizes-de-planos-estadual-e-nacional-para-nao-inclusao-de-ciganos/.

Ribeiro da Silva, Raymundo. "O trachoma na Bahia" [Trachoma in Bahia], 1916. *Gazeta Medica da Bahia* 48(2) (2016): 68–93.

SEPPIR (Secretaria Especial de Políticas de Promoção da Igualdade Racial). *Brasil cigano: Guia de políticas públicas para povos ciganos* [Gypsy/Romani Brazil: Public policy guide for Romani people]. 2013. Retrieved 15 September 2022 from: http://www.amsk.org.br/imagem/marcosLegais/SEPPIR_relatorio-executivo-Brasil-cigano.pdf.

SESAP. *Plano emergencial para prevenção e enfrentamento da Covid-19 para a população cigana do Rio Grande do Norte* [Emergency plan for the prevention and confrontation of COVID-19 for the Romani population in Rio Grande do Norte], April 2020, Secretaria de Estado da Saúde Pública do Rio Grande do Norte. Retrieved 15 September 2022 from https://portalcovid19.saude.rn.gov.br/wp-content/uploads/2020/04/Plano-Emergencial-para-prevenção-e-enfrentamento-da-COVID-19-para-a-população-cigana-do-Rio-Grande-do-Norte.pdf.

Shimura, Igor. *Ser cigano: A identidade étnica em um acampamento calon itinerante* [Being Cigano: Ethnic identity in a camp of itinerant Calon]. Maringá: Amazon, 2017.

Trevisan, Paola. "Austrian 'Gypsies' in the Italian Archives: Historical Ethnography on Multiple Border Crossings at the Beginning of the Twentieth Century." *Focaal* 87 (2020): 61–74. https://doi.org/10.3167/fcl.2020.012806.

CHAPTER 8

"GET OUT OF HERE!"
Discrimination and Prejudice against Ciganos in the Context of the Pandemic

Igor Shimura

Early in 2020, soon after the first infections by the new coronavirus were reported in Brazil, the itinerant Ciganos (Romanies) from the Calon ethnic subgroup began to face restrictions on stopping in some Brazilian cities, mainly in the South Region of Brazil (*Região Sul do Brasil*). As they live in constant transit, remaining only for short periods encamped on vacant lots, they felt especially exposed to contamination by the new coronavirus. The fear of contracting COVID-19 so alarmed Calon community leaders that several groups distanced themselves from the larger, more crowded cities, and sought sanctuary in countryside municipalities.

This dynamic combined with the preventive measures taken by local and municipal authorities, and greatly affected the economic possibilities for these Cigano communities as they depend on small-scale trading. The communities are made up of sets of nuclear families (basically father, mother, and children) that create a network of broader groups of extended families. Actual living arrangements are constantly changing, with families moving depending on new opportunities for local commerce. The closure of commerce, the recommendations—and in some cases, public orders—to physically isolate and distance, led many itinerant families to seek out other alternatives that would both enable the preservation of their businesses and minimize the risk of infection.

In addition to moving into small towns in the interior, these communities also sought out plots of land located on urban outskirts, far from the density of city centers; and as much as possible they avoided contact with locals. Commonly, itinerant Calon groups have leaders (*chefes*) who determine general rules of conduct whenever, for instance, their groups find themselves in difficult situations. In the context of the pandemic, families were instructed by them to pitch their tents in chosen areas, to remain there, and to avoid unnecessary outings beyond the camps. Generally, only male traders were allowed excursions outside the camp premises.

These intra-community measures were aimed at both collective health preservation as well as the search for more flexible and decentralized commercial areas without the presence of agents of the government, which would provide Calon individuals, or so it was hoped, with more opportunities to maintain their informal economic activities necessary to support their families. In general, itinerant Brazilian Calon live as peripatetic traders, selling various products such as jewelry, shoes, towels, herbal teas, sweets and candies, bedding, bath products, and so on, as well as offering divinatory art services, particularly palmistry (*quiromancia*).[1] For this purpose, these communities usually split into smaller groups that settle in different cities for some time. Their decisions are determined by factors such as access to water and electricity, the availability of basic health services, the receptiveness of locals and the attitudes of public authorities, and the existence of commercial opportunities—that is, the level of interest of local residents in their products.

In the context of the spreading coronavirus, while seeking safer places that would offer them better economic conditions, many Cigano communities have also suffered ethnoracial discrimination. Since the beginning of the implementation of preventive measures by public authorities at various levels, except the federal one, several cases of discrimination against Ciganos, mainly itinerant Calon, drew the attention of activists, researchers, media, and sectors of the government.

Some of these cases occurred in the south of Brazil, to be more precise in the states of Paraná and Rio Grande do Sul, and in localities that stand out for the frequency of cases of *ciganofobia* (antigypsyism);[2] that is, prejudice and discrimination against individuals and groups of Romani background. One of the cases that received the most attention and generated complaints to the federal government and the federal Public Prosecutor's Office occurred in April 2020, in the municipality of Dois Vizinhos, in the state of Paraná, when a group of itinerant Calon Ciganos were expelled as they tried to set up their temporary camp on a vacant lot.

I have known this group since 2002, when the NGO Instituto PluriBrasil, of which I am a president, started its activities aimed at supporting and promoting human rights.[3] In 2017, I published an ethnography about this community, known as *"Povo do Biráco"* (Biraco's people),[4] a network of about seven hundred people. These families frequently experience expulsion. Since my first contact with them, in the city of Araucária, Paraná, I have often heard them complain about threats from police officers and neighbors who did not want them around. In 2016, while doing fieldwork for my book, I witnessed an antigypsyist attack on one of their itinerant camps, in the municipality of Rolândia, Paraná, an occurrence that led us to file a complaint to the Paraná State Government, asking for police protection for the community. In view of this, the case that occurred in the municipality of Dois Vizinhos, on 1 April 2020, may appear to be just "another" act of antigypsyism. However, this time Ciganos were blamed for the circulation of a disease, as if Ciganos could enhance the spread of the coronavirus, just because they were Ciganos.

What happened on that day was that a small group broke away temporarily from the rest in search of a place with better business possibilities. Shortly after arriving in the municipality of Dois Vizinhos the group was approached by the Military Police (*Polícia Militar*)[5] and municipal officials who expelled them saying "Get out of here!" Cigano leaders were given a notice to "abandon the town at once," on the grounds that "they could infect the inhabitants of the town." According to one of the Calon leaders, Rogério Alves, aged 30, the approach of the public agents made it clear that this was a case of antigypsyism associated with the fear of the spread of COVID-19, a kind of "Cigano-COVIDophobia."

As the Calon group included children and elderly people, and did not have enough fuel to continue their journey to a town where other families from their community were staying, they asked the agents for permission to remain in the town—this was vehemently refused. Fearing that they were running the risk of being physically threatened, and to prevent a possible escalation of violence, as well as to demonstrate that they had legal backing, they immediately contacted a Cigano lawyer, Marcelo de Almeida, whom they had known for many years. The lawyer spoke with one of the municipal officials on the phone but there was no negotiation.

Marcelo de Almeida, who at the time was in the city of Curitiba, 460 km away, advised the group to record what was happening on their mobile phones, which could serve as testimonial evidence in a possible lawsuit. While the events were taking place, the lawyer contacted the Public Prosecutor's Office, as well as several partners of our institute, of which he is a member. Additionally, he appealed to the federal government through the National Secretariat of Policies for the Promotion of Racial Equality (SNPIR) for immediate help.

The expulsion from Dois Vizinhos, however, was carried out quickly, and the attempts made by the lawyer to mobilize outside support were not effective. The small group left the locale even though they hardly had the means to do so, as they had no money for fuel, nor even a destination. Faced with this situation they sought refuge among their relatives who at that time were encamped in the city of Guarapuava, about 215 km away. Their departure from the municipality took place under police escort, and they were ordered not to return. Everything was recorded in short videos on cell phones.

The next day, 2 April 2020, they found themselves in a larger community of about one hundred individuals, sheltered by their relatives. Everything seemed calm, as the group they joined had already been in Guarapuava for a few weeks and had had no problems with the local authorities. However, in the early afternoon the group was approached by Military Police officers who demanded their immediate departure from the site. The Cigano leaders became indignant at the order and tried to negotiate with the police officers, especially with a female commander of the operation.

Ironically, one of the leaders of this camp, 46-year-old Claudio Mota, is a representative of the Cigano peoples on the Paraná Council of Indigenous Peoples and Traditional Communities,[6] but this fact made no impression on the police and did not exempt his community from the unjustified and unexpected police order. As Calon attempts at a dialogue were unsuccessful, the community leaders contacted our institute, which in turn quickly attempted to mobilize our contacts within the federal and state governments.

This time, contacting other institutions produced quick positive results. It made the police forces on the ground realize that this community was capable of mobilizing other public institutions and, even though considerably anxious, the community was eventually able to buy time while hoping for a potentially more favorable resolution. The SNPIR played a special role in the process when it contacted the 16th Military Police Battalion in the city of Guarapuava, demanding explanations about the operation. This resulted in an immediate halt to the police operation, and about an hour later the community leaders were invited for a conversation with the commander of the battalion.

At the meeting, the commander mandated that the camp be moved within "twenty-four hours" to another piece of land which could be close to where they were encamped at that moment. He argued that the community could end up spreading COVID-19 to others: "Imagine you all over there? One that has [COVID-19] will pass it on fast, pass it on to everyone." In stating this, the commander of the 16th Military Police Battalion revealed that at the time the Cigano community was seen as a public health risk and so should ideally abandon the city. The only reason why this did not happen in the end was the intervention of other public authorities, in particular the SNPIR. Upon hearing the commander's requests and instructions, the chiefs were relieved that they did not have to leave in a hurry and under police escort. The next day, 3 April, they moved to another vacant lot about three hundred meters away.

The two cases above have generated much discussion on social media and led to an open letter from researchers working with and among Ciganos.[7] They warned of "racism against Cigano groups," and demanded that public authorities, especially the federal ones, develop an emergency action plan to protect Cigano communities that would reflect their specific needs.

This pandemic era has been very difficult for Brazilian Ciganos, especially the itinerant ones who live in the South Region of the country. The two cases of prejudice and discrimination demonstrate the vulnerability of these groups, as well as the unpreparedness of public institutions to assist them. The work of our institute assisting Cigano groups that suffer discriminatory acts has been arduous. In these and other cases we have worked towards opening channels for dialogue between Cigano leaders and public officials, particularly municipal officials, and towards looking for practical solutions to any problems that might arise.

Although tensions and chaos dominated relations between Ciganos and non-Ciganos during the pandemic, various cases of discrimination also seem to have provided a greater visibility to the human rights issues related to Ciganos. In a sense, this also seems to be an opportunity to further advance activist agendas for affirmative action and to develop policies that promote ethnoracial equality. Relatedly, the experiences of Brazilian Ciganos during this pandemic have also served to empower Cigano leaders, who have been learning to access public arenas and defend themselves more effectively than before. The context also tests the capacity of associations and NGOs to responds to community needs, and provides a background against which we can evaluate the efficiency and effectiveness of their approaches when resolving future problems similar to those described in this chapter.

Igor Shimura is a lecturer, researcher, human rights advocate, and doctoral student in anthropology at the Federal University of Paraná (UFPR). He holds a master's degree in social sciences (Universidade Estadual de Maringá, UEM), a specialization in cultural anthropology (Pontifícia Universidade Católica do Paraná, PUC-PR), a degree in theology, and he also trained in nursing. He serves as a president of the PluriBrasil Institute, which is a member of the National Council for the Promotion of Racial Equality (CNPIR) and the National Council for Traditional People and Communities (CONPCT/MMFDH).

Notes

1. The art of predicting the future through reading palms. A divinatory art also known as *buena-dicha*.
2. This term is used in the draft bill 2703/2020 proposed by the federal deputy Filipe Barros, which institutes the Brazilian Romani Statute. "II—*Ciganofobia*: any exclusion, restriction or distinction against an individual or a set of individuals that is made based on their Cigano identity in order to restrict their recognition, enjoyment and exercise of human rights and fundamental freedoms in the political, economic, social, cultural or any other field of public or private life." See "Estatuto dos Ciganos. Projeto de Lei 2703/2020." Câmara dos Deputados [The Chamber of Deputies], last accessed 9 September 2021. Available at: https://www.camara.leg.br/proposicoesWeb/prop_mostrarintegra;jsessionid=64A925BB65CA08661F1B830EFB343493.proposicoesWebExterno2?codteor=1894363&filename=Tramitacao-PL+2703/2020.
3. The Instituto PluriBrasil, previously called Associação Social de Apoio aos Ciganos (ASAIC), is composed of people of different ethnic origins, including Romanies, and has been monitoring cases of antigypsyism in the South Region of Brazil since 2002. It has been active promoting the defense of human rights, especially for itinerant communities, and mediating between their leaders and public authorities.
4. Shimura, *Ser Cigano*.
5. A preventive state police responsible for ostensive policing and the maintenance of public order.
6. Conselho Estadual de Povos Indígenas e Comunidades Tradicionais do Estado do Paraná (CPICT/PR), see, for instance, CPICT/PR, "Composição da Gestão."
7. AEECMT, "Nota Pública." For more details, see also the chapter by Gabriela Marques, Aluízio Silva Júnior and Aline Miklos in this volume.

Bibliography

AEECMT. "Nota pública: pesquisadores e ativistas alertam para racismo contra grupos cigano durante a pandemia e cobram plano emergencial" [Public statement: Researchers and activists warn of racism against Romani groups during the pandemic and demand an emergency plan]. Associação Estadual das Etnias Ciganas, last modified 8 April 2020. Retrieved 9 September 2021 from https://aeecmt.blogspot.com/2020/04/nota-publica-pesquisadores-e-ativistas.html?m=0.

CPICT/PR. "Composição da gestão 2019–2021" [Composition of the Board 2019–2021], last accessed 9 September 2021. https://www.justica.pr.gov.br/sites/default/arquivos_restritos/files/documento/2020-03/composicaocpict.pdf.

Shimura, Igor. *Ser cigano: identidade étnica em um acampamento calon itinerante* [Being Cigano: Ethnic identity in a camp of itinerant Calon]. Maringá: Amazon, 2017.

CHAPTER 9

✺ ✺ ✺

"Everything Is on Hold"
The Pandemic and the Ciganos in Minas Gerais

*Valdinalva Barbosa dos Santos Caldas
and Juliana Miranda Soares Campos*

The following two accounts were written in June 2020, less than four months after the first case was confirmed in Brazil, at a time when the number of cases and deaths from COVID-19 across the country was on a steep increase. Starting from different loci of speech (*lugares de fala*),[1] standpoints, this text features two voices. In the first part, Calin[2] Valdinalva ("Nalva") Caldas narrates how she has experienced the pandemic over recent months. It describes her struggle for public health measures to combat the coronavirus within Cigano encampments, as well as her personal struggle when she was diagnosed with a suspected case of COVID-19. In the second part, anthropologist Juliana Campos recounts how she was asked by several of her Calon interlocutors to assist them with their requests for the emergency financial assistance that had been released by the Brazilian government, exposing the difficulties that the state imposed on access to the benefit by the Cigano population.

Nalva Caldas is a resident of the São Pedro Calon encampment, in the municipality of Ibirité in Minas Gerais, and is a vice president of the *Associação Estadual Cultural de Direitos e Defesa dos Povos Ciganos* (State association for the cultural rights and defense of Cigano peoples), of which husband, Itamar Soares, is a president.

The São Pedro settlement is one of those where, for several years, Juliana Campos has been conducting her anthropological research and where she has acted as a partner and ally in the Cigano struggle for their rights. The settlement is connected to various other encampments in Minas Gerais, forming a network linked by ties of kinship, alliances, friendship, and economic exchanges.

Struck by the Virus
Valdinalva Barbosa dos Santos Caldas

When the news reached us that we were facing a pandemic, it gave rise to great fears in our midst. I live in a camp located on an open lot, facing a central avenue in Ibirité. Currently there are twenty-three tents and about sixty Ciganos, including adults and children. In my tent I live with my husband and my stepdaughter. The tents are at a certain distance from each other. Inside each tent, one family lives together, without partitions. Recommendations about social distancing and isolation can only be applied with much difficulty here because we are used to always living close together and to socializing with barbecues, drinks, and music. But we have made a collective effort, because we are aware of the possible consequences of an outbreak of COVID-19 in the camp, especially for the many elderly people and those in other risk groups. Celebrations have stopped happening, especially those that we used to attend in other camps. Weddings have been postponed until later in the year. Sometimes we get together to listen to music and drink beer outdoors in the camp, each family in front of their own tent, and keeping a good distance from each other. We also keep ourselves closed to outsiders, except for health workers who come to the camp to provide care.

Despite all these precautions, in mid-April I began to experience some of the same symptoms as those described for COVID-19. First, I was constantly short of breath and had a slight headache. I decided to go to the hospital of Ibirité because I have diabetes and thus belong to a risk group. The first doctor who examined me said it was a diabetes crisis and sent me home. Two days later my inability to breathe intensified, the headache became unbearable, I coughed a lot and had a high fever. I returned to the hospital and this time the doctor diagnosed my condition as coronavirus, prescribed me some medicine for fever and breathlessness and sent me back to camp, telling me to monitor my state for the next few days. If it worsened, I was to return to hospital again.

The hospital informed the municipality, the health workers and even the military police that there was a Cigana with COVID-19. They all started to watch me: the police so that I would not leave the camp, and the health agents checking to see if my condition was worsening.

I spent many days showing several symptoms, especially a huge shortness of breath. It was a horrible feeling. Apart from medicines that the doctor prescribed, I began to treat myself with natural medication. I took a lot of pigeon pea leaf infusion—bad, bad! I thought it was important to improve my immunity, as the coronavirus attacks those with low immunity. I used all the natural remedies that we usually use for people with dengue. After a few days, the symptoms disappeared. I thought to myself: "I am cured." But, a little more than a week later, I started to deteriorate again. I went back to the hospital and they made me sign a statement not to leave my tent for the next fifteen days. All in all, I suffered for about one month with symptoms that variously came and went—fever, cough, shortness of breath. Only in the very last days in which I was still showing symptoms, which were already weak, was a health agent sent to test me. They did a rapid test (IgM/IgC), which came back negative. They never repeated the test, so I never received any more reliable information that could confirm the result.

Other Ciganos in Minas Gerais and in Brazil have also had experiences like mine and, from what I know, so far at least nineteen Ciganos have died due to the virus. Near our settlement, in a *turma*[3] encamped in the municipality of Betim, one Cigano had to be intubated, but fortunately survived. Luckily, in our camp, so far I am the only one who has presented such strong symptoms of COVID-19; but we have had cases here of Ciganos suffering from something like flu, with fever, but no tests have been done.

As a state-level leader of Ciganos since the beginning of the pandemic, I have been concerned about its effects on the Cigano population. As if all the difficulties we face—lack of opportunities, specific public policies for us, and racism—were not enough, I have also increasingly realized how we as a population are being affected by the coronavirus in specific ways. The pandemic prevention campaigns have said that the main measures were to stay at home and wash your hands well. I immediately thought: how can we stay at home if our livelihood depends on our trading on the street and in marketplaces? We women need to go out to sell dishcloths and cleaning products. And the men need to go out to trade various other products. Today, to survive, we are totally dependent on donations from others. Our tents have no partitions, and we live very close to our relatives. And there is still the question of hygiene, in a context where most of the camps do not have basic sanitation. We do not have bathrooms, so we use the bush, which spreads contamination.

Through the association that I chair together with my husband, we have appealed to public authorities—municipal, state, and federal—and to other partners in civil society asking them to develop some more adequate measures. For several camps in Minas Gerais, we have managed to secure donations of basic food baskets and hygiene products. We have also asked for a vaccination program to be carried out in the settlements, as many Ciganos do not even have basic vaccination against the other diseases that affect Brazil at this time of year, which leaves us even more vulnerable at a time when there is a shortage of hospital beds. We are currently receiving flu and hepatitis A vaccinations here in Ibirité, and we have requested vaccinations for other camps as well. We continue our struggle.

Barriers Faced by Ciganos When Accessing Public Policies during the Pandemic
Juliana Miranda Soares Campos

I have always viewed my work among Calon Romanies in Minas Gerais as a two-way street, in the sense that the trust that the Calon placed in me as an ethnographer implies expectations that I would be useful to them somehow, especially as a mediator between them and the non-Calon world. Thus, over the past seven years I have been assisting my interlocutors with various demands they have addressed to public authorities. Among these I would highlight the preparation of anthropological reports to support requests for land regularization of areas where they had been encamped for several years. I participated in the process of regularization, now completed, of the first two Calon encampment areas in Minas Gerais. With the arrival of the coronavirus pandemic in Brazil, my work has turned more to supporting requests for emergency policies for Romani peoples, for basic hygiene kits and food baskets, and to advising the state association led by Nalva; also, responding to ad hoc requests from various Calon individuals.

On 30 March 2020, just over a month after the confirmation of the first case of coronavirus in Brazil, the Brazilian Senate approved emergency aid for the most vulnerable people: for three months, eligible adults would receive R$600 each, and single mothers R$1,200. Despite some resistance from the federal government, the president approved the aid within two days. In Brazil, the coronavirus could not have arrived at a worse time, given that our current government is characterized by an obscurantist anti-science attitude, by support for conspiracy theories, by denial of the seriousness of the pandemic, and by an ultra-neoliberal economic policy that tries to relieve the state of responsibility for minimizing the pandemic's harmful effects. In this context, it is not surprising that the approval of the emergency aid, crucial for the survival of the country's most vulnerable people, was accompanied by a series of mechanisms that made actual access to the benefit difficult. Such mechanisms of exclusion became clear to me in the case of the Cigano families I accompanied.

The news of the approval of the emergency aid was widely reported in the media. Soon afterwards I began to receive calls and messages from several Calin friends (my closest contact is mainly with the women) asking me for help in applying for it. In these phone conversations, the reports from Calins from different camps converged: because they feared the virus, they were confined to their tents and no longer moved about towns in order to sell dishcloths. Their husbands' dealings (*catiras*) had also diminished considerably. "Everything is on hold," they said. Money for food was running out and some started to cook with wood, as there were no resources to buy natural gas. It was therefore crucial for them to receive this aid. However, many of them did not understand if they would receive it, or what they needed to do to claim it. Three reasons contributed to the difficulties for Ciganos in this network of settlements when accessing the benefit: high degrees of illiteracy, digital exclusion, and frequently a lack of necessary documents. These should not have been obstacles if the access process created by the government was simple and democratic. Added to this were delays in transferring the money to a population that needed to put food on the table immediately.

Many Cigano families in the Minas Gerais settlements are already beneficiaries of the federal government's *Bolsa Família* Program,[4] which in theory should have facilitated access to pandemic emergency aid, as payment to these families was to be automatic and to the same bank accounts used by *Bolsa Família*. However, many Calon found it difficult to access information about when the money would be available. The first portion of the aid took about a month to be transferred to these families, in some cases even longer, which generated great anxiety and concern among those whose food supplies had already run out. On payment days, some Calon recounted the difficulties when facing long queues and crowding at doors of banks, which inevitably exposed them to the virus.

Moreover, a portion of Calon families were not beneficiaries of the *Bolsa Família* or were not included in the federal government's unified register of low-income families. They needed to file a separate request to receive aid. The government set up an electronic site to register such people. This is where I made my main contribution: I was asked by Calon to help them to get around the obstacles in accessing this money, as the government's registry required knowledge of how a website works, and it obliged the applicant to have a telephone number and an email address, and to download a mobile phone app to access a bank account. In this sense, the state bureaucracy proved to be totally disconnected from the reality of many of the most vulnerable Brazilians, including many Ciganos. Some of my interlocutors did not even have documents like social security numbers or photo IDs, required to withdraw the aid. Although most Ciganos have mobile phones, many do not know how to download or use a banking app. And virtually none of the Calon I work with have email addresses. Even after assisting my Calon friends with these issues, in a few cases the aid was denied, and it took more than one attempt to get it approved. It was a marathon in every case I followed, overcoming hurdles along each step of the process until the actual receipt of the money, and it involved a network of collaborative work within and among Calon families.

Although the Brazilian state has historically insisted on excluding part of the population from its public policies, and although Ciganos occupy a unique place of invisibility within this process, the creativity of Ciganos in continually producing new and thriving modes of resistance amazes me. At this present moment, the spread of coronavirus occurs in the context of the rise of activism by Calin women in the state of Minas Gerais. Several Calins have taken on the role of mediators of their communities' demands vis-à-vis the Brazilian state. Nalva is one of the most visible ones, and her work has been fundamental in mitigating the economic and social impacts of the pandemic among Ciganos. The power, energy, and creativity of women like her is what gives us hope in this gloomy scene that is Brazil today—at the crossroads between the devastating pandemic and an extreme right-wing neoliberal government.

Valdinalva Barbosa dos Santos Caldas, a Calon Romani, is one of the leaders of the São Pedro Calon camp (Ibirité, MG). She is vice president of the State Association for the Rights and Defense of Cigano Peoples, a representative of Romanies (Ciganos) in the State Commission of Traditional Peoples and Communities of Minas Gerais (CEPCT-MG) and chair of the State Council for the Promotion of Racial Equality of Minas Gerais (CONEPIR). She has been active in movements seeking rights and public policies for Ciganos in Minas Gerais and in Brazil.

Juliana Miranda Soares Campos obtained a PhD in anthropology from the Federal University of Minas Gerais (UFMG). She has been working with Calon Romanies in Minas Gerais since 2013, conducting research and advising several Calon communities on issues related to the struggle for specific rights and for regularization of their territories. Her research among Calon focuses primarily on marriage, territoriality, kinship, and gender.

Notes

1. Ribeiro, *O que é lugar de fala?*
2. Fem. of Calon.
3. A family cluster usually around a group of male siblings.

4. *Bolsa Família* was a cash transfer program created by the government of the president Luiz Inácio Lula da Silva (known as Lula) in 2004, and was aimed at providing monetary assistance to families living in poverty or extreme poverty. It was ended by Jair Bolsonaro on 30 December 2021, and replaced by a new program.

Bibliography

Ribeiro, Djamila. *O que é lugar de fala?* [What is place of speech?]. Belo Horizonte: Letramento, 2017.

CHAPTER 10

THE CREATION OF THE #*ORGULHOROMANI* COLLECTIVE AMID THE PANDEMIC

*Gabriela Marques Gonçalves,
Aluízio de Azevedo Silva Júnior, and Aline Miklos*

Across Latin America, the political and human-rights mobilization of Romani communities as an institutionalized social movement is a recent development when compared with the history of Indigenous or Afro-descendant movements. This does not mean, of course, that Cigano (Romani) resistance—although maybe not always in easily recognizable forms—is something new. Over the ages, Cigano families and communities in Brazil have organized themselves autonomously to overcome persecution and to deal with the consequences of discrimination. We could mention here specificities of Cigano family economy, the role of intra-family networks, practices of mutual care between families, spatial flexibility, and even the countless times when Ciganos have had to hide their identities so that they could move freely, claim their rights or, simply, avoid prejudice.

The first Cigano organizations emerged in Brazil in the 1990s, but it was only in 2006 that the *Dia Nacional do Cigano* (Romani National Day) was instituted by a presidential decree. The date was a turning point marking the official ethnocultural recognition of Ciganos at a national level. The decree followed the creation by the federal government, in 2003, of the Special Secretariat for Policies Promoting Racial Equality and Human Rights (SEPPIR), whose task it has been to elaborate and implement race equality policies (such as the Racial Equality Statute and the creation of state and municipal bodies to promote race equality). Another decree, in 2007, on the "National Policy on Sustainable Development of Traditional Peoples and Communities," recognized Cigano peoples as pertaining to Brazil's so-called "traditional peoples and communities" (*povos e comunidades tradicionais*) alongside Indigenous peoples, riverine communities, and maroons. But it was only as late as 2013 that Cigano activists and representatives from all over the country gathered in Brasília for the first national Cigano Peoples Week, primarily in order to discuss public policies for Cigano communities. In addition to these initiatives, the Cigano Statute is currently being drafted by the Federal Senate while the federal government is considering adopting the National Policy Plan for Cigano Peoples.

Besides broader social and political changes in countries where Romani people live, and which shape their ethnopolitical mobilization—in Brazil, for example, the adoption of the democratic constitution in 1988—it is also important to highlight parallel changes related to new forms of organizing social and community life in recent years. The Internet has been one of the main drivers of this reconfiguration, stimulating activism across different social movements. The possibility of networking among individuals from different locales has facilitated coordination of activities from the local to the international level.

For communication scientist Jesús Martín-Barbero, the Internet and social networks represent "a 'meeting place' for minorities and marginalized communities, and for collectives engaged in research and educational or artistic work."[1] Within this space, realities and experiences of different social groups, and narratives and knowledges produced by them, enter into dialogue with one another, enabling these groups to explore what they share in their struggles for equal opportunities and in their work to end ethnoracial, class, gender, or other discrimination. Such networking has intensified during the COVID-19 pandemic. As virtual discussions, debates, and congresses became normalized, which eliminated travel distances and significantly reduced costs, multicultural events and discussion forums bringing together Cigano, descendants of quilombos (maroon settlements), Indigenous peoples, *caiçaras*,[2] and other traditional peoples living in Brazil proliferated. In this way, activists constructed new forms of mutual support that have enabled them to promote their activities, articulate common agendas, and share experiences and knowledges, as well as exchange practical advice and tactics of resistance.

On the other hand, the advance of the coronavirus has also magnified the impact of racist and xenophobic ideology within the wider Brazilian society, which is increasingly expressed throughout the media and social networks. It is in this context that the *#OrgulhoRomani* (Romani Pride) collective emerged.[3] It has been formed by us three—by two "artivists" and researchers Aline Miklos and Aluízio Silva Júnior, and by a journalist and researcher Gabriela Marques. We initially met in the virtual environment, and from early 2019 we started to discuss the role of media and of social networks in the propagation of antigypsyism, as well as ways these forums could be utilized to fight it. Since then, we have developed a series of initiatives linking activism in social networks with our academic knowledge and our own experiences. But the pandemic disrupted our initial plans and we were forced to reinvent the group. The popularization of Instagram broadcasts provided us with inspiration as to how we could carry out our joint activities. It was on Instagram that the first events of the *#OrgulhoRomani* collective took place in March 2020. Gradually, we expanded our activities. We created and posted content related to Cigano rights on other social networks such as Facebook, produced journalistic and scientific texts, participated in events organized by other institutions, and contributed to and elaborated advocacy documents.

The personal trajectory of each one of us shapes the articulation of *#OrgulhoRomani* and its aims. Gabriela draws on her personal experiences as a Black woman involved in debates on racism, as well as on knowledge, skills, and contacts gained within the Romani movement in Spain, where she did her PhD. Aluízio brings to the collective his expertise of working within his own Calon community (especially in the State of Mato Grosso and the Federal District) when developing his master's research on environmental education and Cigano mythology, in addition to the knowledge he gained alongside Ciganos in Portugal, where he spent time during his doctorate in health communication. Aline's work is shaped by her Rom family belonging, her work in the Romani movement in Argentina where she lives, and her encounters with the Romanies in France, where she completed her master's and doctoral studies.

Production of Social Media Content

From the beginning, one of the main needs we identified has been the lack of reliable online information in Portuguese on themes such as history, culture, language, and other aspects of the Romani world. The existing Internet content is usually based on stereotypes and unverifiable material. Thus, as a collective our objectives became to disseminate information about Romani cultures and, especially during the ongoing pandemic, to denounce problems faced by communities, and to combat the spread of both false information about Romanies on social media, and racist and stereotypical views about these communities.

The first action proposed by the collective was the realization of live video broadcasts on Instagram. We used Aline's profile, which at the time had more than seventeen thousand followers, but encouraged by the positive reception, we soon created our own channel on Instagram, Facebook, and YouTube, called in all cases "*@OrgulhoRomani.*" In these spaces we broadcast what we call "lives" (livestreams)—that is, interviews with Romani personalities under the title "*Uma Cigana Me Contou*" (A Romani woman told me), as well as creating two kinds of weekly posts. The first is called "*Da Borra do Café*" (From the coffee grounds) and presents Romani artists and arts from around the world. The second, "*Da Barraca aos Livros*" (From tents to books) focuses on scientific works on Romanies. In addition, in our social media profiles we publicize events and activities where we have been involved as activists and researchers of Romani-related issues. Let us discuss these various activities in a bit more detail.

"*Uma Cigana Me Contou*" consists of interviews that we conduct with Romanies and researchers working in Romani studies on various topics, taking advantage of our contacts, primarily in Brazil, Argentina, Portugal, and Spain. It was initially prompted by cases of racism suffered by Romani populations during the COVID-19 pandemic, both in Brazil and Spain, and this was the topic of the first interview addressed by the Spanish Romani activist Celia Montoya. These interviews have offered us an opportunity to create an environment for debate that would reflect perspectives and interests that the three of us share, such as intersectionality, social inequality, public policies, activism, and gender. The initiative raised the interest of researchers, Romani people, and the general public alike. Between March and October 2020 we conducted around twenty interviews, with an audience size of 20–35 who were watching live, plus another 150–400 visitors later. More than half of the "lives" were recorded in the "IGTV" long-form Instagram platform, where videos longer than one minute are saved and can still be accessed.

Instagram and Facebook posts "*Da Borra do Café*" feature Romani artists. Traditionally, in the countries where they live, Romanies have perhaps had the most visible influence in the fields of art and culture, and this reality is no different in Brazil. However, most representations of Romanies continue to trade with stereotypes, and so Romani artists themselves often remain invisible. For this reason, our aim in these posts has been to promote Romani cultural production and artists—whether known or not, whether contemporary or not—as well as to disturb misperceptions in order to stimulate more positive social imaginaries about Romani communities.

The "*Da Barraca aos Livros*" bulletin, originally every Monday, consists of a recommended reading about Romanies from around the world. The authors we choose are both Roma and non-Roma, and our aim is to disseminate these works in order to make accurate information about Romanies more accessible to the general public. The purpose has also been to challenge the racist lenses through which much of the Brazilian majority society view Roma people.

Academic and Advocacy Activities

Another kind of activity carried out by our collective has been the development of jointly authored texts, both academic and opinion pieces. One example is the article "Media and Romani Communities," which tackled, among other things, the construction of the Western imaginary of Romanies and the continued antigypsyism.[4] Another is an article published in the newspaper *Brasil de Fato* on the occasion of the Dia Nacional do Cigano in 2020 in which we highlighted the urgency of talking about Romani futures without stereotypes.[5] We argued in that article that "this year, however, the date [24 May 2020] leads us to other reflections. The COVID-19 health crisis has exposed the cracks in our society and the inequalities that affect a huge part of our population.... [I]t is no longer possible to put off taking certain political and social decisions until later, especially those regarding the Romani peoples."[6]

Besides this, the collective initiated and drafted an open letter denouncing the situation of economic and health vulnerability in which some Brazilian Cigano communities found themselves, condemning cases of racism that itinerant families have faced during the pandemic. The idea of the letter arose when one of the members of the WhatsApp group *Estudos Ciganos* posted information about the expulsion of Cigano families from several towns in the South Region of Brazil.[7] We decided to systematize the information about how the situation of these families unfolded from debates that took place among nearly one hundred members of the group. Our aim was to denounce these cases of racism and to suggest measures that could be taken to minimize the impact of the pandemic on the most vulnerable Romani communities.[8] The draft letter ended up being signed by over thirty researchers and twenty Cigano associations. We then sent it to the two most relevant ministries—the Ministry of Health, and the Ministry for Women, Family, and Human Rights—as well as to the Office of the Federal Public Prosecutor and media, and promoted it via social networks and institutional channels available to other researchers.

These two ministries were selected because the first is responsible for managing of the pandemic in the country, and because, since 2018, the Brazilian publicly funded Unified Health System (*Sistema Único de Saúde*, SUS) has had a National Comprehensive Health Care Policy for Cigano/Romani People (*Política Nacional de Atenção Integral à Saúde do Povo Cigano/Romani*), the objective of which is "to promote the comprehensive healthcare for the Cigano/Romani people, respecting their practices, knowledges, and traditional medicines, and giving priority to reducing and combating antigypsyism or Romaphobia."[9] The second ministry, on the other hand, includes among its responsibilities the development of public policies regarding the Romani people. But the response from the ministries was not very satisfactory. The Ministry of Women, Family, and Human Rights argued that these cases of racism were not within its competence. As for the Ministry of Health, the response was an email sent by the Secretariat of Primary Healthcare on 22 April 2020 with the Advisory Note 002 in order to "provide recommendations to the states and municipalities, especially to primary healthcare professionals and other professionals in the healthcare network, with the purpose of paying attention to the necessary conduct for the prevention, detection, care, and containment of the coronavirus (COVID-19)."[10] A few days later, the National Health Council published a recommendation "concerning the health of the Roma/Romani people in the context of the COVID-19 pandemic, caused by the new coronavirus, SARS-CoV-2."[11]

The advisory note provided background information on history, culture, racism, and social exclusion of Romanies, and even drew in parts from the open letter. But it and the recommendation had no effect. Despite recognizing and advising federal organs that, for example, "it is necessary to take into account the precariousness in which they [Romanies] live, that is, their living in tents, camps (sometimes in irregular places), peripheral areas, among other situations of vulnerability,"[12] the Ministry of Health has not adopted any concrete policies to combat the impact of the pandemic on Brazilian Romani communities. Rather, it has shifted the responsibility, including for the food security and the provision of cleaning and personal hygiene products, to states and municipalities. For their part, however, state and municipal governments have hardly acted, the one exception being the state of Rio Grande do Norte, which developed a plan to address the impact of COVID-19 on Romani peoples.[13]

International Reverberations

Besides the repercussions that the open letter developed by the #*OrgulhoRomani* collective generated within the Brazilian Romani movement, it also resonated with Romani activists in Argentina, thanks to the efforts of the association ZOR—*Asociación por los derechos del pueblo Gitano/Romani*.[14] Inspired by our letter, ZOR made a formal complaint about the very vulnerable situation of some Romani families during the pandemic, which received a positive response from the municipal government of Buenos Aires and the national government. Thanks to this initiative and the constant dialogue that ZOR has had with the national government, the state has begun distributing food baskets to Romani families living in the situation of socioeconomic vulnerability. The government has also launched a campaign in Romanes, together with the Pan American Health Organization, to prevent COVID-19 in Romani communities. For its part, the Commission on Human Rights of the Buenos Aires City Legislature assisted and provided technical experts for the ZOR association to launch its own prevention campaign in May 2020.

Lastly, the National Secretariat for Human Rights established a roundtable to debate and propose public policies for Romani peoples in Argentina. Because the Romani movement emerged in Argentina later than in Brazil, and because less progress has been made regarding the inclusion of these peoples into the political agenda, the arrival of the pandemic generated debates questioning the role of the state that are not present in Brazil. While some Argentinian activists believed that it was the duty of the state to prevent the spread of coronavirus, to assist communities during the pandemic, and to help them face its consequences, others advocated minimal state involvement. Some activists advocated the publication of information material in the three languages spoken by Argentinian Romanies—Roma, Calo, and Ludar—others believed that such action was unnecessary, and even inappropriate.

Final Thoughts

The activities of *#OrgulhoRomani* are the result of our efforts to rethink Romani activism, to give value to the work done by others, to contribute to the construction of a novel narrative about Romani populations by sharing Romani stories and images in their diversity, and to combat the racist imaginaries about Romani peoples in Brazil, Portugal and the Western world more broadly. Echoing Martín-Barbero,[15] we could say that we have been working towards a valorization of differences that would not result in new inequalities: towards a space of encounter in which the identities and interests of different Romani groups meet and organize themselves to face the majority. It is this approach, we believe, that led to the actions of the collective being positively received within the Brazilian Romani movement. The fact that the open letter was signed by different Romani groups and communities, with different histories and different approaches, demonstrates that despite differences it is possible to find common ground in order to demand fairer and more equal living conditions.

Moments of crisis, such as the coronavirus pandemic, call for immediate cooperation to adopt measures to contain the problem and to reduce harm. For us, this sense of urgency transformed into the *#OrgulhoRomani* collective. The activities of the collective were concentrated between the months of March and December 2020. They combated the enforced social isolation by making greater use of social networks. Although the rhythm of updating social network pages has now reduced considerably, we still believe that the actions carried out have contributed to the construction of a community interested in the themes related to the Romani peoples, especially in Brazil. It has also opened ways towards other initiatives. *#OrgulhoRomani* pages continue to function, sporadically disseminating our work, but they also remain available as a location for future projects and partnerships.

Gabriela Marques Gonçalves holds a PhD in audiovisual communication and advertising from the Universidad Autónoma de Barcelona (UAB-Spain), and an MA in communication from the Federal University of Juiz de Fora (UFJF-Brazil). She is a journalist, and a collaborating researcher of the UNESCO Chair in Communication at the Instituto de Comunicación (InCom-UAB).

Aluízio de Azevedo Silva Júnior holds an MA in education and a PhD in communication and health. He is not only a Romani activist, but is also as a journalist, social scientist, and film specialist. He serves as a communications advisor at the Ministry of Health in Brazil, as an associate collaborator at the Universidade Aberta (UAb), Lisbon, and as a member of the Communication and Health Working Group of the Brazilian Association of Public Health (ABRASCO).

Aline Miklos is an art historian, a cultural producer, composer, singer and PhD candidate at the École des Hautes Études en Sciences Sociales, France. She currently works as a senior fellow at the United Nations (OHCHR / South America). Since 2016 she has been coordinating a project in Argentina entitled "Kalo Chiriklo—Latin American Romani Music" from which she released an album *Pájaro Negro* in 2021.

Notes

1. Martín-Barbero, "Globalização comunicacional," 59.
2. The traditional communities of the Atlantic Rainforest along Brazil's south and southeast coast.
3. *#OrgulhoRomani* can be found and contacted via Facebook https://www.facebook.com/OrgulhoRomani, or Instagram https://www.instagram.com/orgulhoromani/.
4. Miklos, Marques, and Silva Júnior, "Mídia e comunidades ciganas."
5. Marques, Silva Júnior, and Miklos, "A urgência."
6. Ibid.
7. See the chapter by Igor Shimura in this volume.

8. AEECMT, "Nota pública."
9. Ministério da Saúde, "Ordinance No. 4,384."
10. Email from the Secretariat of Primary Healthcare, 22 April 2020.
11. Pigatto, "Recomendação N° 035."
12. Email from the Secretariat of Primary Healthcare, 22 April 2020.
13. SESAP, *Plano emergencial*.
14. See e.g., the petition "¡Políticas públicas para pueblos gitanos en Argentina! # COVID19 #gitanofobianuncamas." Retrieved 15 September 2022 from https://www.change.org/p/a-las-autordades-y-organismos-competentes-del-gobierno-federal-provincial-y-municipal-políticas-públicas-para-pueblos-gitanos-en-argentina-covid19-gitanofobianuncamas?recruiter=1090291064&utm_source=share_petition&utm_medium=copylink&utm_campaign=share_petition.
15. Martín-Barbero, "Globalização comunicacional," 60–61.

Bibliography

AEECMT. "Nota pública: pesquisadores e ativistas alertam para racismo contra grupos cigano durante a pandemia e cobram plano emergencial" [Public statement: researchers and activists warn of racism against Romani groups during the pandemic and demand an emergency plan]. An open letter signed by various individuals and organizations, Blog of the Associação Estadual das Etnias Ciganas de Mato Grosso, 8 April 2020. Retrieved 20 December 2021 from https://aeecmt.blogspot.com/2020/04/nota-publica-pesquisadores-e-ativistas.html.

Marques Gonçalves, Gabriela, Aluízio de Azevedo Silva Júnior, and Aline Miklos. "A urgência em se pensar no futuro das populações ciganas, sem estereótipos" [The urgency of thinking about the future of Romani people, without stereotypes]. *Brasil de Fato*, 24 May 2020. Retrieved 20 December 2021 from https://www.brasildefato.com.br/2020/05/24/a-urgencia-em-se-pensar-no-futuro-das-populacoes-ciganas-sem-estereotipos.

Martín-Barbero, Jesús. "Globalização comunicacional e transformação cultural" [Globalization in communications and cultural transformation]. In *Por uma outra comunicação: mídia, mundialização cultural e poder*, ed. Dênis de Moraes, 57–86. Rio de Janeiro: Record, 2003.

Miklos, Aline, Gabriela Marques Gonçalves, and Aluízio de Azevedo Silva Júnior. "Mídia e comunidades ciganas: a construção do imaginário ocidental e o (anti)ciganismo" [Media and Romani communities: The construction of the Western imaginary and of (anti)gypsyism]. Blog Estudos Ciganos Brasileiros, 7 July 2020. Retrieved 20 December 2021 from https://estudosciganosbrasileiros.blogspot.com/2020/07/serie-ativismo-e-representacao-artigo-1.html.

Ministério da Saúde. "Ordinance No. 4,384, 28 December 2018" [Instituting *Política Nacional de Atenção Integral à Saúde do Povo Cigano/Romani*]. Biblioteca Virtual em Saúde. Retrieved 20 December 2021 from https://bvsms.saude.gov.br/bvs/saudelegis/gm/2018/prt4384_31_12_2018.html.

Pigatto, Fernando Zasso (President of the National Health Council). "Recomendação N° 035" [Recommendation No. 35]. National Health Council, Ministry of Health, published on 11 May 2020. Retrieved 20 December 2021 from http://conselho.saude.gov.br/recomendacoes-cns/1166-recomendacao-n-035-de-11-de-maio-de-2020.

SESAP. *Plano emergencial para prevenção e enfrentamento da COVID-19 para a população cigana do Rio Grande do Norte* [Emergency plan for the prevention and confrontation of COVID-19 for the Romani population in Rio Grande do Norte], April 2020, Secretaria de Estado da Saúde Pública do Rio Grande do Norte. https://portalcovid19.saude.rn.gov.br/wp-content/uploads/2020/04/Plano-Emergencial-para-prevenção-e-enfrentamento-da-COVID-19-para-a-população-cigana-do-Rio-Grande-do-Norte.pdf.

CHAPTER 11

INTERLACING BLACK AND ROMANI EXPERIENCES DURING THE CORONAVIRUS PANDEMIC IN PARAÍBA, NORTHEAST BRAZIL
A Personal Reflection

Edilma do Nascimento Souza

"Edilma, is everything all right, my child? Where are you?"

"Hey, Dona Maria José Silva, we are in São Paulo. Our flight was cancelled; we are trying to reschedule. I think we will arrive in Paraíba tomorrow."

"Come here now, my daughter! This is no time for us to be far from our people, from our family, so when you arrive, let us know. I pray to God that you arrive soon and in peace. Have a good trip and God be with you!"

"Thank you, Dona Zeza. A kiss! And see you soon."

—Maria José "Zeza" Silva, WhatsApp conversation with the author, 18 March 2020

The SARS-CoV-2 coronavirus hits Brazil during the second fortnight of March 2020.[1] In the middle of an ongoing economic and political crisis, I decide to return to the Northeast Region, the area where I was born and where I lived for most of my life. On 18 March, while changing planes in São Paulo, I learn that Florianópolis, the city in the South Region of Brazil where I had been living until the day before, had implemented strict measures to comply with the protocols of social isolation. At the same moment, I receive a message from Dona Zeza, one of my long-term research interlocutors, who asks me for updates about my return to the Northeast. Over the years, the relationship with Dona Zeza and other Calon Ciganos with whom I maintain almost daily contact has been constructed through a double affective dynamic, both in the sense of creating a relationship of interlocution underwritten by respect, consideration, and care for each other, and in the sense of being affected in our shared as well as distinct vulnerabilities due to the actions or inactions of the Brazilian state.

I, Edilma do Nascimento—Black, poor, and *Nordestina*,[2] the first and so far the only one in my family (on both sides) to enter public higher education—have occupied the societal fringes as much as the people with whom I have been involved ethnographically throughout my academic career. Black people and Ciganos in Brazil have historically been located at what have been called the "margins,"[3] a social location whose residents in recent years have felt an increased sense of fear and anxiety. During my hasty return from Florianópolis, Santa Catarina, to João Pessoa, Paraíba, this sense intensified in at least two ways: first, as a fear of contagion by COVID-19, whereby I redoubled efforts to protect my health while travelling; and second, as uncertainty and anxiety arising from unemployment and the lack of job prospects due to the continued assault on, and dismantling of, public education and research in Brazil.

The necropolitics, the environment conducive to suffering and death, is shaped by the day-to-day workings of the Brazilian federal government, and today, during the COVID-19 crisis, mostly by its refusal to take adequate measures to protect the population. In his speeches, the president of the Republic, Jair Bolsonaro, often repeated phrases such as: "The virus is there, we are going to have to deal with it ... That's life, all of us will die one day" (29 March 2020), or "I'm sorry. I'm sorry about the deaths. People die every day from all sorts of causes. It's life, it's life" (31 July 2020). Such pronouncements, through which the president had been exempting himself from any responsibility for anyone in the name of economy and individual choice, hide the fact that the poor, disadvantaged and vulnerable have no choice and no means to protect themselves. They bear the costs of the pandemic. At the same time, we are witnessing a continued effort by Bolsonaro and his government to undermine and annul any previous gains in public healthcare and prevention: "So what? I am sorry. What do you want me to do?" (4 April 2020).

Staying at home is not an option for Ciganos or for millions of other people who survive through informal commercial work that necessitates daily outings. For them, the instruction to stay at home has turned into an economic disaster. The way emergency aid is provided, through a mobile app, privileges those sections of the population who are at least minimally literate and who have access to technology. The government's emergency policy often failed to reach some of the neediest Ciganos because of strict bureaucratic criteria and policy design: the requirement to have official documents (ID, work card, etc.), a degree of literacy, access to a cell phone, and a good Internet connection put many of them at an impossible disadvantage.

Exclusion and suffering are bureaucratically invisible. The absence of the category of race on the form produced by the Ministry of Health, which is where health professionals record the care of people infected by or suspected to have COVID-19, speaks for itself. In trying to administratively erase race and class, the state has made it impossible to ascertain what other indicators are suggesting: that there has been a disproportionate number of deaths among those people who simply cannot afford to stay at home or for whom a home is an overcrowded space in an overcrowded slum without basic amenities.[4] The sociologist Jaciane Milanezi argues that in Brazil, the resistance to thorough systematization of certain routine practices within the healthcare system, such as filling in race on forms, precedes the current pandemic.[5] It usually passes unnoticed, despite the repeated demands raised primarily by Black feminists, and speaks to the state's refusal to implement concrete policies to confront the deadly reality of inequalities.

Experiences with related but distinct forms of everyday racism can be discerned in seemingly banal situations that reveal Ciganos' distrust of the public health system. For instance, in Paraíba and other places in Northeastern Brazil, Cigano identity is associated with negative stereotypes that tend to devalue or diminish their experiences and needs. When Jaqueline, a young Calin, was recounting to me the measures her family network undertook to isolate itself in a municipality of Rio Grande do Norte, she described how they hid their identity as Ciganos for fear of being refused local health assistance. Or take the extra precautions that Sidnei, a Calon living in the hinterland of Paraíba, undertook in anticipation of care in the public hospital during the early weeks of the pandemic when anxiety was high. After a public hospital diagnosed him with a mild flu, he suspected negligence and decided to get himself tested at a private one, only to be told that he was at an intermediate stage of COVID-19 infection.

The condition of being on the margins, which constructs and configures our social places and our reactions, makes me reflect on the ways in which Black, Romani, and other bodies are being made vulnerable by the state in its formulation (or, rather, lack) of attention, care, and treatment measures during the coronavirus pandemic. In what ways do our social, economic, racial, and ethnic situations intersect? How are they similar, and how are they different?

It was Tuesday 4 May 2020. I was in the city of João Pessoa, and it was there at my mother's house that I got sick. I relieved the discomforts of sore throat, fever, and nasal congestion by inhaling Penetro, massaging with Vick's, having some serum for the upper respiratory tract, and taking Nimesulide and Dipyrone, and by trying to sleep more, all of which made me believe that I would wake up the next day feeling better. As the days went by, however, the intensity of the symptoms increased, and my physical condition deteriorated. Although every dawn I woke up feeling a little better, over the course of the day the symptoms always worsened. On the sixth day, I woke up feeling terrible and with strong pains in my stomach. By the end of the day, I had started to feel an intense pain in my chest, something I could compare to a heavy concrete block sitting on my chest. The weight of this "concrete block" made it difficult for me to breathe, and I started to grow increasingly anxious. On the seventh day, the symptoms were even stronger, and the concrete block made it even more difficult for me to breathe. With difficulty, it could be somewhat handled by my body and by the meditation exercises I was trying to do, as well as by prayers and chants to God, and to the Orixás to grant me physical strength.

The pain and all the deaths by asphyxiation happening around me during this period, either by COVID-19 or by racism,[6] make me think of what the Cameroonian philosopher Achille Mbembe has to tell us, categorically and metaphorically, about the right to breathe. Even prior to the pandemic, he observes, "humanity was already threatened with suffocation."[7] Throughout 2020, fires of historic proportions were raging throughout the Amazonian rainforest, the "lungs of the Earth," adding to respiratory problems in the region, destroying Indigenous communities,[8] and ending life. Beyond the limits of our physiological body, the philosopher asks us to reflect on breathing as a common ground that belongs to every person, but also stands for life itself, making us reflect on breathing and life in the context of subalternity. Thinking with Mbembe, I ponder: What processes condition the breathing of people who have their bodies racialized? How do the racialized and vulnerabilized majority of humankind become continually condemned "to a premature cessation of breathing" and "to a difficult, panting breath and life of oppression"?[9]

While struggling with the virus in my body, I maintained regular daily contact with my Cigano friends through social networks. They shared with me their fear of using public health facilities. Dona Zeza emphasized daily that I should treat myself at home, that going to the hospital was too risky. As an unemployed person without financial autonomy, living at my aging mother's house in the capital of Paraíba, I did manage to treat myself at home for the first few days. As the symptoms worsened, I decided to visit the UPA (Emergency Care Unit) located in the neighborhood of Cruz das Armas on the city's urban periphery, a short commute from my mother's house. When I arrived, I was unable to stand and so had to sit while a nursing technician checked my blood pressure and other vital signs. Immediately, I was classified as a high-risk case. The doctor ordered a blood test and chest/thorax X-ray, and prescribed a serum with vitamin B complex, intravenous dipyrone, and omeprazole. I was soon called to be medicated and tested, and with the result of the X-ray in hand, the second doctor who attended me prescribed 500 grams of azithromycin for five days and said, "Your picture suggests a possible diagnosis of coronavirus, but we cannot perform more exams here at the moment because you are on the eighth day. You should call the coronavirus service and inform them of your situation, explaining that you came to the UPA and that based on the X-ray you were prescribed antibiotics and that you needed to be tested [for COVID-19]." I thanked him and left the consulting room. A few days later, when I returned to the UPA because I could not breathe properly, there was no doctor there that day, and so I and countless other people had to return home without a diagnosis or medical relief.

Situations of precarity and shortage were already common in the healthcare system throughout the Northeast prior to the pandemic. On "normal" days, Célia, a Calin living in Mamanguape, a municipality near João Pessoa on the coast of Paraíba, had often talked to me about the lack of care at public hospitals. Fearing the infection, the chaos caused by the pandemic, and the fragility of health infrastructure, Calon opted for isolating themselves from urban centers. Célia and her family went to a city in Rio Grande do Norte, where many of them own *pousos*:[10] "In Mamanguape there are many people with this disease, Edilma. We cannot risk it," she stressed. Like Célia's family, who are from the family network of Calon on the coast of Paraíba, Maria Jane Soares, a Cigano leader from the hinterland of Paraíba, also explained to me that her family's plan was to move away from urban areas. In our WhatsApp conversation, she highlighted that the situation of the Ciganos in Condado-PB was one of apprehension: "We fear for our elders." She told me, "Edilma, many of our cousins are becoming infected with this disease and we don't even have the right to take the test—you know how it is, you have experienced this disease and seen the prejudice with which they treat us."

The difficulty faced by Ciganos and others in situations of social and economic vulnerability, without access to tests, hospital beds, respirators, adequate hygienic conditions, and so on, are outcomes of the ways in which health policy has been managed in relation to such populations. The continuous layering of various aspects during the pandemic—the denial of healthcare, the absences of specific health measures for these communities, and the lack of support for those who belong to economic risk groups—has turned the pandemic into a threat to life in two ways: on the level of the body and illness, as well as on the level of family and community survival. On both levels, Ciganos and Blacks are at high risk.

In the months following my infection, I became a point of reference for Ciganos—a small resource through which they managed community survival, one could say. Virtually every day during the first peak period (May–October 2020), a Calon would contact me wanting to check what I thought about symptoms they or their relative were showing.[11] I confess that having been ill and having experienced how the virus impacts each body differently, it has made me uneasy about my new role. In those early months, I realized that the strategy of Calon in Paraíba to abandon urban centers and to limit their contacts had some effect, and the virus did not spread very much among them. Maybe, being historical victims of innumerable forms of racism, the fear of prejudice, the increased persecution, and the accusation of disseminating the virus also played a role. For some time, many Calon thought COVID-19 was being caused by a lack of care for oneself, and this led to a certain distancing from one's extended family. To have COVID-19 was to be isolated, and to have the fear that one might die without having family members around.

Throughout the whole pandemic, the main problem has continued to be the dearth of institutional measures and specific care protocols. As attempts at improvement came only from the affected communities themselves, they drew on their repertoire, social contacts, limited resources, and sources of information. Additionally, suggestions came primarily from individuals such as Cigano activists and researchers who have been denouncing the state's neglect, but they were generally ignored by public health institutions.

For Cigano, Black, and other minorities made vulnerable within the Brazilian necropolitical framework, survival strategies and ways of coping with the pandemic emerge intertwined due to the history of the oppression and neglect that they experience. While my Calon friends and I have been racialized differently, our experiences and knowledge belong to the same field of power relations. I reflect on these relationalities today during the current pandemic, not only as an anthropologist, but as a Black woman from the lower working class in the northeast of Brazil, which shapes my perception of the relations that intersect our conditions of existence: both mine and those of Calon Ciganos. I think of ways in which, in Brazil today, Blacks and Ciganos are submitted to a classificatory system that tends to oppress, underestimate, and neglect access to our basic rights, and the ways this has materialized during the pandemic. Ultimately, I attempt to trace the space of what Black Brazilian writer Vilma Piedade (2017) has termed *dororidade*: a space of empathy born of shared pain.[12]

This space leads us to ponder the conditions of subalternity within this power relationship vis-à-vis dominant segments of society, the state, and its agents. Who are we—Blacks, Ciganos, Indígenas, and other vulnerable populations—to the governmental administration? Who are we to health officials? Are we always already dead bodies, counted or hidden in statistics, but never existing for the state as individuals who belong to our communities? How should we manage the lives of those who have no rights guaranteed? Our racial, ethnic, social, and economic conditions have put us in this place of subalternity and non-care, mediated by the fact that our existence is not framed in a way that would substantiate us as people. It is through management of the conditions of deprivation, and on the basis of our specific historical experiences with racialization, that we are trying to survive and breathe.

Edilma do Nascimento Souza is a lecturer in anthropology at the Federal University of São Francisco Valley (UNIVASF). She holds a PhD in social anthropology from the Federal University of Santa Catarina. She is a member of the Committee of Black Anthropologists, the Committee for Anthropology and Health, and the Education, Science and Technology Committee of the Brazilian Anthropology Association.

Notes

1. I thank all Calon Ciganos (Romanies) who continue to be involved in this relationship of doing anthropology out of an ethnography of engagement. I also thank the colleagues within the research project "Social and moral regulations of the new coronavirus in Brazil: An intersectional and ethnographic perspective," funded by the Wenner-Gren Foundation and coordinated by Flávia Medeiros dos Santos.
2. *Nordestina* refers to a woman from the Northeast Region of Brazil (*Nordeste*), one of the five regions of Brazil and the poorest. It consists of nine states structured under the conditions of strong internal colonization and socioeconomic exploitation. Most Brazilians native to this region do not enjoy economic privileges but face continuous generational scarcity. Within Brazil, and especially in relation to the economic centres of the South that are framed as modern, industrial, and White (European), the Northeast is racialized as a place of backward Others (and non-Europeans). Being in the South as a doctoral student was a strong experience for me.
3. Das and Poole, "El estado y sus márgenes."
4. Araújo, Medeiros, and Mallart, "As valas comuns;" Caponi, "Não existe salvação;" Werneck and Carvalho, "A pandemia de COVID-19."
5. Milanezi, "'Eu não vou parar.'"
6. Suffocation by anti-Black racism is not a figure of speech. Three weeks after I started to have symptoms, on 25 May 2020, George Floyd was suffocated by a police officer who kept kneeling on his neck. In Brazil we have had similar cases, but they have not had any national or global repercussions (a question to consider).
7. Mbembe, "O Direito à respiração."

8. These fires are man-made. While their likelihood and frequency of fires is exacerbated by global climate change, they are being set by ranchers and miners who have simultaneously brought COVID-19 to Indigenous communities.
9. Mbembe, "O Direito à respiração."
10. A *pouso* is a place for temporary residence.
11. This contact is ongoing, but the topic of discussion has changed. Now (December 2020 – April 2021), it is more about vaccination.
12. This intersectional feminist concept, which could be translated as "sorrowity" or "painhood," is composed of *dor* (pain, sorrow) and *sororidade* (sorority, sisterhood). It interpolates feminist calls for sisterhood through unique historical experiences of colonialism as they become petrified in continued pain and suffering. "Dororidade," Piedade writes, "is established and runs through lived trajectories of us as Black people, and here, especially, Us—Women—Black Women, White, of Axé, Indigenous, Ciganas, Quilombolas, Lesbians, Trans, Caiçaras, Ribeirinhas, Slumdwellers or not, we are Women" (Piedade, *Dororidade*, 19). The term also allows me to appreciate how our scarcity becomes a creative power in moments of crisis.

Bibliography

Araújo, Fábio, Flávia Medeiros, and Fábio Mallart. "As valas comuns: Imagens e políticas da morte" [The mass graves: Images and politics of death]. *Dilemas: Revista de Estudos de Conflito e Controle Social* (Reflexões na Pandemia, 2020): 1–12. Retrieved 20 April 2021 from https://www.reflexpandemia.org/texto-33.

Caponi, Sandra. "Não existe salvação individual na pandemia de COVID-19" [There is no individual salvation in the COVID-19 pandemic]. *ANPOCS Boletim Especial* 8 (30 March 2020). Retrieved 20 April 2021 from http://www.anpocs.com/index.php/ciencias-sociais/destaques/2317-boletim-n-3-as-ciencias-sociais-e-a-saude-coletiva-frente-a-atual-epidemia-de-ignorancia-irresponsabilidade-e-ma-fe-6.

Das, Veena, and Deborah Poole. "El estado y sus márgenes: etnografías comparadas" [State and its margins: Comparative ethnographies]. *Cuadernos de Antropología Social* 27 (2008): 19–52.

Mbembe, Achille. "O direito universal à respiração" [The universal right to breathe]. Translated by Mariana Pinto dos Santos and Marta Lança. *BUALA*, 9 April 2020. Retrieved 20 April 2021 from https://www.buala.org/pt/mukanda/o-direito-universal-a-respiracao.

Milanezi, Jaciane. "'Eu não vou parar por causa de uma raça': a coleta da raça/cor no SUS" ['I will not stop because of one race': The collection of race/colour in the SUS]. *Blog DADOS*, 4 June 2020. Retrieved 20 April 2021 from http://dados.iesp.uerj.br/coleta-da-raca-cor-no-sus/.

Piedade, Vilma. *Dororidade* [Painhood]. São Paulo: Editora Nós, 2017.

Werneck, Guilherme Loureiro, and Marilia Sá Carvalho. "A pandemia de COVID-19 no Brasil: crônica de uma crise sanitária anunciada" [Pandemic of COVID-19 in Brazil: Chronicle of an foretold health crisis]. *Cadernos de Saúde Pública* 36(5) (2020). https://doi.org/10.1590/0102-311X00068820.

CHAPTER 12

ROMANIES IN BRAZIL AND THE ESCALATION OF NECROPOLITICS DURING THE PANDEMIC

Aluízio de Azevedo Silva Júnior

"It was difficult for our people already—persecuted, discriminated against, expelled from towns—and now it is even more difficult with this pandemic. In Ceará, a family of mine has more than fifty Ciganos with COVID-19. One went to a hospital, [it] got complicated, [he] died and was buried without his family knowing!" This testimony, given to me on 12 July 2020, comes from Calon[1] activist Antônio Pereira. Born in the state of Ceará, Pereira now lives in Paraná, where he represents Cigano (Romani) peoples at the State Department for Traditional Communities and Peoples.

Ten days before, the Calon community to which I belong had experienced the pain of losing a cousin, 30-year-old José Martins Júnior, to COVID-19. Our community comprises about three hundred people, concentrated primarily in the municipalities of Rondonópolis, Cuiabá, and Tangará da Serra in the state of Mato Grosso. The event was devastating to the parents, Abigail Pereira, who works as an accountant, and José Martins, a police officer. They saw the life of their *chavon*, their son, taken in the worst way: at a moment when health measures did not allow us to perform funerary rites, thus prohibiting the consolations and *janhar*, mourning laments, which are important processes within the Calon cultural ethos.

True, the psychological and social vacuum left by the absence of funeral rituals affects the population in general,[2] but it impacts Cigano peoples and other minorities in a specific manner.[3] The fine cloth of the Calon social fabric was torn: our dead could not receive tributes in accordance with the traditions of Caloninity (*calonidade*) so as to become mythical ancestral figures within the collective memory of our communities. Indeed, the pandemic, which has had an immense impact on the Brazilian population as a whole, has caused immeasurable damage to communities in situations of vulnerability. This impact is not only physical, but also emotional, cultural, economic, and social.

Perhaps these two deaths—as well as thousands upon thousands of others in Brazil—could have been avoided if the federal government had implemented a policy of COVID-19 prevention, and adopted specific plans for vulnerable groups, such as Romani communities. Instead, Bolsonarism[4] has reinforced a politics of death that we could see as a politics of "*extermínio*" (destruction, extermination),[5] a diffuse and inexplicit regime of population control aimed at subalternized groups. As Cruz-Neto and Minayo affirm,

> the Brazilian social scenario has had the art of constructing exclusion, without the need to make it explicit in doctrines, in trained militias and in leaders capable of justifying it. If such gimmicks and techniques of the dominant power have been able to hide the horrors of discrimination, at this moment, an effort of unveiling is needed, a political and social effort capable of naming the evil and making this "necrotic" face explicit.[6]

Historically, ethnic minorities in Brazil, such as Blacks, Indigenous people, and Romanies, endured colonialist policies—persecutory or exclusionary, some directly exterminatory—that placed them in the position of extreme social exclusion and inequality, and this is where they find themselves today. With lower educational levels and less access to adequate housing, formal employment, social services, and leisure and cultural facilities, they are more likely to die from preventable diseases, have lower life expectancy, and experience higher infant mortality rates.[7] Since 2019, the policies of the Brazilian presidency have further pushed the working classes and ethnic minorities into poverty or extreme poverty, stalling their social reproduction and offering them a vision of the future that only involves exclusion or even destruction.

To understand how this reality manifests itself today, I propose a dialogue between the analyses of Otávio Cruz Neto and Maria Cecília Minayo on the extermination policies in Brazil, on the one hand, and those of Achille Mbembe on "necropolitics" and sovereignty in "post-colonial" societies on the other. However, before I approach the policies of death via these authors, I will reflect on how Cigano people perceive and live death and mourning, which emerges from what I have called elsewhere the "Calon philosophy (of life)."[8]

Section 1: The Place of Death within the Calon Philosophy

"There are various ways of dealing with the fact that we are all going to die," observe Mattedi and Pereira.[9] Death and the way it is dealt with "comprise a fundamental aspect of the process of human socialization."[10] All peoples and cultures have narratives, mythologies, cosmologies, and rituals that give meaning to dying. These change over time, like culture, identities, and societies themselves.

Calon communities too have their own ways of understanding life and death, perceiving them as sacred and interconnected, and as belonging to the normative framework set forth by the Calon philosophy. The first point to emphasize is that this framework centers on the family, the main entity of Calon sovereignty, which consolidates traditions that demarcate forms of acting and behaving. Thus, all family rituals, especially those relating to death, are vital.

The Calon philosophy places emphasis on ancient and ancestral wisdom, with uncles and aunts of honor and shame (*tios e tias de honra e vergonha*) as the highest authorities. Elderly men and women are treated in the most respectful ways and act as counsellors and peacemakers, guardians of culture, knowledge, and tradition. Because they are perceived as being closer to death, they act as guardians of collective memory and memories of ancestral spirits.

Dying does not stand in opposition to life; rather, it is one of life's stages. This is the reason for the elaboration of mortuary rituals, of the mythology and cosmology of death, which produce meanings that unite the community. When a Cigano person dies, all members of the group undergo a process of death. During mortuary rites, moments of passage and initiation, we rediscover a sacred knowledge and relive what was manifested for the ancestors (*revivendo o que se manifestou para os ancestrais*). With a looming death, a magical recreation of the world begins. An ill or dead Calon individual does not plunge into the primordial wholeness alone; the whole community takes part. The ritual process begins when an illness is diagnosed, with the unfolding of healing rites and alternative treatments. Then the news spreads throughout the community, and the forebodings of death—materialized in a bird that is spotted, in a premonition felt, in a dream—multiply...

It is a grave offense to miss the wake and funeral of a relative: these events are surrounded by commotion, tension, actualization, socialization, grief and lamentation, unity and separation—processes that are central for the Calon drama. As the Cigano family is structured by age, gender, and kinship, relationships need to be revised with each death. The role played by the dead person is realigned.

The *mulon*, the deceased, is the center of Calon mortuary rituals. Relatives start recalling memories of the deceased person from the very moment of death, and continue to do so throughout the duration of the mourning, which is relatively long and takes years or even a lifetime. The Calon philosophy admits a mystery immanent to the body, associated with the fate of the spirit. Despite the corpse's bankruptcy, the deceased remains in the ancestral cult and collective memory.[11] If the body is not properly ritualized, however, the spirit of the *mulon* will not find peace, and the living will not find it either. Hence the importance of a proper funeral, so that the mourning and the repositioning of the living in the face of death can both occur properly.

This has not been possible with the pandemic. The living are being isolated from each other and completely cut off from those who die. The body of the deceased is hidden, but there is no concern regarding what happens to the spirit of the *mulon* or the way we Calon express grief and feeling for the death of a *chaburron* (relative). When the state bars these ritualizations, even if justified to prevent contagion, there is a strong symbolic impact on the whole Calon culture beyond the physical impact, as people cannot properly hold a wake for—and mourn—their dead.

Such ways of seeing death contrast with the views characteristic of hegemonic modernity, where death is not so openly acknowledged in public, but is hidden by means of sanitary policies that accompany medicalization and commodification processes.[12] At the same time, colonial empires and authoritarian governments have also imposed this on millions of non-European peoples and on those considered external to European modernity, such as the Romanies.

This commodification-medicalization is thus part of a much larger scheme of colonization and oppression. Indeed, the very presence of Cigano peoples in Brazil is a result of Portuguese colonialist policies, which over a period of three hundred years expelled thousands of Romanies, mainly of the Calon ethnic group, to the colony. Many antigypsy laws were enforced throughout the colonies. These policies were inherited after administrative independence by the Brazilian state, which continued to harass Ciganos and issued numerous antigypsy decrees, mainly at the state and municipal levels. The result is not an explicitly declared extermination, but a situation of exclusion and lack of access to citizen rights and services, alongside social inequality and misery.

Along with Latin American decolonial thought,[13] it is clear that, while historical colonialism ended with the administrative independence of former colonies, including Brazil, the colonial logic remains in place. It is being recreated in the coloniality of power, knowledge, being, arts, and sciences. All these people in Brazil who have been persecuted by historical colonial power—and who, as a result, now find themselves in a situation of social vulnerability—are also the preferred victims of both the politics of destruction and of the necropolitics of the Bolsonarist government in relation to COVID-19.

Section 2: From the Endemic Politics of Extermination to Necropolitics as a Program of the Bolsonarist Government

In Brazil, e*xtermínio*, extermination or destruction, is a fact that is always present: an "endemic" fact, to use healthcare jargon.[14] These insights offered by Cruz-Neto and Minayo help us to understand what has been happening in Brazil in the current pandemic scenario, when the exclusionary structural and historical bases of social life in the country are exposed more than ever. Extermination is "part of a political project of those groups" that, considering themselves superior and holders of justice and truth, "arrogate the right and the power to select layers of society to be eliminated."[15] Citizenship and subjectivity of the excluded groups are denied through a "dehumanization of social relations and actions" based on the "philosophy of banalization of life and death." The policy of extermination in Brazil manifests itself "as a process of annihilation, exclusion, and elimination of socioeconomic and cultural groups considered 'marginal,' 'superfluous,' and 'dangerous,'"[16] among which I include ethnic minorities and Romani peoples, given the history of the state's antigypsyism and exclusionary politics.

From a structural-health perspective, this politics of death is shaped by various devices, including: the naturalization of poverty and its effects; forced birth control; infant mortality and low life expectancy, which disproportionately affect poor and racialized populations such as the Romanies, and which are seen as a form of social selection; or by an attitude that these "generators" of misery, epidemics, and violence should be "eliminated."[17]

This historical project of destruction of segments of the population deemed "superfluous," including Cigano communities, has recently been greatly intensified. The pandemic is having serious consequences across several domains, but especially on the economic activities of Cigano peoples, who traditionally engage in informal commerce. At the same time, there are no policies to confront or mitigate these impacts; this reflects a government program that emerges from a necropolitical model implemented by the current president of the republic, Jair Bolsonaro.

I use the concept of "necropolitics," as coined by Achille Mbembe,[18] to further the reflections of Cruz-Neto and Minayo. Mbembe presents "politics as the work of death," arguing that "the ultimate expression of sovereignty resides, to a large degree, in the power and the capacity to dictate who may live and who must die."[19] In this understanding, to "kill or to allow to live" are the fundamental attributes and "the limits of sovereignty." "To exercise sovereignty" is, in his words, "to exercise control over mortality and to define life as the deployment and manifestation of power."[20]

The Cameroonian philosopher correlates Foucault's notion of biopower to two concepts: the state of exception and the state of siege. He analyses "those trajectories by which the state of exception and the relation of enmity have become the normative basis of the right to kill."[21] According to Mbembe, in such instances "power (and not necessarily state power) continuously refers and appeals to exception, emergency, and a fictionalized notion of the enemy."[22] This is a very pertinent reflection through which to analyze the state of exception and generalized emergency caused by the pandemic in Brazil, and the politics of death implemented or tolerated by the current government:

> I have put forward the notion of necropolitics and necropower to account for the various ways in which, in our contemporary world, weapons are deployed in the interest of maximum destruction of people and the creation of "death-worlds"— new and unique forms of social existence in which vast populations are subjected to conditions of life that confer on them the status of "living dead."[23]

For vulnerable populations, the exposure to death is constant, and this is the central mark of necropolitics. It has been present in Latin American countries since the time when they were colonies, and it continues today in different strategies and contexts. In the words of Mbembe, "the colony represents the site where sovereignty consists fundamentally in the exercise of a power outside the law (*ab legibus solutus*) and where 'peace' is more likely to take on the face of a 'war without end.'"[24]

We can encounter necropower applied in Brazil throughout the entire colonial period: in the processes of domination of Indigenous peoples, in the enslavement of Blacks, and in expulsions and persecutions of Romani peoples. As Cruz-Neto and Minayo show, a systematic politics of extermination is still in place today against its poorest and most racialized populations.[25]

There are several elements of extermination operating against Calon communities. Historically we have been linked to stereotypes reducing us to bandits and cheats, to being dirty, immoral, and so on. In the context of Brazilian colonization, for three hundred years it was Portugal that dictated the rules. This racist structure, which considers Romani people to be uncivilized, inferior, dangerous bandits and therefore subjects of annihilation, whether physical or symbolic, originated in Portugal.

The Lusitanian country drew up numerous antigypsy laws, which prohibited Romani people from maintaining their customs, speaking their language, travelling in groups, practicing traditional professions—in short, from being Ciganos. These laws justified the seizure of their property, imprisonment, galleys, physical punishment, banishment to the colonies in Africa and Brazil, and even death.

For centuries, Brazil used the same racist policies that aimed at the destruction of the Romani people, both physical and symbolic. A striking example of this involves the episodes known as "Gypsy Chases" (*Correrias Ciganas*).[26] These were real hunts that the police promoted, entering the encampments and murdering those they met on the way, causing Cigano people to flee.

The re-democratization of Brazil and the adoption of the new federal constitution in 1988 opened new paths to equity and ethnoracial diversity. This also paved the way for the election of the Workers' Party government and the presidency of Luis Inácio Lula da Silva, which inaugurated a new chapter in the state's treatment of Cigano populations. As a result, the first pro-Cigano state policies were created, such as the declaration of a Romani National Day in 2006, and the adoption of Decree 6040 in 2007, which included Ciganos among traditional peoples and communities alongside Brazil's Indigenous peoples, quilombolas, and riverine communities.

Since 1988, however, there has never been a less stable time for democracy in Brazil than today. It began in 2016 with the impeachment of former President Dilma Rousseff, Lula's successor, and it further deteriorated after the election of current President Jair Bolsonaro. On several occasions, the latter has openly declared his admiration for the military dictatorship, and has identified ethnic and gender minorities and social movements as his enemies. In fact, Bolsonarist politics is built through the encouragement of armament, including threats to shoot political opponents and any others who find themselves in the path of his political ideology of hatred.

Applying a colonial historical revisionism, the government's management has been centered on the dissemination of *fake news*. In the name of a God, it defends civil armament and militias. It accuses traditional peoples and communities of reverse colonialism, classifying affirmative policies as "privileges;" in reality we are "the wretched of the pandemic."[27] Contrary to the recommendations of the WHO, the National Health Council, and the Ministry of Health itself, the presidency has repeatedly encouraged the breaking of social isolation and hygiene measures, promoted congregations of people, and has discouraged them from wearing masks.

Additionally, by choosing not to expand on a plan to confront and mitigate the pandemic, the president opted to let people, especially the poorest, die of a lack of adequate prevention and treatment, or to wither away due to a lack of economic prospects, falling deeper into misery and poverty. The first attempt to establish a comprehensive policy to contain the pandemic within Indigenous peoples, quilombolas, Ciganos, and other traditional communities, Law no. 14.021, was promulgated with fourteen vetoes from the president. This removed all state commitment to guarantees of access to drinking water, hygiene and disinfection materials, hospital beds, distribution of basic food baskets, or access to emergency relief.[28]

The situation of Cigano communities during the pandemic was denounced by the Brazilian Association of Collective Health (ABRASCO) in a report aptly entitled "The Unbelievable Invisibility Shrouding Cigano Peoples,"[29] as well as in the *National Plan to Address the Covid-19 Pandemic*.[30] In the latter document, a coalition of public health and medical organizations state that "the pandemic continues invisibilizing and silencing certain segments of the population, such as the Ciganos (Romani, as they identify themselves)," highlighting that many Ciganos "do not have access to water, sanitation or electricity, [or] access to health."[31]

The result has been a social tragedy that seems far from over. It occurs not only on the level of physical violence, but also that of symbolic annihilation: through policies of invisibility, the silencing of traditional peoples and communities, our knowledge and ways of life, our social and cultural organizations, and by preventing us from mourning our dead. But the seeds of this tragedy were not planted at the beginning of 2020. For Romanies and other traditional peoples in Brazil, the mismanagement of the pandemic under the Bolsonaro government does not represent the appearance of some accidental event, but instead an uninterrputed continuation of power relations that have existed since colonial times.

Aluízio de Azevedo Silva Júnior holds an MA in education and a PhD in communication and health. He is not only a Romani activist, but is also as a journalist, social scientist, and film specialist. He serves as a communications advisor at the Ministry of Health in Brazil, as an associate collaborator at the Universidade Aberta (UAb), Lisbon, and as a member of the Communication and Health Working Group of the Brazilian Association of Public Health (ABRASCO).

Notes

1. *Calon* is a self-denomination in the Romanó-Kaló language. It may also be spelled *Kalon* or *Calom* in Portuguese.
2. Pompeu and Tercic, "Pandemia transforma rituais de morte."
3. See Brum, "Mães Yanomami imploram;" or Jucá, "'O coronavírus está quebrando.'"
4. Editors' note: *Bolsonarismo* refers to the far-right and reactionary political agenda associated with the current Brazilian president, Jair Bolsonaro. During the pan-

demic, much discussion in Brazil has revolved around the relationship between Bolsonarism and necropolitics. This chapter belongs to this tradition.
5. Cruz-Neto and Minayo, "Extermínio."
6. Ibid., 207.
7. Silva Júnior, "Produção social de sentidos."
8. For an in-depth analysis of the concept and of what follows, see Silva Júnior, "A Liberdade" and "Produção social de sentidos."
9. Mattedi and Pereira, "Vivendo com a morte," 319.
10. Ibid., 320.
11. Silva Júnior, "Produção social de sentidos," 258.
12. Mattedi and Pereira, "Vivendo com a morte," 320.
13. Quijano, "Colonialidade do poder;" Mignolo, "A colonialidade."
14. Cruz-Neto and Minayo, "Extermínio," 206.
15. Ibid., 203–4.
16. Ibid., 207–8.
17. Ibid.
18. Mbembe, "Necropolítica."
19. Ibid., 123.
20. Ibid.
21. Ibid., 128.
22. Ibid., 129.
23. Ibid., 146.
24. Ibid., 132.
25. Cruz-Neto and Minayo, "Extermínio," 199.
26. Editors' note: "Gypsy Chases" occurred at the end of the nineteenth and the beginning of the twentieth centuries.
27. Sato, *Os condenados da pandemia*.
28. Câmara dos Deputados, Law no. 14.021.
29. Flaeschen, "A inacreditável invisibilidade."
30. Frente Pela Vida, *Plano nacional*.
31. Ibid., 81.

Bibliography

Brum, Eliane. "Mães Yanomami imploram pelos corpos de seus bebês" [Yanomami mothers beg for bodies of their babies], *El País Brasil*, 24 June 2020. Retrieved 10 December 2020 from https://brasil.elpais.com/brasil/2020-06-24/maes-yanomami-imploram-pelos-corpos-de-seus-bebes.html.

Cruz-Neto, Otávio, and Maria Cecília de S. Minayo. "Extermínio: violentação e banalização da vida" [Extermination: Violence and the banalization of life]. *Cadernos de Saúde Pública* 10 (suppl. 1, 1994): 199–212. https://doi.org/10.1590/S0102-311X1994000500015.

Flaeschen, Hara. "A inacreditável invisibilidade que cobre os povos ciganos" [The unbelievable invisibility shrouding Romani people]. *Notícias ABRASCO (Especial*

Coronavírus), 5 May 2020. Retrieved 10 December 2020 from https://www.abrasco .org.br/site/noticias/especial-coronavirus/a-inacreditavel-invisibilidade-que-co bre-os-povos-ciganos/47544/.

Frente Pela Vida. *Plano Nacional de Enfrentamento à Pandemia da COVID-19* [National plan to confront the COVID-19 pandemic] (Version 2). Published on 15 July 2020. https://frentepelavida.org.br/uploads/documentos/PEP%20COVID-19_v2.pdf.

Jucá, Beatriz. "'O coronavírus está quebrando a nossa crença': o luto imposto aos povos indígenas na pandemia" ['Coronavirus is shattering our belief': The grief imposed on Indigenous peoples during the pandemic]. *El País Brasil*, 11 July 2020. Retrieved 10 December 2020 from https://brasil.elpais.com/brasil/2020-07-11/o-coronavi rus-esta-quebrando-a-nossa-crenca-o-luto-imposto-aos-povos-indigenas-na-pand emia.html.

Mattedi, Marcos Antonio, and Ana Paula Pereira. "Vivendo com a morte: o processamento do morrer na sociedade moderna" [Living with death: The processing of dying in the modern society]. *Caderno CRH* 20(50) (2007): 319–30. https://doi .org/10.1590/S0103-49792007000200009.

Mbembe, Achille. "Necropolítica: biopoder, soberania, estado de exceção, política de morte" [Necropolitics: Biopower, sovereignty, state of exception, politics of death]. *Arte & Ensaios* 32 (December 2016): 123–51. https://www.procomum.org/wp-con tent/uploads/2019/04/necropolitica.pdf.

Mignolo, Walter. "A colonialidade de cabo a rabo: o hemisfério ocidental no horizonte conceitual da modernidade" [Coloniality from top to tail: The Western Hemisphere in the conceptual horizon of modernity]. In *A Colonialidade do Saber: Eurocentrismo e Ciências Sociais: Perspectivas Latino-Americanas*, ed. Edgardo Lander, 34–54. Buenos Aires: Clacso, 2005.

Pompeu, Daniel, and Laura Segovia Tercic. "Pandemia transforma rituais de morte e luto no Brasil" [Pandemic changes death and mourning rituals in Brazil]. LAB-19, UNICAMP, 8 May 2020. Retrieved 10 December 2020 from https://www.uni camp.br/unicamp/noticias/2020/05/08/pandemia-transforma-rituais-de-morte-e- luto-no-brasil.

Quijano, Aníbal. "Colonialidade do poder, eurocentrismo e América Latina" [Coloniality of power, Eurocentrism and Latin America]. In *A Colonialidade do saber: eurocentrismo e ciências sociais: perspectivas Latino-Americanas*, ed. Edgardo Lander, 107–30. Buenos Aires: Clacso, 2005.

Sato, Michèle, ed. *Os condenados da pandemia* [The wretched of the pandemic]. Cuiabá: GPEA, UFMT & Ed. Sustentável, 2020. https://editorasustentavel.com.br/os- condenados-da-pandemia/.

Silva Júnior, Aluízio de Azevedo. "A liberdade na aprendizagem ambiental cigana dos mitos e ritos Kalon" [Freedom in Romani/Gypsy environmental learning of Kalon myths and rites]. Master's thesis, Universidade Federal de Mato Grosso, 2009.

———. "Produção social dos sentidos em processos interculturais de comunicação e saúde: a apropriação das políticas públicas de saúde para ciganos no Brasil e em Portugal" [Social construction of meanings within the intercultural processes of communication and health: The appropriateness of public health policies for Romanies in Brazil and Portugal]. PhD diss., Fundação Oswaldo Cruz, 2018.

PART III

SLOVAK CHRONICLES

CHAPTER 13

Introduction to the Slovak Chronicles
Indifference, Securitization, and Antigypsyism

Andrej Belák and Tomáš Hrustič

> Because in the Roma settlements, the coronavirus spreads thirteen-times faster. In other words, a person from the majority will infect approximately one person. A Rom who returns from abroad, for instance from England where he was working for a longer period, if he comes back to where he used to live, will, with a great probability, infect more than twenty people.
> —Peter Pollák, Member of the European Parliament, 4 April 2020[1]

> I refuse the circulation of information, according to which Roma communities are places in which the COVID-19 disease spreads. This information contributes to the stigmatization of Roma men and women as propagators of the disease in the society.
> —Andrea Bučková, Plenipotentiary of the Slovak Government for Roma Communities, 2 November 2020[2]

COVID-19 Meets Roma Inclusion: Between Securitization and Covert Support?

In Slovakia, there are approximately 400,000 to 450,000 Roma people, making up roughly 8 percent of the country's total population.[3] Approximately half live trapped in intergenerational poverty, in over five hundred neighborhoods where practically no non-Roma live, mostly on the outskirts of small villages and towns.⁴ Most residents of these poor, ethnically segregated enclaves face extremely harsh living conditions, including physical seclusion barriers, substandard infrastructure, environmental hazards, anti-Roma discriminatory practices, and racist hatred and stigma.⁵ The remaining half of the Slovak Roma live much closer to or are dispersed among the non-Roma, approximating or sharing the latter's standards of living. Nevertheless, these Roma—often referred to in bureaucratic parlance as "integrated," in contrast to those "marginalized"—face ethnic discrimination, racist microaggressions, and stigma too.

The public statements quoted above regarding the Roma and the SARS-CoV-2 pandemic in Slovakia do not come from political adversaries. How come they present opposing views, then? The answer has to do with the fact that the pronouncements were made at different times: they document a shift that the state administration has undergone in its approach to the pandemic control within segregated Roma enclaves during the eighteen months since the virus was first detected in Slovakia in March 2020 until the time of writing in the autumn of 2021.

Initially, at the outset of the so-called first wave in March and April 2020, leading state representatives, including the then Slovak prime minister Igor Matovič, his party's leading expert on Roma, MEP Peter Pollák, and the government's new plenipotentiary for Roma communities ("Roma Plenipotentiary", RP), Andrea Bučková, argued for the prioritization of segregated Roma settlements in the control of the epidemic, as these were seen as places that presented an acute public health risk for the whole society.⁶ Reflecting this securitization rationale, between 3 and 26 April—when testing for the new coronavirus was still unavailable for most Slovaks—4,784 people living in 162 segregated enclaves were RT-PCR tested for SARS-CoV-2 in a highly publicized military operation. In one of his early related public presentations, trying to better explain the need for the running operation, the prime minister likened Roma communities to "Molotov cocktails threatening to burst our common field of wheat into flames."⁷

Named "Carousel,"⁸ the operation focused on the identification, testing, and isolation of recent returnees from countries where the pandemic was already widespread or on the surge, such as the UK, Italy, and Belgium. Carousel was announced as a military operation led by army generals, MEP Pollák and RP Bučková, alongside representatives and staff of the targeted municipalities. Infrastructurally, however, Carousel was also supported by a dense network of community workers from diverse so-called "national Roma inclusion" projects, funded primarily by the European Commission (EC).⁹ For example, which enclaves needed to be visited and which people needed to be prioritized for testing was decided primarily on the basis of information provided by these workers. Also, it was mainly they who negotiated compliance with testing by the enclaves' inhabitants, as, from a legal point of view, taking part in the testing was voluntary. Eventually, some people tested positive for the virus, but only in 16 of the 162 enclaves. In 5 of them, however, their numbers and those of their close contacts (dozens and hundreds, respectively) were considered so high by the local public health authorities that they ordered a quarantine for all residents of these Roma neighborhoods.

Although the operation proved effective in quickly identifying and preventing possible transmissions from segregated Roma enclaves, it resulted in harsh humanitarian and epidemiological collateral damage. The community quarantines in particular presented an appalling failure of planning, as the Carousel's managers turned out to have had no strategies in place regarding any of the following: communication with those quarantined; prevention of the disease's spread within the quarantine zones; the provision of basic food supplies for those quarantined; a process for ending the quarantines; or the management of public relations. As a result, nearly seven thousand predominantly healthy people ended up suddenly sealed off in their neighborhoods by army and police forces for weeks (in one case for over two months), frustrated by the lack of reliable information regarding their options and prospects, and by the poor supply of food, fuel wood, medicines, protective equipment, and so on. Many (possibly hundreds) eventually contracted the virus from their infected relatives and neighbors. Moreover, all along until the last of these community quarantines were lifted in June 2020, the operation continued to be publicly presented as a success by its convenors. This strongly encouraged a nationwide fear of Roma, tensions between non-Roma and Roma, and related non-compliance among the Roma (e.g., internal conflicts, avoidance of testing, increased mobility), as well as the adoption of evermore repressive measures and attitudes by local authorities.

However, controversial government measures were not only introduced with regard to the management of the pandemics in Roma communities. For example, as discussed by Albín Peter in his chronicle, in April and May 2020 the Slovak government introduced a measure dictating that all people entering Slovakia from abroad, regardless of their ethnicity or citizenship, must be placed in state quarantine centers. Various state facilities, private hotels and dormitories were repurposed to welcome these unlucky incomers who had to wait there for six days to be tested, and were only released after receiving a negative PCR test result. Police and border police were involved in the logistical operations, and many escorts from border crossings were organized for incomers to Slovakia. In the end, tens of thousands of people were involuntarily placed in these facilities in the spring of 2020.

Months later, in October 2020, when the number of COVID-19 cases in the country started to climb to unprecedented levels after an epidemiologically quiet summer, the public rhetoric by central state officials regarding the segregated Roma enclaves appeared rather transformed. In late October and early November, the first countrywide mass testing for antigens revealed particularly high rates of positivity in dozens of segregated Roma enclaves.[10] Poorly managed community quarantines returned immediately and eventually became a common practice: forty-nine community quarantines were ordered and implemented by local authorities during the second wave, of which only one was not in a segregated Roma enclave. Yet, this time the central state representatives in charge—including those who had previously endorsed the Carousel operation—refrained from any public statements with respect to segregated Roma. On the contrary, any attempts to bring the topic back into the public debate were now quickly denounced by these same representatives as stigmatization.

Despite this changed public rhetoric, and as data on Roma community quarantines, excess hospitalizations and deaths amassed, behind-closed-doors officials continued as before trying to establish whether and how any countrywide decisions should consider eventual "Roma specifics."[11] Meanwhile, the Office of the Plenipotentiary of the Slovak Government for Roma Communities resumed and intensified their direct negotiations with the local authorities that were dealing with outbreaks in Roma enclaves, pushing for softer approaches and more effective humanitarian support. However, for the rest of the second wave, all these central state activities regarding the Roma remained practically covert, as there was little public media coverage. Remarkably, this also applied to the (abundant) cases where such negotiation activities helped protect the affected communities to the satisfaction of everybody directly involved.

The quick pace of this policy metamorphosis is not surprising, given the then fast-evolving biomedical information and experiences regarding the pandemic itself, and the related global turmoil. But what about its nature? Does it not appear surprisingly confused in its methods, and unambitious in its aims? To anyone familiar with the history of modern state politics targeting Roma in the region, it might not. Indeed, against a historical background, the pandemic developments merely offer an exceptionally concise distillation of the (rather limited and incoherent) *standard* repertoire of local hegemonic political discourses and practices with respect to Roma.

Firstly, ever since the very birth of the modern state in the region, rulers have depicted Roma as a people escaping standard state control measures and (thus) presenting a danger to public safety and requiring targeted interventions, including in the name of public health.[12] Secondly, for such interventions, rulers have always been able to mobilize considerable public funding and infrastructure, including the military.[13] Thirdly, whether involving Roma political representatives or not, these interventions never included an explicit focus on the countering of anti-Roma racist ideas and discriminatory practices, despite such practices being endemic among non-Roma and thus also encouraging biomedical "nonadherence" among segregated Roma. Moreover, to facilitate their local implementation, any initiatives that aimed to challenge Roma exclusion (e.g., financing housing desegregation) have not been presented as such but rather as security measures.[14]

Segregated Roma Face COVID-19: Diverse Mitigation Tactics and Obscured Impacts

How did the segregated Roma themselves respond to the pandemic and related state measures? As the chapters gathered in these Slovak chronicles document, the response was proactive, imaginative, dynamic, and diverse. Although fully aware of how little they knew (about viruses, the inner workings of their bodies, non-Roma authorities' plans, etc.) and how miserably little they had at their disposal (in terms of food, water, fuel wood, cash, health, non-Roma neighbors' solidarity, etc.), everybody kept trying their very best to devise the right personal solutions for an unprecedented crisis that was being touted everywhere as something that was overwhelming the whole world. To achieve this, they followed TV and social media, discussed their experiences with others, asked their few educated acquaintances or local professionals for advice, and so on.

Some communities hesitated to believe COVID-19 would affect Roma too, quoting a myth of superior Roma immunity to infections, popular among local physicians. In other communities people immediately started to make their own facemasks. There were families who avoided testing or who chose to travel abroad because they feared community quarantines. Other families helped in the local organization of testing. There were individuals who sold fake negative test results, believing they were helping everyone involved. Others passionately joined vaccination campaigns, maybe following a death from the virus among their relatives. And as in the rest of the world, there were hardly any communities, families, or individuals who did not gradually adapt their initial guesses, views, and behaviors regarding the pandemic.

As for the immediate health impacts of COVID-19 on segregated Roma, at first sight they seemed surprisingly light. According to the unique data collected by the Healthy Regions organization (HR),[15] out of the 12,544 deaths from COVID-19 in the country during the first two pandemic waves, only 198 had occurred within the 450 segregated Roma enclaves in which HR works, which constitute two-thirds of the total number of segregated enclaves in Slovakia.[16] This means that although the segregated Roma make up almost 4 percent of the total Slovak population, deaths from COVID-19 within them constituted only about 2 percent of all COVID-related deaths in the country.[17]

A closer look at other related figures reveals, however, that concluding that segregated Roma communities were impacted more lightly by the virus is false. Foremost, making crude comparisons per person does not make epidemiological sense here, as COVID-19 disproportionally affects the elderly. With an average age of twenty-four, the population in segregated settlements is much younger than in the general Slovak population (average age of forty-one). In Slovakia as elsewhere, most deaths from COVID-19 took place amongst the elderly (98 percent of deaths were among those aged above sixty-five). Yet, segregated Roma make up only 1 percent of all Slovaks aged above sixty: this means that about half of the reported 2 percent Roma deaths *present a staggering excess.*[18] Next, other HR figures show that younger people in the Roma enclaves were affected more when compared to the general population: 21 percent of the Roma deaths from COVID-19 (and 43 percent of COVID-related hospitalizations) concerned people below the age of fifty. Finally, HR data also indicates that far too few segregated Roma were hospitalized in a timely manner, given the seriousness of their COVID-19 condition: on average, nearly 40 percent of segregated Roma reported as hospitalized due to COVID-19 died.[19]

In sum, the direct health and fatality impact on segregated Roma was disproportionately harsh. What caused it? Available data and observations point to three key determinants. Firstly, due to substandard infrastructure, poverty, and related poor adherence to preventative measures within some communities,[20] infection rates were extremely high within dozens of large, segregated Roma enclaves, compared to equally large communities elsewhere.[21] Further, due to a combination of anti-Roma discrimination, endemic in many local healthcare services, and poor health literacy among the segregated Roma, some of the excess fatalities might be attributable also to belated hospitalization or its avoidance. Also, due to their harsher living conditions and a much higher burden of diseases across the life course of the segregated Roma, faster deterioration of their bodies is another likely factor.

The Slovak Chronicles: Accounts of Isolated Discontents

The following chapters on Slovakia present a collection of parallel, stand-alone personal accounts. Nonetheless, together they present a conversation around the pandemic, and one that is very timely. It unprecedentedly brings together the firsthand experiences of a small group of people, all of whom played different roles in the management of the pandemic within segregated

Roma enclaves. The accounts have something crucial in common: they all show the passionate, at times successful, but ultimately deeply frustrating personal struggles of authors who witnessed how insensitively the pandemic was managed by those in power. At the same time, the texts also reveal some considerable differences, even tensions—especially in how different actors experienced and understood the contributions of (other) people in positions of authority.

The Slovak chronicles thus reveal how chroniclers from very different walks of life coped with the changing priorities of the state as they tried to help control the epidemic across a historically contentious ethnic divide. Most importantly, we would like readers to reflect, not just on the very different standpoints taken by us chroniclers, but on the fact that we did not manage to establish fruitful conversations whilst the pandemic raged. As we were all so discontent with the actions of state decision makers, why were we unable to collaborate successfully with each other, and why have our accounts ended up seeming so mutually isolated and even hostile towards each other's positions? How can collaboration be cultivated in the future?

The chronicles start with an account by Alžbeta "Haľka" Mižigárová, who reflects on her and her community's frustration, anger, fear, but also resistance following the violent isolation of their neighborhood by army and police forces. Žehra, located in the Spiš region of northern Slovakia, was among the first five entirely quarantined Roma enclaves in March 2020. Literally overnight, people living there lost their freedom of movement. They had been given no warning and were offered no timeline for release. Yet, as Haľka shows, the community did not fall into despair. They mobilized their most precious resources—intense mutual compassion and affection—via seemingly small everyday acts of unconditional mutual support. In detail, she shares how this helped her not to give up but to continue to successfully negotiate with local authorities and other stakeholders in her role as a local community health worker.

In a similar vein, the text "Coffee and Cigarettes in State Quarantine" offers the view of Albín Peter, an ordinary Roma man, on another unprecedented public health measure, experienced as extremely frustrating to his family and friends. In the form of a diary, which he was encouraged to keep by the chapter's co-author, Tomáš Hrustič, the chapter traces the return of the author's family from England to Eastern Slovakia, interrupted at the Slovak border by mandatory placement into a state quarantine facility. The chronicler focuses on the six days involuntarily spent in a prison-like dormitory. As in the previous account, the narration is interwoven with glimpses of the strong urge of the Roma to withstand and resist against a violent predominance, here using "weapons of the weak"[22] such as constant humor and a children's protest.

Mapping in detail examples of early civic engagement among Roma that emerged in Slovakia in the wake of the pandemic, in his contribution Tomáš Hrustič offers a somewhat broader, non-Roma ethnographer's overview of Roma proactivity and self-organization related to COVID-19. Focusing on the development of self-help groups aimed at raising awareness and at the distribution of protective equipment, he discusses how the Roma response contradicted the hegemonic stereotypical expectations of them as a group requiring repressive control, for instance during the distribution of social welfare benefits in the pandemic. In this way, the paper adds another layer to the previous accounts of spontaneous engagement and resistance. It shows how, at times of uncertainty and shortage, segregated Roma did not wait for state or municipal help but were capable of temporarily self-organizing to address the failures in emergency supply.

Jurina Rusnáková and Zuzana Kumanová present a different kind of Roma concern with the pandemic developments in Slovakia, focusing on the outpouring of numerous hoaxes regarding Roma in relation to COVID-19 (for example, depicting state quarantine facilities as a new form of concentration camp). They argue that, because of the failure of the state and health experts to prevent Roma from becoming seen as a public security threat, the public health crisis contributed to deepening the pre-existing stigmatization and marginalization of Roma. In addition to revealing how the pandemic has fed the symbolic vulnerability of Roma in the country, the authors also express their reservations about the role of state representatives and experts in fostering such scenarios.

Andrej Belák's chapter offers more of a direct insider perspective and a critique of the state approach to segregated Roma during the pandemic. The contribution revolves around his discontent, as a non-Roma health expert, with how the state officials managed COVID-19 prevention and control within segregated Roma enclaves, as well as with his own role in the process. In the form of a "diary of hopes and disappointments," the author recapitulates his partly unsuccessful efforts to use his dual position as an expert working both in academia and in state public health to make the authorities' approach more nuanced and thereby also more effective. After briefly discussing the detachment, disinterest, and normalized racism on the part of many state officials, he focuses on what surprised and frustrated him the most: the resistance to his approach on the part of many prominent pro-Roma political representatives and activists.

Andrej Belák, MSc, PhD, is a medical anthropologist and social epidemiologist working at the Slovak Academy of Sciences. Since 2015, he has been working (in various roles) in academia and on behalf of the Slovak Ministry of Health as an expert and researcher specializing in the health of Slovakia's Roma.

Tomáš Hrustič, PhD, is a senior researcher at the Institute of Ethnology at the Slovak Academy of Sciences in Bratislava, focusing on different aspects of life within Romani communities. He also works for the National Democratic Institute (NDI), mainly facilitating workshops and training on various aspects of Romani issues, and leading training for locally elected Roma representatives and Roma youth leaders.

Notes

Work on this chapter and on Slovak chronicles was made possible thanks to funding from the project VEGA nr. 2/0066/19: "Patterns of Social mobility of the Roma in the Light of Empirical Research. Critical Reflection of Existing Practices and Collection of New Data."

1. Chalupka, Pollák, and Rafael, "Z Prvej Ruky." Peter Pollák is the first Slovak MEP of Roma origin. In the spring of 2020, he was appointed by the Slovak prime minister to manage the pandemic control within segregated Roma enclaves during the first wave.
2. Splnomocnenec Vlády SR, "Podiel."
3. This is according to data provided by the so-called Atlas of Roma Communities (MVSR, "Atlas."). Underlying data was collected in 2013 and then in 2019 to identify the most critical infrastructural and social challenges facing Roma, with the intention to better target measures and policies towards the improvement of the situation in disadvantaged enclaves. Roma communities were identified on the basis of ascribed ethnicity.
4. Settled Roma enclaves had already started to form in the area of today's Slovakia in the fifteenth century, and segregation has remained a dominant Roma residential pattern ever since. According to a recent survey, only 1.5 percent of such enclaves' residents do not consider themselves to be Roma.
5. These neighborhoods lack basic key facilities such as public water supply, sewerage, waste disposal schemes, asphalted pavements, and sometimes roads. Most families live in provisional buildings that lack legal approval, access to running water, bathrooms, and insulation. They use harvested wood and waste for both heating and cooking, and often only possess provisional electricity sources, sometimes none. Physical barriers keep most of the places isolated, including distance from the nearest residential areas, poor (or no) roads, fences and seclusion walls, and some are separated by railroad tracks. Nearby environmental hazards can include industrial waste, flood zones of rivers, and landslide zones.
6. See the press conference announcing "the action plan for Roma settlements" at: TA3 News, "TB I. Matoviča, A. Bučkovej;" and the official document supposedly justifying "the action plan": Mikas, "Plán Riešenia." See also a newspaper article: Vražda and Hrivňák, "Ohniská nákazy."

7. See the very end of the video, from the press conference on 17 April 2020: TA3 News, "TB I. Matoviča a J. Mikasa."
8. Officially, the name refers to the operation's logistics, consisting of a rolling rotation across Roma enclaves by eight army ground units, supported by two special forces helicopters. The Slovak term *kolotoč*, however, also evokes traveling entertainment enterprises traditionally run in the country by Roma.
9. As part of the European Union admission process over a decade ago, a Slovak National Roma Integration Strategy (NRIS) was set out, committing to work on the alleviation of inequalities between local Roma and non-Roma. Since then, hundreds of millions of euros (e.g., €400 million for the period 2014–20) are being made available in seven-year periods to the local ministries to update and implement their developmental NRIS "action plans," mostly via "national projects" focused on interventions and development in specific key areas, including health (see European Commission, "Roma Inclusion").
10. According to data from the monitoring system of the Slovak Ministry of Health's contributory organization Healthy Regions (internal report), during both rounds of the mass testing there were more than thirty segregated Roma enclaves with Ag positivity rates above 3 percent (and up to 23 percent). By contrast, the average and the highest municipality rates detected were below 1.5 percent and around 3 percent respectively (with the averages already including the extreme numbers for the Roma enclaves).
11. For example, the Ministry of Health's board of epidemiological experts and the Pandemic Commission both returned to discussing the Roma enclaves regularly, and a "Panel of experts on marginalized Roma communities" was eventually set up by the latter. There were also government-level meetings, with the continued involvement of the plenipotentiary Andrea Bučková and the MEP Peter Pollák.
12. The first documented public health ban aimed specifically at Roma in Slovakia (forbidding them to eat cadavers) was issued as early as the eighteenth century, by the then ruling Habsburgs (Tkáčová, "The Roma," 24).
13. Such initiatives specifically targeting Roma communities in Slovakia included: interwar "edification" and "decontamination" campaigns; interwar Nazi, Communist, as well as post-Communist eugenic policies and institutions; and Communist and post-Communist field nurses and health mediators, respectively (Donert, *The Rights*; Shmidt and Jaworsky, *Historicizing Roma*).
14. During the Communist period, for example, for the first time the rulers' ideology explicitly portrayed segregated Roma as victims of previous racist oppression. Yet, in the public presentation and planning of interventions, Roma themselves and their "lacking awareness" remained the primary target, while local implementation of any structural support for them continued to struggle in silence in the face of resistance from most local non-Roma.
15. Healthy Regions is a state contributory organization of the Ministry of Health focusing on participatory health promotion across segregated Roma enclaves in the country.
16. With no Roma deaths reported prior to the major, second wave (i.e., none before September 2020).
17. This figure of 2 percent has been calculated by increasing the HR-reported number of deaths by 25 percent to 250 in order to account also for the remaining communities where the organization is not present. Data is based on the Healthy Regions'

COVID-19 monitoring system (https://www.zdraveregiony.eu/). See also Holt, "COVID-19 Vaccination."
18. Moreover, since the Healthy Regions' criteria for reporting a death from COVID-19 were strict (it had to be confirmed to the HR fieldworker as such by local authorities), and as it is likely that not all suspected deaths from the disease were identified as such by the community workers, especially in large enclaves, the real number of deaths was probably even higher.
19. This is a rather high average ratio, approximating local fatality rates for COVID-19 patients on ventilation in intensive care units during the pandemic peaks. This observation was also confirmed in a personal communication to Andrej Belak by leading Slovak epidemiologists Prof. Pavol Jarčuška, Dr Alena Koščálová, and Dr Peter Sabaka.
20. According to the direct experience of the authors, consulted fieldworkers and municipality representatives, throughout the pandemic the preventative measures were upheld by most Roma coming from segregated enclaves when leaving their neighborhoods, but they were generally poorly adhered to within most such enclaves (Belák et al., "Pandémia COVID-19").
21. Up to 70 percent, according to MoH immunological pilots carried out in four enclaves showing previous antigen positivity >5 percent. Based on evidence from the HR monitoring system (see footnote 10).
22. Scott, *Weapons of the Weak.*

Bibliography

Belák, Andrej, Peter Marko, Ivan Solovič, and Tomáš Hrustič. "Pandémia COVID-19 v prostredí marginalizovaných rómskych komunít (MRK): Zhodnotenie rizík a návrh postupu pre Ústredný krízový štáb SR" [COVID-19 pandemic in marginalized Roma communities (MRC): Risk assessment and proposed action for the Central Crisis Staff of the Slovak Republic]. Analysis requested by the Pandemic crisis management team of the Slovak Prime Minister, 2021. Retrieved 21 July 2021 from https://www.zdraveregiony.eu/wp-content/uploads/2018/04/MRK-C19_ZhodnotenieRizikNavrhPostupuPreUKS_V3_31.3.pdf.

Chalupka, Radovan, Peter Pollák, and Vlado Rafael. "Z prvej ruky" [From firsthand]. Discussion moderated by Marta Jančkárová, *Rádio Slovensko*, 4 April 2020. Audio, 31:59. Retrieved 20 August 2020 from https://www.rtvs.sk/radio/archiv/1175/1312353.

Donert, Celia. *The Rights of the Roma: The Struggle for Citizenship in Postwar Czechoslovakia.* Cambridge: Cambridge University Press, 2017.

European Commission. "Roma Inclusion in Slovakia." Funding, Strategy, Facts and Figures, and Contact Details for National Roma Contact Points in Slovakia, European Commission. Retrieved 24 November 2020 from https://ec.europa.eu/info/policies/justice-and-fundamental-rights/combatting-discrimination/roma-eu/roma-inclusion-eu-country/roma-inclusion-slovakia_en.

Holt, Ed. "COVID-19 Vaccination among Roma Populations in Europe." *The Lancet* 2(7) (July 2021): e289. https://doi.org/10.1016/S2666-5247(21)00155-5.

Mikas, Ján. "Plán riešenia ochorenia COVID-19 v marginalizovaných rómskych komunitách" [Plan for addressing COVID-19 in marginalized Roma communities]. A plan approved by the resolution of the government of the Slovak Republic nr. 196 on 2 April 2020, Public Health Authority of the Slovak Republic, 3 April 2020. Retrieved 7 June 2022 from https://www.uvzsr.sk/index.php?option=com_content&view=article&id=4166:plan-rieenia-ochorenia-covid-19-v-marginalizovanych-romskych-komunitach&catid=250:koronavirus-2019-ncov&Itemid=153.

Ministerstvo Vnutra (MVSR). "Atlas rómskych komunít 2019" [Roma Communities Atlas 2019]. Ministry of Interior of the Slovak Republic. Retrieved 3 September 2021 from https://www.minv.sk/?atlas-romskych-komunit-2019.

Scott, James C. *Weapons of the Weak: Everyday Forms of Peasant Resistance*. New Haven, CT: Yale University Press, 2008.

Shmidt, Victoria, and Bernadette Nadya Jaworsky. *Historicizing Roma in Central Europe: Between Critical Whiteness and Epistemic Injustice*. London: Routledge, 2020.

Splnomocnenec Vlády SR pre Rómske Komunity. "Podiel pozitívne testovaných na COVID-19 v rómskych komunitách sa pohybuje približne na úrovni pozitívnych prípadov v majorite" [Proportion of positive COVID-19 tested cases in Roma communities is approximately at the level of positive cases in the majority]. Press release, The Office of the Plenipotentiary of the Government of the Slovak Republic for Roma Communities, 12 November 2020. Retrieved 20 January 2021 from https://www.minv.sk/?spravy_rk&sprava=podiel-pozitivne-testovanych-na-covid-19-v-romskych-komunitach-sa-pohybuje-priblizne-na-urovni-pozitivnych-pripadov-v-majorite.

TA3 News. "TB I. Matoviča, A. Bučkovej a P. Polláka o Akčnom pláne pre rómske komunity" [Press Conference of I. Matovič, A. Bučková, and P. Pollák regarding the action plan for the Roma community]. *TA3 News*, 4 April 2020. Video, 56:34. Retrieved 20 August 2020 from https://www.ta3.com/clanok/172964/tb-i-matovica-a-buckovej-a-p-pollaka-o-akcnom-plane-pre-romske-komunity.

———. "TB I. Matoviča a J. Mikasa o výsledkoch krízového štábu" [Press Conference of I. Matovič and J. Mikas regarding the results of the crisis team staff]. *TA3 News*, 17 April 2020. Video, 55:19. Retrieved 20 August 2020 from https://www.ta3.com/clanok/174104/tb-i-matovica-a-j-mikasa-o-vysledkoch-krizoveho-stabu#article-wrapper.

Tkáčová, Anna. "The Roma from the Reign of Empress Mária Terézia until the First Czechoslovak Republic." In *Čačipen pal o Roma: A Global Report on Roma in Slovakia*, ed. Michal Vašečka, Martina Jurásková, and T. Nicholson, 23–34. Bratislava: Institute for Public Affairs, 2003.

Vražda, Daniel, and Tomáš Hrivňák. "Môžu sa stať z osád ohniská nákazy? Štát sa zatiaľ nespamätal, rúška tam prenikajú pomaly" [Can settlements become outbreaks of contagion? The state is yet to wake up, the masks are penetrating there only slowly]. *DenníkN*, 17 March 2020. Retrieved 20 August 2020 from https://dennikn.sk/1806084/mozu-sa-stat-z-osad-ohniska-nakazy-stat-sa-zatial-nespamatal-ruska-tam-prenikaju-pomaly/.

CHAPTER 14

QUARANTINE, SEGREGATION, AND RESISTANCE
The Case of Žehra

Alžbeta "Haľka" Mižigárová

I will never forget how my father came out of the house. He was in local quarantine.[1] I looked at him, he looked at me.

"Gosh, what are you doing here, Haľka?" he asked. They call me Haľka.

I approached him in that protective wear. He was standing at the gate, and I couldn't go to him. I was afraid that he could possibly get it [infection] from me because I was spending time with people with a positive test. My father had worked all his life, trying his best to feed us with his hands. He is seventy years old, and we know older people have weaker immunity, and they have a harder time coping with the disease. I thought these might be the last moments I would see him alive. I figured he could get that Covid. I have it all in my heart. It has left its mark on me. Nothing—food, car, money—is more important than life. Life and health.

I am twenty-nine years old and work as a Roma health mediator for Zdravé regióny (Healthy Regions).[2]

We take care of Roma communities and try and improve their health conditions. Our work involves inviting people to get various vaccinations, providing education regarding personal hygiene, preventive medical examinations, and advice on medication use and breastfeeding.

There are about three hundred of us, and we are of their kind: we are all Roma. We come from the environment in which Roma live. That's why they trust us. I used to live in Žehra. Then I moved to Dobrá Voľa, which is a part of Spišské Vlachy. I lived there for ten years. For the last three years I have been living with my boyfriend in Spišský Hrhov. We have a house there, but no children yet.

For many people working for Healthy Regions, this is their first regular employment in their life. I used to take care of my mom, who was tied to her bed, then after her death I joined Healthy Regions. I've been working there for four years now. I'm in charge of Spišské Vlachy and Dobrá Vôľa. During the pandemic, I was also helping in Žehra. I caught the first news of the coronavirus in the media. In China, it started big. Then came Italy and other countries. And when we saw that it was in the UK, we expected it to come here as well. There are a lot of people from here in the UK. We knew they would start returning home and could bring the virus to the settlements here as well. I listened to such talk at my job. And I was scared. Of course, I was scared.

When I saw the mortality rate, I realized that it could be dangerous. Yes, people die of the common flu too, but there were more deaths due to coronavirus. You may tell yourself, *Well, this is not a common flu.* The virus really came. And then they cut off all of Žehra from the world. It was like that. No one knew about it when they closed off the settlement. People just got up in the morning and found that the settlement was closed. No one told them that they were closing the settlement because there were a certain number of positive cases inside. In short, people got up in the morning and could not leave the place.

Easter was coming, but people had no chance to buy any groceries, any medicines. They wouldn't tolerate it. They didn't know what was going on. They knew someone must be positive, but they didn't know who, or how many other people around them might have it. The authorities didn't tell them so that they couldn't riot against those who were positive.

It was a critical situation. In the first week, it was a surprise and a shock. By the second week, people were becoming fully aware that they could not go out. And in the following days and weeks, the situation turned out to be immensely bad. People kept asking: when will they let us out? Some wanted to go and fight. Even though we kept explaining it to them, they couldn't figure out in their heads why they were being kept in isolation, shut away. It was a big struggle for those two months.

There was no day when I wouldn't cry. I was sorry, I wanted to help people, but I didn't know how. I knew I had to explain things to them, bring them medications, and buy groceries for them. Some didn't have any food, even basic food. We were telling them what we knew. But they wanted concrete information that we didn't have access to either.

We wore protective overalls and went from house to house. We were such a mixed group—someone from the armed forces, a medical doctor, Andrej

Belák, the guys from local Roma civic neighborhood watch. We went to see the people we had been informed had tested positive—to tell them the news that they were positive. We told them to stay in home quarantine as no quarantine village had been set up yet.

But let's face it. Some didn't follow the guidelines. No matter they were positive, they went out anyway. But we couldn't tell the others the names of those who were positive. And they didn't tell others about themselves either. They didn't say: "I'm positive, be careful, don't come close to me while I'm out, because I also need some fresh air for a while." They would disappear into their houses as soon as they saw me, because they knew that I knew they were positive. But later on, I would see them outside, mixing with those who had tested negative. We had to keep our mouths shut, because otherwise conflicts could arise.

People thought if they didn't have any symptoms, such as fever or shortness of breath, then they were sound and they didn't have COVID-19. But the tests showed many such people to be positive. Of course, I was angry with them when I saw them among the healthy. Very much so. They were putting other people at risk.

Later, even we didn't know anymore who was positive because the mayor took it into his own hands and didn't share the information. However, we continued doing our job. We are like the extended arm of health professionals: we explained what measures needed to be followed and why. We talked to people about hygiene, washing hands, wearing facemasks, and washing clothes, because the virus also sticks to clothes. We kept repeating to them not to gather in groups, and to disinfect their homes.

We gradually distributed facemasks, gloves, disinfectants—a few of those items to each family at a time.

When Žehra was in quarantine, we entered the settlement only in full-body protective overalls. It was a novelty for me. I had only seen it on TV before. At first, I wanted to try it, but when I was dressed and entered the quarantine zone, I had butterflies in my stomach. Suddenly I saw many faces were staring at me. But even so, everyone recognized me right away. "Hal'ka is coming, Hal'ka is coming," they said.

I was surprised. I don't know how it's possible because I was as much covered as I could be. But still they recognized me. "Hal'ka, will everything be all right? All will be well, won't it? When will they let us go?" they were calling at me.

That's when I realized that it's not about the outer appearance but about the people who look at you. They recognize you despite that protective wear. You are one of them. And they keep asking you, they keep telling you how sad they are, how afraid they are.

In Žehra, I have my brother, my sister, my niece, my uncle... I could only approach them, as well as the others, in the overalls. It was a strange feeling. My sister and I grew up in the same house, and now I was standing next to her in a kind of protective overall, afraid I might get infected. And there's nothing you can do about it; you can't stay and talk—just announce what you need, and leave.

I cried every day, like when I was sitting in the car on my way home. I felt sorry for those people. They were asking for information, but there was no one who could give it to them. I felt awfully sad because they are humans too, and yet we often treat them like monkeys. I told myself that only the inscription "Zoo" was missing there.

When people from the UK returned to Žehra, there were no problems at first. But then, when the settlement was kept locked down for a longer time, the locals blamed those who had come from abroad, asking why they had come back and brought the virus, and why they hadn't stayed there. There was tension, people had arguments. They shouted, yes, but there were no other incidents.

Some people in Žehra live in shacks, others are better off, and yet there was cohesion between them. For that, I am extremely proud of them; they tried to help each other. The Roma are very direct and sociable, but that is the problem in this pandemic. It was extremely difficult to get across to them to stay at home, to not gather in large groups of even fifty, to wear facemasks. At first, they complied, then not, then again. Some were neglecting the measures. When no one was looking, they didn't follow them. They had no symptoms, they felt well, and they didn't care. Others followed the measures. It was about halfway through.

There were mood swings—good for five minutes, and then bad for another five minutes. They joked, too, and they sang. There was also a celebration when the isolation ended. People knew around 10 o'clock in the morning that the quarantine would be lifted. I don't know who had told them, but they already knew. The music went on, then MEP Peter Pollák came and announced: from 3 pm you will be free, you can go wherever you want. We were incredibly happy, people danced. And me with them. I didn't even need that protective suit then.

There only remained one quarantine village,[3] in which we had fifty-four people. We tried to motivate them, encourage them, because they had already been kept locked down for two months. They needed someone to talk to them, even more than before, so that they would know they had not been forgotten. We were available to them around the clock: when they had a problem, needed to have their temperature taken, or their medication brought. We tried to make them feel like we weren't afraid. We walked among them, albeit in special clothes. They appreciated it very much. And we were happy to be able to help them with the stress and fear they were experiencing. Because everyone is worried about their children, their health.

When we came out, they disinfected us, took our overalls off us, and we went home. We had something to eat, and then went back out to other locations to provide help there. Our usual work hours were from eight to four, but we were now making ourselves available twenty-four-hours a day. I told everyone: "Whenever you need something, I'm at your disposal."

I was afraid that there would be many victims, but thankfully, we didn't have a single death in Žehra.[4] If someone had died, it would have intensified the emotions even more. Of course, you're scared within because you can get infected yourself. I was afraid I would get it. I was worried about my boyfriend, my father, my family. And that fear is still there, because it's not over yet. But that job made me grow. I am here for people, and now we must be strong to give them that strength as well. They need us. We younger ones will somehow make it, we have a stronger immunity, but we have to think of the older people who are more at risk. And when they smile and thank us, it's the most beautiful feeling for us.

Initially, there were fears about testing the Roma, and many Roma opposed it.[5] I was in six settlements where testing took place. The people were mostly ready; it went smoothly, everyone came. At first, some didn't want to, but then they themselves asked to be tested. What matters is how the mayor approaches it and how it is presented to people. When it works and they feel trust, it's not a problem.

I have been for tests four times myself; they were all negative. The same for my colleagues. We figured we could eventually be positive, but we were simply there for the people who needed us. I think these were the most intense two months of my life. I don't regret any of it when I see people smiling at me, thanking me. I am proud of my people.

And I think this experience can help to improve the standard of living in the settlements and facilitate trust between people. I saw that they were trying. I think it will progress. That period changed me. It is important to tell the truth. Yes, you are positive, your life is at risk, it can change from minute to minute, you have to double-protect yourself, follow the measures and all will be well. You have to trust yourself, me and others. I learnt over those two months to tell the truth. I will try twice as hard in future, so that I don't find it hard telling the truth to people who need to hear it.

I would like to thank Tatiana Hrustič, the Director of Healthy Regions, as she has awakened great trust and an even greater willingness in us. I would like to thank all my colleagues, field expert Richard Koky and coordinator Peter Molek for their everyday support in the most difficult moments. And most of all, I would like to thank the people who are called Gypsies—that is, the Roma. They are the winners. Not us, but them. They did a great job.

Alžbeta "Hal'ka" Mižigárová is a Roma health education assistant for Healthy Regions. She comes from the Roma community in Žehra, where she has worked on health education since 2015. She is active in the community, and currently serves as a board member at the elementary school in Spišské Vlachy. She also works with young mothers as a lactation consultant.

Notes

1. Note by Tomáš Hrustič: The Romani settlement in Žehra, in the Spiš region of northern Slovakia, was locked down and put into quarantine on 17 April 2020. No warning was given, and no timeline for release; and, unlike the rest of the village, the Romani inhabitants of this neighborhood lost their freedom of movement. This situation of deep uncertainty lasted for four weeks until the authorities began to test inhabitants and gradually open the village, zone by zone. Žehra is a village composed of two main parts. There is a historical part where mostly non-Roma live, and then a Roma settlement approximately 2 km from the center of the village. The Roma settlement is divided into two parts: one is composed of blocks of flats and municipal apartment houses, and the other is full of wooden shanty cottages and huts without any basic infrastructure. Right next to this Roma settlement there is a neighborhood called Dobrá Vôľa, which is technically part of another municipality, Spišské Vlachy. During the chaotic times at the beginning of the state quarantine, Dobrá Vôľa was also closed without any warning, despite the fact that it is part of a different municipality and no infected people were identified there.
2. Note by Tomáš Hrustič: Zdravé regióny (Healthy Regions) is an organization affiliated to the Ministry of Health that manages the program of health mediation in marginalized Romani communities in Slovakia. It is a low-threshold participatory program employing Roma health assistants from more than 250 Romani communities in Slovakia, with emphasis on employing people living directly in these neighborhoods and speaking the language of these communities.
3. Note by Tomáš Hrustič: a special zone with temporary housing units for people who had tested positive. They were then isolated away from the rest of the population so that the whole neighborhood did not need to be closed off.
4. Note by Tomáš Hrustič: this text was written after the first wave in spring 2020. However, unfortunately, there were some casualties during the second wave in autumn of that year.
5. Note by Tomáš Hrustič: Slovak authorities introduced targeted testing in Roma communities in spring 2020 with the help of military medical teams to get information on the coronavirus infection among marginalized Roma communities.

CHAPTER 15

COFFEE AND CIGARETTES IN STATE QUARANTINE
Stuck on the Way Home

Albín Peter and Tomáš Hrustič

This chapter was written as a collaboration between two authors who have known each other since January 2004: Albín Peter, a local Roma leader in a small town in Eastern Slovakia, and Tomáš Hrustič, an academic who enjoyed Albín's and his family's hospitality during his long-term research in 2004 and 2005. Since then, although their paths have led them to different parts of Slovakia and Europe, both have remained in frequent contact and try to see each other at least once or twice a year. The first part of the chapter ("Preparations for the Journey and the Journey Itself") is based on an interview and debate between Albín and Tomáš, and was written in July 2020 when both authors met in Eastern Slovakia.[1] Albín describes the reasons for him and his family deciding to leave England and all the preparations for the trip, and Tomáš transcribed and edited his account. The second part ("State Quarantine") is a transcription and translation of Albín's diary, written when he and his family had to be isolated in a Slovak state quarantine center during the first wave of COVID-19 in spring 2020.

Preparations for the Journey and the Journey Itself

Many Roma from east Slovakian cities, such as Košice, Trebišov, Sobrance, and Michalovce, live in Gravesend, in Kent. Many of these families have lived there permanently: the men often work in construction companies or in waste separation, and the women in food companies. I have lived there since 2009, but with small breaks such as when I tried to find a job in Slovakia (without success). I had a good job in Gravesend, working as a driver and dispatcher for a construction company; I had a very good salary, in local terms, from which I was able to support a wider household.

After the outbreak and spread of COVID-19, we followed the news from Slovakia where there was a lockdown, with closed schools and, most importantly, closed borders. Other European countries had also closed their borders. We were uncertain about whether to return to Slovakia or stay in England. We didn't know how the situation would develop, or what the future would be like for us in either country.

In May, several Roma met in the town center in Gravesend. There were about seven fathers of the families that came to the meeting, and we talked and discussed what would be the best thing to do. We were all worried about kids—I was personally worried what would happen to Ryan, my six-year-old grandson. It was rumored that the authorities would test the children and then take them away from us. They said that if the father of the family became ill, they would come to test the whole family, and even if the children were not sick, they would say they were sick and take them away for adoption.[2]

We agreed that we had to leave. The ones from Trebišov left first, the second ones to leave were from Košice, and then we left. We told each other that we were going home. Mostly, the only Roma who remained in Gravesend were those who did not have their own place or anywhere else to return to in their home country. For example, all those from Luník IX continued to stay in Gravesend.

We decided to return to Sobrance in five cars: we were about five families, with twenty-three members. I was personally afraid of the journey because it was a long way and I had to drive it on my own. I didn't have a car, but all five of us said we would buy cars. My manager, who comes from India, had given me a car a long time ago to drive people to work. He was immensely helpful in this situation. He wrote off the car from the company accounts because it was old, and he had already registered it in my name. However, the car was good and reliable, and it cost me just £150 in all.

During preparations for the journey, we all called our families and friends all over England. Some called Derby, others Sheffield and Bradford. We were inquiring in this way who was going home, how they were going, and what their travel plans were. We were looking for information about the borders that were open. First, we checked if there were any buses that could take us home. We called the Ministry of Foreign Affairs in Bratislava about repatriation schemes. They told us that we could come back, but only on our own, and only by car. Secondly, like all citizens of Slovakia, we would have to go through the state quarantine after entering Slovakia.

On the morning of Saturday 16 May 2020, we set off from Gravesend to Dover, from where we boarded a ferry to Calais. Then, via Belgium and Germany as far as Dresden, and from there via Poland to Slovakia. We had unverified information that if we crossed into Slovakia via Poland, we would not have to go to quarantine—which, of course, we wanted to avoid if possible.

We were stopped for the first time in Belgium—but not at the border—by traffic police. They had noticed that the passengers in the back seats in two cars did not have seat belts fastened, so René and I each had to pay a €116 fine. The journey then continued without any further problems until we stopped at the border between Germany and Poland. They kept us there for about three hours. I stood outside because I was nervous about having to wait for that long. The border officer said they would let us go, but first they must call Warsaw to check if they could let us go. But it seems he tricked us and instead of Warsaw he called Bratislava, where he informed them that we were returning to Slovakia. Hence, Slovak police officers were already waiting for us at the Slovak border in three police cars. I'm assuming this was the case, because all the cars except ours were being allowed to go through—just not us, because we had English license plates on our cars.

When we came to the Slovak border, they made us park our cars next to portable toilets, so I knew we were going to be quarantined. We arrived at the border at 3 p.m. and were kept there until 10 p.m. We were hungry and waited there like morons. We were not allowed to leave our cars. We were mainly waiting for a police escort because the police present at the spot did not have adequate resources. When I asked how long we would have to wait, I received a polite answer that they were sorry for the delay, but we would just have to wait. Finally, the police escort arrived to shift us from there. Before that I had told them we were hungry, to which they replied they would provide us with food at the hostel in the morning. However, the police escort made an exception. When we stopped at a gas station, they allowed the drivers to buy food and especially cigarettes. When we reached the hotel, we had to wait outside in the cold for another two hours until they allocated us rooms. We were tired and didn't know who was staying where. But in the morning, when we went out onto the balconies, we were glad to see we were close enough to each other to be able to talk.

State Quarantine

Monday, 18 May 2020

Having left the Polish border, we arrived at the state quarantine center in Stará L'ubovňa on 17 May at about 10:30 p.m. It was our first day there. They brought us breakfast, but we Roma want coffee and cigarettes in the morning. I called the front desk to bring us coffee or a coffee machine, but were told we couldn't have a coffee machine. I saw that Darinka (my wife) and everyone was nervous, and it seemed as if we were being treated like prisoners. So I made an immersion water heater from the kit that Darinka had brought for her nail care. I took out tweezers and the cable from the night lamp—and there we had the immersion water heater. Then we made coffee and we were happy; we all went to the balcony, drank coffee and smoked. Only Jožko (Jogi) didn't join us as he likes to sleep late. Soon, however, we got upset again after we saw the police guarding us downstairs. We cursed them and that helped us to calm down as we could vent our anger. Then we joked again and forgot about the problems for a while. Suddenly we saw a Gadjo[3] from the balcony, who was going to mow the grass. We all (each of us from our own balcony) were looking at him. For fun, I told the Gadjo not to buzz as it would wake up Jožko. This made everyone laugh, and we were in a good mood again.

Tuesday, 19 May 2020

We woke up about 6 a.m. I made coffee for Darinka, and then had to quickly pass the water heater on. As I lowered it down to the balcony of the room below, I asked for my "horse" back. This made all of us laugh because the "horse" is how prisoners call such a string or rope in jails. Although I had never been in a jail, I knew of this word from my friends. It was 10 o'clock and Jožko (Jogi) was still asleep. Everyone envied him for being able to sleep for so long, as the quarantine would pass away faster for him than for us. We had new neighbors; they spoke Russian or maybe they were Ukrainians. And here it is again: questions about when they would let us go home, and politics. Everyone was talking about the parliament, especially about Matovič and Pollák.[4] I said to myself, "Poor Matovič, he has just taken office, and he already has a problem. He is all cursed, everyone swears at him, they curse him (*koškeren les*)." Darinka knew everything the best, as always (and she cursed him the most). I felt sorry for him, but Darinka cursed him. When he was elected, I was happy; I had kept my fingers crossed for OĽANO. Just then, Ryan cried. He was talking on the phone with his mom, who had stayed in England. Čopak (Jančo) kept eating. The children put on a protest, chanting across the balconies, "Let us go home, damn it!" Darinka had told them to do so. All the Roma children from several floors joined in. The protest was loud and strong. And then the staff brought us dinner, mashed potatoes (thickened with milk, broth) with one egg. It was good as we had not eaten it for a long time. We didn't have such food in England; we didn't have Slovak food there. Only Ryan sneered (he didn't want to eat). So, I ordered a kebab. I also bought cigarettes through a taxi service. They brought up the cigarettes, but the kebab ended up at the reception desk and wasn't brought to us, so I had paid in vain. But when a friend ordered the packaged food, it was brought to him, so it was clear we weren't allowed to order any unpackaged food. Now we were all talking with each other on the balconies. Maroš, "the fucker," told Jančo (Čopak) to send the "horse" so he could pass me things to wear, as I didn't have a T-shirt. He then tied rubbish in a black bag to the string and told me to pull it up, so that he could get rid of his trash. But Jančo (Čopak), "the mad moron," pulled it up and everyone laughed at him.

Wednesday, 20 May 2020

I got up at six and wanted to drink coffee. I had coffee but no sugar, so I was a little nervous. Then they brought breakfast at eight. We had yogurt, butter, and one slice of ham. Čopak said he didn't want it because he had Ryan's leftovers from yesterday. So, I gave Čopak's breakfast to Ryan. I was happy because Ryan likes ham, and he finally ate for the first time. Bogár was the first to ask for the water heater; he went out onto the balcony and shouted: "Albín!" We went out too, and started talking about Jožko (Jogi), that he was getting all benefits of sleep—he was still asleep. We all envied him. Then I went to my room, and my Indian boss in England called me to say that my colleague Jaro was not coming to work. To this, I said to myself that I did not have peace even while in quarantine. That is my punishment. Finally, I shouted "Fucking hell, I don't even have peace in quarantine!"

I called the reception desk to ask when we were to be tested; they said the next day, and we were all happy and thanked God.

We were in a crisis then, as although we had money, we didn't have what we needed. Because we didn't have sugar, it was a "sugar crisis." I called the front desk, and they told me they didn't have any sugar either. Finally, I got sugar via the taxi service, but it cost me 11 euros. Sugar at 11 euros is a blast. At home, I would have a liter of vodka for that. Damn it. It was 1 o'clock, and we were waiting for lunch. The lunch was good. Finally we had Slovak food, Szeged goulash, which we all appreciated, especially as it came with dumplings. Maroš, the moron, asked me if I wanted more because the children weren't eating theirs. I said good, I will eat it then. So, I sent him the horse. When I pulled it up and opened it, everything was empty—just paper packages. Everyone started laughing. I wished him in turn that he and his family would have to stay in quarantine for an extra week. That when we go home, I don't want to see him for at least a month. Fuck again! Then I ordered for Ryan the "Man, Don't Get Angry" board game. The taxi brought it, but again it got stuck at the front desk with the explanation that this was not allowed.

Thursday, 21 May 2020

I got up late. René shouted that he didn't have the water heater. So, I gave it to him. I named him "neighbor Záviš"[5] because he was grumpy about everything. I said he was more of a moron than his father, to which everyone laughed. Then the sad mood returned again. We counted the hours because they had already told us that they would be taking us for tests the next day. We hoped the tests would go well; may God help us.

At 5 o'clock, some new clients arrived. We shouted at them in Slovak, but they didn't react. They were kind of conceited. When we cursed them in Gypsy *o Rat len te marel*;[6] they immediately looked around and told us that they were not Gypsies. But I think they were.

Friday, 22 May 2020

We got up at 6:30 a.m., had breakfast, and waited to get tested. We were looking forward to it. We had our lunch and still nothing happened. We were told to wait. Some people in the hotel were going home, but we were all still stuck up there. Out of nervousness, we started shouting and cursing. It was all in vain. I was so nervous my head was spinning around. I was worried, hoping that I had not fallen sick. Ryan was going mad. I couldn't bear it mentally anymore. At 2:30 p.m., they finally came to test us. We each wondered how it would turn out. We, especially I, begged God that all tests would be good. Darinka went and was well behaved. She was not hysterical, even though she was very afraid that it would be painful. I was nervous imagining Edy and Lila drinking in England around then (because we drank every Friday), while I was in such a soup. Everyone on the balcony reminded me that if I were in England still, I too would be drinking now. I hoped everything would turn out to be good the next day. The Lord God will help us, and we will get out of there. Then, I'll finally have a drink and see my grandchildren.

Saturday, 23 May 2020

We had a dry breakfast—dry bread and a slice of cheese, with tea. I ate, but Jančo didn't. "Why don't you eat, Jančo?" I asked. "Will I eat dry bread? Fuck them." He started complaining: "Who do they think we are?" Then I calmed him and said, "Let us survive and it will be good." I was afraid that he might get screwed up and do something wrong. They called our room number and announced that we were negative. We went downstairs and they had us sign a check/invoice for food—13 euros for six days per person.

We started going home. We started our cars, pulled out, and stopped at the nearest gas station—so that we could all meet, shake hands, and hug as if we hadn't seen each other for a year.

Albín Peter is a Roma activist from Eastern Slovakia. In the past he was elected as a local councilor in his hometown, and was active in local level politics and civil society. Since 2011 he has mostly been residing with his extended family in the United Kingdom (sporadically returning to Slovakia), where he works to provide a better life for his family than they had in Slovakia.

Tomáš Hrustič, PhD, is a senior researcher at the Institute of Ethnology at the Slovak Academy of Sciences in Bratislava, focusing on different aspects of life within Romani communities. He also works for the National Democratic Institute (NDI), mainly facilitating workshops and training on various aspects of Romani issues, and leading training for locally elected Roma representatives and Roma youth leaders.

Notes

1. Writing of this chapter was made possible by the project VEGA nr. 2/0066/19: "Patterns of Social Mobility of the Roma in the Light of Empirical Research. Critical Reflection of Existing Practices and Collection of New Data."
2. Note by Tomáš Hrustič: Whilst doing research in both Slovakia and the UK over the last ten years, I have seen how the possibility of Roma children being taken away by English authorities (for various reasons, but most often for neglect of care or domestic violence) is considered a very real threat by Roma families. In particular, families with young children often live in tension that social workers, together with the police, will take their children away and give them up for adoption. This fear has been exacerbated by the firsthand accounts of several Roma families to whom it has really happened. Roma remind each other that the authorities assess Roma families very strictly, and they can get into a very unpleasant situation even for a small offense. For example, during my visit to Gravesend in May 2017, I witnessed Albín's son pack up everything within two hours, get in the car with the whole family and return to Slovakia after their children had got into a routine child-conflict with their Pakistani neighbors, and the neighbor had threatened to call the police.
3. Note by Tomáš Hrustič: A Romani term used for any non-Roma. It is usually used to refer to a person when emphasizing ethnic difference—in this context, it was a nameless person, a non-Roma, who became a target of their joking.

4. Note by Tomáš Hrustič: Igor Matovič was the Slovak prime minister at the time. His political party, OĽANO, had unexpectedly won the elections in February 2020, and the new government was appointed in March 2020 to govern the country during the pandemic crisis. Peter Pollák is a Romani MEP for OĽANO, and a close ally of Igor Matovič. The prime minister entrusted Pollák with the management of pandemic measures in Roma communities.
5. Note by Tomáš Hrustič: After a Hungarian cartoon series character, popular in Slovakia.
6. Note by Tomáš Hrustič: Local Romani dialect. The literal translation would be "let the blood drench you."

CHAPTER 16

"IN DIFFICULT TIMES WE SHOULD STICK TOGETHER"

Roma Self-Help Initiatives and Awareness Raising Activities as an Immediate Reaction to the Spread of COVID-19 in Early March 2020

Tomáš Hrustič

Introduction

In March 2020, just as the first news about the pandemic began to spread in the Slovak media, I noticed that my Roma friends and acquaintances—like myself and everybody else I knew—became extremely interested in learning how to avoid becoming ill with COVID-19 and how to prevent the virus spreading within their communities. Everyone, whether living in segregated settlements or living among the general population, was very keen to access the most up-to-date and accurate information. Although I am not an expert in public health, from my position as someone who has been engaged in several academic and non-academic projects among Roma communities throughout Slovakia over the last twenty years, I could observe how various Roma communities responded to the new situation, the uncertainty it brought and the implicit and often explicit manifestations of racism and antigypsyism that emerged in the context of the COVID-19 pandemic.

In those early days, those professionals and organizations working with Roma communities were developing, and expressed their own preoccupations. Many feared that the spread of this virus would be relatively fast in many Roma settlements. They believed that this spread could not be effectively prevented due to a number of challenging factors: poor material conditions (substandard housing, lack of infrastructure), population density in the settlements, overcrowded housing, and certain sociocultural predispositions—for example, unlike most of the Slovakian population, for Roma their daily contact with relatives within the extended family living in other households is essential. The experts feared that under such conditions it would be impossible for individuals and families to accept the measures required to slow down the spread of the virus, in particular through social distancing and physical isolation.

Experts in public health were concerned about the increased risk for Roma living in segregated and marginalized communities due to their significantly shorter life expectancy in comparison to the majority population outside these settlements.[1] They have higher infant mortality and are affected by diseases to a much greater extent, including chronic diseases associated with poverty such as diabetes, hypertension, and chronic respiratory problems.[2] In other words, their average life expectancy is shorter because this is a population generally more heavily burdened by health inequalities.

Although the Roma population in Slovakia is younger than the non-Roma population, which some politicians and public health authorities argued put Roma at a lesser risk, all these other circumstances served as warning factors for aid organizations and individuals working in Roma communities—and also, I would argue, for the vast majority of Roma people themselves, who are well aware of the conditions they live in and the effect they may have on their health. They responded proactively through multiple initiatives and activities to mitigate the spread of the virus. Their resilience, ingenuity, and civic engagement, which I document throughout this chapter, challenges head on the dominant stereotypes of Roma passivity and unruliness, which have been prominent in the media both before and during the pandemic.

Health-Related Concerns and Awareness-Raising Campaigns

> Romale. Aven ajse láče, na phiren avri kaj namušinen. A te mušinen te džan nakuposke, thoven tumenge rúškos, te tumen nane, šalos, alebo šatka. Častones morkeren o vasta, sapuňiha, doležito hiňi osobno hygiena. Naphiren pal o Roma, pal e famelija. Nasikeren tumen ode kaj hin o but ňipos, but l'udos. Naphiren kanake pal o zabavi, nakeren bare hoscini, bo koronavirus. Sikeren tumen andro kher, sako khejre, peskere čavenca. O Del amenca![3]

> (Roma, please, don't go outside if you don't have to. And when you have to go shopping, put on a mask. And if you don't have one, take a shawl or scarf. Wash your hands frequently with soap, as personal hygiene is important. Do not go to

see people, do not visit family, and do not show up where there are many people. Don't go to parties or arrange big feasts, because coronavirus isn't easy. Stay at home with your children. May God be with us!)

These are the words of Magdalena Beláková, a Roma health support assistant at the hospital in Michalovce and an employee of the Healthy Regions organization of the Ministry of Health in Slovakia.[4] In a short video in the Romani language, she encourages people to take the current epidemiological situation seriously. The video was posted on 17 March 2020 on the organization's Facebook page. Within three days, it had been shared over 1,300 times and been seen over 47,000 times.[5] Along with this video, over twenty further videos featuring Romani health mediation coordinators and assistants, doctors, and influential personalities have appeared on the Healthy Region Facebook site as part of an information campaign put together by Healthy Regions, People in Peril,[6] and a volunteer organization Bystriny.[7] Within a few days, they had devised the campaign strategy, its visuals and graphics. They launched a website www.koronatemerel.sk ("let corona die") that contains videos and information about the virus for Roma in marginalized communities.

Besides the one featuring Magdalena Beláková, several other videos were very widely shared. For instance, the message from Jarmila Vaňová, the first Roma woman elected to the National Council of the Slovak Republic, was viewed by more than 44,000 people and was shared 434 times. To assess the relative success of this campaign, I compare these most successful videos with videos shared by publicly known Roma during the protests against rising fascism in January and February 2020. The wave of Roma civic engagement during the election campaign, in response to the growing popularity of the extremist "People's Party Our Slovakia,"[8] has been one of the most significant manifestations of Roma participation in Slovakia to date. Interestingly, only some of the videos from that period (e.g., Peter Pollák jr. and his speech against Our Slovakia's Marian Kotleba reached 72,000 views)[9] were viewed and shared more often than videos from the COVID-19 information campaign. And only a few of these political videos were recorded in the Romani language.

In the early weeks of the first wave, the biggest challenge was a lack of centrally coordinated plans by state authorities, and a lack of material supplies to tackle the pandemic. The Healthy Regions organization, despite being part of the Ministry of Education, did not get any instructions on how to proceed and deal with new circumstances. Consequently, they elaborated their own crisis plans and instructions for their employees to follow. In a similar way, other organizations with social workers or community center workers in the field also elaborated their own crisis plans. A huge problem in March 2020, however, was that none of these organizations had access to personal protective equipment. Without PPE, the fieldworkers were not able to maintain any regular direct communication with their clients. On the other hand, health education assistants were living directly in these communities (as 94 percent of them are Roma), and so they could not avoid daily contact with people in the settlements. They were not, however, allowed to visit their clients inside their homes, and even communication outside without protective equipment was risky. Although they worked in a limited mode, in these segregated Roma settlements they served as vital channels for sharing information about the spread of the virus and about ways of protecting against it.

Roma living in settlements, local leaders and activists also responded to the unprecedented situation. Within a few days of the first reports of the spread of coronavirus in Slovakia, many spontaneous civic initiatives emerged. In many Roma settlements and communities in Slovakia, Roma activists started to organize grassroot action groups, trying to contribute to the improvement of the situation. Most of these activities were initiated not only by community center workers, Roma health mediators, municipal office staff, and local politicians, but by many individual Roma in communities who had the capacity and will to help and contribute. In essence, most of the tasks were focused on crafting protective face masks, which were badly lacking. Roma women organized themselves to start sewing, and they gradually gained further support and material. In many places (e.g., Kecerovce, Ostrovany, Rudňany, Sečovce, and Jarovnice), the initial need to provide a few masks for family or local community developed into more organized sewing activity for nearby towns and villages.

Responses to the Securitization Discourse on the Roma

The visibility of Roma in Slovak public spaces is interpreted through a racist lens and is strongly resented by large sectors of the non-Roma population. Groups of Roma standing in front of supermarkets or post offices in rural areas often leads to disapproving looks from passersby, and to negative or racist remarks and comments. Roma are aware that they have never been welcome in many public spaces, and that they have extremely limited possibilities to change this situation. This makes Roma the object of local policies, but without even limited powers to participate in decision-making processes related to their own communities. In the context of the Slovak countryside, the position of Roma is thus characterized by a significant power asymmetry (non-Roma decide on resources for Roma) and inequality over the control of symbolic representations (the stigmatization of Roma ethnicity). The system of unequal power distribution and access to public space along ethnic lines is so deeply ingrained in Slovak society that, in the past, it was only rarely questioned by either side. For Roma actors, transgressing the unwritten rules of where Roma ("Gypsies") belong, which are defined by the dominant non-Roma population, is invariably a tense act with unpleasant consequences. For the non-Roma, it is certainly an unwanted phenomenon.[10]

When the lockdown[11] was imposed, many municipal and political authorities throughout the country became concerned because Roma were scheduled to receive their social benefits during that first week. Not only they were afraid that there would be many Roma in public spaces, but moreover that they could become potential virus spreaders. They feared that Roma would gather in large numbers outside post offices and subsequently make large purchases in stores and shopping centers, and that these would work as super-spreader events. Although Roma from the settlements were not the only group receiving social benefits, these concerns were explicitly associated only with them. Roma have been portrayed (repeatedly) as a threat and as intruders into public space rather than as a vulnerable group. Despite the coordinated efforts of several Roma activists and academics (including myself) to push for rhetoric change at the top, and to adopt more adequate welfare distribution solutions, the Central Crisis Staff[12] decided instead to strengthen the presence of the armed forces (police and army) outside post offices to oversee security and to ensure compliance with the new measures.

This decision gave rise to several responses, with most Roma activists expressing anger and concern about the possible escalation of tensions and local conflicts. However, due to the time pressure and oft-stated seriousness and unprecedentedness of the situation, the Roma local leaders, either from NGOs or locally elected representatives, decided to comply with the authorities. Rather than resisting, they initiated spontaneous information campaigns for people in settlements to explain the presence of police officers. They tried to shift the paradigm in terms of the protection of the Roma themselves. People received information that they would only be able to enter the post offices individually and with protective masks, keeping safe distances between each other and taking other relevant measures. The local Roma leaders also tried to explain the importance of family members going shopping alone, and of not taking children to the shops. This information campaign was conducted literally in just one day. In most communities, it was mainly fieldworkers from various helping professions who disseminated this information locally, and who coordinated and organized the groups receiving social benefits. Thanks to the (unrecognized) work of these fieldworkers, there were no incidents, and most of the Roma from segregated settlements received their benefits in compliance with the measures. This is in stark contrast to the humiliating and unjustified portrayal of Roma as troublemakers and a potential threat.

On her Facebook profile, Jana Gáborová Kroková, a Romani PhD student at the Institute of Romani Studies at the University of Prešov, compared the way Roma made their purchases with the shopping spree that had engulfed the general Slovak population a week earlier:

> I decided to replenish supplies in a department store in Košice. When I saw so many cars in the parking lot and plenty of Roma, I thought, "Well, I would rather pick another day to replenish my supplies." I compared it to the panic shopping wave I witnessed last week. Everybody was shopping as if it was the end of the world. The most hectic days were Thursday and Friday. You should have seen it: head-to-head, trolley-to-trolley, dribbling, and buying everything: from toilet paper to all types of disinfectants. In each cart, at least enough to last for a year. What if the cart next to it had to go without soap, without disinfectant? Today, it was different. Also, the Roma from the communities have abandoned shopping for fun, which they use to do once a month. Families walked around with children, aunts, and... Today, however, these people were shopping individually. I saw only one member of the family, buying with a mask on their face, with sufficient distance, sophisticated and quiet. And... they didn't need any control from the department store, the police or the soldiers. I wondered how nicely these "inadaptable"[13] had adapted, and how those supposedly "adaptable" required regulations and coordination.

Examples of Mutual Support

To get an overview of the pandemic situation in Romani communities around Slovakia, I contacted my friends, acquaintances, and other contacts in many villages in Eastern Slovakia. I asked them about self-help activities in Roma communities. Their reactions only confirmed to me that these forms of mutual support and encouragement were spreading at least as fast as the virus itself. Roma shared their Facebook stories and posts, commented on those of others, and inspired others to follow. One Roma social worker told me in her Facebook message:

> In those localities where the cooperation of local government and field social workers, community centers, and a local neighborhood watch is good, the situation there in prevention is much better ... I am pleased that the call "ačhen khere!" [Romani for "stay at home"] is being listened to ... and I am glad it does not confirm that our Romani people [reinforce negative stereotypes]. ... With God's help and the protection of the Virgin Mary, we will make it! (23 March 2020, personal communication)

Finally, in March and April 2020, when there were practically no protective masks available in Slovakia, people had no choice other than to help themselves. It was extremely encouraging to see many photos in which Roma and non-Roma were sitting together behind sewing machines, cooperating at the local level. Many people from various villages, regardless of ethnicity, worked together to distribute masks in settlements and communities. They were all together in this catastrophe: the virus does not choose.

Many activities were not limited to just sewing the protective face masks. Some Roma helped with translating information into the Romani language, for example. Zuzana Blaháková, a non-Roma field social worker from Nitra, wrote to me about her experience:

> "*I was happy to do it* [to help with the translation of these materials]. *In difficult times we should stick together, and everyone should contribute to the common goal as much as possible.*" A member of the Vlax Roma community wrote this message to me after I thanked him for his cooperation in translating the C19 info material into the Vlax variant of the Romani language. Another person contributed by recording his message for the local radio in the Romani language. These are just some examples of the COVID-19 activities taking place in this community. All these people are to be respected for their willingness and sincerity to help without seeking reward. If the approach is rational and immediate, everything is possible. It is not just about the coronavirus—it's about people and attitudes. Del o del! [Romani phrase for "Let God helps us"] (20 March 2020, personal communication)

Another exciting and spontaneous activity was, for example, the Facebook page of Romani Fairy Tales (Romane paramisa),[14] founded by Roma pedagogy student Michal Sivák. Fairy-tale readings were being uploaded to the site, with the aim of entertaining children who were at home being quarantined. It should be noted in this context that the education of children from segregated and marginalized Romani communities during the first and second waves of the pandemic in 2020 was very problematic because Slovakia closed all schools very early in March 2020, and many of them stayed closed until April 2021. The learning process was dependent on online teaching tools and the existence of some working space at home. This situation excluded children from poor communities, without access to the internet or to mobile devices, and often living in overcrowded huts. In some cases, teachers attempted to mitigate this systemic failure and unequal access. Many of them distributed homework via field social workers or community centers, so that the children had at least some portion of the distant education. The public Slovak Television also broadcast some online teaching classes in Romani language during the first wave of the pandemic in spring 2020.

Conclusion

Many activities and initiatives undertaken by local activists and politicians, individuals and families could be listed. But the brief discussion above sufficiently conveys the breadth of Roma civic engagement and responsibility in Slovakia. It should be remembered, however, that the situation in Roma settlements in the spring 2020 Covid wave was diverse, and that in some areas it was more challenging than what is described above. Nevertheless, what all these examples show is that, contrary to the discourse in the Slovak media, it is not possible to generalize how an ethnic or social group will respond to the pandemic measures. In this short chapter there are several examples of how Roma at the local level reacted to the new and unprecedented health-related threats from the coronavirus pandemic. I have provided examples of how Roma self-organized, both as individuals and as groups—for example, producing protective equipment such as face masks, setting up information sharing campaigns, and mobilizing alongside non-Roma allies. Moreover, these examples of engagement were not directed only against health-related risks. They became also a tool for confronting the antigypsyism and racism of those who view Roma only as a threat (and a potentially infectious one, in this instance) to Slovak white society.

It is evident that the symbolic power asymmetries in municipalities around Slovakia and at the central level placed Roma in a degrading position: the symbolic dominance and power of non-Roma still persists. "White" hegemony and systemic racism still defines how the Roma are portrayed, and how they are perceived in the public arena. I hope that this text has shown that there were a large number of engaged Roma, often from poor and excluded settlements, who organized and created initiatives, together with their non-Roma allies, helping to slow down the spread of the epidemic. These stories can thus serve as examples of Romani resistance against local and central non-Roma political and social hegemony, and as a counterbalance to the symbolic power asymmetry between Roma and non-Roma in Slovakia.

Tomáš Hrustič, PhD, is a senior researcher at the Institute of Ethnology at the Slovak Academy of Sciences in Bratislava, focusing on different aspects of life within Romani communities. He also works for the National Democratic Institute (NDI), mainly facilitating workshops and training on various aspects of Romani issues, and leading training for locally elected Roma representatives and Roma youth leaders.

Notes

The finalization of this chapter was supported by the project VEGA nr. 2/0066/19: "Patterns of Social Mobility of the Roma in the Light of Empirical Research. Critical Reflection of Existing Practices and Collection of New Data."

1. Cook et al., "Revisiting the Evidence."
2. Hajioff and McKee, "The Health of the Roma."
3. See *KoronaTeMerel* website: https://koronatemerel.sk/wp-content/uploads/2020/03/07.mp4 (last accessed 20 August 2020).
4. Zdravé regióny (Healthy Regions) is an organization of the Ministry of Health that focuses mainly on support and education in the field of health and access to healthcare for people living in marginalized Roma communities. The organization has approximately three hundred employees, and most of them are Roma who live and work within marginalized communities, working in the language of the community. For more information about the organization, see the chapter by Andrej Belák in these Slovak chronicles.
5. In August 2021 the post was seen by more than 72,000 people.
6. People in Peril (Človek v ohrození) is one of the most influential Slovak NGOs, with focus on humanitarian activities around the world. They also run a dozen community centers in Roma communities in Slovakia.
7. Bystriny is a networking organization with a focus on linking individuals and organizations who seek professional help with those who offer it for free.
8. The political party was founded by neofascist Marian Kotleba, who increased his popularity on an anti-Roma platform. The party had been elected to Parliament for the first time in 2016, and in their election campaign in 2020 they organized large gatherings around Slovakia. Many Roma individuals and activists along with other human rights advocates protested against these gatherings, and hate speech spread at these rallies.
9. Peter Pollák, "Kotleba Vyrástol Na Rómoch," Facebook, 19 January 2020, https://www.facebook.com/peter.pollak.37/videos/vb.100000169281164/3235576889791255/?type=2&video_source=user_video_tab.
10. For more on power asymmetries related to the political participation of Roma at a local level, see Hrustič, "Roma Mayors."
11. In Slovakia, "lockdown" meant that only essential shops like groceries and pharmacies were open; all other shops and public spaces were closed. People could only go shopping for their basic supplies.
12. So called Central Crisis Staff was a body appointed by the prime minister to submit proposals and measures to mitigate the pandemic in Slovakia. It was composed of representatives of key governmental institutions, epidemiologists and crisis managers. They did not have a direct responsibility but had to submit their proposed solutions for adoption to government. However, their competencies and responsibilities were often blurred and unclear, and many chaotic activities and decisions ensued.
13. In Slovak context, the word "inadaptable" is often used to refer to Roma by spokespeople from the majority. In their general ignorance, they consider it to be more polite than "Gypsies."
14. See https://www.facebook.com/romskerozpravky/.

Bibliography

Cook, Benjamin, Geoffrey Ferris Wayne, Anne Valentine, Anna Lessios, and Ethan Yeh. "Revisiting the Evidence on Health and Health Care Disparities among the Roma: A Systematic Review 2003–2012." *International Journal of Public Health* 58 (2013): 885–911. https://doi.org/10.1007/s00038-013-0518-6.

Hajioff, Steve, and Martin McKee. "The Health of the Roma People: A Review of the Published Literature." *Journal of Epidemiology & Community Health* 54 (2000): 864–69. https://doi.org/10.1136/jech.54.11.864.

Hrustič, Tomáš. "How Roma Mayors Penetrate the Municipal Power Structures: Resisting the Non-Roma Dominance in Slovak Local Governments." *Slovenský národopis* 68(4) (2020): 397–411. https://doi.org/10.2478/se-2020-0023.

CHAPTER 17

THE HOAXES AND INCORRECT INFORMATION RELATED TO COVID-19 SHOWED A LACK OF TRUST BETWEEN THE MAJORITY AND THE ROMA, AND A LACK OF KNOWLEDGE

Jurina Rusnáková and Zuzana Kumanová

Introduction

In Slovakia, during the first wave of the pandemic, Roma became the main protagonists of negative prognoses about the development of the disease. Predictions of an uncontrollable spread of COVID-19 within marginalized Roma communities were strongly voiced by both professional and political authorities. The main concern was the idea that poor settlements would become a threat to others if nothing was done to prevent it. Consequently, Roma quickly became seen as a public health threat within the public debate. This resulted in, among other things, the cordoning off of dozens of Roma settlements, and the imposition of community quarantines on them at various times. As the Public Defender of Rights of the Slovak Republic ("Ombudsperson"), Mária Patakyová, argued, these community quarantines were discriminatory: they had a "selective character" as they were being imposed exclusively on "marginalized Roma communities."[1] They led to the scapegoating of marginalized Roma, and further exacerbated their economic deprivation and exclusion.

Both authors of this article are Roma, and we care very much about how Roma are depicted and perceived. We would like to warn our readers that what follows are our opinions, observations, and experiences, and so we ask you to read the chapter as a subjective statement rather than an objective report. It reflects our overall conviction that hatred is also a pandemic, which, if uncontrolled, will affect very large numbers. While we can have some protection against the spread of COVID-19 (masks, hygiene, social distancing) and we can even get vaccinated against it, we have yet to find a vaccine for hatred.

We believe it is not appropriate to ask what is more dangerous, the risk of COVID-19 or the risk of an even stronger exclusion of Roma from society. The dangers of setting these options against each other have increasingly become clear to representatives of Roma civil society who, through 2020, changed their positions between the first and the second waves. While in the spring of 2020 they demanded that special measures be taken with regards the inhabitants of poor settlements, by the autumn they had grown more cautious. Like us, they became reluctant to repeat the situation from spring 2020, when Roma were portrayed as likely to spread the infection, and they did not want to support what ultimately was a campaign of fear. Meanwhile, the COVID situation in autumn 2020 and especially spring 2021 became demonstrably worse throughout the country, and disproportionately so in Roma settlements.

Roma Settlements as a Threat

Today we know that the supposed threat that Roma were meant to pose to the rest of Slovak society did not materialize. In spring 2020, thousands of Roma in the east of the country were placed in community quarantines for several weeks without good access to basic amenities such as drinking water. Yet in Roma settlements themselves, and throughout the country, the first wave developed relatively "calmly"—although, of course, every life lost is a tragedy.

The pandemic has shown that a large part of the dominant society, including its elites, can easily and perhaps willingly believe unsubstantiated reports about Roma as a threat. Once the situation calms down, it will be important to analyze and understand what led the authorities to take the decision to quarantine whole Roma settlements, to what extent the threat of uncontrolled spread in segregated settlements was real, and how exactly the narrative of Roma as public health threats contributed to the decision to impose community quarantines. We suspect that, in addition to the damage to the health and the worsening of already poor living conditions of a large part of the Roma population, the pandemic has brought a deterioration in the ways Roma are perceived in the country, and in interethnic relations.

We do not have quantitative evidence to support this idea, but the indications are convincing. We draw on the individual experiences of rejection in shops and pharmacies reported by Roma activists, and on our knowledge of heavy-handed policing of whole communities, which were designated as risky even though there were very few cases. Indeed, the government approved specific measures for managing COVID-19 in marginalized Roma communities, which allowed quarantining of whole communities whenever 10 percent of the people became infected: for no other local communities or neighborhoods in the country was such an order developed. Equally, one example of local over-policing we could mention is the physical police violence against children in the town of Krompachy, when the policemen who patrolled the community quarantine in the city attacked a group of children who overstepped the borders of the quarantined area.

As noted previously, the topic of marginalized Roma communities in relation to the pandemic featured strongly in public debates in the first half of 2020. There was an appeal on the part of Roma and pro-Roma activists, and a section of the media, to protect the vulnerable inhabitants of poor Roma settlements where, because of poor living conditions, basic prevention measures could not be implemented. The prime minister, the minister for health, and the Pandemic Commission tasked with controlling the pandemic, all warned about the risk of the virus spreading from Roma settlements to the majority environment. They also argued that specific measures for Roma were necessary, in particular a targeted testing for COVID-19 within Roma communities. The discussion was not helped by media statements about the irresponsibility of settlement residents, and about high levels of uncontrolled mobility to and from countries heavily affected by the pandemic, such as Great Britain. These reports were received and interpreted by the public with a great deal of negative emotion towards the Roma.

A letter from several Roma and pro-Roma activists at the end of March stated: "We, the representatives of civil society, therefore appeal to the Government of the Slovak Republic to pay due attention to the potential impact of the pandemic on marginalized communities." They also asked the government "to invite organizations that were already actively helping to address the most pressing ongoing problems to focus now on the pandemic situation in poor localities."[2] This was the first challenge to the state during the pandemic coming from representatives from civil society. In later months it was followed by a series of criticisms of the state's actions against Roma, specifically regarding the closure of Roma settlements through community quarantines without evidence of the need for such action; and regarding the lack of effective and humane measures to protect settlements.[3] Instead, activists proposed measures based on their own professional knowledge and experience. They generally argued for closer cooperation between NGOs and the state, and for the creation of informed crisis plans so that measures could be applied ad hoc. In our view, these were not voices that had any real influence on decision making—and probably not on public opinion either.

On the other hand, the forecasts produced by state health analysts and epidemiologists, who also received much attention in the media at the time, were more effective at reaching a broader audience and persuading both politicians and the public.[4] For example, when the Public Health Authority published their analyses modeling the spread of the virus, their most pessimistic projections always stressed the risk arising from Roma settlements. Some of these forecasts were presented to the public by the media and at press conferences of high-ranking politicians, including the prime minister. Probably under the influence of these estimates, members of the expert council set up by the prime minister recommended that targeted measures be taken "specifically" for Roma in the settlements, which resulted in the adoption by the government of the "Plan for addressing COVID-19 in marginalized Roma communities" on 2 April 2020.[5]

The public did not have the opportunity to assess the accuracy of these forecasts: the accompanying published information was very general and did not provide the data on which the decision to target Roma communities was based. Data on the diversity of living conditions of the Roma population—such as on those Roma who live in ethnically homogeneous or in ethnically mixed villages, or on access to basic infrastructure, or on different capacities to adhere to pandemic mitigation measures (such as social distancing)—seem not to have been considered at all. We should stress here that detailed data on living conditions in Roma communities was already publicly (and readily) available, and could easily have been taken into consideration.[6] In our opinion, all of this had a significant impact on the decision to quarantine Roma communities, which was taken by several regional public health authorities. Indeed, there has been no quarantine at a community level anywhere else in the country except for Roma settlements.

We can only assume that these trends are signs of an entrenched, generalized view of Roma in Slovakia, based on poor knowledge and on a tendency to take negative depictions of Roma at face value and without evidence. This is particularly worrying in the case of politicians, experts and policy makers, and we believe that if they had used data on Roma communities more responsibly, their forecasts would not have been so negative. The careless approach to the protection of Roma rights by those at various levels of state governance comes as no surprise to us, as there is ample evidence that the violation of Roma rights is viewed as less problematic than for other population groups; examples include the ethnic segregation of Roma children in schools and the lack of access to drinking water in poor communities.

In particular, it was reckless of these experts and policy makers to refer to the possible irresponsibility of Roma in settlements as a motivating factor in their decisions, even though there was no evidence to support such claims and no data to compare the behavior of marginalized communities with that of the general population. On the contrary, Jurina Rusnáková carried out a simple survey in April 2020 for the then newly appointed[7] Government Plenipotentiary for Roma Communities. The survey aimed to elicit the estimates and observations of professionals working in 411 Roma communities in 278 municipalities, which is half of the Roma communities in Slovakia: 60 percent of social workers estimated that everybody in their communities was maintaining regular hand hygiene, 80 percent that they were all using masks, and 52 percent that everybody in their communities was practicing increased social distancing; in addition, 77 percent of respondents explained that everybody in the communities was worried about the pandemic and its effects.[8] For comparison, in March 2020, sociologists from the Slovak Academy of Sciences conducted a nationwide survey that revealed, on the basis of self-declaration, that the vast majority always wore face coverings outside their homes (90 percent), that half had reduced their social contacts significantly (47 percent), and that many worried significantly about the pandemic (39 percent).[9] While different methodologies do not allow us to compare the results directly, they do suggest similar trends for the same period among the Roma as well as among national populations. Taking into account the serious obstacles to compliance with measures based on the poor housing conditions in many Roma communities (such as the impossibility of individual quarantine, or the lack of running water), it can be concluded that Roma in marginalized communities nevertheless behaved in a similarly responsible way in relation to the pandemic as the majority population.

In the interest of fairness, we should stress that the first wave of the pandemic was accompanied by a high level of stress and a fear of the unknown, which must have played a role in the events we are describing, shaping the decisions of policy makers. It is also true that the Roma were not the only group considered to be a threat. There were also the so-called "pendlers" (cross-border commuters), homeless people, and those traveling for vacation abroad. However, unlike Roma, who underwent nationwide testing with massive media coverage, the proposed stringent measures targeting these groups were not implemented. Although we do not necessarily consider the testing carried out in the settlements to have been harmful in itself, we do think that it contributed to the stigmatization of their inhabitants.

It certainly could have been implemented more sensitively, such as paying more attention to the ways it might increase the stigmatization of Roma.

This stigmatization is not new. Instead, it builds on entrenched and widespread notions about Roma that have permeated policy making during the pandemic. One of the results of this stigmatization is the high level of distrust in the state and its authority on the part of Roma, who, unsurprisingly in view of what we have described, do not feel part of Slovak society. This distrust was made palpable in a series of hoaxes that circulated during 2020 and 2021 among Roma.

Fear and Distrust among the Roma

The first of the hoaxes or myths were reported to us by social workers during the survey mentioned above. According to them, COVID-19 did not pose a threat to Roma because they had different genetics from the majority, and so they were immune to the disease. It appeared to be supported by the fact that the numbers of those infected in the Roma settlements seemed low, and by the fact that, at least to start with, most people did not know anybody who had been infected. However, a reflection on the structure of such rumors (Roma as specifically protected from coronavirus) invites us to wonder to what extent it is related to the desire of Roma to subvert the existing hierarchies, to be protected and "at an advantage," at least in this case. We do not have the answers but ask the reader to treat these questions as food for thought.

Distrust in the state and a sense of threat were also contained in a second hoax, which emerged from the April 2020 survey mentioned above. It warned Roma against testing that was being rolled out in the spring of 2020. According to this hoax, either Roma would be infected during the test, or the tests were in fact a cover for carrying out an experiment on them. We believe that this rumor was the result of the fact that the testing was insensitively organized and communicated by the state authorities, which created fertile ground for misinformation. The process of testing Roma communities did not do much to strengthen the already fragile trust of the Roma in the institutions of the state—indeed, it rather had the opposite effect.

At a certain stage of the first wave of the pandemic, it was reported that policy makers were considering creating a quarantine center for Roma in the Lešť military area. While in fact the plans to set up a mobile hospital and quarantine center were not aimed at Roma specifically, a rumor developed that Lešť would be a concentration camp, where the Roma were going to be imprisoned or liquidated. Here the collective memory of the events of the Second World War and the fear of the contemporary actions of the state seem to have blended together. It is a pity that a high-quality information and awareness-raising campaign was not provided by the authorities. On the other hand, it must be acknowledged that the country found itself in a situation for which it was not prepared, and that many measures were having to be decided during a time of stress. Unfortunately, it cannot be said that the time between the first and second waves was used effectively. In any case, all the actions of the actors involved (including media outlets) will need to be seriously analyzed in order to have a chance to learn for the future—especially how to communicate about these vulnerable groups in times of crisis.

Conclusion

The pandemic has revealed how vulnerable the marginalized Roma in Slovakia are, as well as how society views them in times of crisis. It presents us with a very serious warning that Roma will continue to be exposed to a disproportionate risk in the event of any further pandemic waves or other social crises. Support for the inhabitants of marginalized Roma communities was not well received by the public. In public discussions, such as on social media, but also in opinion polls, it becomes clear that a significant part of society perceives the promotion of support for Roma negatively, as evidence of undeserved preferential treatment. Yet practical experience from municipalities and cities suggests that the attitude of the majority is very important for development and planning—for example, when deciding how to invest in infrastructure projects—and it can be central to decision making by local governments.

Fake news circulating among the Roma during the pandemic suggests that they do not always feel part of society and that they are suspicious of the actions of the state. This is probably the result of intergenerational memories of tragic historical periods, but also of currently lived experiences of exclusion and discrimination. Generalized reports "about the Roma" speak of a high degree of social distance between the majority and minority, and of the presence of prejudices in the attitudes of the majority population. It is particularly regrettable that the public pronouncements of some politicians and experts involved in forecasting the development of the pandemic also generalized about Roma or the inhabitants of Roma communities, without taking into account their diversity or their social position. These two points we consider to be an important finding. The legacy of hoaxes and rumors *among* the Roma, as well as *about* the Roma, must be taken into account when developing public policies for the support and inclusion of Roma, and also when communicating publicly about them.

The second wave was different. The country was hit harder, the numbers of hospitalizations and deaths were high, and the restrictions affected everyone. The Roma were no longer an ever-present issue, nor were there any specific measures for them (except for outreach projects with very little media coverage). This correlated with the decrease in rumors and hoaxes about Roma that we observed. At the same time, there has been a growing acceptance of untruths throughout society in general, not excluding Roma. For example, in the aftermath of several months of nationwide testing, which was received very negatively by part of the population, various rumors emerged associated with it (e.g., about microchipping in order to bring the population under stronger control, or about an intention to misuse the biological material taken for unfair scientific purposes). The vulnerability of Roma to rumors and conspiracies is probably not higher than that of the rest of the country's population (the level of distrust in the state is generally low anyway in the Slovak Republic), but their content and effects on interethnic relations is worthy of more attention.

Doc. Mgr. **Jurina Rusnáková**, PhD, is a university teacher, and director of the Institute of Romani Studies at the University of Constantine the Philosopher in Nitra, Slovakia. She has studied social work with a focus on Roma communities. In her scientific and pedagogic work, as well as in practice, she deals with issues to do with Roma integration.

Zuzana Kumanová, PhD, completed her doctoral studies in ethnology in 1998, on the topic of the Roma family. She has since been working in the non-profit sector, but also in the state sphere, where she has focused on the design of public policies in relation to the Roma. She lives in Bratislava.

Notes

1. TASR, "Ombudsmanka."
2. Kosová, "Výzva."
3. See for instance the petition initiated by the some activists: https://www.peticie.com/vyzva_mimovladnych_organizacii_vlade_sr_k_bezodkladnemu_odstraneniu_diskriminanych_opatreni_voi_romskym_marginalizovanym_komunitam (last accessed 21 June 2021).
4. Also, the expertise of the Office of the Plenipotentiary of the Government of the Slovak Republic for Roma Communities, the highest state body dealing with public policies for the inclusion of marginalized Roma communities, was not widely used

in decision making. She argued for a need (a) to base decisions on the specificities of local conditions and against blanket decisions, given that the diversity of living and housing conditions across Roma communities is high; (b) to use the capacities of the helping professions; (c) to avoid adopting repressive measures (such as curfews, community quarantines); and (d) to set up a system of humanitarian aid and access to services in those settlements that were closed off. She also considered community testing (back then a novel idea, it should be remembered) a good step, and so participated in it. We share her sentiment but wish to suggest that the whole process was communicated badly, and the hullabaloo around it had the effect of mobilizing anti-Roma sentiments, which in turn became further entrenched.
5. UVZS, "Plán riešenia."
6. See MVSR, "Atlas."
7. Ms. Bučková was appointed a plenipotentiary on 1 April 2020.
8. Posting by Andrea Bučková on Facebook from 29 April 2020 (date of last access: 23 June 2021): https://www.facebook.com/andreabuckovaRK/posts/125270525 799514.
9. Results are available on the website of the Sociological Institute SAS. "Výskumníci sa pýtajú: Ako sa máte Slovensko?" [The researchers ask: How are you Slovakia?]. Last accessed on 21 June 2021 http://www.sociologia.sav.sk/cms/uploaded/3129_attach_TS_ASMS_Marec2020.pdf.

Bibliography

Kosová, Ingrid. "Výzva zástupcov a zástupkýň občianskej spoločnosti k vláde Slovenskej republiky" [Appeal of the civil society representatives to the government of the Slovak Republic]. *SME*, 23 March 2020. Retrieved 23 June 2021 from https://komentare.sme.sk/c/22365845/musime-chranit-aj-ludi-v-osadach.html.

Ministerstvo Vnútra (MVSR). "Atlas rómskych komunít 2019" [Atlas of Roma communities 2019]. Retrieved 3 September 2021 from https://www.minv.sk/?atlas-romskych-komunit-2019.

TASR. "Ombudsmanka sa pre karantenizáciu rómskych osád obrátila na generálneho prokurátora" [The ombudswoman turns to the prosecutor general regarding the quarantine of Roma settlements]. *RTV Správy*, 25 February 2021. Retrieved 23 June 2021 from https://spravy.rtvs.sk/2021/02/ombudsmanka-sa-pre-karanteniza ciu-romskych-osad-obratila-na-generalneho-prokuratora/.

UVZS. "Plán riešenia Ochorenia COVID-19 v marginalizovaných rómskych komunitách" [Plan for addressing COVID-19 in marginalized Roma communities]. Last modified 3 April 2020. Retrieved 23 June 2021 from https://www.uvzsr.sk/index.php?option=com_content&view=article&id=4166:plan-rieenia-ochorenia-covid-19-v-marginalizovanych-romskych-komunitach&catid=250:koronavirus-2019-ncov&Itemid=153.

CHAPTER 18

OH, MY ANTIRACIST FRIENDS, WHERE ARE YOU?

A Health Expert's Diary of Hopes and Disappointments Regarding Pandemic Prevention and Control across Segregated Roma Enclaves

Andrej Belák

I am a health policy expert and, when the SARS-CoV-2 pandemic reached Slovakia in March 2020, willy-nilly I became co-responsible for the state's controversial approach to prevention and control of the virus's spread into, within, and from segregated Roma enclaves across the country. In search of useful lessons from this personal entanglement, in this chapter I briefly recap what frustrated me the most along the way, and contemplate the broader societal forces that might have shaped my experiences.

Exposition: Why I Got Involved and What I Hoped For

What were my initial concerns with regards to the pandemic? I feared that segregated Roma would inadvertently start bringing the virus home with them from abroad as part of their international migration. Slovak Roma seeking decent pay, and a modicum of respect and tranquility, were migrating to and from countries where the epidemic was already widespread or on the rise.[1] I was afraid that the virus would spread especially fast in segregated enclaves, mostly due to overcrowding, substandard infrastructure, and low levels of health literacy, combined with a common resistance towards many hegemonic biomedical standards of care.[2] I was frightened that the spread would stay unrecognized for too long, because I knew that Roma face complex barriers to access healthcare, including basic diagnostics, and I expected that they would come last regarding testing. I also feared that, despite the much younger age of segregated Roma compared to the national average, the spread might still turn deadly in the settlements given that biological wear and tear, including from chronic comorbidities, tends to be much greater among them, even in the younger age groups. Also, I expected the Roma would, by default, not be viewed, labeled, or approached by most other Slovaks as "at risk" but rather as "risky," due to the tradition of antigypsyism, firmly entrenched in all of Central and Eastern Europe. Finally, I feared that the local state officials and experts likely to be in charge would fail to mitigate all of these problems because of poor motivation, inadequate information, and a lack of tools.

Where did I get such specific concerns from? Determinants of the poor health status of segregated Roma in Slovakia have been the main subject of my academic research career since 2004.[3] In parallel, since 2014 I have worked as the lead public health consultant for an EC-funded "national project" called Healthy Communities, providing health promotion and mediation directly within 450 of the poorest Roma enclaves in the country via nearly three hundred community fieldworkers. In 2017, the project was fully adopted by the Slovak Ministry of Health (MoH), and it has since continued to be managed by the ministry's contributory organization called Healthy Regions, where I continue my expert role. Thanks to these engagements, during several years leading up to the pandemic I was increasingly invited as an external expert to central policy-making processes addressing health inequalities between Roma and non-Roma. For example, between 2014 and 2020 I actively participated in two rounds of revision and external evaluation of the Slovak National Roma Inclusion's Action Plans regarding health.[4]

What did I envision as the prevention and control features necessary for a successful mitigation of all the risks I have mentioned above, and why? I put all my bets on what I had learned to view as crucial over the previous two decades of related work: the more one works empirically, openly, and inclusively, the better for everyone involved. Under "working empirically," I meant planning any interventions based on what was already known regarding the causes of the poor health status of Roma in the country (Figure 18.1), combined with current pandemic-related data, ideally monitored down to the level of single communities. This, I thought, would base the interventions on solid evidence. By "working openly," I meant making it always publicly explicit which interventions targeted marginalized Roma enclaves as such—that is, as places being marginalized *because* they were inhabited by Roma.

Andrej Belák

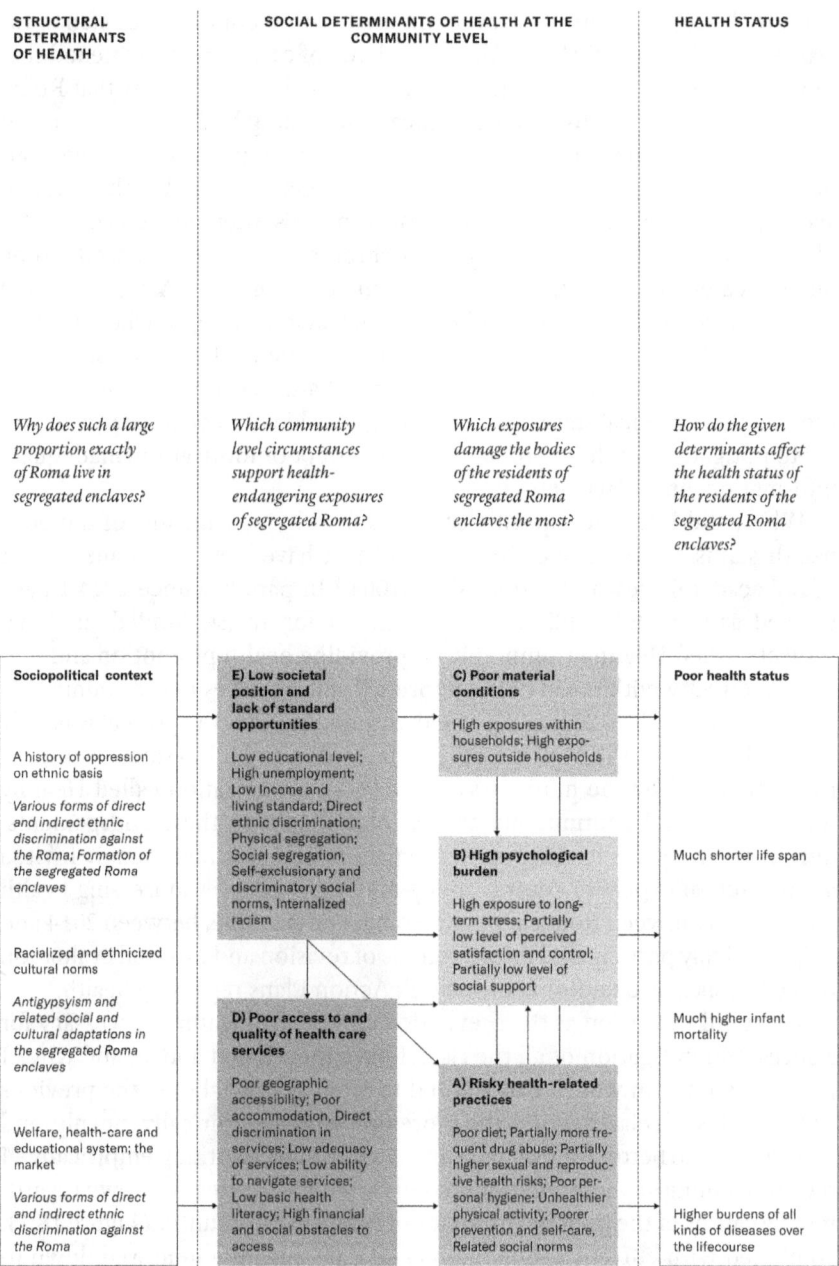

Figure 18.1 Determinants of the poor health status of segregated Roma enclaves in Slovakia. See also Belak, *The Social Determinants*, 11.

This, I believed, could prevent the usual silencing of what has previously been identified as the root cause behind the poor health status of the Slovak Roma—the various forms of both direct and indirect anti-Roma racism (see Figure 18.1)—and might allow us instead to mobilize more of the critically needed non-Roma solidarity with segregated Roma. Under "working inclusively", I meant ensuring that anybody with stakes in the epidemiological situation of the segregated Roma, including the Roma themselves, would become partners in the state's prevention and control approach throughout the whole cyclical process of its conception, implementation, and evaluation. Only such radical collaboration, I was convinced, could enable the ethical and (thus also) practical feasibility of the prevention and control approach.

What made me think that my requirements might eventually become adopted by the state officials and experts in charge of the pandemic management? I recall three main reasons. Firstly, I expected that the imminent threat of a highly infectious and potentially deadly epidemic reaching segregated Roma enclaves would be considered so urgent by the state agents and experts alike that they would be attentive to *any* informed and constructive ideas.[5] Secondly, I felt that, through our common expert work, both myself and the Healthy Regions organization had earned an unprecedented level of trust among state agents and experts within and outside the MoH, as they had increasingly started to approach us for consultations on matters that they openly understood as urgent and highly contentious.[6] Lastly, it seemed to me that the grand political shifts that Slovakia had gone through just before the pandemic might bring more direct support from the political hierarchy, precisely for the kind of principles I stood for.[7]

Rise and Climax: How I Got Involved and What Disappointed Me the Most

How did I try to push for what I thought was needed? From the very first days of the pandemic in Slovakia, I kept producing analyses, methodical proposals, revisions of others' analyses and proposals—all informed by the above principles—and I used them to keep bothering all the relevant actors I could think of, both within and outside my two related jobs, formally as well as informally. Eventually, I also tried to use these same principles to evaluate any implementations I could "in the field," in person in selected Roma enclaves.

For example, to secure the needed current data, during the first week of the pandemic I convinced the director of Healthy Regions to set up a system of continuous reporting via fieldworkers on the basic pandemic-related indicators for all the Roma enclaves in which the organization worked (approximately 75 percent of all poor segregated Roma enclaves in the country). To render the focus and purpose of this monitoring clear, it was explicitly dedicated to "COVID-19 within *marginalized* Roma communities." To enable feedback from the monitored people, prior to sharing any reported data with anyone outside Healthy Regions, several rounds of focus groups were held with the organization's fieldworkers regarding technical as well as ethical questions.[8] After the system was approved in-house, I started to bother other MoH departments (e.g., the public health authority) to connect with it as part of the general epidemiological surveillance system on COVID-19 that was already being set up across Slovakia.

Over the first year of the pandemic, I insisted on applying this style of work to all the COVID-19-related agendas that were targeting segregated Roma enclaves. These were (in chronological order): risk awareness campaigns; mass testing led by the Slovak army; health promotion, testing, clinical screening, psychological and humanitarian support for quarantined households (both individually and within community quarantines); management of the largest quarantine camp; design and implementation of several MoH-led intervention studies; conception and implementation of MoH pandemic control guidelines for municipalities; and vaccination campaigns and implementation.

Was my activity successful? It was in part, mostly thanks to the devoted engagement of the hundreds of fieldworkers from Healthy Regions. As usual in public health, we cannot know how much damage has been prevented through specific health-promotion and prevention activities, whether direct or online. Nevertheless, we do know that, in many of the segregated enclaves, basic preventative measures were adopted early as a direct result of these activities. We also know that in many places Healthy Regions succeeded in negotiating and assisting safer quarantine management with the local authorities; thus, access to testing, clinical examinations, medication, and psychosocial support remained available within most community quarantines.

Some structural advances were achieved, too, especially thanks to the usefulness of the Healthy Regions' COVID-19 monitoring system that I have described above. Based on the data generated through this system, the day-to-day cooperation between the organization and other major actors—state, municipal, and non-governmental[9]—quickly became systematic. Referring to the data provided by Healthy Regions, in October 2021 the then minister of health appointed Healthy Regions to set up and lead a collaborative expert panel on COVID-19 within marginalized Roma communities under the MoH's Pandemic Commission.[10] In turn, during the second wave between October 2020 and June 2021 the state interventions increasingly used local epidemiological evidence and the recommendations made by local fieldworkers. Drawing on successful interventions of this kind, the MoH expert panel issued *Recommendations Regarding COVID-19 for Municipalities with Marginalized Roma Communities*[11]—a pandemic control manual eventually endorsed by both the Slovak Chief Public Health Officer and the Office of the Public Defender of Rights of the Slovak Republic. As I write these lines, a successful pilot of "low-threshold mobile vaccination units" dedicated to vulnerable communities, including segregated Roma, working along the principles I pushed for, is being upscaled to the national level.[12]

So, why do I need to write about and emphasize my disappointments? Because throughout the pandemic, all the effort described above also met with continuous resistance and even misuses, which sometimes added to the negative impact of the pandemic on segregated Roma communities. For example, during the first wave, the data on returnees from abroad obtained by Healthy Regions were misused by the then central pandemic crisis management to justify the implementation of the first poorly prepared and oppressively managed community quarantines. Meanwhile, the same central crisis management obstructed the interconnection of the (mis)used monitoring system with the national surveillance system on COVID-19, significantly delaying the generation of more precise comparative analyses, better tailored interventions, and more accurate public reporting on the pandemic situation in segregated Roma enclaves.[13] During the second wave then, for most decision makers the continuing practice of poorly managed community quarantines did not become an impetus to support the proposals of Healthy Regions for more sensitive control measures, but rather was an argument against any prevention and control measures targeting marginalized Roma whatsoever. As a result, most recommendations of the MoH's collaborative expert panel were not systematically adopted into local municipal and public health authority practices until after the second wave had faded out.

But, to be honest, what frustrated and disappointed me most was that the fiercest and most successful opposition I encountered came from those pro-Roma activists and political representatives who were also state officials or experts, and whom I had originally expected to be my closest allies. For example, the initial central crisis management that failed to prevent the quarantining of segregated Roma settlements during the first wave was led by a Roma MEP from the government's leading party, with the public support of the newly appointed government's plenipotentiary for the Roma community. Throughout the pandemic, the most powerful and effective opposition to any collaborative proposals put forward by me or the Healthy Regions came from the plenipotentiary herself and from the first ever Roma state secretary (of the Ministry of Culture). Meanwhile, similarly to a wide range of other previously publicly active pro-Roma actors, the new president and her office refrained from making any public comments regarding how the pandemic was being managed by the state within segregated Roma enclaves.[14]

Epilogue: What Might Be Making Such Disappointing Experiences Likely?

Why did the other professional pro-Roma activists in power oppose the kind of approach to epidemic prevention and control that I was pushing for with respect to segregated Roma settlements? What was seen to be insufficient about my way of lobbying for evidence, transparency, and collaboration, and why?

Over the course of my involvement, I kept witnessing large-scale decisions concerning the segregated Roma being made in haste, mostly following only informal lay discussions, uninformed by related science or data, behind closed doors, and by a handful of people who were obviously overwhelmed by their workloads. No matter how hard I tried, and often contrary to previous agreements, most proposals I put forward from within these "decision-making processes" were eventually completely ignored, and with no explanation. On many occasions, some of the other decision makers would be openly unfriendly.

In such a context, it is hard not to reply to the above questions with yet more questions: Was it just something personal? Something I did in the past? Or something somebody said I did? Or something somebody said I was? Or was it, in fact, something about who I was? Was it my style or my motivations? Was the way I wrote and spoke too unclear, complicated, confusing? Was I coming across as arrogant? Or too candid? Was there something perhaps that made me seem untrustworthy? Or dangerous? Or was it rather about them, personally? Were some of them just too lost and too insecure? Or, on the contrary, were they just too polite to embarrass me with explanations of something I obviously did not understand? Maybe it was just too unbearable for them to have to deal with a (middle-class, anarchist?) non-Roma man who thought that he could understand (segregated, Catholic?) Roma? And so on... I only wish I knew!

But perhaps it is more useful to ask instead what social forces might be capable of setting different pro-Roma activists against each other even in the midst of an epidemiological crisis. Regarding this question, I am haunted by many worrying hypotheses, too. What if those in charge believed that some of my proposals would have been better for the segregated Roma but felt that they had no choice but to reject my ideas? What if opting for what I proposed would have jeopardized their positions of power? What if it were still impossible in Slovakia to occupy a position of power whilst insisting on evidence-based, transparent and inclusive decision making regarding the segregated Roma?

I wonder whether it is at all possible here to have a position of authority and yet insist that epidemiological evidence must be taken seriously in the Roma case. I wonder whether it is at all possible for those in authority to demand explicitly that that the quarantine policies of public health offices be systematically evaluated and disciplined for anti-Roma bias. And I wonder if it is at all possible for these authority figures to insist that segregated Roma must be personally present, and respectfully consulted too, in discussions regarding prevention and control targets and measures planned for their neighborhoods.[15]

It seems impossible in our country to become a powerful person—Roma or non-Roma—unless you avoid having any strong reservations about the segregated Roma. Perhaps this has something to do with the absence from public school textbooks of any discussion of the long history of Slovak racism. Perhaps it is just too complicated and embarrassing, even for intelligent and brave influential people, to talk publicly about how Roma ethnicity is conceptualized in Slovakia both by non-Roma, and by Roma themselves. Or perhaps it is much easier for everyone to believe that racist conceptualizations have already been phased out, or will eventually go away on their own, if we just stop talking about them. What if most of us believe that this is better than seeking ways to get rid of all racialized and racist understandings about any ethnic group?[16] And what if, in such a country, some Roma, including some of those in power, had become incapable of believing that they can ever trust and/or rely on any non-Roma?[17] I hope that one day we will all become brave enough to talk about these things.

Andrej Belák, MSc, PhD, is a medical anthropologist and social epidemiologist working at the Slovak Academy of Sciences. Since 2015, he has been working (in various roles) in academia and on behalf of the Slovak Ministry of Health as an expert and researcher specializing in the health of Slovakia's Roma.

Notes

The finalization of this chapter was supported by the project VEGA nr. 2/0066/19: "Patterns of Social Mobility of the Roma in the Light of Empirical Research. Critical Reflection of Existing Practices and Collection of New Data."

1. United Kingdom, Austria, Germany, Belgium, Italy, etc.

2. Some of the care standards—such as prevention, or seeking medical care for frequent respiratory infections, diarrhea, tooth decay, and obesity—are often viewed by my Romani interlocutors as too non-Roma (*gadžikane*), meaning exaggerated.
3. See, e.g., Belak et al., "Segregated Roma," and Belak et al., "Health Care Frontline Professionals." During the pandemic, I was employed in an academic capacity as a researcher at the Slovak Academy of Sciences.
4. This created some important personal challenges and tensions for me, because through my experience as an ethnographer working among segregated Roma I have come to appreciate resistance to the dictates of the state as a valuable political stance.
5. I did not expect decision makers to feel solidarity with the people living in the segregated Roma enclaves. Instead, I expected that most decision makers would be guided by the fear that epidemic hotspots within segregated Roma enclaves would easily lead to other people in the country being endangered.
6. For example, regarding remedial actions by the state to compensate for previous failures and to prevent future ones concerning the forced sterilization of Roma women in the country.
7. Following mass anti-corruption protests, in early 2020 a brand-new coalition of parties replaced the previous administration after thirteen years. Openly critical of the previous government's struggle with Roma inclusion, the leading party appointed a new Roma plenipotentiary, and brought three Roma MPs into the parliament—which is unprecedented. Also, shortly before the pandemic, the country's new president had publicly expressed her personal interest in the situation of the marginalized Roma, via public visits and references in speeches.
8. The vast majority of the nearly three hundred fieldworkers employed by Healthy Regions are themselves Roma from the same segregated enclaves in which they work.
9. Several major NGOs (especially People in Need, Way Out, ETP Slovakia, and Medicines Sans Frontiers), MoH's COVID-19 Intervention team, and regional offices of the Office of the Plenipotentiary for the Roma Community kept providing segregated Roma with humanitarian and clinical support throughout the pandemic. Collaboration between all the actors was coordinated through regular online meetings.
10. Organized to be led by the Healthy Regions' director, the panel quickly brought together experts from across the various disciplines—both academic and employed by the state public health authority, representatives of major NGOs involved in pandemic control within segregated Roma settlements during the first wave, and representatives from the Government's Office of the Plenipotentiary for the Roma Communities, including the plenipotentiary herself.
11. https://www.zdraveregiony.eu/odporucany-postup-pre-samospravy/.
12. Moreover, data from the monitoring system provided unambiguous evidence that, compared to the general Slovak population, people in the same age groups in segregated Roma enclaves were impacted about twice as harshly by COVID-19-related health problems (for more details, see the chapter "Introduction to the Slovak Chronicles").
13. After my direct appeals to the crisis management team failed to lead to any changes, I started to criticize the management publicly. In turn, both myself and Healthy Regions stopped being approached by the central state crisis management team until the management of the pandemic had been turned over to a new minister of health during the second pandemic wave six months later.

14. As for the forms of the resistance I encountered, they varied. Sometimes my invitations to meet to discuss proposals were politely refused, and at other times my suggestions were criticized in informal settings. I struggled to find a platform where I could openly debate with those who disagreed with my standpoint.
15. During the pandemic, I have been to numerous official meetings where 'activist' proposals of this kind—no matter by whom or how logistically detailed—were followed by people in charge, including current Roma political representatives, silently looking at their feet, sneering, or raising their eyebrows. The proponent would often not be invited back the next time.
16. One of the arguments I kept hearing against any tailoring of interventions according to the current living conditions of the segregated Roma was that, in a country that allows oppressively managed community quarantines, not speaking about Roma at all will bring them less harm than even the best intended attention.
17. Throughout the pandemic, some of the Roma in power were organizing parts of the decision-making processes along ethnic lines. For instance, the Roma MEP leading the initial state crisis management with respect to segregated Roma convened brain-storming discussions "to get feedback from the field," but involving only Roma mayors, even though most poor segregated Roma settlements do not have a Roma mayor. The same holds for most pandemic-related implementation pilots organized by the Office of the Plenipotentiary for the Roma Community.

Bibliography

Belak, Andrej. *The Social Determinants of Health and Health Needs across Segregated Roma Enclaves in Slovakia. Final Report from the Initial Phase of the Evaluation and Systematic Needs Assessment of Target Locations of the National Project Healthy Communities*. Kosice: UPJS University, 2020.

Belak, Andrej, Daniela Filakovska Bobakova, Andrea Madarasova Geckova, Jitse P. van Dijk, and Sijmen A. Reijneveld. "Why Don't Health Care Frontline Professionals Do More for Segregated Roma? Exploring Mechanisms Supporting Unequal Care Practices." *Social Science and Medicine* 246 (2020). https://doi.org/10.1016/j.socscimed.2019.112739.

Belak, Andrej, Andrea Madarasova Geckova, Jitse P. van Dijk, and Sijmen A. Reijneveld. "Why Don't Segregated Roma do More for Their Health? An Explanatory Framework from an Ethnographic Study in Slovakia." *International Journal of Public Health* 63 (2018): 1123–31. https://doi.org/10.1007/s00038-018-1134-2.

PART IV

POLISH CHRONICLES

CHAPTER 19

INTRODUCTION TO THE POLISH CHRONICLES
Digital Kinning and Care

Kamila Fiałkowska, Michał P. Garapich, Ignacy Jóźwiak, Elżbieta Mirga-Wójtowicz, Sonia Styrkacz, and Monika Szewczyk

Introduction

The Polish chronicles focus on the experiences of Polish Roma living in Poland, Britain, and Germany as they navigated, negotiated, and resisted mobility restrictions during the first months of the COVID-19 pandemic. While not essentially different from non-Roma Poles in their abilities to resist hostile migration regimes, Roma, due to their disadvantaged position and the discrimination they face, rely to a greater degree on migration social capital, and to a lesser extent on formal opportunities. As a result, it is even more important to focus on the role of migration culture—by which we mean norms, values, practices, and meanings related to mobility—in more ethnographic detail.[1] Whilst we call on the need to see Polish Roma migration as part of broader processes of migration from Poland, we also advocate exploring its specificity regarding practices of bordering, racialization, and securitization of migration regimes, which disproportionately affect Roma and can be seen as manifestations of antigypsyism. Our two chapters thus focus specifically on pandemic (im)mobilities of Polish Roma, analyzing them in the wider context of the changing atmosphere around the mobility of new EU citizens and around pandemic mobility restrictions, both of which contribute to the anxieties and insecurities that come with living transnational family lives. The second part of the Polish chronicles specifically looks at the attempts to maintain transnational bonds via the internet, and at practices of digital kinning.

Migrations of Polish Roma

In Poland, Roma constitute a highly heterogenous, albeit small, minority.[2] Numerous groups, sometimes referred to as *nacje* in Romani, inhabit Poland: Bergitka (known as Carpathian Roma or the self-ascribed Amare Roma), Polska Roma, Lovari, and Kalderasha. Dispersed across the whole country, this diversity reflects a complex Polish history as it points to a broader feature of Roma culture: their ability to adapt to complex new environments and challenges in an often hostile world without losing a sense of self or the continuity of certain traditions, meanings, and practices.[3]

The migration of Polish Roma follows a familiar pattern across the region of Central and Eastern Europe. The collapse of the socialist welfare system and the "shock therapy" of the introduction of free-market reforms meant that Roma who were employed by state industries[4] were losing their jobs, housing, and social assistance. Others were the target of aggression by local impoverished Gadje (like in the infamous town of Mława).[5] During the 1990s there was a massive outflow of Polish Roma seeking asylum or better opportunities in Western Europe and North America, with some communities rapidly depopulating, and even disappearing from the Polish social map.[6] Urban centers like Nowa Huta lost around half of their Roma. Unlike in Slovakia or Hungary, ghetto-like settlements physically separated from Gadje are rare in Poland. Across neighborhoods in almost all large and medium-sized towns, as well in some rural areas, especially in the south of the country, we find clusters of Roma households. The next large outflow of Roma and non-Roma alike began in 2004 with new access to the labor market in Britain, Ireland and Sweden and later in other EU member states. However, as a result of the economic crisis of 2008, social welfare cuts in Britain, uncertainties around the consequences of the Brexit referendum, and the rise of child benefit payments in Poland, there has been a noticeable number of returns.[7] The COVID-19 pandemic added yet another layer of uncertainty and, overall, due to migration processes that have spanned over at least thirty years, it has affected the lives of Polish Roma in Poland, Germany, Great Britain and elsewhere in a specific manner.

Our central contention is that mobilities and immobilities are connected, interdependent, and relational. In our two chapters we look into their various facets, having investigated, since 2016, recent experiences of im/mobilities of several Polish Roma families living not only in southern Poland, but also in Greater London and in Germany, many of whom we have known from our previous research[8] and maintain contact with, or are part of our networks of families and friends. Our current, much wider, research project has been to analyze how Polish Roma adapt and negotiate their group cohesiveness and group identity in the face of challenges posed by living transnationally across several social spaces anchored in several nation-states.[9] These challenges are locally and historically grounded, stemming from economic and social exclusion, racism, the welfare state transformations in post-1989 Poland,[10] pressures from within the group due to the erosion of established sources of authority, and the negotiation of gender roles, power structures, and cultural values.[11] As we have learned over the last several years, Roma families in Poland have migrated more often than their Gadjo neighbors, and this is in the context of Poland being traditionally seen as a migrant-sending country, both during the post-1989 transition and after the EU accession of 2004. Thus, it seems shortsighted, if not impossible, to study the impact of the pandemic on Polish Roma without considering the transnational dimension of their lives, as they navigate multiple social, political, and local contexts.

Due to the transnational living of many Polish Roma, they are uniquely positioned to discuss, exchange views, and decide what to do at times such as these, having several points of reference in terms of state structures, health systems, and discourses (Polish, British, and German in our project's case). To some extent, we have seen some returns during the pandemic, but overall, Roma have complied with the requirements of social isolation. What is certain is that they have adapted extremely quickly, with some fascinating outcomes visible online, like digital kinning practices, allowing for the celebration of family and religious holidays, and with online activities such as "challenges," some of which we discuss in individual chapters. In order to be able to continue our fieldwork and eventually to capture these processes, however, we have also had to adapt our project's methodological focus during the pandemic.

In Search of a Lost Fieldwork

Since 2016, the authors of our two chapters have been working on a collaborative research project[12] aimed at exploring and analyzing identity and boundary-making mechanisms in the transnational context in which many Polish Roma live. The project is sensitive to the complexity of Roma social realities, and it looks at migrants and non-migrants, young and old, men and women. We focus on the social and cultural consequences of migration and transnational living of Polish Roma, looking into various groups and family networks in Poland, Germany, and Britain, taking an intersectional and relational perspective on boundary making, both those demarcating Roma and Gadjo worlds, and boundaries within Roma groups as they become reformulated and negotiated as a result of transnational circulation. In the process, we attempt to fill a void in Romani studies as well as in migration discourse regarding the migration of Polish Roma.[13]

Taking an agentic and actor-centered approach, we examine how and what contemporary Roma actually do and say, instead of being constantly tossed around by the discourses, stereotypes, and policies invented and applied by the institutions, and by, broadly speaking, Gadjo worlds. We are convinced that to be able to do this requires not only the ethically sensitive recognition of postcolonial power relations and domination of the knowledge-production about Roma,[14] but something more obvious, albeit uncommon: the construction of a mixed Roma-Gadjo research team that takes dialogical intersubjectivity seriously, and labors towards discussing ideas and the power relations underpinning them in an egalitarian manner.

Our team includes both Roma and non-Roma researchers, thus gaining an additional aspect of trust from our respondents, and providing a response to the call for more researchers of Roma origin to take part in the production of knowledge about contemporary Roma.[15] This is a particularly important issue in Polish scholarship, where Roma voices have, until very recently, been remarkably absent.[16] However, the nature of the mixed team also means that we are constantly testing, questioning, and unpacking our own assumptions and stereotypes—whether they concern Roma, Gadjo, men, women, or (as researchers) ourselves. This self-reflexive mode of dialogical debate also keeps us attentive to what happens in the field. For the Roma researchers in our team, this is about extended family connections, the ability to carefully navigate between being Roma and being a researcher, and being a member of a particular Roma group while also studying it. For the Gadjo researchers in our team it is about recognizing our own positionality, privileges, and unrecognized power relations—and crucially, how previous discourses and social science work on Roma in Poland have been biased, racist, and classist. Apart from being Roma and Gadjo, we are also men and women from various class backgrounds. Testing these multiple facets of our identities is also part of the process.

The pandemic has thrown our project planning into disarray. The early lockdown of March 2020 ensured a relatively mild first wave of COVID-19 in Poland. Some restrictions were lifted in May, and after summer holidays the country continued to open up. In autumn 2020, however, a second wave struck the country very hard, with numbers of infections rapidly increasing and the health system coming under considerable pressure. In October 2020, the Polish government therefore announced a "zero tolerance" policy, and divided the country into zones, only later to declare the whole country a most restrictive "red zone." As of April 2021, more than sixty thousand have died of the disease, making Poland one of the hardest-hit countries in the EU.

The eruption of the pandemic coincided with our fieldwork entering the ethnographic phase. Faithful to Judith Okely's famous call for "ethnography without notes,"[17] a metaphor for an ethnographic practice that aims at minimizing the legacy of the dominance of Gadjo-the-professor-producer-of-knowledge-about-the-Roma (to which Roma respond in their own ways), we began a slow process of immersion into the lives of several family networks, known through personal contacts or from previous projects, and with whom a rapport of trust and understanding between research participants and researchers has been built over the years.

However, instead of slow immersion into the field—which means visiting friends, friends of friends and family, drinking lots of coffee (ground coffee put directly into a glass and boiling water poured over it) and endless talking, gossiping, chatting, and nodding—we found ourselves facing various degrees of lockdown and were forced to isolate. As of late March 2020, when time zones came to be more important than physical distance (people from the neighborhood and people from other countries seemed equally distant or equally close), the internet and social media became a legitimate, and sometimes the only, way to spend time with people outside one's household, By default, this became the only possible way for us to do ethnography. Lockdowns with their restrictions on mobility and social encounters meant that we needed to shift our approach entirely, moving mainly to online communications, conversations via Zoom or Skype, and observations of the very dense and active Roma social media. The initial sense of disappointment of not being able to fully immerse ourselves in the social lives of our respondents and "getting caught up in the daily life of the research subjects"[18] gave way to a realization that ethnography is about following people and the ideas and practices they engage in, wherever and however they manifest themselves. After all, the lives of the people we were meant to talk to and observe have also been disrupted (*toutes proportions gardées*), and for these the internet has emerged as *the* place to be, talk, and socialize. Thus the shift to online social interactions in order to construct and deconstruct boundaries, continue maintaining family relations, deal with community politics, resolve disputes, gossip, have romance and so on, was their way of dealing with that disruption.

From our standpoint, the internet is simultaneously a source of information, a field site and a means of mediated contact with our research participants.[19] Under the global online shift, the role of social media has increased in our daily lives and our research practices alike. This shift became magnified during the pandemic. Those of us who speak and understand Romani are also active social media users, and we participate in various Roma groups on social media. Discussing, commenting on, and sharing content related to Roma culture, community politics, and Romani studies is a part of our lives (literally, as we use our actual names in our accounts). This digital participant observation thus entails some aspects of auto-ethnography, because while doing research online we not only observe the practices that negotiate the identity and continuity of the group; we actively take part in that process, engaging in lively debates, comments, and exchanges of opinions about Roma lives, and about the status of Roma researchers, women, and individuals who have both Roma and Gadjo family roots. This observation part leans heavily on participating, as in the end we are often describing ourselves and our own families and friends. This ubiquitous online location pushes our multi-sited ethnography towards possible non-sitedness,[20] where spatial frames are no longer crucial for intimate relations and practices to occur, and where in addition the researchers' personas and identities are also a subject of reflection and auto-ethnographic self-evaluation.

Our move towards e-ethnography was not therefore borne out of convenience or unwanted necessity but was precisely because, especially during the pandemic, much of the social lives of the people we study—and our own as well—moved into that sphere. The Polish chronicles that follow are our unfinished, interpretatively raw, and unpolished attempts to conceptualize and make sense of how the consequences of the pandemic have caused turmoil for Polish Roma, wherever they may be.

Conclusion

The social, political, and cultural effects of the pandemic will be felt for years, even decades. The ways people, communities, and systems eventually adapt to new circumstances will probably take some time to make sense of sociologically, but what we can do as researchers is to document, report, and analyze how people reacted in the initial stages of the pandemic, as this was the moment the "not normal" becomes normalized, and the challenge of the unfamiliar new turns into the known routine. In face of the pandemic, Roma in Poland have been demonstrating tremendous resilience, but they also are being affected in new and unprecedented ways. As the old boundaries and alliances are being tested and tried, potentially new ways of doing Roma things, and relating to the Gadjo world, emerge. These Polish chronicles, we believe, provide just a glimpse, and signal the start, of a wider discussion in Poland not only about Roma—although this is much needed—but about minorities in general, which in the light of the increasingly dominant right-wing identity politics in this country is becoming quite challenging.

Kamila Fiałkowska is a researcher at the Centre of Migration Research, University of Warsaw. Her research focuses on migration from Poland. Currently she focuses on Polish Roma migration, inequalities, gender, religion, and national and ethnic identities of migrants from Poland.

Michał P. Garapich is a social anthropologist working at the University of Roehampton, London, associated also with the Centre of Migration Research at the University of Warsaw. He has published dozens of articles on issues to do with migration from Poland, transnationalism, far-right radicalization, homelessness, the politics of diasporic engagement, and auto-ethnography.

Ignacy Jóźwiak is a sociologist and social anthropologist (ethnologist). His research is centered around migration, transnationality, and translocality. His interests also include the areas of state borders and borderlands, ethnicities, and labor migration. He works as a researcher at the Centre of Migration Research, University of Warsaw.

Elżbieta Mirga-Wójtowicz is a cultural animator, political scientist, and researcher at the Centre of Migration Research, University of Warsaw. She holds a PhD in social sciences from the Pedagogical University of Cracow. She is the author of evaluation reports on Roma integration policy in Poland for the EC within the Roma Civil Monitor project in 2017–20 and for 2021–25.

Sonia Styrkacz is a psychologist and a pedagogue. She is a PhD candidate in social psychology at the University of Warsaw, Institute of Social Studies. Her research focuses on the Roma lifestyle phenomenon. She works at the Centre of Migration Research, University of Warsaw, on a project concerning the transnational lives of Polish Roma.

Monika Szewczyk is a PhD candidate at the Jagiellonian University. She is also a researcher at the Centre of Migration Research, University of Warsaw, focusing on the migration and ethnic boundary making of Polish Roma. Her research interests involve Roma migration, national and ethnic issues, and the role of oral history in identity politics.

Notes

1. For further analysis of the concept, see Cohen, *The Culture of Migration*.
2. According to government figures, officially around seventeen thousand Roma live in Poland, but with NGOs putting this figure closer to thirty thousand.
3. Stewart, "Roma and Gypsy Ethnicity."
4. This refers mostly to Bergitka Roma, who in general were more likely to be employed during socialism.
5. Some Roma families in Mława were well known for their used car dealership businesses, importing cars from West Germany. During their time of prosperity of the 1980s, several of those families built huge, baroque-style houses, which are still standing today, although in decay. By the end of 1980s, these Roma families in Mława were a relatively wealthy and influential group in the town. With the collapse of communism and subsequent economic shock therapy, this turned against them. In 1991, after a local Roma had caused a car accident in which a local Gadjo was killed, the local Gadje population organized an anti-Roma riot, targeting affluent Roma in the town, and resulting in major property damage (see Giza-Poleszczuk and Poleszczuk, "Cyganie i Polacy;" Kapralski, "Evolution of Anti-Gypsyism"). As a result of the ease of travel to the West and international attention, many Roma in the aftermath of the anti-Roma pogrom asked for asylum in Sweden, Germany, and Canada.
6. Fiałkowska, Garapich, and Mirga-Wójtowicz, "Polish Roma Migrations;" Fiałkowska, Garapich, and Mirga-Wójtowicz, "Why Do Roma Migrate?"
7. Fiałkowska, Garapich, and Mirga-Wójtowicz, "Polish Roma Migrations."
8. The research project "Continuity or Change – Anthropological Analysis of Polish Roma Migration Paths to Great Britain" was realized between 2016 and 2018 with the financial support of Polish National Science Centre, grant no. 2015/19/P/HS6/04125. The project has also received funding from the European Union's Horizon 2020 research and innovation programme under the Marie Skłodowska-Curie grant agreement No. 665778.
9. Anthias, "Where Do I Belong?" Glick Schiller, Basch, and Szanton Blanc, "From Immigrant."
10. Bartosz, *Nie bój się cygana*; Mirga and Mróz, *Cyganie*.
11. Fiałkowska, Garapich, and Mirga-Wójtowicz, "Polish Roma Migrations."
12. Project "Transnational lives of Polish Roma – Migration, family and ethnic boundary making in changing European Union" is funded by the National Science Centre, Poland, OPUS 16, grant no: UMO-2018/31/B/HS6/03006, duration 2019–22.
13. Fiałkowska, Garapich, and Mirga-Wójtowicz, "Why Do Roma Migrate?"
14. Kóczé, "Race;" Mirga-Kruszelnicka, "Challenging Anti-Gypsyism."
15. Mirga-Kruszelnicka, "Challenging Anti-Gypsyism."
16. With the exception of Andrzej Mirga, the first Polish Roma university graduate and an ethnographer. Recently, more Roma researchers have been entering the academia, including Tomasz Koper, Joanna Talewicz-Kwiatkowska, Anna Mirga-Kruszelnicka and three of the coauthors of these chronicles—Elżbieta Mirga-Wójtowicz, Sonia Styrkacz, and Monika Szewczyk.
17. Okely, "Knowing without Notes."
18. Del Baso and Lewis, *First Steps*, 212.

19. Caliandro, "Digital Methods;" Pink et al., *Digital Ethnography*.
20. Airoldi, "Ethnography."

Bibliography

Airoldi, Massimo. "Ethnography and the Digital Fields of Social Media." *International Journal of Social Research Methodology* 21(6) (2018): 661–73. https://doi.org/10.10 80/13645579.2018.1465622.

Anthias, Floya. "Where Do I Belong? Narrating Collective Identity and Translocational Positionality." *Ethnicities* 2(4) (2002):491–514. https://doi.org/10.1177/146879680 20020040301.

Bartosz, Adam. *Nie bój się cygana* [Don't fear the Gypsy]. Sejny: Pogranicze, [1994] 2004.

Caliandro, Alessandro. "Digital Methods for Ethnography: Analytical Concepts for Ethnographers Exploring Social Media Environments." *Journal of Contemporary Ethnography* 47(5) (2018): 551–78. https://doi.org/10.1177/0891241617702960.

Cohen, Jeffrey. *The Culture of Migration in Southern Mexico*. Austin: University of Texas Press, 2004.

Del Baso, Michael, and Alan D. Lewis. *First Steps: A Guide to Social Research*. Scarborough: International Thomson, 1997.

Fiałkowska, Kamila, Michał P. Garapich, and Elżbieta Mirga-Wójtowicz. "Polish Roma Migrations: Transnationalism and Identity in Anthropological Perspective." *Ethnologia Polona* 40 (2019): 247–75. https://journals.iaepan.pl/ethp/article/view/33.

———. "Why Do Roma Migrate? A Critical Analysis of Academic Silence in Polish Scholarship." *Critical Romani Studies* 2(2) (2019): 4–22. https://doi.org/10.29098/crs.v2i2.37.

Giza-Poleszczuk, Anna, and Jan Poleszczuk. "Cyganie i Polacy w Mławie: Konflikt etniczny czy społeczny?" [Gypsies and Poles in Mława: Ethnic or social conflict?]. In *Trudne Sąsiedztwa: Z Socjologii Konfliktów Narodowościowych*, ed. Aleksandra Jasińska-Kania, 221–47. Warsaw: Scholar, 2001.

Glick Schiller, Nina, Linda Basch, and Cristina Szanton Blanc. "From Immigrant to Transmigrant: Theorizing Transnational Migration." *Anthropological Quarterly* 68(1) (1995): 48–63. https://doi.org/10.2307/3317464.

Kapralski, Slawomir. "The Evolution of Anti-Gypsyism in Poland: From Ritual Scapegoat to Surrogate Victims to Racial Hate Speech?" *Polish Sociological Review* 193(1) (2016): 101–17. http://www.jstor.org/stable/44113928.

Kóczé, Angéla. "Race, Migration and Neoliberalism: Distorted Notions of Romani Migration in European Public Discourses." *Social Identities* 24(4) (2018): 459–73. https://doi.org/10.1080/13504630.2017.1335587.

Mirga, Andrzej, and Lech Mróz. *Cyganie: Odmienność i nietolerancja* [Gypsies: Difference and intolerance]. Warsaw: Wydawnictwo Naukowe PWN, 1994.

Mirga-Kruszelnicka, Anna. "Challenging Anti-Gypsyism in Academia: The Role of Romani Scholars." *Critical Romani Studies* 1(1) (2018): 8–28. https://doi.org/10 .29098/crs.v1i1.5.

Okely, Judith. "Knowing without Notes." In *Knowing How to Know: Fieldwork and the Ethnographic Present*, ed. Narmala Halstead, Eric Hirsch, and Judith Okely, 55–74. New York: Berghahn Books, 2008.

Pink, Sarah, Heather Horst, John Postill, Larissa Hjorth, Tania Lewis, and Jo Tacchi. *Digital Ethnography: Principles and Practice*. Thousand Oaks, CA: Sage, 2016.

Stewart, Michael. "Roma and Gypsy 'Ethnicity' as a Subject of Anthropological Inquiry." *Annual Review of Anthropology* 42(1) (2013): 415–32. https://doi.org/10.1146/annurev-anthro-092010-153348.

CHAPTER 20

PANDEMIC (IM)MOBILITIES OF POLISH ROMA

Sonia Styrkacz, Michał P. Garapich, and Kamila Fiałkowska

Introduction

Over a year into the COVID-19 pandemic (we write this chapter in late summer 2021), it is now obvious that the pandemic has affected us all, but not to the same extent. Many of the ongoing policy and social debates have revolved around the issues of mobilities and immobilities: why we move, why we should not move, who can move, who should stay in place, who cannot afford not to move. Some people have been able to work from home, safer from the dangers posed by the virus, while others have not had much scope for negotiation, especially when the work has required their physical presence (particularly in professions labelled "essential" to the functioning of their society, which did not translate into safer working environments). All of this has impacted the everyday functioning of families, including those who are living transnationally—apart, yet together.

The Polish Roma families who are the focus of this chapter live spread across Poland, Germany, and the UK. They are sustaining togetherness while being physically separated due to their permanent or temporary migrations. Like a growing number of people, they have learned how to practice togetherness through various means of communication, family visits, and reunifications, as in their everyday lives physical copresence has become a rare luxury. In addition, especially in countries more peripheral to global capitalism, absence and presence increasingly become markers of social inequality.[1] The pandemic and its aftermath have brought to light, more acutely than perhaps before, the unjust power relations of uneven mobility, inequality and power exercised through mobility regimes,[2] and their differential impacts on family relations.

Inevitably, the experiences of our family members have become an intrinsic part of our own journeys through the pandemic—this is how we have learnt what has happened with the relatives of our Roma team members, those working temporarily in Germany, visiting family in the UK, living in London or Sheffield, or remaining in Poland. In particular, Sonia's mother Tala, in her early 50s, has been a close collaborator, sharing many of her thoughts and experiences with us during the pandemic. She has offered an especially rich and informative account of how she and her multigenerational family experienced different stages of the pandemic. Whilst Tala lives in the south of Poland, members of her family live in different towns in Poland, as well as in Germany and the UK. Some relations have remained close, while with others the long absences have widened the emotional distance. The complexity of family relations with those family members who have never migrated, those who were temporarily moving back and forth, and those more recently arriving at their respective destinations in the UK has revealed itself during recent months. Their experiences of returning to Poland and quarantine, of enforced immobility under lockdown, and later of recurring migration, will guide us through this chapter. The chapter encompasses the struggles for the well-being of family members, the inability to get together with those who are away, and the economic difficulties that have affected much of the Roma population in Tala's city of residence. For those who have remained in Poland, the physical separation and inability to be with loved ones has proved particularly problematic during lockdowns.

For the time being, the pandemic, lockdown policies, and imposed immobility have somewhat overshadowed the other momentous changes shaping everyday lives within these transnational families: the Brexit process and the new emerging migration regime. Prior to the pandemic, the implications of these changes were already palpable in the tightening access to welfare for many EU migrants who are low paid and in precarious employment, including Roma. We are witnessing a process of bordering EU Roma citizens within the UK through covert state practices against families and households that discourage them from exercising the free movement rights guaranteed under EU law.[3] The impact of this bordering on the EU citizens living in Britain can be profound, particularly on those with limited language and digital skills. As reported by the Roma Support Group NGO, based in London, European Roma living in the UK face difficulties in presenting proof of their residence status within the new EU Settlement Scheme.[4]

Given this limbo, some have chosen to return to their home countries, while others have been waiting to see how things develop.[5] With Brexit and its effects receding into the background at the time of writing, the pandemic has been producing very tangible and immediate effects that are impacting the everyday realities, plans, and functioning of people. Centered on Tala's narratives, we want to zoom in on some of these aspects, documenting the reactions, fears, conversations, and actions of some research participants in our project.[6]

Transnational and Translocal Care

Lockdowns, both in Poland and abroad, were widely discussed and commented on both transnationally online[7] and in face-to-face meetings by the Polish Roma migrants we are in touch with. Like for other migrants, for Polish Roma migration is seen as a step towards financial independence or a means for emancipation from the confines of family obligations. At the same time, however, it brings risks to the maintenance of the social and family ties that are so central to Roma families. These families are often extremely close-knit despite being widely spread across Poland and abroad, and they provide individuals with social support and space for being Roma (although not always understood in the same way across all generations or among the different Roma groups in Poland). For many of our respondents, the effort maintaining family links sustains their social status, just as respect within the community is linked to their socioeconomic position, gender, family status and age. This in turn translates into support networks within families and the wider Roma community, both in their hometowns and abroad.

During our research we have witnessed how Polish Roma families, not without problems, manage these tensions, diffuse conflicts, and maintain solidarity and cohesion, as well as how individuals negotiate space for some independence. We have observed how some family members have attempted to influence the behavior of others living outside of Poland, not only to preserve norms and traditions but also to confirm the intragroup relations between the two largest Roma groups: Polska Roma and Bergitka Roma. Inevitably, however, some ties have become loose due to prolonged absence, distance, and fewer opportunities to interact. For our Roma collaborators, just as for other migrants, migration is a potentially disruptive situation, but the strain on family ties has been exacerbated by the pandemic.

Migration brings changes to the everyday functioning of the families, which are commented on and variously resisted, anticipated, and feared. Many Roma talk about these changes as they relate to the perceived evolution of traditional ways of life. Tala and her cousin Szandor, a man in his mid-40s, recount, at times nostalgically, their childhood memories or the stories of their elders as they speak about the changes, which are linked with migration and are caused by their immediate social environments. Their words reflect their ambivalence about attempts to reconcile modernity with the Romani way of life:

> **Tala:** Times have changed, become modernized. Everyone wants to improve their lives. We have the internet, these new technologies, younger ones don't listen to the elders, and Romani people are becoming more modernized too, less traditional.
>
> **Szandor:** It was unthinkable back in my days that Roma didn't know how to play music, how to dance. They are not interested in it [now]; luckily they still speak the language, but they live more like Gadjo now ... Young people look at how others live.
>
> **Sonia:** And how about migration, has this affected how they live?
>
> **Szandor:** For sure ... Romani people, just like in music, it changes under the influence of the local music ... so is the way in life, they go there [abroad]. Some things are kept, but all else changes to how it is in these new places. They evolve, they move on, but it is not sure if this progress is so good. Life becomes ... running after money ... and they don't take care of their spiritual development, they don't take care of their relations, they don't call, don't have the time.
>
> **Sonia:** So this is what you fear, that this younger generation will forget?
>
> **Szandor:** Yes, that they will forget that they are Gypsy, or will be ashamed of this.

Tala and Szandor refer to their relatives with whom, after years of them living in the UK, the contact has loosened up. This is their firsthand experience of how migration puts pressure on social fabrics. However, as the conversation progressed, they both admitted that despite these ongoing changes in their social-family circles, they have witnessed significant "Roma" ways of caring for one another, which they put at the center of their understanding of *Romanipen*, as they explain below:

> **Szandor:** We can argue, not talk with one another; sometimes when I am angry with my brother and don't talk with him, he calls our friend and this friend calls on me to check on me if I am healthy and alright ... this is our *Romanipen*, sometimes we fight, we argue, but then...
>
> **Tala:** Is he not hungry, doesn't he suffer?... We care about one another, like our mother, she is very caring, but she doesn't show emotions, she is tough, to show that we are faring well. But we are very caring, old generations are like that.

As Tala and Szandor explain to Sonia and Kamila, mutual support and care are at the center of how the Roma should be. Especially during the challenging times it is important to reaffirm that no one is left behind. This is the core of *Romanipen*, the uncodified common law that defines the Roma ways of living and being, and the boundary between Roma and Gadjo. In the past, *Romanipen* proved essential for survival in the hostile social environment. It has also become central to the maintenance and reconstruction of social life during the pandemic, although the lockdown and social distancing measures have put it under strain.

Romanipen during the Pandemic

Enforced immobility during the pandemic has affected those who lived in Poland, as well as their relatives abroad, whether temporarily or permanently. It has impacted family and community lives and caused great anxiety about how to continue living according to Roma life cycle rhythm and rituals. The anticipation of the inability to get together—whether for a funeral, to meet elders to show respect (*paćiw*, in Romani), or to discuss important family matters—has generated deep distress not just to individuals; it has threatened the very survival of family bonds, which are central to our interlocutors' sense of self, as they directly link it with their understanding of *Romanipen*. In the next chapter, our colleagues Monika Szewczyk, Elżbieta Mirga-Wójtowicz, and Ignacy Jóźwiak capture ways of managing tensions and expectations through, for instance, streaming funerals or saying prayers for someone's health on behalf of any members of the family who could not attend in person; through posting pictures of newly engaged couples to spread the news among the community members; or by simply connecting celebrations (like an Easter dinner) in Poland, Germany, and the UK via video-conferencing. Here we want to focus on the economic aspects of social support and recognition.

From mid-March until June 2020, when the strictest lockdown measures were being implemented in Poland, many livelihood options were cut off, especially for those without stable jobs or incomes. Many of our respondents in Poland had worked in local bazaars, trading in textiles and other housewares, and they found themselves in a particularly troubled position. During the months when they could not make money, the social network provided them with much needed support. This was *Romanipen* translated into action:

> **Tala:** We were supporting one another back then. For instance, when the bazaars were closed, someone got their pension or some benefits, "Do you have food? You don't? Ok then, have this" . . . , and life goes on, we need to get by, it is good that family holds us together. It doesn't matter if you are angry with someone, we still care that everyone has the means to survive.

As Tala explains, family conflicts and personal animosities should be put aside when people need to get by. When the lockdown and social distancing measures made physical presence and meetings impossible, people maintained contact via frequent phone calls, sent money to the close ones in need, or did shopping for neighbors, leaving groceries by their doors. The importance of sharing, care, and support, whether in-kind or financial, came to the fore as an expression of *Romaniness*,[8] especially among those of our respondents who experienced financial problems during the pandemic. This applied as much to those who were in lockdown nearby, in the same town or city, as to those living away in different countries.

In the face of the unknown virus and the threat it posed, transnational contacts with some family members have been revived during these months. As Sonia told the rest of the team, when she reflected on her own family members, many of whom have been living in the UK for years, "people were afraid, some panicked that there will be deaths, and they will not manage to meet with one another." This sense of uncertainty has pushed people to reach out to one another, thereby intensifying contacts, even those that earlier may have been sporadic at best.

"Half of the People Are Going to Die Here"

The pandemic and the dangers it brings have been widely commented about on social media among Polish Roma, both in Poland and abroad, as people have been exchanging information, and sharing news and fears. During the early months of the pandemic (between March and May 2020), when people were trying to find out what was happening and were learning how to navigate their fears, we came across a statement in one of the Facebook group discussions by a Polish Roma living in the UK: "Half of the people are going to die here." Within a discussion about the lockdowns and the state of the national healthcare system, his was the voice of despair about the overall situation in the UK and its poor management of the enormous health crisis. This perceived ill management (and Brexit) has undermined the already fragile trust both our Polish Roma respondents and their Gadjo compatriots in the UK have for the British healthcare system.[9]

The various developments and timelines of implementing social distancing measures and lockdowns in Poland, Germany, and the UK matter. Starting in early March 2020, the Polish authorities implemented a series of social distancing and lockdown measures (obligatory masks in public spaces, closure of schools and universities, suspension of public events, and restrictions on gatherings; even some public parks were closed). The implementation of the social distancing and lockdown measures took place at a similar time in Germany. While this was reassuring for many of our respondents, providing, it seems to us, some sense of security, the situation in the UK was strikingly different. The UK entered lockdown roughly two weeks after most EU states, and even after the initial actions towards curbing the virus were taken, people expressed their worries and insecurities both in person and through social media, and thus some felt urged to take matters into their own hands, opting to return to Poland. A year later, in early 2021, the situation has strikingly changed, with the UK implementing and enforcing lockdowns and effectively curbing the infection levels. In Poland, prolonging lockdown (from October 2020) had little or no effect on the infection rates or on preventing excess deaths (over 68,000 deaths as of 4 May 2021, and an especially high numbers of deaths in March and April, with weekly averages ranging between 250 and 600).

The constant messaging from the media about the prohibition of family visits and the widely reported common instances of people dying alone, or among strangers in hazmat suits, has exacerbated the fear and anxiety among our respondents. In the opinion of those who have been living abroad, they would receive better healthcare in Poland. Perhaps it is important too that insufficient language has made some unable to communicate well with doctors.

Fearing that borders would be closed and that some would be stuck without a chance to be reunited with families in Poland, some planned an organized route out of the UK. These fears were fueled by social media and by the constant exchange of news, comments, pictures, and live streams. Posts on social media called for organized convoys with cars, perhaps because of having heard about such arrangements among Roma from neighboring Czechia and Slovakia. In reality, a month into lockdown, when the darkest predictions vented on social media had not taken place in reality, we and our respondents started to settle into the "new normal."

The implementation of lockdown in Poland meant that all borders were temporarily closed and only Polish citizens (and some categories of foreigners) could enter the country. Upon doing so, they then had to undergo a fourteen-day quarantine. In her fieldnotes, Sonia captured how this affected her family: "From December to beginning of March [2020], my mum's partner was in Canada. He feared that he wouldn't be able to return home. It was clear from his observations that in Canada the situation didn't seem as dire as in Europe back then, at least as it was shown in the media ... My mum was very worried by all this, that he would get infected."

The communication about closing the land and air borders was somewhat chaotic, making many people genuinely afraid they would be stuck without any prospect of returning home. As the last commercial flights were entering Poland, the government started bringing its citizens back with special flights, adding to the drama of these moments. Tala's household, as was expected, needed to quarantine for fourteen days, as reflected in Sonia's fieldnotes:

> So when he finally got back [March 2020] he had to undergo a quarantine, for two weeks. Also my mum. It was VERY stressful for us all. We needed to logistically sort out the days when we did shopping for them, and the police would come daily to check on them ... To the neighbors it was clear that there were people in quarantine on the block, and this caused discomfort. The neighbors know that we are Roma, as they have lived here many years, and they have got used to it, but I feared there would be some troubles.

They were the only family in the neighborhood under quarantine and the police were checking on them daily, just as they did in all cases of official quarantine in the country. Sonia recalls how she was worried that her mother and her partner could easily be accused of spreading the disease by their Gadjo neighbors. Sonia's family paid careful attention to the rules of the quarantine so as not to make the slightest slip, but not knowing if it would be enough. COVID-19 stigma and prejudice has been widely reported from many parts of the world, and worryingly enough, it has been for the most part the experience of migrants and ethnic minorities.[10] The introduced measures affected them, as they would affect anyone else in a similar situation, but given their experiences with the Gadje world they also anticipated additional troubles caused by their belonging to a minority that was commonly stereotyped as not playing by the rules.

Oblivious Summer

Summer 2020 brought a much-needed break to living under confinement, and fear of the coronavirus in Poland soon decreased because of the relatively low levels of infections and deaths. The warm days enabled people to socialize outdoors, making them feel more secure. Many among us had missed the regularity of social life and meeting people physically instead of seeing them on laptop or smartphone screens, and we hurried to reestablish a sense of normalcy. This is perhaps why the initiative to stage the Roma music festival in Nowa Huta, as it had been for the previous six years, was met with much enthusiasm. The event would have occurred in late July, but there were prolonged discussions about whether it was safe to hold it or not. Finally, however, after seeing that many other summer festivals were taking place (although on a smaller scale), the decision was made to hold it. Elżbieta Mirga-Wójtowicz, a member our project team, was in the audience, and this is how she reflected upon the event in her field notes:

It started at 6 p.m., and despite the pandemic so many people came, more Roma than at the previous editions! Older ones, often not in good health, families with children, all came near to the stage, even though that evening was a bit chilly. Besides Roma from Kraków, there were many from other towns in Poland, [later she explained that a few had also come from England for family visits]. People were tired with the ongoing state of insecurity and tensions. They often repeated that they miss contacts with families and friends. Communions had been postponed, and a few weddings ... We were afraid, but we hadn't seen each other for so long.

One family I talked to said that they normally go between Poland and England, and they noticed that now in Poland people were not taking all the restrictions seriously, and that in England they wore masks and were much more careful. There were moments during the concert that I had the feeling that the pandemic had ended.

One family we met at the festival had come from England for the summer, to the Polish Tatra Mountains where their relatives live. Before they boarded their plane in Kraków to return to England, they visited the festival. For them, as for many participants, the festival and above all the time with others was a symbolic end of the summer and its relatively joyful and less stressful atmosphere. Quite ironically, many of our Roma respondents who visited Poland during the summer were astonished by the cavalier attitude towards wearing face masks and restrictions regarding public gatherings they observed in many places in Poland. This was in sharp contrast to the different approaches that had been taken by the two countries in the early months of pandemic, during the so-called first wave.

In the early autumn of 2020, the pandemic was still there, yet distanced: everyone knew about it, yet it was easy to forget. The cooler and shorter days heralded the end of the season of lifted restrictions and from day to day we were faced with the second wave, and eventually a third wave, of the pandemic. In October, with worryingly high numbers of deaths and skyrocketing levels of infections, Poland and neighboring countries entered a long and ever-extending lockdown. The prospects of the winter loomed dark on the horizon.

"Off We Go, to Get Back the Jobs We Once Had"

Those of our informants who had temporarily migrated to Germany or the UK felt doubly trapped by measures taken by governments in the first months of the pandemic. Along with their colleagues, they had travelled from their homes in Poland to workplaces abroad, but then their work ended abruptly—for some, as early as March 2020. With lockdown policies rapidly changing across the EU countries and being communicated in a chaotic manner, they encountered troubles getting back home. At that time, it was unclear whether the borders would be closed to everyone, when closures would be enforced, how long they would last, and many other uncertainties. While the Polish government published new instructions, some contradicting earlier ones, the internet blossomed with interpretations, often distorted news, and fake news. Initially, "door-to-door" international shuttle buses stopped operating as the drivers were unsure if they needed to undergo quarantine when crossing the border, the popular online Bla-Bla car-sharing platform was of no help, it was difficult to buy train tickets, and there were no flights. Contacts with people returning to Poland with their own cars were worth their weight in gold.

One problem was how to return home; but another was the lack of jobs and offers in the coming weeks and months (typically in the building and service sectors) back in Poland. The pandemic brought stresses not only related to health but also to economic existence. This applied to both the long- and short-term Roma migrants we were in touch with, as well as to their non-migrating family members.

Potential temporary migrants who found themselves still in Poland, on the other hand, were also waiting to hear more convincing news that the pandemic was being curbed in their intended destination in the UK or Germany, and that death levels there had fallen. At least for some time, these fears prevented some from going abroad, even though in some cases we know employers had contacted the workers and asked them to return. Slowly, however, the typical routes for temporary migration both to Germany and to the UK reopened. The internet forums provided instructions on how to organize a stay, find a flat and insurance, and fulfil the other administrative tasks needed under the current circumstances. Nearing the summer of 2020, different restrictions were being lifted each week, especially for workers in certain sectors of the labor market. Those Roma we are in touch with, working for example in the construction sector, report that the demand for skilled workers has been stable despite the pandemic, and that only coronavirus restrictions were making temporary work abroad more complicated to organize.

"I Wouldn't Go There If Not for the Coronavirus"

The pandemic exacerbated the existing inequalities and systemic problems the Roma face on a daily basis. Especially for those who had already been in a precarious position prior to the pandemic, its outbreak and the lockdowns have had a tremendous impact on their well-being. Anxiety over being able to satisfy the financial needs of their families, especially after the several difficult months, led some to decide to move abroad temporarily. Sonia and Kamila had discussed these matters with Tala two days before she departed for the UK to join her partner in September 2020:

Tala: I'm afraid of one thing really, [which is] catching this coronavirus. I'll manage the rest somehow. My husband works, so we'll have just enough to buy bread.

Sonia: And if it wasn't for the coronavirus, would you go?

Tala: Well, I guess not, because it's not so bad in Poland, well . . . but I'll tell you, I won't go to stay there permanently, only for a few months, because I have a daughter, a granddaughter, the whole family here, and although we live a bit further away, we are close. We always call each other, whether my sister, or daughter, or brother or whoever—that's how it is. He [her husband] has a family there [in England], he has children there from his first wife, [so] he is close to this family. He went there because for almost a year he didn't see his children or his granddaughter or anyone. So I will go there, you know, you need to compromise a bit.

In this segment, Tala thinks out loud that perhaps if not for COVID-19 she would have stayed in place and continued working in the marketplace in her hometown in Poland. But this, as she explained earlier, was made almost impossible during the pandemic—first because the market was shut down, then because people were afraid to come close and see the products they were selling. She explained: "It's difficult these days, because of this coronavirus, people are afraid to approach one another, not to get infected, right? So we had to really encourage them, to come closer, to take a look and buy, and for really low prices."

Economic worries were the primary reason behind her visit to the UK, but no less important were the needs of the transnational family. Tala explained that her partner had returned to Poland in Spring 2020. But as his long-planned journey to the UK, where he had been living for more than a decade, had been postponed for several months by the lockdown, he had not seen his children for some time. When the travel restrictions were lifted, he decided to join them, as well as to find employment and support his relatives in Poland. Some months later, perhaps fearing that more mobility restrictions would be introduced, and—not without reason—anticipating a worsening of the general pandemic situation, Tala decided to join him. She stresses, however, that it will only be temporarily, and it has been caused by her understanding of the complex situation and the family needs of her partner.

Conclusion

Pandemic (im)mobility is far more complex than our brief ethnographic sketches allow us to present in this chapter. We are all, to different degrees, affected by this complexity, and in our team we, along with our Roma research participants, are constantly trying to make sense of what is happening around us and to our own lives. As some of our respondents returned to the jobs they held before the pandemic, or were making their way back and forth between their temporary work in Germany, others returned back to their homes in the UK after a period visiting their families in Poland. These returns or short-term stays have not been caused by economic factors alone, but also by the need to be with close ones during these difficult times.

While writing this conclusion in late summer 2021, the pandemic is entering its next wave (third and counting), with the numbers of infections increasing in many countries, including Poland, Germany, and the UK. The months ahead will certainly bring more uncertainties regarding personal well-being and worries about the well-being of family and social networks, but we are also witnessing enactments of agency on the part of our participants who attempt to exert a degree of control over their socioeconomic environment. The relaxation of summer 2020 was much needed, but eventually, the relatively calm period of the pandemic and its first wave in Poland came to an end. Perhaps for some it seemed that the infections were not that deadly, and the precautions taken were not that necessary. Currently we are observing that awareness of the dangers is much higher with those people—including our team members—who have had firsthand experience of the impact of COVID-19. We see and hear about infections in our immediate social environments, with our friends, neighbors, family members, and distant kin going through the sickness, and sometimes the death of loved ones, and the mourning. The experience gathered in recent months is crucial—it is one of struggle and fear, but also of care and support, which, importantly, help to reassert the notion of *Romaniness* transnationally among the people we have been in touch with. For the months to come, with worryingly high numbers of infections and deaths, and what seems now like an endless lockdown, the modern means of communicating, just like in the spring of 2020, will serve as crucial "social glue" through which bonds can be reaffirmed, redefined, and tested.

Sonia Styrkacz is a psychologist and a pedagogue. She is a PhD candidate in social psychology at the University of Warsaw, Institute of Social Studies. Her research focuses on the Roma lifestyle phenomenon. She works at the

Centre of Migration Research, University of Warsaw, on a project concerning the transnational lives of Polish Roma.

Michał P. Garapich is a social anthropologist working at the University of Roehampton, London, associated also with the Centre of Migration Research at the University of Warsaw. He has published dozens of articles on issues to do with migration from Poland, transnationalism, far-right radicalization, homelessness, the politics of diasporic engagement, and auto-ethnography.

Kamila Fiałkowska is a researcher at the Centre of Migration Research, University of Warsaw. Her research focuses on migration from Poland. Currently she focuses on Polish Roma migration, inequalities, gender, religion, and national and ethnic identities of migrants from Poland.

Notes

1. Beck and Beck-Gernscheim, *Distant Love*, 162; Palenga-Möllenbeck, "Unequal Fatherhoods."
2. Sheller, *Mobility Justice*.
3. Greenfields and Dagilytė, "I Would Never Have Come."
4. Roma Support Group, *Brexit*.
5. Clark, "Stay or Go?"
6. Project "Transnational lives of Polish Roma—Migration, family and ethnic boundary making in changing European Union" is funded by the National Science Centre, Poland, OPUS 16, grant no: UMO-2018/31/B/HS6/03006, duration 2019–22.
7. See the next chapter by Monika Szewczyk, Elżbieta Mirga-Wójtowicz, and Ignacy Jóźwiak.
8. Bartosz, *Nie bój się cygana*, 170–71; Mirga and Mróz, *Cyganie*, 127; Koper, "Strategie adaptacji," 170.
9. Osipovič, "If I Get Ill."
10. Bilewicz and Olko, "COVID-19 stygmatyzuje."

Bibliography

Bartosz, Adam. *Nie bój się cygana* [Don't fear the Gypsy]. Sejny: Pogranicze, 2004.
Beck, Ulrich, and Elisabeth Beck-Gernsheim. *Distant Love*. Cambridge: Polity Press, 2013.
Bilewicz, Michał, and Justyna Olko. "COVID-19 Stygmatyzuje imigrantów i mniejszości etniczne" [COVID-19 stigmatizes immigrants and ethnic minorities]. Foundation for

Polish Science. Published 18 February 2021. Retrieved 25 August 2021 from https://www.fnp.org.pl/covid-19-stygmatyzuje-imigrantow-i-mniejszosci-etniczne-2/.

Clark, Colin. "Stay or Go? Roma, Brexit and European Freedom of Movement." *Scottish Affairs* 29(3) (2020): 403–18. http://doi.org.10.3366/scot.2020.0331.

Greenfields, Margaret, and Eglė Dagilytė. "'I Would Never Have Come If We'd Known It Might Be like This': On the (Un)Intended Consequences of Welfare Governance of EU Roma Migrants in Britain." *Intersections. East European Journal of Society and Politics* 4(3) (2018): 81–105. http://doi.org/10.17356/ieejsp.v4i3.447.

Koper, Tomasz. "Strategie adaptacji Romów w Polsce na przykładzie grup Polska Roma i Bergitka Roma" [Roma adaptation strategies in Poland on the example of Polish Roma and Bergitka Roma Groups]. PhD diss., University of Warsaw, 2018.

Mirga, Andrzej, and Lech Mróz. *Cyganie: Odmienność i nietolerancja* [Gypsies: Difference and intolerance]. Warsaw: Wydawnictwo Naukowe PWN, 1994.

Osipovič, Dorota. "'If I Get Ill, It's onto the Plane, and off to Poland.' Use of Health Care Services by Polish Migrants in London." *Central and Eastern European Migration Review* 2 (2013): 98–114. Retrieved 19 October 2021 from http://www.ceemr.uw.edu.pl/vol-2-no-2-december-2013/articles/if-i-get-ill-it-s-plane-and-poland-use-health-care-services-polish.

Palenga-Möllenbeck, Ewa. "Unequal Fatherhoods: Citizenship, Gender, and Masculinities in Outsourced 'Male' Domestic Work." In *Paid Migrant Domestic Labour in a Changing Europe: Questions of Gender Equality and Citizenship*, ed. Berit Gullikstad, Guro Korsnes Kristensen, and Priscilla Ringrose, 217–43. London: Palgrave Macmillan, 2016.

Roma Support Group. *Brexit, EU Settlement Scheme and the Roma Communities in the UK*, London, June 2020. Retrieved 25 August 2021 from https://www.romasupportgroup.org.uk/uploads/9/3/6/8/93687016/roma_brexit_euss_report_16.06.2020_final.pdf.

Sheller, Mimi. *Mobility Justice: The Politics of Movement in an Age of Extremes*. London: Verso Books, 2018.

CHAPTER 21

THE INTERNET AND TRANSNATIONAL POLISH ROMA FAMILIES IN A TIME OF PANDEMIC

Monika Szewczyk, Elżbieta Mirga-Wójtowicz, and Ignacy Jóźwiak

Digital Ethnography for the State of Exception

Dispersed across Europe, as country after country entered into lockdown in March 2020, Polish Roma families made efforts to sustain their ties with each other and with the larger Roma community. In this chapter, we analyze family and community practices of Polish Roma in Poland and abroad, mainly in the UK and Germany. We focus on the pandemic conditions and the accompanying state of lockdown and the need for so-called "social distancing." Our main emphasis is on the period of the strictest safety measures in Poland and the "onlineization" of social and professional life in late March and early April 2020, but we also take the subsequent few months into consideration.

Our observations about the period between mid-March and mid-September 2020 point to the diverse ways Polish Roma coped with the pandemic and the related safety measures through online activities. The practices we identify are not new and they are not exclusively characteristic of the Roma. However, with the lockdown regime in the springtime followed by its relative easing, these practices gained new dimensions. Referring to Roma families with whom we maintain contact, including our own families, we can say that (even before the pandemic context) there has been a drive to create a niche and a safe space for the maintenance of Roma language and culture online. In this respect, the internet has enabled uninterrupted contact with loved ones, and new forms for the cultivation of language and customs, even though they both change.

We are aware that the increased and extensive use of messaging apps and social media, the intersecting of online and offline lives is a universal phenomenon, and it should not be perceived as something distinctive for Polish Roma. Before the pandemic, digital interactions and extensive use of the internet were already essential for Polish Roma, whether in Poland or abroad. In the age of the general digitalization and transnationalization of life, the internet is helpful in maintaining language, traditions, and the feeling of group affinity among Roma in Europe and worldwide.[1] It allows individuals to stay in contact, exchange vital information, uphold intimacy, and cultivate family bonds.[2] What appeared novel for the non-migrant global majority has long been the norm for migrants and their families.[3] Lockdowns in the spring of 2020 turned migrants into a type of global pioneers in online technologies of digital kinning. Polish Roma in the UK and Germany are no exception in this regard. As we suggest, it does not mean that there is no difference between the digital lives of the Polish Roma and that of the Polish Gadje (non-Roma). The most notable aspect is the use of language or languages (different Romani dialects mixed with Polish to varying extents). Another refers to the bonds worked out by decades of living as a minority among a potentially hostile milieu. This has resulted in intensive sociability with other Roma in everyday life, to which migration presents a challenge and the internet a solution.

This chapter also contributes to the debates that mushroomed on various humanities and social science blogs and across social media in the spring of 2020.[4] Multiple concerns were raised about the lockdown and "social distancing" becoming the new norm, about citizens' vulnerability in the face of state apparatuses, and about the limits that anti-epidemic measures put on mutual care and solidarity.[5] Reading these interventions helped us theoretically to unravel our "exceptional" situation. At the same time, our online observations and participation help us fill the empirical gap that emerged in the research process during our current project.[6] Through observing and participating in online activities we also try to grasp the process of digitalization of everyday life and of social relations in a period when imposed isolation caused by policy restrictions on gatherings came into tension with the increased longing for personal encounters (related to calendar festivals and other events). We are interested in the general shape that community and family life have taken during this exceptional time. We also note the consequences of the partial lifting of lockdown measures, and the return to the supposedly "normal" at the expected end of the pandemic.

This chapter is based on various kinds of online-generated content on large public sites and online groups. Some of them are frequented by Roma visitors from all over Europe, some are focused on Poland and are also visited by Polish Roma abroad, while some are run by Roma organizations. We focus on social media posts and streams created by ordinary individuals, as well as on statements by Roma activists and celebrities. Nevertheless, we also refer to our own activities on social media and the individual profiles of our friends and families. All these activities helped to alleviate the anxiety and fear surrounding the new and potentially dangerous disease in the early months of the pandemic. They achieved this by transposing, to the sphere of social media, the familiar embrace of kinship and community that is so essential for Roma.

Social media users were well informed about the social and political situation in Poland, and extensively shared information about it. They also shared personal events and statements, especially when Easter, one of the key yearly events for Poles, was approaching. Initially, posts focused on topics such as religion (posting pictures of holy figures, texts of prayers), news about the pandemic (including conspiracy theories and fake news), jokes, and politics. Religious ceremonies in Romani languages were also broadcast live. Social media were full of pictures and short videos showing hospitals, and people who had reportedly died from COVID-19. Posts related to politics and policy referred to statements by Polish and foreign politicians about the number of infections, and comparing the situation in different countries.

The internet is a main communication platform for Roma leaders (including religious ones) and celebrities, and it should be stressed that they are closely followed by Polish Roma living abroad. We have identified in particular six such leaders, all of them males in their 50s and 60s, who are NGO activists, sportspersons, or musicians. They often combine their roles as community leaders and elders, moral authorities, NGO leaders, and (in at least one case) policy advisors with parallel careers in entertainment and sport. Using pseudonyms when writing about them and their activities allows us to focus on the phenomena under study instead of on the specific individuals. It also permits us to secure anonymity for the internet users who visit their public profiles and leave their comments there. One of them, let us call him *Celebryta*, is particularly active on social media, building his position not only as a Roma leader but also as an intermediary between Roma and non-Roma (Gadje) in Poland. *Celebryta* combines his stage charisma with policy advising, which makes him a popular figure among the Polish Roma (although controversial, and not necessarily admired by everyone). Aiming at both Roma and non-Roma, he manages to simultaneously perform his message as a kind of respected elder of the Roma community and a noble citizen and religious Pole.

Messages from leaders and activists, and videos of online games (nominations and challenges which we describe below), are publicly available, as are the related comments posted by users. This is not the case with a Facebook group dedicated to Roma: this group, which has over ten thousand members, is "closed" (has a restricted access) although there are no strict membership criteria. We anonymize the names of users and content producers, including publicly recognized personalities, and we do not reveal the names of websites or Facebook groups.

The Internet and the Everyday Life of Polish Roma: Chance or Challenge?

Digital presence has become an integral part of everyday life across Europe, and it is fostered by practically unlimited access to the internet and the popularity of smartphones, even among the underprivileged. Thanks to this increasing onlineization, social media and discussion groups have become an integral mechanism of maintaining social bonds, contributing to identity and solidarity on local, transnational, and translocal levels. The process has, however, also raised concerns among Roma about exposure to content that might be harmful or dangerous to the community through the erosion of traditional values and norms. The COVID-19 pandemic has accelerated a process which already existed. This is where we turn to the concept of *Romanipen*. This uncodified common law assesses group identity and delimits its boundaries, and is central to Romaniness. It can be perceived as a kind of philosophy of life, and as such it differs among different groups of Polish Roma. Therefore, its interpretations in Romani studies differ.[7] On visual and performative levels it is manifested for example in clothing, jewelry, furniture, and interior design, the way of setting the table during celebrations, and the ingredients used for food.

Social media also allow the expression of care for family and community, and, as a consequence, facilitate the reproduction of minority culture, even if in a transformed shape.[8] A study by Markéta Hajská is particularly inspiring for our impressions and analysis here.[9] Hajská analyzes the role of the internet and social media (she focuses on photographs, and selfies in particular) in upholding culture and group bonds. She also acknowledges the opportunities for self-creation (creating the image of oneself) through generation of content that meets the supposed expectations of the Slovak Vlach Roma community in Slovakia and the UK. These expectations reflect tradition and the image of migrants as people of success.

The internet emerges as a relevant site for observing changes in and challenges to Roma everyday life. It is a space where elements of different Polish Roma cultures (e.g., Polska Roma, Bergitka Roma, Lovari, Kelderari), languages, and lifestyles (also generational) intersect. Young people transmit elements of Roma customs, concurrently redefining and contesting them. Those belonging to older generations observe these trends and some try to put them on halt or at least "censor" some of them. Despite these controversies, the internet enables the consolidation of Roma communities and the securing of a safe space for the use of language and for the preservation of everyday culture without interference from Gadje outsiders. For the expanded family networks in Germany, Sweden, and the UK, the easily accessible virtual space allows for wide-ranging digital kinning.

The use of social media for trade, this time more pragmatic than symbolic, has also increased under the lockdown. Trade is one of the traditional Polish Roma professions respected by all group members. In the past, it was performed in marketplaces or directly at the homes of customers. With the development of the new technologies and with wide access to potential customers, social media has presented an alternative. One of the most popular Roma online groups is devoted to buying and selling. Before the pandemic, a large number of advertisements for buying and selling cars and furniture could be found online. Final transactions are agreed upon and made in private, so the success level of these sales are not known to other registered users or the public. During the pandemic, the number of trade and business-related videos and live streams increased. This is nothing more than an online marketplace offering real time, direct sales. Some Polish Roma women in Poland, Germany, and the UK conduct live streamed sales at their home boutiques to sell clothes, shoes, and household items. This kind of sales session is usually conducted in both Polish and Romani, and the products can be shipped to Poland or abroad. The buyers declare an intent to buy by posting comments under the video stream. Most popular online shopping sessions gather up to two hundred people from all over Europe. Language appears to be an important part of these interactions: it is a mix of Polish and Romani, with a general predominance of the latter. The products for sale are in line with the fashion attributed to traditional Roma, and with the requirements of more conservative Roma communities towards female clothing, like long skirts and dresses.

The unevenness of social norms comprising *Romanipen* is also evident in the different approaches to the internet and its users. It is particularly nuanced among seniors and women.[10] We have come across opinions that a *paćiwali Romni* (a respected woman of high social esteem) should not use social media, or at least not be seen doing it. This is why fake accounts are often used within Roma groups on social media. A person using his or her real name and profile picture knows that they will be judged by family members. Women are exposed to higher pressure than men, so they use fake accounts more often. Sharing accounts with spouses is also a popular thing to do. This kind of account protects individuals from slander or misunderstandings concerning their online conduct. Senior community members often do not understand and sometimes fear social media, but some can also see their advantages. For young people, the use of social media in daily life has become an indicator of belonging, and it impacts social relations, including their emotional and sexual lives, interests, and professional activities. In a similar way to seniors and women, a fear of being ostracized can lead young people to also use fake accounts.

The order of conduct comprising the code of *Romanipen* includes the need for control over online activity. The internet has become a powerful tool for maintaining tradition while simultaneously tightening social bonds, thus becoming a possible means of control. The symbolic boundaries separating the Roma and Gadje worlds are constructed and maintained through daily practices, including online activity. These activities allow one to preserve the feeling of belonging despite the changing conditions and intensive contact and cultural exchange with the Gadje world. Generating online content in Romani languages can be seen as constructing an ethnic boundary. A potential observer who does not understand the language or the cultural context of its use consumes the entire audiovisual text in a different way than its intended recipients. Sometimes, the message is purposely distorted in order to make it less comprehensible to Gadje, further reinforcing the feeling of belonging.

This contextual entanglement of verbal (language) and nonverbal (visual) messages in the construction of online communication can be described as "*e-Romanipen*", a term coined by Monika Szewczyk. On the visual level we observe signs and symbols that point to Roma identity. Individual visualization of certain events for the wider Roma audience is aimed at stressing group belonging and upholding tradition. Some of these messages seem staged, with well-selected stage props, costumes, decoration, and music—all of it aimed at demonstrating one's Romaniness. The intensification of online interactions also entails the intensification of nonverbal expression of Roma identity and intimacy within the community.

The Internet and Transnationality among Polish Roma in Poland and Abroad

The use and nonuse of the internet raises many controversies within the community of Polish Roma, revealing the diverse challenges that this medium poses to traditional Roma hierarchies of power. The threat is seen to come from the universal and uncontrolled access to information, and the ability to share it, that the internet offers. For example, among the elders of the Polska Roma, there have been serious discussions on imposing customary Roma law restrictions on internet users. In 2019, a ban on the use of the internet for all but income-generating purposes was announced on YouTube by the Śero Rom.[11] In the words of the elders, this move was aimed at protecting young people and women from immoral conduct that could bring shame upon their families and the Roma community as a whole. Although the Śero Rom's judgments are only binding for one group of Roma in Poland, the Polska Roma, he is also respected by other groups. Regardless of the Śero Rom's reasoning, the use of social media is widespread among all groups of Roma in Poland.

Our research and our everyday life experiences show that online communication with the use of Messenger, Skype, WhatsApp, and Facebook is crucial for many Roma families and kinship groups. It is reflected in the adaptation of such words as *mesendżeris, fejsbukos,*[12] *skejpos,* and *wotsapos* into Romani dialects. For elders and community leaders, social media can be used as tools for surveillance with regard to social norms and customs associated with *Romanipen*. In the migratory context, the internet is a very important space for communication and social/family life for both migrating and non-migrating Polish Roma. It is also a space for unbounded use of the Romani language.

The young generation use social media platforms to get to know new people, perform courtship, and maintain existing relationships. Dating sites have long replaced traditional forms of matchmaking, which raises some concerns among the older generations, who in turn tend to identify social media with dating sites. For many traditional Roma, using Facebook is perceived as tantamount to looking for a relationship. In traditional matchmaking, parental responsibility and involvement was crucial for the entire process. In the digital age, offline matching has not disappeared, but instead has gained new elements provided by online transitions and Facebook posts. Sometimes young people take the initiative, but later on the engagement and marriage ceremonies are conducted in accordance with custom, albeit with additional online streaming. Under lockdown, the impossibility of holding an engagement party has led people to advertise news about engagements and parental consent to as many people as possible, and pictures of the young couple are often shared online.

The Internet as a Chronicle of the Plague Year

Online interactions became even more important once the lockdowns and restrictions started. Several Roma organizations raised funds for masks and hygiene products through the internet and social media. One of them joined forces with organizations working with migrant communities in Poland, including Romanian Roma, to publish practical information about COVID-19 in Polish and in two Romani dialects.

After the state of epidemic was declared by the Polish government, Roma leaders joined the #*stayhome* campaign and encouraged Roma communities to follow the instructions from the medical experts. They withdrew from meetings and all other forms of non-internet activity. *Celebryta*, whom we have introduced above, organized a fundraiser among Roma and Gadje to support public health institutions. Apart from providing help, the goal was also to break the negative stereotype of the Roma people as a passive minority dependent on social welfare. In a similar manner, a man we call *Muzyk*, 'the musician,' auctioned off his musical instruments and stage costumes in order to raise funds for his local hospital. It was just before Easter that *Celebryta* initiated popular games of nominations and challenges, which involved performing and filming certain activities. To make lockdown and quarantine more bearable, nominees were encouraged to sing and play music. This entertainment was quickly picked up by other Roma artists, both professional and amateur. Nominations and challenges soon reached the wider strata of internet users, and included non-musical activities such as toasts, cooking, physical exercise, and putting curses on the coronavirus to make it go away.

These kinds of online games, competitions, and speeches replaced streaming of the feasts, parties, and other joyful social events that were popular among the Polish Roma on the internet before the pandemic. In the process, the Polish-Romani dialects became enriched with such words as *nomineł, nomininaw, czelendżos,* and *czelendżo*. Even if some of them are playful and funny, on the basis of our own affective understanding of the situation, we claim that they also represented a reaction to anxiety and the feeling of being endangered, which was further amplified by the lack of direct contact with loved ones.

In one of these videos, a man greets his family in the UK and Germany, and raises a toast to end the *koronawirusos*. Another video shows a well-dressed man sitting by a posh table with a bottle of fine liquor in front of him and baroque porcelain figures behind him, with the theme music from Francis F. Coppola's "The Godfather" in the background. The man greets his online audience and (with a calm but firm voice, in the Romani language) thanks others for their nominations, toasts the well-being of all people and God's care over them, and wishes everyone a peaceful and vigorous Easter. Toasts and alcohol consumption were performed mostly by men, but women (even if less visible) were responsible for filming, suggesting the people to be greeted and Romani equivalents for the Polish or English words related to social media.

Both men and women took up online challenges related to food preparation. Female participants baked cakes (the most popular were yeast pastries filled with dried fruits) and other sweet snacks, while men were encouraged to make dumplings. The most popular dumplings were those filled with black pudding or with mashed potato and cottage cheese (so-called *pierogi ruskie*, or "Ruthenian dumplings," an iconic Polish dish). The dumpling challenge was introduced by Polish Roma families living in Poland and in the UK. In one of the videos, a man in his forties living in England can be seen making *pierogi ruskie*. The man is wearing a traditional Tatra-highlander hat (which points to part of his family's origin from the Podhale region in the south of Poland), a chef's apron, and rubber gloves (supposedly contributing to the safety measures under the pandemic). The performance was filmed by his wife, who was also giving him some practical tips. In another video, a young man in Kraków who used to live in England made dumplings, accompanied by his daughter who was also responsible for filming. In both cases, the people involved were mixing Romani and Polish languages. These cooking activities were also accompanied by wishes of good health and protection against *koronawirusos*.

Such live streams and videos conveyed to the friends and relatives: "we" are fine, healthy, and safe, and "we" stay at home, therefore so should "you." They served as community-building/affirming rituals where people met and did something together according to a particular pattern, and in so doing strengthened the social bonds and the feelings of belonging. Live streaming of important events was also a way to show other people (in Poland, the UK, and other countries) that the customs were being upheld, appropriate food was being placed on the table, proper toasts were being made (with proper drinks), proper clothes worn, and people were behaving themselves. The presence of all these elements in place, live streamed to numerous Roma households in England, Germany, and Poland, was also a way of demonstrating mutual respect. In a period of limited opportunities of getting together, marked by anxiety over each other's health and well-being, these rituals became more frequent and even more important than before. The message about the need to stay connected in order to maintain group intimacy intensified with the approach of Easter, which, even for non-believers, is an important get-together celebration all over Poland. In the pandemic year, this getting together just took a rather unconventional form.

Digital Easter 2020

As a means of auto-ethnography of family celebrations amid lockdown measures, below we present our own accounts from Easter Sunday. Our personal experiences are employed in an analysis of pandemic events in Poland, and their impact on transnational families. We treat these vignettes as links between the single experiences of individuals and the broader social and cultural shifts triggered by the pandemic. They show how the internet enabled mediated intimacy at a time of expected festivity, which was characteristic for Roma and non-Roma alike. To underline the individuality of each fragment, we turn to first-person narratives.

Monika: The family meeting was a video call attended by my aunts and cousins living in and calling from two towns in England and two towns in Poland. The atmosphere was festive and familiar. There were jokes, toasts, and showing and sending old pictures. Some people sang and danced, and one cousin played the accordion. Another cousin was present on three different calls at the same time using two telephones and one computer. After a while, the older generation left the video call, leaving more freedom to the younger generation. One of the aunties kept dropping by in order to check if everything was fine. Another auntie appeared for "inspection," and suggested that it was late and that the call could be continued the next day. I should stress that this kind of video call is not a new phenomenon in my family. What was new was the online meeting around the table. It was the first time in my life that we hadn't visited each other at Easter. It was conscious isolation driven by the fear of the disease. It's quite common among Roma to fear diseases and hospitals. And this fear made them stay home.

Elżbieta: I spent this Easter with my in-laws who live close to us, just a few blocks away. I abandoned my initial plans to go to the mountains, where I come from and where my father's family, the Roma part of my family, lives. As my siblings have been living abroad (England, France, and Sweden) for many years, I'm the one responsible for taking care of my parents. Luckily, they don't need direct care but they do expect frequent contact and visits from their daughter and grandchildren. Unfortunately, they had to spend last Easter on their own. It was the same with my aunts and uncles living in the same mountain town. All of them are in the high-risk group because of their age and health issues, and they take social distancing recommendations quite seriously. I want to stress that since the young generation, meaning my siblings and cousins and me, have left our hometown, holidays and family events are always an occasion to visit our family home. Of course, on Easter Sunday there were phone calls; we exchanged good wishes, and regrets that we could not meet in person. My cousin, who works in Berlin and had not seen her parents for a long time, came up with the idea of holding a family meeting via Zoom. We managed to connect with Berlin (Germany), Czarna Góra (Poland), Cieszyn (Poland), Radom (Poland), Stockholm (Sweden), Kraków (Poland), and Rotherham (UK). The idea was spontaneous, so not everyone attended, but still the opportunity to see and talk to even a part of the family was both touching and funny.

Ignacy: Because of divorces (which have multiplied family cells) and geographical dispersion (both national and transnational), we don't get together for large Easter (or Christmas) gatherings in my family, which (unlike Monika's and Elżbieta's families) is entirely Gadje. Instead, the celebrations are divided into smaller subgroups, so every year there are questions about whom to spend Easter and Christmas with. For many years, phone and video calls have been a part of these celebrations (the latter usually concerned parts of the family in the UK and US). They have always been an addition to physical meetings, and have never lasted longer than fifteen minutes, mainly for exchanging courtesies, showing the dishes on the table, and all that. This time it was different. Eight of us gathered in front of four computer screens (three in Warsaw, one in a small town in northern Scotland). A lot of the time and energy devoted to this meeting was spent on technical issues: making sure that everyone was onboard, and double checking the connection and transmission quality. The main challenge was to instruct a family elder on the use of Skype, which required an additional phone call—a kind of a double mediation (or mediation within mediation). Other groups of my family were reached on the phone, and our conversations were dominated by the coronavirus and the impact the pandemic was having on our lives.

Lockdown, increased controls at the state borders, mandatory quarantines for travelers, and other restrictions in different countries made Easter 2020 exceptional for everyone, including transnational families. Most people in Poland, Roma or non-Roma, stayed home and resigned themselves to not receiving any guests, and this enforced separation from others and the threat of loneliness led to certain levels of anxiety. This might be the reason why, in comparison to previous years, live streams and videos shared on the social media were scarce. Instead, people gathered in front of screens for more direct contact with their loved ones.

Filming, live streaming, and sharing life events and calendar celebrations on social media has long been popular among Polish Roma families. In the communities of diverse and territorially dispersed family networks, the internet appears as a functional tool for cultural reproduction, social control, and group integration. Feasts and other gatherings reinforce group solidarity, and remind people of the existing common law that requires certain behaviors and respect towards elders. As such they are an important part of Roma culture (or cultures, as it is difficult to speak of one Roma culture). It is worth noting that they are also crucial for many, if not most, people in Poland, where family life is influenced by Roman Catholicism, leaving an imprint even among non-believers. Live streaming from dinners and feasts can also serve as a message to friends and relatives in different locations that everyone is fine and, no less importantly, that the traditions and customs are being maintained, securing the affinity among the Roma communities.

Respect for norms and customs can also be expressed, like in the videos and challenges described above, through serving particular kinds and proper amounts of food, raising toasts, and following proper dress codes and use of language. It is a way of expressing mutual respect (*paćiw*) among the recipients and transmitters of the videos.

What Was the (New) Normal, and What Comes Next?

In mid-September,[13] we managed to catch some fresh air, both real and metaphorical, at a music festival. After facing countless dilemmas, the organizers presented the 9th annual International Roma Culture Days in the Nowa Huta district of Kraków.[14] The festival has always been thought of as a holiday event, and as such is usually held on the first weekend of July. Every year it gathers Roma and Gadje from Nowa Huta, and is also frequented by people who live in the UK and Germany but who are paying a summer visit to their hometown. The pandemic nearly led to the cancellation of the 2020 edition, but finally, under strict sanitary and hygiene requirements and at a later date than usual, it did take place. It seemed to us that all the Roma from Nowa Huta were there. There were also some participants from other towns, and some foreign musicians. One could easily feel the atmosphere of festivity, joy, and emotion caused by the opportunity to get together after the period of isolation and social distancing. That year, only a few people from Nowa Huta living in England and Germany attended the event. However, technology was once again helpful. Parts of the event were transmitted live by attendees sharing it on Facebook. In this way, those not present could also take their mediated part. The concerts were commented on in real time, and mutual greetings were shared. These kinds of hybrid solutions were worked out as an answer to the challenges presented by this exceptional period. They mediated between the "(new) normal," where gatherings in physical space were held, and the state of exception, where participation (if even possible) was limited.

As we write this, the coronavirus is still with us. Two of us have already had COVID-19, but recovered from it, and we keep experiencing the pandemic through the daily news about the number of cases and deaths, the first- and secondhand testimonies of those who have suffered the illness, new restrictions, and the growing concerns about the future. With the increasing number of cases and deaths in the spring of 2021, social media were still full of pictures of the diseased, and invitations to prayers. Our site-bound fieldwork (unlike the digital fieldwork) has been postponed, and we continue to have our team meetings online. In this way, the spring of 2021 is similar to that of 2020.

Over one year into the pandemic restrictions, we are still observing a flourishing of online initiatives among Polish Roma, both in Poland and abroad. Apart from communication, the internet is also used for trade, which was not common before the pandemic. Romani language is used for the item descriptions and for the transactions themselves. Different groups of Central and East European Roma in the UK organize online lotteries (again, mixing Roma dialects with the languages of their respective countries). Religious institutions have also developed online initiatives aimed at Polish Roma. That is especially true of the Jehovah's Witnesses,[15] who have long been open towards spreading their message in different languages and through online platforms. Lockdowns, even if partial, created new opportunities for the followers, and there are Romani-speaking online congregations aimed at Polish Roma broadcasting from both Poland and the UK. This is only one of many examples of how the internet is being used for tightening the existing bonds and maintaining community boundaries.

With the apparent ease of the internet fitting into the social life of the Polish Roma and vice versa, the adaptation of Roma everyday life and meaningful events to the new technologies confirm the significance of digital tools for these communities. They also point to individual and collective agency during a state of exception, which—let us not forget—has long been the everyday reality of many people worldwide, especially of ethnic and racialized minorities.

Monika Szewczyk is a PhD candidate at the Jagiellonian University. She is also a researcher at the Centre of Migration Research, University of Warsaw, focusing on the migration and ethnic boundary making of Polish Roma. Her research interests involve Roma migration, national and ethnic issues, and the role of oral history in identity politics.

Elżbieta Mirga-Wójtowicz is a cultural animator, political scientist, and researcher at the Centre of Migration Research, University of Warsaw. She holds PhD in social sciences from the Pedagogical University of Cracow. She is the author of evaluation reports on Roma integration policy in Poland for the EC within the Roma Civil Monitor project in 2017–20 and for 2021–25.

Ignacy Jóźwiak is a sociologist and social anthropologist (ethnologist). His research is centered around migration, transnationality, and translocality. His interests also include the areas of state borders and borderlands, ethnicities, and labor migration. He works as a researcher at the Centre of Migration Research, University of Warsaw.

Notes

1. Hajská, "The Presentation;" Nagy, "Roma Networks."
2. Bielenin-Lenczowska, *Spaghetti z ajwarem*, 53–54; Patzer, "Napotkanie przedtekstowego."
3. Baldassar and Krzyżowski, "Not Social Distancing."
4. Debates we find the most intriguing can be found at: Allegra Laboratory—Anthropology for Radical Optimism (https://allegralaboratory.net/category/thematic-threads/corona/), The Coronavirus and Mobility Forum (https://www.compas.ox.ac.uk/project/the-coronavirus-and-mobility-forum/), Critical Legal Thinking (https://criticallegalthinking.com/), and "Coronavirus and Philosophers" thematic thread on the website of the European Journal of Psychoanalysis (https://www.journal-psychoanalysis.eu/coronavirus-and-philosophers/).
5. See, e.g., Foucault, Agamben, and Benvenuto, "Coronavirus and Philosophers;" Laszczkowski, "Brave New Normal;" Sotiris, "Thinking Beyond."
6. Project "Transnational lives of Polish Roma—Migration, family and ethnic boundary making in changing European Union" is funded by the National Science Centre, Poland, OPUS 16, grant no: UMO-2018/31/B/HS6/03006, duration 2019–22.
7. Cf. Koper, "Strategie adaptacji;" Koper, "Romanipen."
8. Nagy, "Roma Networks."
9. Hajská, "The Presentation."
10. Women are often perceived as tradition-bearers. They are responsible for taking care of the family and its public image upon which the family and community respect is built. Social control concerning accordance with *Romanipen* often takes the shape of observing and assessing one's behavior and the way of communicating with other Roma and with Gadje.
11. Śero Rom (literally the Head of the Roma, sometimes referred to as a Roma King) is a common-law authority of the Polska Roma group of the Polish Roma.
12. Applications are used by different groups of Roma who speak different dialects of the Romani language. According to the dialect, the most popular social medium can be called *fejsbuko*, *fejsbukos*, or *fejsbukura*.
13. As some readers may guess, this section title has been inspired by Catherine Verdery's *What Was Socialism, and What Comes Next?*
14. Nowa Huta, which means "New Steel Mill," is a district in the city of Kraków in Poland built in the late 1940s around a newly developed industrial complex. Roma from the Polish highland regions of Spisz and Podhale were among the first settlers, and to this day, this is where most of the Roma in Kraków live (Szewczyk, *O Romach*).
15. We have identified the participation of Polish Roma in Poland, Germany, and the UK in the Jehovah's Witness movement as an important aspect of their transnational lives and migratory encounters. This issue will be developed in our further studies.

Bibliography

Baldassar, Loretta, and Lukasz Krzyżowski. "Physical, Not Social Distancing: What We Can Learn from Migrants." *UWA Social Care and Social Ageing Living Lab News*, April 2020. Retrieved 25 April 2021 from https://livinglab.com.au/4548-2/.

Bielenin-Lenczowska, Karolina. *Spaghetti z ajwarem: Translokalna codzienność muzułmanów w Macedonii i we Włoszech* [Spaghetti with Ajvar: The translocal everyday life of Muslims in Macedonia and Italy]. Warsaw: Wydawnictwo Uniwersytetu Warszawskiego, 2015.

Foucault, Michel, Giorgio Agamben, and Sergio Benvenuto. "Coronavirus and Philosophers." *European Journal of Psychoanalysis* (online), March 2020. Retrieved 25 April 2021 from https://www.journal-psychoanalysis.eu/articles/coronavirus-and-philosophers/.

Hajská, Markéta. "The Presentation of Social Status on a Social Network: The Role of Facebook among the Vlax Romani Community of Eastern-Slovak Origin in Leicester, UK." *Romani Studies* 29(2) (2019), 123–58. https://doi.org/10.3828/rs.2019.6.

Koper, Tomasz. "Romanipen. O Dwóch strategiach 'bycia Romem' we współczesnym świecie" [Romanipen. On Two Strategies of 'Being Roma' in the Contemporary World]. *Studia Romologica* 13 (2020): 85–124.

———. "Strategie adaptacji Romów w Polsce na przykładzie grup Polska Roma i Bergitka Roma" [Roma adaptation strategies in Poland on the example of Polish Roma and Bergitka Roma Groups]. PhD diss., University of Warsaw, 2018.

Laszczkowski, Mateusz. "Brave New Normal World." *AllegraLab*, 3 April 2020. Retrieved 25 April 2021 from https://allegralaboratory.net/brave-new-normal-world/.

Nagy, Veronika. "Roma Networks: Ethnic Solidarity in an Internet Age?" *Intersections. East European Journal of Society and Politics* 4(3) (2018): 158–79. https://doi.org/10.17356/ieejsp.v4i3.440.

Patzer, Helena. "Napotkanie Przedtekstowego. Budowanie wiedzy etnograficznej o migranckich światach troski" [Encountering the pre-textual: Building ethnographic knowledge of migrant worlds of care]. *Teksty Drugie* 1 (2018): 111–26.

Sotiris, Panagiotis. "Thinking Beyond the Lockdown: On the Possibility of a Democratic Biopolitics." *Historical Materialism* 28(3) (2020): 3–38. https://doi.org/10.1163/1569206X-12342803.

Szewczyk, Monika. *O Romach w Nowej Hucie słów kilka* [A few words about the Roma in Nowa Huta]. Kraków: Integracyjne Stowarzyszenie Sawore, 2019.

Verdery, Katherine. *What Was Socialism, and What Comes Next?* Princeton, NJ: Princeton University Press, 2014.

PART V

CZECH CHRONICLES

CHAPTER 22

INTRODUCTION TO THE CZECH CHRONICLES
Of Loss and Silence

Yasar Abu Ghosh

There is no mention of Roma in relation to the pandemic whatsoever in the media. The authorities haven't addressed the specific circumstances of socially excluded localities under the pandemic. The Roma suddenly don't exist.
—Gwen Albert, human rights activist, December 2020[1]

I never did better.... There is work everywhere, we eat what we want, I go shopping every second day. I have never earned as much as I do now. I hope this will never end.
—Petr Kaliňák, young Roma man from South Bohemia, June 2020[2]

Introduction

In contrast with the other countries discussed in this volume, the case of Czechia is paradoxical in two respects. Firstly, it is probably the only country with a significant Roma minority where the register of biopolitics that emerged during the pandemic has not identified Roma as the weak link in the prevention of contagion. As chronicler Gwen Albert explains in the first quote above, the attitude of the state and of major media outlets during the pandemic has been characterized by an almost complete lack of interest in the plight of people living in so-called "socially excluded localities" (SELs)[3] with heavy Roma overrepresentation. This neglect contrasts with how Roma have been feared, besieged, or attacked in connection with the pandemic elsewhere.

The second quote draws readers' attention to another paradox. It comes from a conversation I had with Petr, a young Roma man from a community in South Bohemia. I have been in contact with this community since my doctoral fieldwork, and in June 2020, with the easing of pandemic measures after the first wave, I was planning a visit. Before arriving and with some trepidation, I asked Petr how he was coping during the just-ending first period of hard lockdown. I had expected sighs of resignation and apathy that, I assumed, would result from the impossibility of maintaining the usual survival strategies. Scrap collecting, wild-berry picking, occasional gigs for unskilled construction workers, and debt optimizations through pawnshops had to stop during this period because most of these places had been closed. To my surprise, Petr did not complain at all, and nor did his two cousins who worked with him. He described this period of crisis as a time of abundance that he had been eager to reap without any reluctance.

Petr's detour from the path of irregular jobs and economic uncertainties has an explanation, of which he is aware. As I could verify from some videos he shared on social media and, later, in person, the pandemic had indeed opened unexpected possibilities of change for some marginalized Roma. For example, after the temporary outflow of foreign workers back to their home countries (most often to Ukraine), who had worked in sectors such as construction, Roma occasionally took their place. The labor shortage led to another effect: previously considered an unskilled worker, Petr was given the opportunity to perform much better paid work assignments such as tiling. Consequently, Petr and his young family moved out of an SEL, and (as I am writing, at the end of 2021) he seems to be maintaining his newly changed status and expanding his future opportunities by passing a driving license test, a much-valued achievement perceived as transformative among marginalized Roma.

The dynamics of the labor market that created these temporary windows for individuals like Petr were consistent with how the epidemic was handled by the authorities in its first wave, from March to June 2020. The declaration of a state of emergency, the severe lockdown, and the closure of borders, along with a collective optimism that the situation would be resolved, contributed to the relatively successful management of the first wave. The Czech prime minister was thus able to boast in an international forum that the Visegrád Four countries (Czechia, Hungary, Poland, and Slovakia) were "the best in COVID." However, the subsequent easing of almost all restrictive measures during the summer months, when I visited Petr, proved to be a fatal mistake. From the beginning of the autumn 2020, the number of reported COVID cases began to rise until they were surpassing fifteen thousand per day by the end of November 2020. The second wave proved particularly severe, with the number of deaths reaching around five thousand by the end of the year. "The best in COVID" became the worst hit country in Europe. In fact, as of 1 November 2020, Czechia had the highest weekly number of deaths per capita in the entire world. Then, in the winter months from January to March 2021, the third wave hit, and was characterized in particular by a high number of hospital admissions compared to the previous wave. The fourth wave culminated in December 2021; it was no longer accompanied by measures such as lockdown or school closures, due to the increasing vaccination coverage of the population (approaching 70 percent of the population at the end of 2021); but once again, hospital intensive care units were at their limits.

In relation to labor market dynamics, however, it is interesting to note that households and businesses used this time to plan construction projects. There is therefore talk of a construction boom and a large demand for labor from spring 2021. This explains that even as workers who had previously vacated the labor market began to return, there was no loss of positions such as those acquired by people like Petr.

Both paradoxes become more comprehensible the moment we place them in the same story. Petr's successful escape is the flip side of a complete disregard for both the impact of the epidemic on the majority of Roma living in the SELs and the measures to mitigate it. For those among them who are long-term unemployed and who need to complement their welfare checks by engaging in temporary jobs or other livelihood strategies outside the taxed economy, the situation became particularly deadlocked. Their predicament during the pandemic is evocatively described by representatives of the Manusha, an organization of Roma women dedicated to social assistance among poor Roma in the Ostrava region: "If a man is working on a contract or 'under the table' and now cannot work due to lockdown, then the problem arises of where they will get money for housing and food."[4] And Aurélie Balážová, from the same organization, adds: "For several Romani families I had to ask the head of the OSPOD[5] if she could provide basic food from the food bank."[6] The resources that the government started to spend to ease the effects of the anti-pandemic measures, like subsidies to employers to cover wage costs during the shutdown or one-off allowances for the self-employed, did not help people who, at best, worked on temporary work agreements or without any contractual security. Although the inattention of the authorities or the media to the plight of the marginalized Roma may have seemed benign at first, their silence and inaction have nurtured an acute distrust among the Roma towards official discourse.[7] Given this historically learned skepticism, it was not surprising to see some Roma themselves retreating into silence. But it was "a sharp silence," a silence that is kept in order to hear what is being said.[8]

Recurrent Crisis—Syndemics

Yet my argument is that despite the apparent silence and existential resurgence that the examples point to, a series of pre-pandemic structural conditions—worsening health, deterioration in access to education, and increasing poverty—which are often invisible and normalized, transpire and inform a crisis of a different scale. Despite the invocations of an unprecedented emergency, it is the pre-existing conditions that become actualized and magnified during the pandemic.[9]

In one of the early and rare instances of any media reporting on the impact of the COVID-19 pandemic on the lives of people in SELs, the Roma inhabitants surprised the journalist by their skepticism regarding the potential consequences of virus contagion for their livelihoods. For them, says the journalist, "possible impoverishment would represent hardly anything new."[10] And when it comes to health issues, within the two years before the pandemic the inhabitants of this SEL had already experienced epidemics of dysentery and hepatitis. In fact, it is appropriate to characterize the situation as syndemic. Although the spreading COVID-19 contagion initially seemed to follow the "great equalizer" logic, very soon it started to chart "the fault lines of society—exposing and often magnifying power inequalities that shape population health even in normal times."[11]

The substandard housing conditions in SELs not only make it impossible to follow the protective public health recommendations related to hygiene and physical distance, but also create favorable conditions for the worsening of certain diseases which, in conjunction with infection from the COVID-19 virus, can synergistically increase the possibility of a dramatic course for the pandemic. The pandemic has affected different communities with different levels of intensity, and the effects have mirrored the structures of inequality that already existed in Czech society. To adequately assess and respond to COVID-19, it is necessary to integrate how other threats to the lives of marginalized people contribute to the unfolding of the pandemic,[12] taking social context and politico-economic inequities into account.[13]

Evidence to this effect is offered by an observation from Jan Dužda, who works as coordinator in a project promoting effective assistance in access to health institutions for people at risk of poverty and social exclusion at the National Institute of Public Health (*Státní zdravotní ústav*).[14] As is documented in various reports and policy papers related to the health status of Roma, there is an entrenched "state of chronic acceptance"[15] of health disparities between Roma and the rest of the population on the part of Czech health authorities. As a result, the Roma Dužda works with are often reluctant to trust healthcare providers. Dužda's project does not accept this situation, and attempts to address the social determinants of health as a key factor in the development of the most prevalent diseases in the populations of SELs. During the pandemic, the activities of project coordinators, who otherwise help build trust in healthcare providers, were limited to making phone calls to clients. According to Dužda, the clients' trust that their needs would be addressed evaporated before his eyes.

Encouraging Roma to seek early medical help and to attend preventive examinations was made impossible due to the critical situation in medical facilities. Moreover, some events further reinforced the perception that the health system was not there for them. For instance, in March 2021, the news of doctors in a hospital in Chomutov refusing to provide care to a young Roma man who was showing symptoms of COVID-19 infection (breathing difficulties, chest pain, tingling in his hand) had a deep effect on Roma. What appeared to the doctors as a non-serious illness and, according to witnesses, even as faking, resulted in Viktor Mikulecký, the father of a three-year-old daughter, dying in silence in the waiting room of the surgery.[16] In the interview in this volume with Jozef Miker, a Roma activist from the same region, he glosses the dynamic in the following manner: "At first the Roma thought Covid did not concern them. And when they started to fear it, they found that nothing could save them."

Although we lack data showing the extent to which Roma in the SELs were affected by the pandemic (in terms of numbers of deaths and hospitalizations), I would conclude from the above that the impact was greater than in other health and social contexts. The notion of "necropolitics," as the power to expose others to conditions of death, comes to mind.[17] For a long time, the substandard and often unhealthy housing conditions in the SELs have not only been overlooked by non-Roma in positions of authority, but even accepted as appropriate for the perceived sociocultural level of poor Roma.

Poverty

In its examination of the effects of the global pandemic on Roma and Traveller communities, the European Union Agency for Fundamental Rights (FRA) observes that "[W]hile it is anticipated that the special crisis measures, and the concomitant economic downturn have negatively affected the lives of Czech Roma, the immediate impact of the measures is unclear."[18] The most up-to-date government document that regularly provides information about the Roma population and that serves as a basis for monitoring the government's Roma integration policy is the 2019 State of the Roma Minority Report. This document states that getting towards half[19] of the Roma population in the Czech Republic—110,000 out of 260,000—live in conditions of social exclusion and at risk of poverty.[20] The Agency for Social Inclusion, the main arm of the state's central Roma policies, produces and annually updates "the index of social exclusion." In its COVID-19 edition from this year (2021), the agency estimates that the expected economic deterioration as a consequence of the pandemic (established at 5–6 percent) will bring an increase of 1–2 percent of people at risk of poverty (i.e., 100,000 to 200,000).[21] If there were any positive trends in the socioeconomic status of people living in SELs prior to the pandemic, the economic turbulences caused by the pandemic have not only halted them, but also put those sections of society that Roma demographically dominate at increased risk of poverty and extreme poverty. Some of the NGOs that help with housing shortages, foreclosures, and debt resolutions are already reporting a growing demand for help, and have been obliged to increase the number of helpline staff.[22]

These figures seem to confirm the worst expectations about the socioeconomic impact of the pandemic on the lives of the socially excluded Roma. And it is also important to remember the situation of those who were devastated by the pandemic measures themselves, and whose situation make the story of Petr so noteworthy. While many owners of small businesses and their employees shared a large part of the crisis expenditures to help companies whose very existence was threatened by the state of emergency, the life-sustaining income from either unskilled labor or the untaxed economy for the long-term unemployed dried up without (or only late-distributed) compensation. As Jozef Miker says in an interview, "my wife, like everyone who worked in the hospitality industry, lost everything from one day to the next … we were threatened with going on the street, with having our child taken away … every month we were locked up at home, our debt grew, and I had to borrow from decent friends." What about those who did not have such loyal—and solvent—friends?

Online Schooling in Segregated Education

In 2007, the European Court of Human Rights ruled in the case of D.H. and Others v. the Czech Republic (No. 57325/00) that the fact it is twenty-seven times more likely for Roma children to end up in "special schools" for mentally disabled pupils constitutes a pattern of segregation that violates the non-discrimination protections in the European Convention on Human Rights. Yet the Czech government has been unable to adopt measures to rectify this pattern. As a consequence, special schools were closed; and so now Roma pupils, especially from SELs, have to attend schools that offer a substandard curriculum and are spatially and racially segregated: there are currently about eighty segregated schools with a majority of Roma pupils; the segregation is either actively encouraged by local municipalities, or is not prevented. Given that the education system was already so markedly reproducing social inequalities, it was predictable that after the government-imposed school closures on 11 March 2020, the existing disparities in educational support, quality teaching, and technical equipment would worsen.[23]

According to the Czech School Inspectorate (CSI), in its interim examination of the initial impact of the pandemic on teaching, "in approximately 1,000 schools, one-third of pupils do not communicate with teachers online, and in approximately 100 schools more than half of pupils are not involved in online remote teaching at all. The main reason for pupils not communicating is either the lack of equipment or insufficient internet connectivity."[24] Given the great efforts of the non-profit sector after the first wave, many disadvantaged households were provided with the necessary technical equipment for remote teaching. Charity collections and donations have also made it possible to mitigate, but not eliminate, this inequality. Yet where there have been multiple children in a household, participation in remote teaching has been further limited.

However, the reasons why the pandemic measures in education will have a far-reaching impact on children growing up in SELs, and why this impact is now difficult to estimate, does not lie in the initial technical or material deficiencies. The shift to remote teaching also has a destabilizing effect in that it requires significant involvement from parents as co-creators of content and knowledge transfer. For parents from socially disadvantaged backgrounds, the situation proved to be additionally challenging in many respects. At the end of 2020, People in Need (Člověk v tísni) and another fifteen NGOs conducted a survey of primary and secondary schools' approach to remote teaching for socially disadvantaged pupils.[25] They were also interested in the conditions that families have for learning, and one of their findings was that a strong factor negatively influencing learning outcomes, as well as a child's attitude to learning, was that their parents could not support them sufficiently due to their own low education levels. Thus, according to the research, up to a third of parents had problems with home preparation because of the complexity of the subjects covered. This makes it very clear how pre-existing conditions of inequality have become actualized and magnified during the pandemic. Before the pandemic, inclusive education programs were put in place to help overcome social disadvantages by providing teaching assistance to pupils. During the pandemic, however, it is these inherited lacunae that re-emerge as crucial in forming children's learning experience.

Chronicles of Loss

Although the contributions to the Czech chronicles vary in content and style, as authors, we initially agreed together on the overall concept. This was going to voice many notions of loss—a loss of time together, a loss of action, a loss of sense of belonging—presented in different ways: a short story, an interview, a reflection, an image. By loss, however, we are not pointing to a cultural concept or a shared perspective on the pandemic experience. Rather, it seems to us that loss is a kind of a vanishing point of the existential dimension of the pandemic experience in general. Whether it is the distress of various losses or the experience of our own losses and the losses of loved ones, we are reminded anew that the post-pandemic situation will require each of us to eventually regain something that has been weakened, endangered, or even lost—a status, a dignity, a sociality.

This may sound paradoxical when speaking of people who were living at risk of poverty and exclusion even prior to the pandemic. But, as we will see in the example of Jozef Miker, even those who experienced a kind of "social death," a loss of such proportions that it cannot be quantified ("I don't know how to tell you that I need to help people... if I didn't, others would abuse them"), are looking towards the end to reclaim what was taken away. Similarly, Iveta Kokyová contemplates on the fear of loss of family, her source of happiness. When I invited Iveta to be part of the Czech chronicles, I presented her with my initial inspiration. Knowing how gatherings of all kinds—ritual or casual—were prominent in the daily lives of Roma, I was wondering what the implications and applications of rules of social distancing would look like? Do the rules of social distancing in fact create any social distances among Roma? To this call, Iveta, who is part of a new generation of female Romani writers,[26] responded with a story inspired by a travel encounter she had at a moment of temporary easing of lockdown measures—a story in which the fear of loneliness haunts both protagonists, the author and her accidental interlocutor. Loneliness, as the product of social distancing, or of "protective asphyxiation," is amplified during the pandemic as a vector of experience so that the existential and pandemic loneliness coalesce.

Paying attention to silence, loss, and the ongoing crisis was enabled by adopting a kind of methodological polytheism. The Czech chronicles are reflexive inscriptions by singular authors who are deeply involved in the lives of their own communities or in working for the Roma community at large. They bring us the experience of the pandemic from a distanced perspective, which is made possible because their reflections were written after the most difficult period of state of emergency. The plurality of genres allows an accentuation of different facets.[27] The urgency in Jozef Miker's testimony runs through the entire interview. The sensitivity and empathy of Iveta Kokyová's narrative style, on the other hand, in a sense brings to the chronicles calm and patience. Gwen Albert's reflective look expands the chronicles in time, and directs the reader's attention to future needs and problems. The denialism and vaccine hesitancy that is at the center of her reflection have been upsetting, and will leave great scars on the body of civil society. The urgency to recover from the pandemic is, however, still in the distance at this moment when our societies are still facing an unpredictable future.

Yasar Abu Ghosh studied ethnology at Charles University in Prague, and social anthropology at École des Hautes Études en Sciences Sociales in Paris. He teaches at the Department of Social and Cultural Anthropology, Faculty of Humanities, Charles University. He has also taught at universities in Munich, Budapest, and Paris. He has been researching Roma since his graduate studies. Among his main research interests are fugitive politics, survival strategies, and politics of commemoration. He has acted as an expert on European as well as national expert and advisory boards.

Notes

1. Personal communication.
2. Personal communication.
3. The term "sociálně vyloučené lokality" (socially excluded localities, SEL) was introduced into Czech policy discourse after a state-commissioned mapping of the people affected by social exclusion in 2006 and again in 2015 (GAC, *Analýza*, 2006 and 2015). The latter has confirmed the doubling of the number of localities (from 310 in 2006 to 606 in 2015) comprising up to 115,000 people, or containing between 30 and 50 Czech Roma (GAC, *Analýza*, 2015, p. 15). Generally, an SEL is a "bad address." However, since 2020, the presence and degree of social exclusion at the municipal level is measured by a "social exclusion index," based on tracking several different indicators (Lang and Matoušek, *Metodika*). The highest concentrations of SELs are in the regions of North Bohemia and North Moravia.
4. Horváthová, "Nejsou vidět."
5. A state authority responsible for the social and legal protection of children.
6. Horváthová, "Nejsou vidět."
7. Gwen Albert (a fellow chronicler in this volume) in fact speaks of the "emergence of a fundamental axiom among many involved with human rights issues and the Romani minority across Europe—namely, that now was the time to double down on skepticism with regard to government action."
8. "Un silence aigu quand, la nuit, on retient son souffle pour entendre" (de Saint-Exupéry, *Lettre à un Otage*).
9. Bratton, "18 Lessons."

10. Dvořáková, "A Vy na virus věříte?"
11. Wade, "An Unequal Blow," cited in Gravlee, "Systemic Racism," 1.
12. Horton, "Offline."
13. Gravlee, "Systemic Racism," 5.
14. See http://www.szu.cz/anotace (last accessed 21 September 2022).
15. Sandset, "Necropolitics of COVID-19," 2.
16. Dlouhý, "Rodina viní."
17. Mbembe, "Necropolitics."
18. FRA, *Coronavirus Pandemic*.
19. "Half of the qualified estimate" is the exact definition.
20. Úřad Vlády ČR, *Zpráva*, 30.
21. Romea, "Agentura."
22. Macháčková, "Bez práce."
23. Apparently, the Czech education system is strongly possessed by Maxwell's demon, as Pierre Bourdieu would put it (Bourdieu, *Raisons Pratiques*, 40). In a summary analysis of inequalities in education, the researchers confirm that the Czech education system reinforces inherited inequalities (PAQ Research, *Nerovnosti ve vzdělávání*). Significant regional and social differences are manifest at all levels of education. Some factors typical of living in socially excluded areas—such as foreclosures, evictions, and housing shortages—contribute up to 46 percent to the educational failure of children from this background (ibid.). Children from a poor background are two to three times more likely to struggle at school if they live in hostels or other facilities typical for those living in SELs (ibid.).
24. Pavlas et al., *Vzdělávání na dálku*, 4–5.
25. Kovalčík, "Více než čtvrtina."
26. Ryvolová, and Houdek, "Literatura Romů."
27. The pandemic period has already given rise to a new field of "genres of the quarantine" (Clover, "Rise and Fall").

Bibliography

Bourdieu, Pierre. *Raisons pratiques. Sur la théorie de l'action* [Practical reason: On the theory of action]. Paris: Le Seuil, 1994.

Bratton, Benjamin. "18 Lessons of Quarantine Urbanism." *Strelka Mag*, 3 April 2020. Retrieved 3 May 2021 from https://strelkamag.com/en/article/18-lessons-from-quarantine-urbanism.

Clover, Joshuar. "The Rise and Fall of Biopolitics: A Response to Bruno Latour." *Critical Inquiry*, posted 29 March 2020. Retrieved 10 December 2021 from https://critinq.wordpress.com/2020/03/29/the-rise-and-fall-of-biopolitics-a-response-to-bruno-latour/.

Dlouhý, Hynek. "Rodina viní ze smrti mladíka chomutovskou nemocnici. Špitál pochybení odmítá" [The family blames Chomutov Hospital for the death of the young man: Hospital denies any fault]. *Litoměřický deník*, 18 March 2021. Retrieved 14 June 2021 from https://litomericky.denik.cz/z-regionu/rodina-chomutov-nemocnice-smrt-mladik-20210318.html.

Dvořáková, Petra. "A vy na virus věříte? Sociálně vyloučené lokality v době pandemie" [And you believe in the virus? Socially excluded locations in the time of the pandemic]. *Deník Referendum*, 7 May 2020. Retrieved 14 June 2021 from https://denikreferendum.cz/clanek/31166-a-vy-na-virus-verite-socialne-vyloucene-lokality-v-dobe-pandemie.

FRA (EU Agency for Fundamental Rights). *Coronavirus Pandemic in the EU: Impact on Roma and Travellers*. Bulletin 5, 2020. Retrieved 14 June 2021 from https://fra.europa.eu/sites/default/files/fra_uploads/fra-2020-coronavirus-pandemic-eu-bulletin-roma_en.pdf.

GAC. *Analýza sociálně vyloučených lokalit a absorpční kapacity subjektů působících v této oblasti* [Analysis of socially excluded locations and absorption capacity of institutions working in in this area]. Prague: GAC spol. s. r. o., 2006.

———. *Analýza sociálně vyloučených lokalit v ČR* [Analysis of socially excluded localities in the Czech Republic]. Prague: GAC spol. s.r.o., 2015.

Gravlee, Clarence C. "Systemic Racism, Chronic Health Inequities, and COVID-19: A Syndemic in the Making?" *American Journal of Human Biology* 32(5) (2020): e23482. https://doi.org/10.1002/ajhb.23482.

Horton, Richard. "Offline: COVID-19 is not a Pandemic." *The Lancet* 396(10255) (26 September 2020): 874. https://doi.org/10.1016/S0140-6736(20)32000-6.

Horváthová, Rena. "Nejsou vidět, přesto pomáhají! členky romské ženské skupiny Manushe podpořily ženy ve vyloučených lokalitách" [They do not see, yet they help! Members of the Roma Women's Group Manushe have been supporting women in excluded locations]. *Slovo21*, 2020. Retrieved 21 September 2022 from https://assets-global.website-files.com/61c1d8d802122cb75d70dc8c/61c1d8d802122c633870dd7f_Archive%20-%20Final-6.pdf.

Kovalčík, Martin. "Více než čtvrtina dětí nerozumí probírané látce" [More than a quarter of children don't understand the learned material being discussed]. Člověk v Tísni, 31 January 2021. Retrieved 14 June 2021 from https://www.clovekvtisni.cz/jak-se-uci-na-dalku-socialne-znevyhodnene-deti-7374gp.

Lang, Petr, and Roman Matoušek. *Metodika pro posouzení míry a rozsahu sociálního vyloučení v území* [Methodology for assessing the degree and extent of social exclusion within a given territory]. Prague: Agentura pro Sociální začleňování, 2020. Retrieved 21 September 2022 from https://www.socialni-zaclenovani.cz/dokument/metodika-pro-posouzeni-miry-a-rozsahu-socialniho-vylouceni-v-uzemi/.

Macháčková, Kristýna. "Bez práce, internetu a s virem. Lidi v ghettech stresuje covid i online výuka, opatřením již nevěří" [Without work or internet, but with the virus: People in the ghettos are stressed by COVID and online learning, and they no longer trust the precautions]. LIDOVKY.cz, 6 April 2021. Retrieved 14 December 2021 from https://www.lidovky.cz/domov/bez-prace-internetu-a-s-virem-lidi-v-ghettech-stresuje-covid-i-online-vyuka-opatrenim-jiz-neveri.A210406_113758_ln_domov_tmr.

Mbembe, Achille. "Necropolitics." *Public Culture* 15(1) (2003): 11–40. https://doi.org/10.1215/08992363-15-1-11.

PAQ Research. *Nerovnosti ve vzdělávání jako zdroj neefektivity. Souhrnná analýza pro Nadaci České Spořitelny* [Inequalities in education as a source of inefficiency: Summary analysis for the Česká Spořitelna Foundation]. Nadace České spořitelny, 2020. Retrieved 21 September 2022 from https://www.paqresearch.cz/post/ner ovnosti-vzdelani-neefektivita.

Pavlas, Tomáš, Dana Pražáková, Tomáš Zatloukal, Ondřej Andrys, Jiří Novosák, Roman Folwarczný, Irena Borkovcová, Zdeněk Modráček, and Karolína Chovancová. *Vzdělávání na dálku v základních a středních školách* [Distance education in primary and secondary schools]. Tématická Zpráva, Česká Školní Inspekce (CSI). Published in May 2020. Retrieved 21 September 2022 from https://www.csicr.cz/cz/Dokumenty/Tematicke-zpravy/Tematicka-zprava-Vzdelavani-na-dalku-v-ZS-a-SS.

Romea. "Agentura pro Sociální Začleňování: Kvůli epidemii může v ČR přibýt až 200 tisíc chudých a sociálně vyloučených lidí" [Agency for social inclusion: A possible surge of up to 200 thousand poor and socially excluded people in the Czech Republic due to the epidemic]. *Romea.cz*, 18 April 2021. Retrieved 14 December 2021 from http://www.romea.cz/cz/zpravodajstvi/domaci/agentura-pro-socialni-zaclenovani-kvuli-epidemii-muze-v-cr-pribyt-az-200-tisic-chudych-a-socialne-vyloucenych-lidi.

Ryvolová, Karolína, and Lukáš Houdek. "Literatura Romů na Československém území po roce 2000" [Romani literature in the Czechoslovak territory after the year 2000]. *CzechLit*, 14 April 2018. Retrieved 14 December 2021 from https://www.czechlit.cz/cz/feature/literatura-romu-na-ceskoslovenskem-uzemi-po-roce-2000/.

Saint-Exupéry, Antoine de. *Lettre à un otage* [Letter to a hostage]. Paris: Gallimard, 1943.

Sandset, Tony. "The Necropolitics of COVID-19: Class and slow death in an ongoing pandemic." *Global Public Health* 16(8–9) (2021): 1411–23. https://doi.org/10.1080/17441692.2021.1906927.

Úřad Vlády České Republiky. *Zpráva o stavu romské menšiny v České Republice za rok 2019* [Report on the state of the Roma minority in the Czech Republic for 2019]. Approved by the Czech Government on 23 November 2020 (resolution nr. 12/14). Retrieved 21 September 2022 from https://www.vlada.cz/assets/ppov/zalezitosti-romske-komunity/aktuality/Zprava-o-stavu-romske-mensiny-2019.pdf.

Wade, Lizzie. "An Unequal Blow." *Science* 368(6492) (15 May 2020): 700–703. https://doi.org/10.1126/science.368.6492.700.

CHAPTER 23

THE IMPACT OF THE PANDEMIC ON ACTIVISM AND THE ACTIVIST
Conversations with Jozef Miker

Yasar Abu Ghosh

Jozef (Jožka) Miker is a native of Slovakia, but he left there at the age of twelve with his parents when his father got a job in Trnovany near the North Bohemian town of Teplice. He graduated from the secondary technical school, and while still a student he started working in opencast mines as a miner. He eventually spent more than thirty years there, working in the shaft and as a highly skilled operator of the mine's big machines. He had to leave his job at the age of forty-five due to advanced Bechterew's Disease. As a pensioner, he took up full-time activism. Especially in 2011 and 2012, during the anti-Roma racist marches in North Bohemia, he was one of the most visible mobilizers of local Roma resistance. He also strongly advocated the removal of the industrial pig farm from the site of the former concentration camp for Roma in Lety u Písku.

I have met with Jožka on several occasions during the pandemic. What follows are excerpts from a series of conversations we had, formally and informally, in person and virtually, between March 2020 and September 2021. Initially, I had intended our conversations to serve as a window into the experiences and viewpoints of a veteran Roma rights activist into the pandemic crisis. Given his strong and long-standing involvement, particularly at the less visible local level, his experiences of how Roma have dealt with the effects of the pandemic are specific. He does not encounter their difficulties as an observer, but as someone to whom those affected turn for help. Moreover, he and his family often share similar difficulties as other Roma in the Ústí region.

During our conversations, it gradually became clear to me that the pandemic, unlike the virus itself, was undermining Jožka's agency. He found it very difficult to cope with not being able to move freely among the people who needed help, as he could not engage in his usual volunteer activities. Although he never used the term himself, the pandemic seemed to me to be leading to his "social death"—his agency was blunted, he could not ameliorate the urgency of the life situations of the people who were turning to him, and he was losing the vital impulse of his own altruism. It was particularly devastating for him when he confronted the death of Stanislav Tomáš.

On 19 June 2021, a year and a half into the global pandemic, Stanislav Tomáš, a Roma from Teplice, died during police detention. The police intervention was captured on the cell phone camera of a local resident, and the video went viral almost immediately. It shows police officers in the infamous kneeling position, putting pressure on the neck of the detainee. As in the case of George Floyd a year before, the detainee warns that he cannot breathe, but the police ignore him and continue the intervention for six minutes until Stanislav stops showing signs of life. Only then is medical assistance summoned. The circumstances of the intervention, as well as the subsequent course of the investigation, raised the suspicion that the responsible authorities were trying to divert attention from their own fatal mistakes. Consequently, a great wave of opposition arose not only in Teplice, but among Roma throughout the Czech Republic and abroad. From that moment on, Jožka, together with his close associate Míra Brož, has been dedicated to helping the bereaved and to demanding a fair, impartial, and thorough investigation of the circumstances.

However, the course of events was influenced by a novel phenomenon, the so-called "lifers" (*lifeři*). These are Roma influencers who comment on current events on social media, most often on Facebook, in live video feeds, and attempt to mobilize Roma people in this manner. This was the case in this instance too, when some influencers, who came from various parts of the Czech Republic, came to Teplice and tried to lead the Roma movement to clarify the circumstances of the death of Stanislav Tomáš. However, the influencers' activity is always accompanied by fundraisers to pay for their activism. Jožka Miker and Míra Brož have thus found themselves in the very unusual situation of competition when attempting to represent the bereaved family. Especially from the lifers' side, this competition was accompanied by an intense denunciation campaign, which took Jožka very much by surprise, and left a lasting impression on him. The lifers' resolve was short-lived, and fizzled out when their activities became suspicious to several donors who began to turn away from them. Nevertheless, in the course of events, words were spoken on social media and trenches dug that significantly weakened the possibility of a radical Romani movement against racial oppression, especially one emerging at a local level and from community organizing.

The death of Stanislav Tomáš occurred at a time when the pandemic measures had already been relaxed, and life was seemingly returning to normal. Jožka Miker was recovering from his pandemic "social death," and was once again finding opportunities to act in the struggle for the human and social rights of the Roma in Teplice. Especially during the first two weeks of the Roma community protests at the end of June 2021, I came to see Jožka in this way. The passages in the interview that follows where he explains his "compulsion to help" correspond with this moment. Yet with the entrance of the lifers comes a significant disillusionment and reassessment of goals, with Jožka lifting his gaze from helping specific actors to higher political and human rights goals.

Becoming a Roma Activist

As interviewer and editor, I have edited our conversation minimally. Additional information regarding specific events can be found in the endnotes.

YAG: Jožka, since when have you been doing activism, and how did you get into it?

JM: I got into activism in the early 1990s. Back then, the skinhead movement was growing here in Teplice. There were already some anarchists there to fight them, but the skinheads were really gaining strength. They started organizing marches.

One such march was organized in Dubská Street, which was a kind of Roma ghetto during the late socialist period. We Roma defended it and didn't want to let the Nazis in. And there was a guy there in his eighties with a pitchfork. The cops warned us against carrying any weapons. The Roma people originally armed themselves with axes and such, and wanted to defend their families, because everyone had threatened to kill them; but then they agreed not to carry any arms. The old guy was a *gadjo*;[1] there was more than one of them, because they used to go to Dubská to the pub. There was a field where they used to play football, it was called the Stará Drozďárna (Old yeast factory). I said to him, "Grandpa, what have you got there? Drop the pitchfork or the cops will pick you up!" And he says to me, "No way, son, we've already allowed this once. We had said to each other, 'It's only the Jews.' But what a horror that was, son! It must never come back."

I took this to heart and asked myself what I could do about it. Then Kuba Polák[2] appeared. He came up to me and introduced himself: "I'm Jakub Polák and I'm an anarchist." So we shook hands and we worked together until his death. We were separated for a while when Kuba was with [Ivan] Veselý. I didn't agree with the politics of ROI,[3] it was all corrupt. They did nothing, they presented themselves very little, they didn't go among the Roma, they despised the poor, they called them *degeš*.[4] I can't say anything to such people who despise the poor. As long as the Roma who have a shirt that costs five crowns more, and think they are worthy people and the others are beggars, then we will never get anything done.

Besides anti-fascist activism, I have also long been dedicated to honoring the victims of WWII with dignity. There are a lot of forgotten camps all around here where not only our people died, but also prisoners of war, and not much is known about them. My friends and I are trying to draw public attention to it.

YAG: How much time do you devote to activism and assistance to other Roma?

JM: I work all the time, there's not a day that goes by that I'm not working on something. Just when it looks like I might be free, some kids show up and say "Uncle, help us fill out the social security paperwork" or "Come with us to the office for social security." It just annoys me how many times they don't tell me the whole truth, you know? How many times do I put my head down at the office, apologize, and walk away, because it's not until I get there that I find out the truth about how these people are. That makes me angry. I tell them: "I'll help you, but I need to know the plain truth!"

YAG: Could you find a way to get them to tell you the plain truth?

JM: No, you just can't get some people to tell the truth. They only tell the truth when they're wrong. Some of them lie so much that they start believing their own lies. People are different, I get that; but if they want my help, they can't make me look like a fool, you know. Some people won't even thank you... If you help them, then you're their "uncle," if you don't, then you're a hunchbacked bastard who's never helped anyone. You give them infant formula that they couldn't afford to buy for their kids, you give them like ten packets because there's two kids—I get it from my friends who have a food bank, I don't buy it with my own money—but then they want twenty more for their relatives.

YAG: I know that you have had to face unexpected negative reactions and questioning of what you are doing in connection with the activities around the death of Stanislav Tomáš. But is it something you must deal with often, and how do you deal with it?

JM: Listen, the worst thing is when nobody appreciates you. We never expected gratitude, we often got scolded... like in the gym, remember?[5] I spent the whole summer on that, I didn't spend any time with my little daughter. My wife ran out of patience—she took the kids and left me. She was gone for three months, and I was alone for three months. No one said "Look, his wife and kids left him because he prefers to look after the vulnerable and puts them before his own family..." The price is terrible. When my daughter was a little girl, she kept asking me, "Daddy will you come with me to the pool, there are other dads there?" But I couldn't, I had to stay there [in the gym] and watch those people; the city police were even there in a van all the time, guarding the facility. A big NGO bought them food, and the women cooked, but they would leave a mess! So I had to go over there and yell at them to clean up after themselves first, and after that to take the food. I had their respect, they obeyed me... because they knew they wouldn't get anything the next day otherwise. Then the NGO ran out of supplies. With the help of a council deputy who borrowed money, I bought food and canned goods for them.

Look, my wife was throwing me out of here yesterday morning. She said, "You promised you'd get the rent. I can't afford it this month, so take your stuff and go to the people you're helping. Everybody promises you mountains and mountains, and you get it in the end, right? Shit!"

Predicaments of Help

YAG: I was intrigued by how you distinguished between the fact that some people help others for their own gratification, but that doesn't mean they are providing real help. What is real help then?

JM: Yes, that's right. For example, I don't have enough money to give someone two months of food, I can only give them a week or two from what I have. The family is taken care of for a few days, but what else? It's not just me that sees it that way, it's the same thing at the food bank, they don't give them a month's worth of food either... Just like that homeless guy I was telling you about. I met him here the other day, the former homeless guy. He was cleanly dressed, accompanied by a woman. He said hello and introduced me, and I could tell by the way he talks that he's a completely different person. Of course, he thanked me, so I told him not to thank me, to enjoy it. He's got a good job; he's just had a pay rise... So, he's left the residential hotel, and he's staying with the lady. She also goes to work, and he says that if it works out, they can't afford it yet, but in the winter, they may go on holiday together, skiing. Well, that's what warms your heart, their success.

YAG: During the Covid pandemic, did people need more short-term or long-term help?

JM: During Covid it was mostly the short-term help that was needed. However, even that couldn't be done for most of the time. People mostly needed help with food, rent, or paperwork. They needed to fill out forms at the welfare office all the time, even though the office was closed to the public. Applications and supporting documents had to be dropped off in the mailbox. It's important for the applications to be filled out perfectly, otherwise they'll get rejected. If the person can't write properly, they'll reject the application and not approve the vital assistance.

The government promised people something, but here in our region, the social assistance department didn't follow through. That's what irritated me the most. Maláčová[6] said on TV that it was possible to submit documents by email and I don't know what, but here they seemed thrilled about the fact that they could stop people from receiving money. Even though nothing was supposed to change in the payment of benefits, many people who had lost their jobs did not receive benefits.

They kept saying that people should visit the office—but they couldn't, could they—or send the documents in by email. I said to them, how are you supposed to get these people to email it to you? I mean, they're on welfare, they don't have Internet or a computer at home. Because if the welfare office inspection found out they had Internet and a computer, they'd tell them it's an unnecessary luxury and they'd cut their benefits.

We're going to have to move to a time when every person has access to the Internet and a computer, because you can't do anything without it these days. I say to them, after all, Minister Maláčová clearly said that the paperwork filed before the pandemic is sufficient for the whole pandemic period. I also complained to the minister. We have the misfortune that in the Ústí nad Labem region the person who oversees national minorities at the regional office is a member of the SPD,[7] so I guess you know what's going on... We have nowhere to complain... On the one hand, they want strong capitalism here, but they forget that strong capitalism is only possible with a strong social assistance network. They would probably prefer to build capitalism without the marginalized.

YAG: *And you personally, how has your life been affected during the pandemic?*

JM: Well, that was the worst crisis for me. My wife couldn't go to work, so we went into a lot of debt. Like everyone who worked in the hospitality industry, she lost everything from one day to the next. We were threatened with living on the street, with having our child taken away... Every month that we were locked up at home, our debt grew, and I had to borrow from decent friends.

YAG: *What happened to your voluntary work?*

JM: I had to stop all that, I couldn't even cook for the homeless... They'd come in here saying they were hungry. I've been cooking for the homeless with Karel Karika[8] for years. I would cook on Wednesdays in Teplice, and he would cook on Sundays in Ústí. Karel kept cooking, but I couldn't help him because we couldn't go out of town.

YAG: When you cooked here in Teplice, how did you pay for it?

JM: Well, on my own and people helped. Karel brought me some groceries, some people would send me money, 200–300 CZK. I tried it twice during the lockdown, but each time the cops came and threatened me with a fine. That was in winter. Luckily the people didn't starve, because there was an eatery for the homeless, where people went in three at a time and they could maintain social distancing. It was run by the NGO Květina, and they could also have a bath there.

People kept calling, of course, despite Covid, but I couldn't help them, I couldn't go to them. I felt sorry every time, but what could I do? Some even got mad at me. I didn't want to take any chances, and the ones who refused to wear masks and disputed the pandemic altogether, they especially didn't believe me.

YAG: What makes you endure in your activism? I noticed that when the Stanislav Tomáš case came up, which was right after the end of the lockdown, you were immediately reinvigorated, and you felt that you could do something.

JM: I don't know how to explain it to you, everybody's got their compulsion. Mine, the thing that drives me on and gives me a purpose in life, is this, that I can help. When I can do that, I have peace of mind. Even if I can't help everyone, and even if I must endure the reproach of my own family for preferring strangers. Besides, if I didn't help the people. . . others would abuse them.

When I can help others, I'm so happy, I can sleep in peace, I don't have to think about anything, I'm just so happy. I dream about it many times! Some people say I'm crazy: these are usually people who've never helped anyone. Most of the time, if I have something to help the poorest people here. But the people who think I'm crazy will come and say, "Why are you giving it to them? Give it to me!" That's what your relatives tell you, "You must take care of your family first." I know they're not as badly off as the people in need, though.

YAG: Do you feel like your volunteering and activism will change after Covid, that it will it be different than before?

JM: Absolutely! Many Roma people have lost hope; they think the government and everyone else is lying and stealing. They think that NGOs are making money off them. They come to me and ask me for the money I am supposedly getting because of them. They have no confidence in anyone, not in any politician or in any advocate. I have now lost a number of friends, both among the whites and the Roma, and we have even had a feud in the family because of this Covid. My sister and her family don't believe in it, they don't want to be vaccinated because they believe vaccines kill people, and they side with Volný.⁹ It may seem that there are just a few of them, but if you count the rise in the voter preferences for the SPD, Volný, and other extremist parties, then you can see that there are a lot of those people.

YAG: *You bring up a specific notion of loss, not just the loss of hope, but the loss of trust among people.*

JM: At first the Roma thought Covid didn't concern them. When they started to fear it, they found that nothing could save them... The people who have left me now—because I'm an asshole who got vaccinated, etc.—are the same people who sewed face masks and gave them away for free in the first wave of the pandemic. Some bought sewing machines and distributed face masks to hospitals and nursing homes... So they weren't bad people. Now, after the second wave, when the authorities said that it's not enough to have face masks, it must be a respirator, etc., and when these people found out how much money is being made from this, who owns the vaccination and testing centers, they lost confidence. Why does one person have to work nights for free while somebody else is getting rich from it? These are not people who live any differently than I do. It's that fucking Covid that's pushed us so far apart. I had my doubts at times too, you know I did... But then I thought, if it was just in one or two countries, maybe, but to have it all over the world? As several of my friends got sick over time, I knew it was true.

As for the loss of people, I'll tell you a story about Pete. He likes to drink, but he never goes to the pub, he only drinks outside because he has always been a sworn non-smoker. We often talked. He had two daughters, grandchildren, great-grandchildren. Nobody came to see him for the duration of Covid, except one of the daughters came once a fortnight to clean his apartment. He only had his wolfdog, so we'd go dog-walking together sometimes. There's a grocery store next door, so he'd always buy a beer, and drink it standing outside the store. During Covid his old dog died. I used to meet him here and I'd see he was just wasting away, as his family couldn't visit him. Then I didn't see him for a long time, and when I asked about him, they told me he had died. He was just miserable; he died a month after his dog. We had had big plans together... He was born in 1936 and lived here as a boy; he remembered that when he was delivering milk with his father, there was a POW camp not far from here, where different nationalities were imprisoned, even Roma. Nobody knows anything about that camp now, as there's no memorial, nothing.

Making Roma Lives Matter

YAG: *The experience of what is happening now, the Stanislav Tomáš case, has taken you quite by surprise. In what way, exactly?*

JM: This is probably the biggest shock for me, I'm terribly disappointed. I was getting depressed about it. How can people I have helped suddenly deny that I got them a place to live, that I helped them with their social security paperwork? All because some thief is ripping them off. In the end, it was us who buried Standa Tomáš, me and my associate Míra. That's how you get to know who people are. Some just follow the guy who is all talk and no action—a good liar. How easily people can be manipulated, persuaded! The worst thing, though, was the abuse during the live online broadcasts, against me and Míra, the implicit incitement to physically attack me.

One is easily disappointed. Listen to what happened to me recently. I got a call from a woman who said her husband had left her and she had nothing to eat with three children. She asked if I could send her some money, she gave me her account number. I told her I didn't have anything myself, but I'd get in touch with friends, and we'd visit her at 6 p.m. I didn't know her at all. Two friends arrived and I told them not to bring anything with us, that we would go and see her and find out what she needed. Well, when I called her at 5 p.m, she said she was no longer interested in our help.

[*Jožka is interrupted by a call*] "We don't have any more apartments, the ones we had a hard time getting were the ones in Bílina. It would be difficult to find two apartments for two big families. . . and what's the reason the owner is throwing her out? . . . Oh, and she has kids, how old? Well, I'll let you know, we'll try to find something. Does she only want it in Teplice, or doesn't it matter? Okay, I'll call you later."

So, another one, imagine this: the landlord kicking out the tenant because she didn't pay him the full rent. She's a *gádji*. I just got a call from my wife, it's her co-worker. I don't know where my head is again. When I have an apartment for one, another one needs money; but if I have money, then it's an apartment that's needed.

YAG: *So now you'll have something to do for at least a week.*

JM: That's gotta be more than a week. . . Because if she hasn't paid all the rent, that means she has nothing. Who's gonna rent to her? Moreover, the shelter for single mothers in Krupka is completely full, places are long gone.

YAG: *What do you think you'll end up remembering about the affair with Stanislav?*

JM: Probably the people who called me names and threatened me. How easily they believed the lies! How a person can be mean and turn around! Otherwise, as far as this thing is concerned, I have only one goal or wish left, which is not completely unrealistic according to what a friend who works in the European Commission told me. That is to have a Europe-wide ban on police kneeling on suspects during arrests. That would be a win for me, and that is what I am going for. I can't bring him back, but this could save more lives.

At a recent meeting, the regional police director himself offered to meet three times a year with other activists who really want to make a difference—not those who just talk the talk. Recently, the regional liaison officer for ethnic minorities got in touch to let us know what has and hasn't been done in recent times at our monthly meetings. The regional liaison seems to be interested in our advice, wants to discuss specific cases with us, and so on. They also proposed that I teach future police officers at the police academy the Romani language. They offered a regular contract for that.

YAG: *Then you'll do it, won't you?*

JM: No, never! Cops don't need to speak Romanes, I would be betraying my own people! The Salesians are building a cultural center across the street from here, and they want me to teach Romanes there too. I don't care who goes there.

YAG: *Not a policeman, though.*

JM: Not a policeman. Again, I don't think I can work very well with a policeman either. That could backfire on me. I'm Roma and an activist, what then? No, it's not possible at any price. There are certain boundaries that can't be crossed.

Now I still want to finish two urgent things. I'm doing a campaign in Romanes to get Roma people vaccinated, and we're making videos that will be broadcast on Facebook and YouTube. I also want to help Míra organize in Krupka and Teplice so that Romani people will come and get vaccinated in the mobile vaccination centers. The ambulance so far has been to two places around. Only twenty people came for vaccinations, though, it was bad publicity.

Jozef (Jožka) Miker is a native of Slovakia. For over thirty years he worked as a miner in North Bohemia, and retired aged 47 due to advanced Bechterew's Disease. He then took up full-time activism and was one of the most visible mobilizers of Roma resistance during the anti-Roma racist marches in North Bohemia of 2011–12. He has strongly advocated the removal of the industrial pig farm from the site of the former concentration camp for Roma in Lety u Písku.

Yasar Abu Ghosh studied ethnology at Charles University in Prague, and social anthropology at École des Hautes Études en Sciences Sociales in Paris. He teaches at the Department of Social and Cultural Anthropology, Faculty of Humanities, Charles University. He has also taught at universities in Munich, Budapest, and Paris. He has been researching Roma since his graduate studies. Among his main research interests are fugitive politics, survival strategies, and politics of commemoration. He has acted as an expert on European as well as national expert and advisory boards.

Notes

1. A term designating "non-Roma" in Romani language.
2. Jakub Polák (1952–2012) was a Czech anarchist and antiracism activist; he often acted as an attorney-in-fact for Roma who had been victims of racial attacks.
3. ROI (Roma Civic Initiative), a Romani political party that was established shortly after the Velvet Revolution but never really attracted a large Roma following. The party was dissolved in 2005. Ivan Veselý served temporarily as its executive secretary.
4. A "low-life" in Romani language.
5. In the summer of 2018, more than two hundred mostly Roma inhabitants of the Modrá residential hotel in the town of Ústí nad Labem suddenly found themselves without shelter when the authorities closed the facility. Jožka and his organization Konexe helped the families, first to find temporary shelter in a school gym and then to place them in new homes.
6. Jana Maláčová, minister of labour and social affairs, 2018–21.
7. *Svoboda a přímá demokracie* (SPD, Freedom and direct democracy), a nationalist, anti-immigration and anti-Muslim party known for its welfare chauvinism.
8. Karel Karika has been a city representative in Ústí nad Labem and a local politician since 2014 (Green and later Pirates party). However, he has been active as a Roma public figure since the 1980s. In 2019 he received the František Kriegel Award, which is handed out annually by the Charter 77 Foundation for human rights activism.
9. Lubomír Volný, until October 2021 an MP, and currently the leader of a fringe, anti-vaxxer, and nationalist party *Volný blok*.

CHAPTER 24

DENIAL OF DANGER
COVID-19, Disinformation, and When to Burst Our Bubbles

Gwendolyn Albert

I live in Prague, Czech Republic, where COVID-19 had devastating results during the country's "second wave" in the autumn of 2020. I have long worked as a human rights activist reporting from this country on the more egregious abuses against the Romani community, such as the denial, until recently, of their suffering during the Holocaust, the forced sterilization of Romani women which is now about to be compensated at long last, and the lack of access to adequate education. Both my husband and I have been working for ourselves online for more than a decade. I am a translator for the news server Romea.cz, so even prior to vaccination being available, the pandemic impacted our own day-to-day lives very little. However, in terms of communicating with our fellow human beings, including Romani community members—and especially before vaccination was available—the pandemic plunged us into what still feels like a never-ending ethical dilemma, as we constantly come up against different states of denial held by those around us about our common situation.

Among those in civil society with whom I usually communicate in the Czech Republic, both Roma and non-Roma, I have been disappointed to observe many who have felt free to express views of the ongoing COVID-19 pandemic that have either flirted with a denial of the reality of the global situation or have outrightly espoused the view that officials communicating about the pandemic to us are a priori not to be trusted. While in many respects skepticism of government can be a sensible attitude, in this circumstance it has veered towards the slippery slope of reality-denying conspiracy theory. I have also observed the drastic contrast between people's actual behavior and their recounting of their own behavior, which is yet another aspect of denying reality. This denialism has presented me with a dilemma that remains unresolved and is perhaps unresolvable: When does it become ethically necessary to try to burst somebody else's denial bubble?

As most experiences of disappointment are related to expectations, it would be appropriate to state the basic expectation I have been holding, albeit one that the reality of the pandemic has greatly challenged: namely, that, by and large, people in the Czech Republic do want their fellow human beings to enjoy good health. The country took the step recently of banning smoking in pubs, but the fact that the number of "private clubs" where smoking over drinks continues unabated should probably have clued me in to the reality that indifference to whether others live or die is more the governing ethos here. But what can I say—I'm slow.

The first moment of confrontation that generated denialism in the Czech Republic was the government's March 2020 decision to declare a state of emergency involving the closing of the country's borders. Of course, discussion of the deadliness of the virus had been percolating since the start of the year, and one of the last indoor, in-person gatherings I attended in February 2020 with the Romea.cz staff before the country went into lockdown involved a colleague returning from a ski vacation in Italy, and those of us greeting her of course made what are now regrettable jokey references to her potential contagiousness, given that the official description of the trajectory of the disease describes it as coming from that country. Indeed, my husband and I had traveled to Italy ourselves over Christmas, when the virus was thought to be "far away" in China, without even giving it a second thought.

The closing of the borders triggered a response among those whom I know here that once again revealed to me how, despite having lived in the Czech Republic for a quarter-century, my mindset differs fundamentally from the non-Roma and Roma who were born here. Following the social media posts among the Roma community members who regularly respond to reporting on Romea.cz, I could see that they and everybody else were full of recriminations against the authorities, and had absolutely no faith in the notion that this could possibly be a plausibly appropriate decision in terms of preventing the spread of a disease for which there is no cure, for which there was at the time no vaccine, and that often spreads asymptomatically. Many middle-aged commenters, whether non-Romani or Romani, were clearly envisioning a return of the restrictions they had to live through during communism. It soon became clear that there was no point in trying to respond to these fears. Pointing out to people that an end date for the border closure had in fact been announced from the very beginning (and that it was eventually honored) seemed to be irrelevant. By contrast, my own assumption was that the authorities would only take such a step if the alternative of allowing uninterrupted travel were logically worse—and in any event, my access to international media made it clear to me that the number of safe travel destinations was rapidly dwindling. However, the environment for comment was highly politicized and so I found myself choosing not to engage in discussions of reality versus the hypothetical dystopia being darkly predicted. The same applied to conversations in which Romani interlocutors began to tell me that this was a sign of the End Times, as foretold by the Bible, a parallel I understand but do not consider as an explanation; or when I saw media reports in which Romani community members had insisted to journalists that COVID-19 was a disease of the non-Roma only. Having little to no standing to refute such nonsense, I was more and more in the position of a silent observer to this loud, proud denial of reality.

As the pandemic dragged on and the situation grew increasingly more deadly, I began to see the emergence of a fundamental axiom among many involved with human rights issues and the Romani minority across Europe, namely, that now was the time to double down on skepticism with regard to government action. The guiding thesis was that the introduction of emergency powers necessarily involved the potential for increased repression, especially of the Roma. Far fewer discussions among that same community came to my attention about how to constructively and effectively recommend the proactive use of such state power for the common good. In the beginning, with respect to Romani issues in particular, a great deal of attention was attracted by the Government of Slovakia deploying the military to test the residents of Romani settlements and the subsequent (evidence-based) recommendations made to quarantine some of them. Media outlets focused on the civil society response, reported in full, on the acrimony between some in the nonprofit sector, including human rights activists, and the authorities. An incident of police brutality against some Romani children breaking the quarantine rules then happened, and the investigation of it has become protracted, although that is no different to every other such incident prior to the pandemic. The Slovak Public Defender of Rights also critiqued the way Romani settlements were quarantined.

At the time that it was happening, I found the critique of the quarantining hard to take in a situation where the ostensible aim of these measures was to save people's lives, and where the bringing of the tests to the segregated Roma seemed predicated upon the idea that they would have difficulty accessing them otherwise. At the same time as I was translating the reporting done about the Roma in Slovakia for Romea.cz, I was fully aware of what the media were relating about the situation of marginalized people of color in the United States, who were and still are dying faster than anybody else, had less access to everything needed to protect themselves, and were disproportionately forced to work in conditions of exposure. The US president was in full denial mode; the powers of the state to help people understand their health status and options were going barely untapped there. In comparison with the denialism of Trump, the actions of the Slovak authorities seemed proactive to me. The fact that the situation of the entire human race worldwide had radically changed, and that the Slovak authorities' measures were likely, on balance, to save lives was not being acknowledged at all by those in civil society from whom I was hearing. It was also not clear to me what their proposed alternative was. I did not comment on this to anybody at the time, but as I rarely find myself in disagreement with others in the human rights field, my own internal reaction to these developments gave me cause to pause, because it made me question how reliable these sources of information were about the situation there.

Towards the end of 2020, I was asked by an international organization to monitor media reporting in the Czech Republic about the Romani minority in the context of the pandemic. Quite surprisingly, according to my survey of the media up until the close of that year, the opportunity for Roma-bashing that COVID-19 could have presented was not really pursued in the Czech media and, when it was pursued, gained little traction. Rather, what we saw here was inaction and, to my mind, a much more insidious silence about how "Roma fellow-citizens" (*Rómští spoluobčané*) have been faring during this particular cataclysm. The issue of the impact of school closures and the digital divide for marginalized Roma remains an extremely neglected topic. The Romani media published a lot of content at the start of the pandemic about Romani people voluntarily sewing face masks and engaging in different kinds of local self-help, but that material was not taken up by the mainstream media, which continued to frame the Roma as outsiders, through the lens of repatriations from the UK or the situation in the settlements of Slovakia. Most regrettably, none of the Czech media, not even those outlets focused on Roma, had any idea about how to report facts about the health status of the Romani community in the aggregate—how many Roma had undergone what kinds of testing, how many had what they needed to keep themselves safe, how many were hospitalized, how many had died?

It would not be until far later in the pandemic, a good six months in, that the issue of the COVID-19 denialism and disinformation being consumed and shared by members of the Romani community online—and not just by them—would begin to be covered by the media outlets interested in Roma. I witnessed more than one person surprisingly share for serious consideration media reports comparing this catastrophe to "the flu" or discussing "herd immunity" in ways that implied we should not be concerned by our fellow human beings dying in this way. Again, I found it best not to engage, but chose the route of making no comment and even, at one point, "muting" some people from my Facebook feed whom I otherwise consider important colleagues, so that I wouldn't have to watch the litany of doubts. The issue of vaccination has only regenerated this pattern.

The exertion of social pressure from others to gather in person waxed and waned, and in the time prior to vaccination being available it was, in retrospect, one of the most upsetting aspects. The handful of times that I agreed to meet with people—always outdoors, and I was always in full mask and gloves—were inevitably followed by the news of yet another near-miss with the virus, as the acquaintances, many of them from the Romani community, who had randomly passed by in the street later got in touch to say they had been officially diagnosed. Some people bragged, in a cavalier fashion at certain times, that the virus would not keep them from doing as they pleased, only to regret it later. Others blithely discussed international travel plans in the pre-vaccination days. Again, I held my tongue after realizing that if somebody was going to dissuade them from putting themselves and others at risk, it was not going be me—my standing did not include that kind of power, and it would have been foolish for me to have made the attempt.

By the fall, COVID-19 denialism had finally found its official political home on the rightward side of the extremism spectrum here in the Czech Republic, with antivaxxers exploiting antisemitic tropes and engaging in violent demonstrations. That and the deathbed Facebook broadcasts by Romani community members seemed to galvanize a refocusing on the issue by the civil society people whom I know, but by then it was far too late to change anybody's behavior. I still recall the shock I felt seeing the release of a Romani music video in the summer of 2020, where a popular performer included a well-known Romani community member and TV journalist in a depiction of face-mask-less partying. I don't know if everybody on the set was tested before filming or not, but the production of such a diversion with the date 2020 on it is unlikely to age well—depending on your perspective, of course. Some will probably only ever see it as a declaration of independence.

It was in September 2020 that I became an official member of the Czech Government Council on Romani Minority Affairs. Once vaccines began rolling out, I endeavored at the beginning of 2021 to reach the Health Ministry about whether or not they were planning a targeted campaign for the Romani community regarding vaccinations. The anodyne, laconic email response that I initially received was confirmation yet again of the "insidious neglect" scenario—the ministry's representative on the council said there were no plans in particular to target messaging about the vaccine to Romani communities that were any different than those to anybody else. It took a great deal of strenuous intervention by colleagues at the Office of the Government for us to finally reach the person responsible for rolling out the mobile vaccination campaign in hard-to-reach locations, which has happened with local Romani nonprofit support in many areas; but the idea of a special campaign, featuring Romani personalities, delivered through Romani media outlets, died on the shakily supported vine that is being a volunteer civil society member on this particular advisory body. There was, however, a new committee set up to do more of the investigative work on how COVID-19 has impacted the Romani community, and I anticipate that information in that regard will be published by the Office of the Government's 2020 Report on the State of the Romani Minority.

I have now received two shots of Moderna and so can meet with people in person, following what I understand the guidelines to be for preventing transmission. The recriminations for corporate and government failures are flying. Romani people living in countries further east, such as Bulgaria and Romania, have indeed been subjected to terrible mistreatment by the authorities all this time—as indeed they always were prior to the pandemic—but that news has been slow to reach any but the experts who communicate amongst themselves. The authorities in the Czech Republic seem unable to stick with anything—one health minister broke the country's guidelines and had to resign, and public communications systems about the development of the pandemic have been launched only to be withdrawn or undermined almost immediately. Mistrust in the authorities was a self-fulfilling prophecy. At the beginning of the pandemic, when people made their own face masks as a gesture of defiance to the authorities after the government mandated the use of something in such short supply, there was a sense of genuine social solidarity, but it proved all too fleeting. Without a foil against which to define themselves, people seem incapable of boosting each other's morale, to say nothing of encouraging each other to do what is actually objectively best for both themselves and others—and yes, figuring that out is not beyond us, and those giving us such advice do not necessarily have ulterior motives. Nevertheless, one dear Romani friend who is the same age as me described to me how she has been vaccinated, whereas both her parents and her own offspring are delaying getting the jab. She has decided that those decisions are theirs to make, and she will not be attempting to persuade them to do otherwise—to each their bubble.

My experience of the pandemic is that despite my tiny household having avoided the disease (so far), I despair of ever again convincing my colleagues in civil society to do the right thing for the right reasons. If enlightened self-interest won't motivate a commitment to respecting reality, then probably nothing will. It apparently takes much less to tip us over into irrational behavior than I ever realized. I hope not to deny that particular reality about my fellow human beings in the future.

Gwendolyn Albert is a human rights activist whose work to secure redress for unlawfully sterilized people has been recognized by the Committee for the Redress of the Roma Holocaust in the Czech Republic (Award for Humanity, 2020), as well as by the Embassy of the United States of America to the Czech Republic (Alice G. Masaryk Human Rights Award, 2021).

CHAPTER 25

LOCKED DOWN IN OUR OWN PERSONAL QUARANTINE
How Nothing Can Be Taken for Granted

Iveta Kokyová

For a moment I believed that everything bad is actually good for something. When the pandemic began, people joined forces. It seemed like all were equal and fighting for the same cause. Gradually all that changed, however, and more and more hateful behavior and ugly opinions have been surfacing in society. Pain, wrongdoing, remorse, even envy. There was so much of it that I began to be very sad.

I embraced my family, even in my thoughts. An unexpected feeling of gratitude and solidarity overwhelmed us. Of course, we argue sometimes, we do not share the same opinions about everything, but we stick together, we are there for each other. This is absolutely a given, especially when times are tough.

At work and in my neighborhood I meet people from different walks of life. Until recently, however, one thing had always eluded my understanding—namely, that family cannot be taken for granted.

Just a couple of days before the state of emergency and quarantine was announced, I was taking the train home to Hradec Králové from Prague. I usually take the bus, but this time everything was different. When I entered the train compartment, a tall and heavyset man was sitting there who quite elegantly and willingly let me sit next to the window when I mentioned that I do not like to sit rear-facing. The entire compartment smelled of his cologne and I said to myself: *"Uf,* that's really strong." After a while, though, the fragrance began to seem pleasant to me. I even remembered black-and-white films and to wondered what gentlemen must have smelled like back in the day. Those fleeting thoughts were then replaced by a brisk chat. The man, now sitting in the seat opposite from me, observed the landscape as it flew past and suddenly leaned towards me slightly, smiled, and asked if I was on my way home.

"Yes, I'm going home. I've been at school for finals, they turned out well, I'm glad to say. I live in Hradec Králové. Where are you going? Are you also from Hradec?"

"Yes, I am also going to Hradec Králové. Imagine, I was meant to be at a conference today, I hadn't even got off the train before I received a text message to say that it was being cancelled due to the state of emergency."

"That's unpleasant," I immediately respond. Personally, I would have been angry to have spent time going there only to turn around and head back. He was not, though.

"It doesn't matter, at least I get to go for a ride," he answered.

The train came to the next stop, the doors opened, and a middle-aged lady joined us. My fellow passenger leaned back in his seat and again looked out of the window in a melancholy way. Her arrival had interrupted our conversation. It seemed he did not want to speak in front of her. So I pulled out a book and began studying. But I noticed that at each station he followed whether the lady would be getting up and leaving. At the same time, I saw in his eyes the wish that nobody else would enter our compartment at any of the next stops. It seems absurd to me, when I write about it now, but at the same time it seems magical. It basically does not matter who believed what. That is how it is in life. We think about things, we have expectations and ideas. Sometimes they are fulfilled and sometimes not.

The lady eventually left the train. The only other person to enter the compartment was a young man with a trolley offering snacks, including iced coffee. Our conversation could continue. We sat there by ourselves and sipped the refreshing coffee.

"Really an unplanned coffee today," he spoke after a moment. It seemed he was searching a bit for words or thinking about what to say.

"What do you mean? Do you have all your coffees planned?" I smiled.

"No, that's not it, I just didn't expect to have coffee on the train today," he said, sipping from the cup, and again averted his gaze. He squinted his eyelids nervously.

You know, I have listened to a lot of life stories. And I have to admit that people routinely reach out to me and talk, spontaneously. I myself really love being with people. Each story gives a glimpse into the lives of others. Recently everything has started to revolve around the pandemic and around our worries; not just about our health, but about jobs and the harmony of relationships related to that. There are fears lurking all around us, and new information, either biased or truthful, is circulating in the media. We have become stuck in our social bubbles—and in our own selves. We curse the situation and wonder why me, why him, why is this happening. We have little joy, we feel ashamed to smile, it is as if COVID-19 has swept away everything that kept us afloat in our ordinary concerns.

We pull down our face masks and sip coffee. I am listening to a sad life story. I am a little paralyzed, I don't know what to say. Why is this person confiding in me, how will this conversation go? It is weird. Maybe he is a colleague, or a friend from past lives—and I smile inwardly at my own justifications for having affection towards this man whom I do not know.

The man was full of pain. But he was not really complaining. Maybe he just needed to talk. He spoke as if reading a book. About the hard work, the wife who cheated on him and had a child with another man, the cancer he had, the stroke and the time he spent in a coma. His family has turned their back on him. And me? My jaw dropped in amazement at the openness of this stranger and the vicissitudes of life. There are things and situations for which there are no soothing, magical words. We all would like the magic words to exist that could heal all wounds.

I am silent, pursing my lips, wishing I could say something comforting. But so what, it is like a story from a novel.

"When I was in hospital, nobody from my family ever came to visit me," the man says, crushing the empty cup in his hand, and even more pain can be felt from his words. It is so piercing that I would like to move one seat over to avoid the arrows of his words. I quickly recover, though. In every novel there is a friend who comforts, listens, helps. I guess that is supposed to be me today. And so I start playing my role in this bizarre game of destiny.

"Why? I don't understand. That could never, ever happen in our family. That is unacceptable!" I hastily exclaim, but immediately add that in our family we are accustomed to solving problems together, even though they are very often hard and unpleasant.

"I don't get it either. I was in the hospital, visiting hours came, I was suffering. I saw families visiting patients, speaking kindly to them, feeding them. Tears were running down my face, I had to turn my back so they wouldn't see me cry. I felt like a little child whose mother had failed to come for him. It's strange, right... To hear a grown man speak this way. But you know, everybody needs to love somebody and to have someone who loves them," he answered.

I immediately felt empathy and sympathy for this story. I felt bad for him, I wanted to help him somehow, even if only by listening attentively. My impression of him was that he was decent.

My intuition told me that this tall, heavyset gentleman was greatly suffering, and his soul was in pain, and I immediately remembered my own son.

This year 2020, in February, my son was diagnosed with schizophrenia. It was a blow. And something completely foreign to us, something unfamiliar. We didn't know what to do, how to help him. I think just about every parent suffers the most when they see their child suffering and are unable to help. I would call it a kind of inner desperation. In my family we are fighters, though, so I always tell everybody never to give up. As long as we have faith, we have hope.

I understood each word the gentleman said to me through the story of my own son, and I empathized. My son, immediately after his diagnosis, lived at home with us for three months, even though he has his own apartment, wife, and a married child. For three months my husband and I gave him safety and love. He was afraid, afraid of everything. You know, we were scared too, but we would never let it show. He needed our support and strength. I cannot imagine that at the time when my child needed the most love I would have turned away from him and left him to fend for himself. I could never, as a mother, have forgiven myself for such a thing. It does not matter how old we are, each of us needs to receive love, to feel that we belong and to know that we have a family, a functional one.

I listen to the man in the compartment, and here and there the stories of other people come to mind. It's as if having a family today were an expensive luxury—a commodity that is not for sale, that each of us has to steal for themselves or go without. No, it cannot be taken for granted! How grateful I am that my family experiences the good and the hard things together.

"One disease came right after another, so I couldn't cope. I began taking antidepressants," the gentleman continues his story.

"Given all you've been through, I would have been surprised if you weren't taking them. I'm sorry," I say, wandering back and forth between our conversation and my own thoughts. The random man on the train has forced me to think about the relationships in our family. They are not flawless, I am thinking, but we learn from each other and when the going gets tough, we definitely get the entire family to help the one in need to get through it.

"We're getting close to Hradec, we have fifteen minutes more to talk. I'm really glad to have been able to meet you," he says with a smile, and it is clear he is doing his best to steer the conversation in a more positive direction. Our time was over.

"I'm glad to have met you too. I wish you all the best! Take care of yourself," I smile back, and head for the door.

We go past the Hradec Králové sign, and the train stops. I briskly put on my coat. My fellow passenger invites me for tea to continue our chat. I decline politely because my husband is waiting for me in the car. We exchange contact information, shake hands, and say goodbye.

On the way home I brooded over this odd encounter. I remembered my children, the events of recent years. My granddaughter contracted diabetes, and my daughter who lives abroad gave birth to a beautiful daughter of her own, but fear of the pandemic is making her parenthood difficult. If only I could be everywhere at once. I do not want to admit to myself that my children are adults, and that I should let them experience some of life's trials on their own. Or should I? No! I do not want to. How happy I am when they call for advice, when I bounce my grandkids on my knee and pick up the toys they have thrown all over, and how sad my husband and I are when the door closes and the house is quiet again.

It seems there is something worse than disease itself. That is loneliness. Nobody in the world should have to be alone. Loneliness is intrusive, it steals away our faith. If we cannot believe in something, then we cannot begin to undertake change, not even in our own selves.

That same evening the man from the train sent me a text message to wish me a beautiful evening. The next day he wished me a beautiful morning, and so our lively communication by text messages began. Because quarantine had been announced and I was not going to work, I had a lot of time to devote to writing these messages. We wrote to each other in the morning, in the mid-morning, in the afternoon and in the evening. There was always something for us to write about, our topics were inexhaustible. Out of a sense of gratitude that I was giving him my time, he began to write me poems, which pleased me very much, and that awakened something surprising in me, something I had not known for a long time.

The gentleman from the train opened up in me a faith, an awareness, an awakening, and a love for all that lives. The poems, which exuded genuine feelings and a longing for a better, less lonely life, forced me to reflect on life as such. Each line confirmed for me that it was high time I reassessed my own values.

Through emails and text messages, we mutually confided in each other and believed that we were of great support to one another, even though we had only known each other for a few days. The gentleman from the train and I had found in each other a confidant, an attentive listener. We developed a special virtual relationship—I mean, how could we not. We discussed different situations, family, castles, rocks, flowers, the sky and stars, all that is animate and inanimate.

When I read these lines, yes, I too have to smile; perhaps some of you will think I have absolutely lost my mind. Sometimes a word is more than a physical touch and more than a whip. It can both caress and slash. Words are stories, hopes, experiences, and without them we cannot live our lives.

I believe the pandemic is influencing our emotional makeup and perceptions. We are both more sensitive and more irritable; more vulnerable and more determined. We are learning to live with new challenges, new situations. We are reassessing our lives, priorities, and values. We perceive the world around us in a much deeper way. We are more open with each other, we have a need to communicate our innermost feelings.

The days went by and I started to really like this man. Maybe our encounter on the train was not an accident, but destiny. Maybe coincidences do not exist, but everything happens for a reason. I had met a man who longed to be heard. He needed somebody to talk with, somebody to visit him in the hospital. I still do not understand why his family is unable to give him that. Have they done something wrong to each other? What can be so bad that it cannot be forgiven? Or maybe it is just the absence of feeling.

What role can I, a distant virtual soulmate, play in his life now? When will my role in this end, or have we perhaps found a friendship for life? Maybe I was meant to fill his life with understanding and recognition, and to deepen his self-esteem and self-confidence. I did everything I could for that. The tall, heavyset gentleman enchanted me somehow. He confirmed to me that I would never want to be left alone in this world, and that what helps us is exactly the safety of a family and a feeling of belonging. Loneliness must be maddening. He intensified my receptivity, compassion, and gratitude.

What is loneliness like in a time of pandemic, when we are all cut off from normal life? Some people are going crazy from being in their family environments because they are unaccustomed to spending time together. Others are bored, and others are enjoying family life as much as possible. But when someone is all alone or maybe loses any social contact, they can experience such overwhelming loneliness that is difficult to fill the hole.

That has led me to many questions. I am reflecting more and more frequently on what our social roles are, how we fulfill them, to what degree we even need social contact. I am not speaking about this on a sexual level. There are also asexual people who do not like any kind of physical contact or touching, and yet still need somebody in their lives who understands them.

And that is basically what I have concluded. Each of us is seeking understanding, and on the other hand we are most afraid of what we do not understand, of what we do not know how to comprehend.

Loneliness cannot be fully understood, it is impossible to grow accustomed to it, and it is not easy to live with it. I believe the same applies to understanding. We long for someone to understand us, to become part of us, whether as a friend or as a life partner.

Right now, it is far more difficult to make such contact. On the other hand, the anonymous gate of the Internet is opening, where it is possible for shy individuals, or for those who find it hard to establish new relationships, to dare to become bolder.

Loneliness terrifies me. I have never been alone. I am rereading one of the recent messages sent to me by this man whom I hardly know. A shiver runs down my spine, I am sad. I feel melancholy for all those who are distressingly alone. One day he wrote me this:

> When I quietly slip away from this world, I know nobody will miss me. Oh, precious human. I'm sinking into darkness and have been for some time. I have dark thoughts. You are my light that brings me joy in life and hopefully still will. You know, my experiences have been absolutely different from your kind words. A complete lack of feeling and concern, or just the minimum, and what's worse, probably feigned. I could go on, but it's not appropriate to mention.

I reproach his family for the coldness they are bestowing upon him. I know very well that there are many such families. They live side by side, they share nothing, they do not care about each other. I have never known that kind of loneliness. We were exchanging emails and our worlds were absolute opposites. That is exactly what brought us together. I have given him a reason, day after day, to sit at the computer and try to write a few nice sentences, and to tear himself away from his oppressive loneliness. And he has held a mirror up to me and has amplified even more my awareness of, and perspective on, what it means to have a complete family full of love.

It did not take long for him to write to me that I am his angel in this world. I do believe in angels, they are hidden within us. Each of us has an opportunity to help others, to empathize.

Sometimes that is enough. I pray for him every night. I would like his broken spirit and heart to heal. I think about how he will yet come to know love, and spend his days with a loved one.

I look around my apartment. The children will come over soon. My husband is already looking out of the window for them. The place is tidied up, there are toys waiting in the corner. Lunch has been ready since the morning. This is nothing unusual, I know. It is just that I have realized that this is what is called the warmth of home. This is my daily faith, seeing the grandchildren's hope, and spending this time together gives loneliness no chance. It is a shame I cannot chop off a bit from my own happiness and give it away. That probably would not be right, though; everyone must, paradoxically, fight for their own happiness. Can loneliness lead to that? I hope so. Difficult moments manage to give us a kick, and we stubbornly tell life: "Not like that! I'm going to grab a piece of my own happiness."

Go on, go on, mysterious friend from the train compartment. Find your happiness in this strange silent time.

Sometimes we are locked down in our own personal quarantines. We are hiding from the world, from our feelings, and absolutely most frequently we are hiding from ourselves. We flee pain and hide from fear. If there were nothing but happiness and joy, though, the scales of fate would not be balanced.

The pandemic and quarantine have brought into my life a lot of space for reflection, and have put a man in my path with a mirror to reflect my life back at me. You know, I am a little embarrassed when I read his words and know that I am so well off.

Many people are angry about the restrictions that are now in place—that they cannot go outside, have fun, and live "normally." But as long as we have others with whom to live and for whom to live, then no quarantine limits our lives that much. It is we ourselves who build these barriers. We have this time to spend together, and some are actually angry about it. Maybe when you next get annoyed, you will recall my friend from the train, who would have given his very life for such a quarantine in the company of his family. Let us stay cheerful, let us keep ourselves in good condition, and maybe we can overcome all gloom and diseases.

I close these lines with humility, and embrace my loving family with each word.

Iveta Kokyová was born in Hořice, her mother a Slovak Roma and her father a Vlach Roma. She speaks both dialects, but uses Slovak Romani as the main language of her literary message, and writes both poetry and prose. Trained as a mechanic, she worked as a cleaner and packer, then as a fieldworker for the Hradec Králové City Council, and now she is an evaluation coordinator for inclusive education. She is also a 5th-year student at the Faculty of Arts at Charles University, majoring in Romani Studies. Iveta Kokyová belongs to the youngest generation of Romani authors who have established themselves on the scene only in the post-millennial era. She draws mainly on her childhood, family stories, and her own experiences.

❊ ❊ ❊

Concluding Reflections

Paloma Gay y Blasco and Martin Fotta

We write these reflections in late April 2022, exactly two years after we decided to gather firsthand accounts of the impact that the pandemic was having on Romani communities in five countries. Back in April 2020, during the first lockdown, we lived the COVID-19 pandemic as a new, overwhelming, all-encompassing, incomprehensible event. Now, with lockdowns a thing of the past, and face masks, testing, and self-isolation phased out in many countries, we are told that the virus has simply become another annoyance to live with. Whereas we used to turn away from the news because of anxiety, we now scroll past the ever-briefer items on COVID out of boredom. Other concerns, in particular the Russian invasion of Ukraine and the accompanying global inflation, have taken over the headlines. It is tempting for us, survivors of the pandemic, to conclude that we have won: Humans 1 – Virus 0. In this apparently changed landscape, what is the relevance of this volume?

No matter what the future holds (whether this is indeed the beginning of the end or just a pause), the chronicles collected in this book have undoubted value as historical documents. They provide windows into irreducible, individual lifeworlds in 2020 and 2021, during a time of great global shake-up. They capture this evanescent moment for Romanies, revealing the intimacy and immediacy of the COVID-19 world crisis as a socially constructed event, embedded in and reproducing specific patterns of inequality and structural harm. They tell about the imprints left by generations-long experiences of marginalization, and also about Romani forms of agency and ethics of care: in the voices and experiences of the chroniclers we find abundant traces of hardship and vulnerability, but also much evidence of resilience, creativity, and resistance. Lastly, the chronicles speak also about a moment in the development of academia, and in particular of scholarship on Romani lives.

We believe that the pandemic will continue in the form of transformed policy approaches, new views of and practices around danger and contagion, and of course in the form of economic consequences. Indeed, we would argue that for the Romani people whose lives are narrated in this volume, the pandemic has not and cannot finish in yet another sense. We explained in the Introduction that the global crisis settled upon the historical experiences of everyday routinized crisis for Romanies: these experiences continue, and they continue to deteriorate, and contributors to the volume are already documenting some of the ways in which Romani lives are currently being damaged by the consequences of pandemic policies and management.

In Spain, for example, the introduction of the Minimum Life Income (*Ingreso Mínimo Vital*) in June 2020 has proven particularly complex. A form of state-guaranteed basic income, it was presented by the left-wing government as a fast, decisive step to tackle the damage that the lockdown was doing to the most vulnerable families, many of them Gitano. The income would level out the disparities in support provided for the poor by the different regional governments, and would supplement rather than replace existing help. This was the government not just addressing the health crisis but devising much-needed fixes for enduring problems: the income was here to stay. Yet the regional authorities were quick to reduce their welfare budgets, and two years on the system continues to suffer crippling practical problems. Thousands of the poorest Spaniards, the same ones who were hit particularly severely by the lockdowns, have been without any state support at all for months at a time throughout 2020, 2021, and 2022. Many have been asked to return payments issued in error. The Gitana community mediators who describe in the Spanish chronicles their harrowing difficulties supporting families during the first lockdown are now struggling to help them survive the debacle of the Minimum Life Income. This is a textbook example of necropolitics.

Thus, whether or not the pandemic is over—whether or not more variants, waves, and mandates appear— there is no doubt that scholars studying Romani lives will have to be attentive to how its ripples mold individuals, families, and communities for decades to come. And, as time passes and knowledge about the pandemic evolves, we very much hope that the testimonies gathered in this volume will serve as a useful starting point for comparison, debate, and critique.

The pandemic has brought into sharp focus the uncertainty that forms the ground on which lives and societies exist, and therefore also the precarity of knowledge. This awareness that understanding, of the pandemic and of human life, is always being produced and therefore always unstable, was central to our ethos when planning and shepherding the *Chronicles*. We were hoping to make the inescapable experience of Romani oppression and marginalization as visible as possible, whilst also foregrounding the moments, standpoints, and positions from which each of the chroniclers knows and speaks. We believe that the significance of this volume lies not just in its content but in its form and method.

We conceived the method of the chronicles as a concrete, practical attempt to give primacy to subjectivity, embodied experience, and witnessing in understanding the pandemic—as an experiment that might work, or not. We were also keen to foreground the analytical, critical contributions of non-academics to debate and to understanding—of people whose experiences are often disregarded as non-analytical, who tend to be considered research objects rather than partners. And so we invited contributors from a wide variety of backgrounds to join our project, and we encouraged the coordinators of each section to devise flexible, collaborative ways of working with authors.

We wanted to see what a conversational, even cacophonic collection of voices (scholarly and not, Romani and non-Romani) might generate. We hoped to be able to include experimental pieces by writers who had not published before—indeed, who had never even contemplated writing—and we were delighted that so many were willing to join us. Whilst guiding our contributors and editing their pieces with them, we encouraged each to write according to their own style, strengths, and position—hence the tremendous diversity of the chronicles. Lastly, we wanted to make space for contrast, contradictions, and dissent, because we knew that Romani experiences of and perspectives on the pandemic are too varied and complex to be captured through the assertive, monolithic discourses so favored by academia.

As editors, we encountered difficulties, and these throw light on the process of collaborative work, its potentials, and its limits and drawbacks. We found that coordinating such a large project, with so many contributors and only one native English speaker, was very time consuming. Even though we set clear goals and deadlines, maintaining synchronicity among thirty-seven contributors turned out to be impossible: in our families, communities, and workplaces we were all dealing with personal losses and problems brought about by the pandemic, all of which followed their own temporalities and rhythms. The fact that many of the chroniclers had never written for academia and that others had never conceived of writing for an audience at all, whilst an undoubted strength of the book, also posed challenges: the collaborative editorial process was considerably lengthier and more detailed than is usual in academic writing, and more invasive and demanding for authors, involving ongoing work with each of them as they produced successive drafts. As we collaborated with the contributors—as their translators, facilitators, guides, and copy editors—we were very aware of the practical and aesthetic constraints that shape publishing, of the ways these constraints build barriers that keep certain groups out. We did our best to balance the need to encourage contributors to develop their own style as authors (to speak with their own distinctive voices and from their own standpoints), with the necessity of making texts clear, accessible, and readable for the audience. As non-Romani editors of a book about Romani experience, we knew that these tensions and processes were not just procedural or stylistic but political.

At times we struggled with our aim to provide space for voices or perspectives we disagreed with. We often found ourselves veering towards the construction of homogeneous, authoritative accounts of the academic kind we were both so familiar with. And, because the project took a relatively long time to finish and the pandemic landscape changed so fast, we were constantly tempted to review our interpretations and those of our contributors, rather than accepting them as emerging from particular spaces and moments. Additionally, many of our contributors are non-English speakers who will not be able to read the book as a whole, thereby limiting the extent to which the volume functions as a conversation for those who have participated in it, as opposed to the wider audience.

We are sure that these challenges have shaped *Romani Chronicles of COVID-19* and are visible to readers. From the start our intention was that any limitations or failures of the book, as much as any accomplishments, would spark debate. Now that the book is finally about to be published, we hope that that it will inspire others to experiment in similar ways.

Paloma Gay y Blasco teaches social anthropology at the University of St Andrews in Scotland. She has authored books and articles on ethnographic methods, collaborative anthropology, and Romani issues, including, with Liria Hernández, *Writing Friendship: A Reciprocal Ethnography* (Palgrave Macmillan, 2020).

Martin Fotta is a researcher at the Institute of Ethnology, Czech Academy of Sciences. He is the author of *From Itinerant Trade to Moneylending in the Era of Financial Inclusion* (Palgrave Macmillan, 2018). His current work explores transformations across the Romani diaspora of the Lusophone South Atlantic region.

Index

❊ ❊ ❊

Page numbers with the letter "n" indicate a reference in the chapter-end notes.

abandoning urban centers, 13, 132
ABC (Spanish broadsheet), 7
Abu Ghosh, Yasar, 13, 18–19, 23, 24, 259–268
AC (After COVID), 17–18
access to public space, 177
access to Wi-Fi, 20, 39. *See also* Internet; social media
activism, 22, 261–66
agency, 260
Albert, Gwendolyn (Gwen), 20, 247, 249n7, 255, 270–76
Alicante, 16
Almeida, Marcelo de, 106
Alston, Philip, 12, 36
Alves, Rogério, 106
Amare Roma. *See* Bergitka Roma
Amazonian rainforest, 95, 130
anti-Gitano discourses, 84–86
anti-mask protesters, 86
anti-Roma riots, 206n5
anti-science attitudes, 113
antigypsy laws, 138, 140–41
antigypsyism, 5–6, 10–11, 21, 105–7, 119, 205
antigypsyist assumptions, 7
antisocial gregariousness, 7
antivaxxers, 274
APROIDEG, 71
Aragón Martín, Beatriz, 9, 12, 40

Argentina, 122–23
Artemisa Network, 44–45, 46, 47–48
Arza Porras, Javier, 70, 73
Asociación Barró, 44–45, 47–49
Atlas of Roma Communities (MVSR), 147n3
authority figures, 199
auto-ethnography, 210, 237–38
Autonomous Federation of Gitano Associations of the Valencian Community (FAGA), 69–75
Ayala Rubio, Ariadna, 36–37

Bahia state, Brazil, 93–94; Public Prosecutor's Office (MPB), 99n21
Baláž ová, Aurélie, 249
banking apps, 114
"Da Barraca aos Livros" bulletins, 120
BC (Before COVID), 17
Belák, Andrej, 12, 24, 154, 160–61, 192–201
Beláková, Magdalena, 175
belonging, 234
Bergitka Roma, 206, 217
Betim, Brazil, 112
the Bible, 83–84
biopower (Foucault), 140
biosecurity preoccupations, 21
Black Brazilians, 94, 128
Black Lives Matter, 22
Blaháková, Zuzana, 179
Blanchot, Maurice, 17
Bolsa Família Program, 114–15

Bolsonarism, 136, 141
Bolsonaro, Jair, 10, 11, 94–95, 96, 128, 141
"bordering," 216
borders closing, 221–22
"Da Borra do Café," 120
Bourdieu, Pierre, 253n23
Brasil de Fato, 121
Brazil, 22; access to emergency relief, 141–42; Advisory Note 002 (Ministry of Health), 122; antigypsy laws, 138, 140–41; Black people, 94, 128; central government approaches, 94; colonialism, 11, 136, 138–39; commodification-medicalization processes, 138; countryside municipalities, 104–5; COVID-19 deaths, 94; COVID-19 prevention, 136; Decree 6040 (2007), 141; emergency aid, 113–14, 128–29; ethnic minorities, 11, 98, 132, 136, 139; Federal Constitution 1988, 99; health policies, 96; healthcare, 131; hygiene, 97, 98; impact of COVID-19, 95; informal workers, 97; Law no. 14.021, 141–42; military police, 106–7, 111; Ministry of Health, 99, 122, 129; Ministry of Women, Family, and Human Rights, 122; mismanagement of pandemic, 10, 20, 96–97, 141–42; National Comprehensive Health Care Policy for Cigano/Romani People, 96; National Policy of Traditional People and Communities, 96; necropolitics, 135–142; racist policies, 118, 141; "Recomendação N° 035" (National Health Council), 122n11; Romani population, 95–96; SEPPIR, 117–18; Sistema Único de Saúde (SUS), 96, 97, 121–22; SNPIR, 106, 107; state violence, 11; stigmatization of difference, 94; trachoma eye disease, 93; "traditional peoples and communities," 94–95, 99, 118; vaccination programs, 112–13. *See also* Calon Romanies; Ciganos
Brazilian Association of Collective Health (ABRASCO), 142
Brazilian chroniclers, 20

Brexit, 13, 19, 216–17. *See also* UK
Brož, Míra, 260
Bučková, Andrea, 147, 148, 187n7
Bulgaria, 6–7
Bystriny networking organization, 175

Caduff, Carlo, 21
Caldas, Valdinalva Barbosa dos Santos ("Nalva"), 95, 98, 99, 110, 111–13
Calon Romanies, 95–96, 104–7; avoiding urban centers, 13, 99; expelled from municipalities, 94; extermination, 140; isolating, 97, 131; leaders (*chefes*), 105, 106; Minas Gerais, 113–15; mortuary rites and rituals, 137–38; movement for social justice, 99–100. *See also* Brazil; Ciganos
Caloninity (*calonidade*), 136
Campos, Juliana Miranda Soares, 16, 98, 99–100, 110, 113–15
Cañada Real, 12, 19, 33–34, 40, 53–54, 60–66. *See also* Gitanos; Spain
caregiving, 14
Carmona, Gregorio "Gory," 10, 40, 81–87
"Carousel," 148–49
Carpathian Roma. *See* Bergitka Roma
Carrón, José, 70
Catalan Association of Young Gitanos of Gracia, 71
catch-22 situations, 11
Celebryta, 231, 236
Célia (Calin, Brazil), 131
Central European Romanies, 13–14
challenging state directives, 22
children: xii, 11, 16, 18–20, 33, 35, 36, 37, 39, 45, 46, 47, 50, 52, 54-6, 57, 58n1, 60, 64, 69, 72, 106, 111, 163, 166, 168, 169, 179, 185, 187, 225, 252, 253, 256n23, 272, development of, 74–75; impact on in SELs, 253; "special schools," 252–53; taking by English authorities, 166, 171n2
Chomutov, Czech Republic, 251
Christianity, 83–84
chroniclers, 1–5, 21, 287–88
chronicles: as method, ix, xi, xii, 2, 5, 17, 24, 39, 210, 254, 287–288; as historical documents, 5, 285

churches, 13, 46–47, 81
"*Uma Cigana Me Contou*" interviews, 120
"Cigano-COVIDophobia," 106
Cigano Peoples Week, 118
ciganofobia. *See* antigypsyism
Ciganos, 10; Brazil, 95; ethnocultural recognition, 117; expulsion of families, 121; family structure, 137; funeral rituals, 135–36; healthcare, 121–22; informal commercial work, 128; and list to receive vaccines, 99; located in the "margins," 128; Minas Gerais, 112; negative stereotypes, 129; nuclear families, 104; pandemic emergency aid, 114; pandemic prevention campaigns, 112; population, 95; Portuguese colonialist policies, 138; portrayed as public health risk, 98, 107; small-scale trading, 104; social and economic vulnerability, 131; social tragedy, 142; trachoma eye disease, 93–94; "traditional peoples and communities," 118; Vitória da Conquista, 99n21. *See also* Brazil; Calon Romanies
collaboration (collaborative methods), 5, 23, 24, 26n40, 39, 153, 165, 207, 287–88
collective health preservation, 105
collective lives, 59–60, 66
colonial historical revisionism, 141
Commission on Human Rights of the Buenos Aires City Legislature, 123
Communist period, 151n14
community quarantines, 21–22, 149–150, 183–84, 185–86. *See also* personal quarantines; quarantining
compulsory quarantine, 6
Comunidad Valenciana, 69, 71
concentration camps, 9, 188–89
continuous reporting system, 195–96
cooking for homeless, 264–65
COVID-19 denialism, 86, 87, 271, 273–74
COVID-19 pandemic: contracting COVID, 111–12, 129–131, 240; exacerbating inequalities, 224–25; health impacts, 151–52; helping others, 263–64; immunity hoaxes, 188; Roma in SELs, 251; as a socially constructed event, 285; as a trial from God, 83–84, 87; vulnerability of Romanies, 8–9, 173–74, 183. *See also* first wave; second wave
critical Romani studies, 4–5
Cruz das Armas, João Pessoa, Brazil, 130–31
Cruz-Neto, Otávio, 136, 139–140
cultural mediators, 21, 56
"culture" and "customs," 8
Czech Government Council on Romani Minority Affairs, 274
Czech Republic (Czechia): Agency for Social Inclusion, 252; "The best in COVID," 249; closing borders, 271–72; denialism, 271; doctors refusing to treat, 251; education system, 253n23; emergency powers, 272; inattention to plight of Roma, 249; National Institute of Public Health, 250; online teaching, 252–53; poverty, 251–52; repression, 272; Roma population, 247, 251–52; segregated schools, 252–53; social assistance, 264; social exclusion, 251–52; state of emergency, 271; State of the Roma Minority Report 2019, 251–52; vaccinations, 274–75
Czech School Inspectorate (CSI), 253

"*Da Barraca aos Livros*" bulletins, 120
"*Da Borra do Café*," 120
data and analysis of Western scholarship, 23
Davies, Thom, 34
deaths: Calon Philosophy, 137–39; COVID-19, 151–52; doctors refusing care, 251; funeral rituals, 135–36; resisting standards of adequate behavior, 8; Slovakia, 160
debts, 18–19, 264
decolonizing academic knowledge, 4–5
degeš ("low-life"), 262
democratic governance, 20
denialism, 86, 87, 271, 273–74
determinants of poor health, 193–95, *194*, 250–52
D.H. and Others v. the Czech Republic (No. 57325/00, ECHR), 252

Dia Nacional do Cigano (Romani National Day), 117, 121, 141
dialects and languages, 234, 236, 241
Díaz Ayuso, Isabel, 86
digital divide, 55–56. *See also* Internet
Digital Easter 2020, 237–240
digital kinning, 230
digitalization of everyday life, 14, 230, 232
disciplinary measures, 8
discussion groups, 232
disinformation, 273–74
Dobrá Vôľa, Slovakia, 159–160
doctors refusing care, 251
Dois Vizinhos, Paraná, Brazil, 105
dororidade, 132
Dubská Street, Teplice, 261
dumpling challenge, 237
Dužda, Jan, 250–51

e-ethnography, 209–10
"*e-Romanipen*" (Szewczyk), 234
East European Romanies, 13–14, 19
Easter Sunday 2020, 237–240
economic crisis 2008, 12, 34, 35
economic deterioration, 252
economic mobility, 19. *See also* migration
economic worries, 225
education, 36, 39, 45, 53–57, 252–53. *See also* online learning; schools
educational gap, 19–20
"Egyptian (eye) disease" (trachoma), 93–94
email addresses, 114
emergency aid, 113–14, 128–29, 141–42
enforced immobility, 219. *See also* social isolation
enlightened self-interest, 275
Equi Sastipen Network, 73
Estudos Ciganos WhatsApp group, 121
ethnic boundaries, 234
ethnic minorities, 12, 38, 136, 139
"ethnography without notes" (Okely), 209
ethnoracial discrimination, 105
EU Agency for Fundamental Rights (FRA), 251
EU Settlement Scheme, 216–17

European Commission (EC), 148
European Court of Human Rights (ECHR), 252
Evangelical churches, 45, 46, 56, 81, 87
Evangelical Gitanos, 40, 85, 87. *See also* Pentecostal Christianity
exclusion, 18, 20–21, 98, 129
experience and academic approaches, 3
expulsions, 106–7, 121
extended families, 14
"*extermínio*" politics, 136, 139, 140

face-mask-less partying, 274
Facebook, 120, 178, 179, 220, 232
face masks, 86, 179
FAGA (Federación Autónoma de Asociaciones Gitanas de la Comunidad Valenciana), 69–75
fake news, 7, 141, 189
false accusations, 7
families, 14, 98, 217–222, 237–240. *See also* kinship bonds
family clusters (*turma* camps), 112
family meals, 64
family visits, 221
Fasenfest, David, 17
fears, 163, 188–89
Fiałkowska, Kamila, 24
financial needs, 225
first wave, 2; Cañada Real, 62; Czech Republic, 248; misused data, 197; Poland, 208–9, 223, 226; Slovakia, 148, 165–171; stress and fear of the unknown, 187. *See also* COVID-19 pandemic; second wave
Flaeschen, Hara, 142
Flores Torres, Dulce, 1, 11, 52–54
Florianópolis, Brazil, 127, 128
Floyd, George, 23, 260
folk antigypsyism, 5–6. *See also* antigypsyism
food banks, 56
Fotta, Martin, 24
Foucault, Michel, 140
full-body protective overalls (see also PPE), 161–62
fundraising, 236
funeral rituals, 135–36

Gáborová Kroková, Jana, 178
Gadjos (*gádje,* non-Romani), 168, 206, 207, 208, 233, 234, 267
García Bizárraga, Pilar, 19, 54–56
Gay y Blasco, Paloma, 24, 38, 39, 44–46, 85
Gazeta Medica da Bahia, 93
gendered division of labor, 15
Germany, 220–21
Gitana mediators, 15, 39–40, 44–57
Gitana women, 15–16, 47, 57, 72
Gitano associations, 35, 56
Gitano children: digital divide, 55–56; education and schools, 6, 36, 39, 52–57; prevention strategies, 64; Singular Specific Group (SSG), 54
Gitano churches, 81, 85–86
Gitano Evangelical churches, 7, 13, 53, 81
Gitanos, 6; behaving as citizens, 85; below-average health status, 64; calls for help, 52; caring for the sick, 47, 78–79; compliance, 10–11, 63; death rates, 38; deprivation, 35, 37; discriminatory representation, 87; perceived as non-citizens, 40; familial solidarity, 40–41; family meals, 64; family support, 70, 78–79; impact of state of emergency, 70–73; impact of the lockdowns, 73–75; impact survey, 74–75; "inclusive exclusion," 38; informal economy, 48; isolation, 52; lockdowns, 38–39, 44–46, 52–53; marginalization, 34, 40, 45–46; and the press, 47; projects supporting, 45; religion, 83; since March 2020, 38–39; social exclusion index, 35–36; social mobility, 36; and social norms, 85; Spanish and non-Spanish Romanies, 35; as spreaders of COVID, 40; state aid, 48–50; street vending, 45, 48, 50; subsistence strategies, 38–39; unruliness stereotype, 40, 61, 65, 85, 87. *See also* Cañada Real; Spain
governance potentialities, 21
Government Plenipotentiary for Roma Communities (Slovakia), 187
Gravesend, Kent, 165–66
group affinity, 230

Guarapuava, Brazil, 106
"Gypsy Chases" (*Correrias Ciganas*), 141
Gypsyness, 8–11

Hajská, Markéta, 232
Haraway, Donna, 97
Haro, Spain, 6
health and poverty, 193–95, *194,* 250–52
Health Group of the State Council of the Gitano People, 73
health practitioners, 21
health videos, 174–75
Healthy Regions (Zdravé regióny, Slovakia), 12n19, 151, 159–160, 175, 193, 195–97
helping others, 263–64
Hernández, Liria, 14–15, 40–41, 77–79
hoaxes, 7, 188, 189–190
homeless, cooking for, 264–65
homework, 19, 53–56, 72, 179
housing: Cañada Real, 60; inner-city ghettoes, 6; living conditions, 186; self-isolating in crowded homes, 56; substandard conditions, 250
housing insecurity, 18
Hrustič, Tatiana, 163
Hrustič, Tomáš, 10, 24, 153–54, 165, 173–180
hunts (*Correrias Ciganas*), 141
hygiene, 8, 40; adhering to recommendations, 97; and basic sanitation, 112; Brazil, 97, 141–42. *See also* personal hygiene; public hygiene

Ibirité, Brazil, 111
Iglesia Evangélica de Filadelfia (IEF), 81, 85–86
Iglesias Pérez, Estrella, 16, 48–50
immersion in the field, 209
immunity to infections myth, 151
indebtedness, 18
Indigenous peoples ("*povos indígenas*"), 11, 94–95
"the infected Other," 84–85
influencers, 260. *See also* social media
informal economies, 59; Brazil, 97; Calon Romanies, 105; Cañada Real, 65–66; Gitanos income, 48; street-

and market-vending, 39, 42. *See also* working in lockdowns
Informe sobre la situación (FAGA), 70–71
inner-city ghettoes, 6. *See also* housing
"insidious neglect" scenario, 274
Instagram, 119–120
Instituto PluriBrasil, 105
International Roma Culture Days (Nowa Huta, Poland), 206, 222–23, 240
international travel plans, 274
Internet, 230–37; access to Wi-Fi, 20, 39; Cañada Real, 53–54; digital divide, 55–56; 'meeting place' for minorities, 118; online education, 20, 53–57; and research participants, 209–10; *Romanipen* code, 233, 234; stereotypes, 119; traditional hierarchies of power, 234–35; virtual discussions, 118; virtual relationships, 281–83. *See also* online communications; social media
interventions, 193
intra-community measures, 105
irresponsibility in settlements, 187
isolation, 6. *See also* social isolation

Jehovah's Witnesses, 241
João Pessoa, Paraíba, Brazil, 128, 129, 131
Johnson, Boris, 13
Jóźwiak, Ignacy, 14, 239

Kalderasha Roma, 206
Kaliňák, Petr, 247, 248, 249
Karika, Karel, 264–65
Khetane Platform, 71
kinship bonds, 7, 14. *See also* families
"kinship gatherings," 7
Koky, Richard, 163
Kokyová, Iveta, 24, 254–55, 277–284
koronawirusos, 236. *See also* COVID-19 pandemic
Košice, Slovakia, 165, 166
Kotleba, Marian, 175n8
Kumanová, Zuzana, 7, 9, 20, 154

La Parra Casado, Daniel, 73
La Pequeña Villa Church, 81

labor market dynamics, 248–49
Law no. 14.021 (Brazil), 141–42
leaders (*chefes*), 105
leadership, 22
Lešť military area, Slovakia, 188–89
"lifers" (*lifeři*), 260. *See also* social media
living conditions, 186. *See also* housing
lockdowns: digital kinning, 230; online interactions, 209, 235–36; Poland, 217, 219–221, 223–24
loneliness, 254, 282–83
Lovari Roma, 206
Luník IX, Slovakia, 166

Madrid, 54–55, 82, 86
making a good life, 14
Maláčová, Jana, 264
Manusha (organization), 249
marginalization, 2, 3, 4, 6, 9, 14, 19, 24, 34, 35, 37, 40, 45, 46, 66, 75, 154, 185, 285
marginalized people of color (US), 272–73
Marques Gonçalves, Gabriela, 22, 99, 119, 121
Martín-Barbero, Jesús, 118, 123
Martins, José, 135
Martins Júnior, José, 135
mask wearing, 13
Mato Grosso, Brazil, 135
Matovič, Igor, 148, 168
Mattedi, Marcos Antonio, 137
Maxwell's demon, 253n23
Mayoral Silva, Francisca, 20, 56–57
Mayoral Silva, Manuela, 10, 15, 16
Mbembe, Achille, 11, 98, 130, 136, 139–140
"Media and Romani Communities" (Miklos, Marques, and Silva Júnior), 121
media reporting, 47, 250
mediators, 20, 44–57, 115; community mediators, 44–45; cultural mediators, 56; health mediators, 46; social mediators, 52
meeting people, 274
messaging apps, 230
methodological polytheism, 254

migration, 205–7, 217–18. *See also* economic mobility; transnational circulation
Miker, Jozef (Jožka), 18–19, 22, 251, 252, 254, 259–268
Miklos, Aline, 22, 95, 99, 119–120, 121
Mikulecký, Viktor, 251
Milanezi, Jaciane, 129
Military Police (*Polícia Militar*, Brazil), 106–7, 111
Minas Gerais, Brazil, 99, 112
Minayo, Maria Cecília de S., 136, 139–140
Minimum Life Income (*Ingreso Mínimo Vital*), 286
Ministry of Health (Brazil), 99, 122, 129
Ministry of Health (MoH, Slovakia), 175, 193, 195, 196–97; Pandemic Commission, 196
Ministry of Women, Family, and Human Rights (Brazil), 122
Mirga-Wójtowicz, Elżbieta, 14, 24, 222–23, 238
mistrusting authorities, 275
misused data, 197
Mižigárová, Alžbeta "Hal'ka," 12n19, 21–22, 153, 159–164
Mława, Poland, 206
mobile apps, 114, 128–29
mobilities and immobilities, 206–7
Molek, Peter, 163
Montañés Jiménez, Antonio, 40, 80–87
Montaño García, Fernanda, 15–16, 50–51
Montoya, Celia, 120
mood swings, 162
mortuary rites and rituals, 137–38. *See also* deaths
Mota, Claudio, 106
mourning rituals, 15
music festivals, 222–23
Muzyk ('the musician'), 236

nacje, 86. *See also* Polish Roma
National Comprehensive Health Care Policy for Cigano/Romani People (Brazil), 96, 121–22
National Health Council (Brazil), 122
National Institute of Public Health (Czechia), 250

National Plan to Address the Covid-19 Pandemic (Frente Pela Vida), 142
National Policy of Traditional People and Communities (Brazil), 96
"National Policy on Sustainable Development of Traditional Peoples and Communities" decree (Brazil), 118
National Policy Plan for Cigano Peoples (Brazil), 118
"national Roma inclusion" projects (EC), 148
National Secretariat for Human Rights (Argentina), 123
National Secretariat of Policies for the Promotion of Racial Equality (SNPIR, Brazil), 106, 107
necropolitics, 4, 11, 13, 15, 98, 128, 132, 135–142, 251, 286
necropower, 140
"the new normal," 17, 18, 240–41
nomadism, 8
Nordestinas, 128n2
Nowa Huta, Kraków, Poland, 206, 222–23, 240
nuclear families, 104

Office of the Plenipotentiary of the Government of the Slovak Republic for Roma Communities, 186n4
Okely, Judith, 209
online challenges, 237
online communications, 209, 234. *See also* Internet; social media
online education, 20, 53–57
online games, 236
online information, 119
online initiatives, 241
online learning. *See also* education; schools
online schooling, 252–53
online shopping, 233
onlineization, 229, 232
#OrgulhoRomani collective, 99, 118–120, 122, 123–24
OSPOD, 249
Ostrava region, Czech Republic, 249
over-policing, 185
overintensive sociability, 8

paćiwali Romnija, 233
palmistry (*quiromancia*), 105
Pan American Health Organization, 122–23
Pandemic Commission (Slovakia), 185, 196
pandemic (im)mobility, 226
pandemic vulnerability, 13
Paraíba, Brazil, 129, 132
Paraná Council of Indigenous Peoples and Traditional Communities, 107
Paraná state, Brazil, 105
parents: educational competence, 20; remote teaching, 253
Partido Popular, 86
past and present harm, 10
Patakyová, Mária, 183
"pendlers" (cross-border commuters), 187
Pentecostal Christianity, 80, 83–84, 87. *See also* Evangelical Gitanos
People in Need (Člověk v tísni), 253
People in Peril (Človek v ohrození), 175
"People's Party Our Slovakia," 175
La Pequeña Villa Church, 81
Pereira, Abigail, 135
Pereira, Ana Paula, 137
Pereira, Antônio, 135
peripatetic traders, 105. *See also* informal economies
personal hygiene, 8, 112, 159, 161, 174–75, 187. *See also* hygiene
personal protective equipment (PPE), 161-162, 176
personal quarantines, 277–284. *See also* community quarantines; quarantining
Pete and wolfdog story, 266
Peter, Albín, 13–14, 149, 153, 165–171
physical separation, 14
Piedade, Vilma, 132
Pigatto, Fernando Zasso, 122
"Plan for addressing COVID-19 in marginalized Roma communities" (UVZS), 186
Polák, Kuba (Jakub), 261–62
Poland: lockdowns, 219–221; social media, 231; #*stayhome* campaign, 236; summer 2020, 222–23; temporary migrants, 224; "zero tolerance" policy, 209
Polish Roma: cultures intersecting on internet, 232–33; digital kinning, 14, 230; dumpling challenge, 237; group cohesiveness and group identity, 207; live streamed sales, 233; migration, 205–7, 217–19; *nacje*, 206; social media and internet, 229–241; transnational living research, 207–8; use of Polish and Romani languages, 233; views on UK, 13, 220
Polish Roma families, 215–220
Polish-Romani dialects, 236
politics of death. *See* "necropolitics" (Mbembe)
"the politics of indifference" (Davies), 34
Pollák, Peter, 148, 162, 168
Polska Roma, 206, 217
Portugal, 119, 138
post-pandemic future, 16–17
poverty: Czechia, 251–52; determinants of poor health, 193–95, *194*, 250–52; and underemployment, 9
"*o povo cigano*" (Romani people), 94–95
"*Povo do Biráco*" (Biraco's people), 105–6
"*povos indígenas*" (Indigenous peoples), 11, 94–95
pre-pandemic structural conditions, 250
pro-Roma activists, 197–98
protecting vulnerable inhabitants, 185
"protective asphyxiation," 254
Public Health Authority (Slovakia), 186
public hygiene, 94, 98. *See also* hygiene
public services, 61, 148n5
punitive containment, 6–7

quarantine centers, 9, 149, 167–171, 188–89
quarantine zones, 149
quarantining, 6, 222, 272. *See also* community quarantines; personal quarantines
quilombolas (maroons), 94

racial segregation, 19
racialization, 21

racism, 4, 8, 12, 16, 18, 22-23, 34, 56, 93-101, 112, 118-22, 129, 130, 132, 141, 154, 173, 180, 195, 199, 207
"Recomendação Nº 035" (Pigatto, National Health Council), 122
Recommendations Regarding COVID-19 for Municipalities with Marginalized Roma Communities (MoH), 197
Red Cross relief packages, 16
refugee camps, 6
Região Sul do Brasil, 104, 121
religious ceremonies, 231
religious institutions, 241
remote teaching, 253
Renta Mínima de Inserción (RMI), 48, 82
Report on the State of the Romani Minority 2020 (Czech Republic), 275
responsible behavior, 10, 187
returning home, 221-22, 224
reverse colonialism, 141
Ribeiro da Silva, Raymundo, 93
Rio Grande do Norte, Brazil, 129, 131
Rio Grande do Sul, Brazil, 105
Rodriguez Camacho, María Félix, 16, 38, 39-40, 69-75, 85
ROI (Roma Civic Initiative), 262
Rolândia municipality, Paraná, Brazil, 106-7
Roma ethnicity, 199
Roma-Gadjo research teams, 208
Roma Lives Matter, 23, 266-68
"Roma Plenipotentiary" (RP), 148
Roma/Romanies: compliance, 10; compliance and exclusion, 11; defined by non-Romanies, 177; denied individuality, 7-8; disempowerment, 4; diversity of living conditions, 186; escaping state control measures, 150; isolation, exclusion and confinement, 6; as outsiders, 273; as responsible citizens, 10; spreading the virus, 7; stereotyping, 5-7; suffering as unfortunate but predictable, 8-9; survival and mutual protection, 14; symbolic boundaries with Gadje, 234
Roma Support Group (NGO), 216
Romani dialects and languages, 234, 236, 241

Romani Fairy Tales (Romane paramisa), 179
Romani National Day (*Dia Nacional do Cigano*), 117, 121, 141
"Romani peoples," 96
Romani rights, 99
Romanian Romanies, 60
Romanipen, 14, 218-220, 232-35
Romea.cz, 271
Rousseff, Dilma, 141
Rusnáková, Jurina, 7, 9, 20, 154, 187

Santos, Vaninalva, 16
São Pedro Calon encampment, 110-11
SARV-Cov infection, 61n7
schizophrenia, 280
school support workers, 21
schools: racial segregation, 19; Spain, 46, 52-56. *See also* education; online learning
second wave, 2; community quarantines, 150; Czechia, 249, 270; Poland, 208-9; poorly managed community quarantines, 197; Slovakia, 12n19, 190, 196-97. *See also* COVID-19 pandemic; first wave
Secretariado Gitano, 36
segregated Roma, 10, 12, 147-152, 192-99, *194*
segregated schools, 6, 19, 54, 187, 252-53
segregation, 5, 6, 10, 12, 18, 19, 21, 36, 37, 54, 61, 62, 115n4, 148, 149, 150-2, 154, 159-164, 173, 174, 176, 177, 179, 184, 187, 192-99, 272
self-help activities, 178
self-isolating in crowded homes, 56
SELs (socially excluded localities), 247, 248, 250; economic deterioration, 252; impact on children, 253; public health and hygiene, 250
Śero Rom (Head of the Roma), 235
sewerage, 148n5
shared standards of adequate behavior, 8-9
Shimura, Igor, 22, 98, 99, 104-8
shopping sprees, 178
Silva Júnior, Aluízio de Azevedo, 10, 22, 95, 98, 99, 119, 121, 135

Silva, Luis Inácio Lula da, 141
Silva, Maria José "Zeza," 13, 127–28, 130
Sistema Único de Saúde (SUS, Brazil), 96, 97, 121–22
situated knowledges, 97
Slovak Academy of Sciences, 187
Slovak National Roma Inclusion's Action Plans, 193
Slovak National Roma Integration Strategy (NRIS), 148n9
Slovak Public Defender of Rights, 272
Slovak Television, 179
Slovakia: anti-corruption protests, 195n7; Central Crisis Staff, 177; challenges to the state, 185–86; coercive dimensions of state care, 8; community quarantines, 183–86; conceptualization of Roma ethnicity, 199; COVID-19 deaths, 151–52; COVID-19 information campaign, 174–75; determinants of the poor health, 193–95, *194*; education, 19–20; fear of Roma, 149; forcefully quarantine, 8; Healthy Communities project, 193; Healthy Regions (Zdravé regióny), 12n19, 151, 159–160, 175, 193, 195–97; Ministry of Health (MoH), 175, 193, 195, 196–97; mortality rates, 160; negative depictions of Roma, 186–87; Pandemic Commission, 185, 196; proactive authorities, 273; Public Health Authority, 186; quarantine centers, 9, 149; Roma as a threat, 184–88; Roma people, 147–48; Roma plenipotentiary, 187, 195n7, 196n9; Romani women, 6; Romanies returning to, 166; SARS-CoV-2 pandemic, 148; segregated Romani settlements, 12, 148-150; social distancing measures, 10; spontaneous civic initiatives, 176; targeted testing, 163n5; testing for COVID, 148–150, 272; unequal power distribution, 176–77
slow harm, 4, 9, 13
slow death, 13

slums, 6, 10
small-scale trading, 104
Soares, Maria Jane, 131
Sobrance, Slovakia, 165, 166
social control, 233n10
"social death," 254, 261
social distancing: Britain, 13; in camps (Brazil), 111; Poland, 220–21, 229; "protective asphyxiation," 254; Slovakia, 10; street- and market-vending, 39
social exclusion, 74, 122, 136
social exclusion index, 35, 247n3, 251–52
social isolation, 35, 98, 99, 123, 207
social media: care for family and community, 232; fake accounts, 233; fake news and false accusations, 7; influencers "lifers" (*lifeři*), 260; kinship ties, 14; and *paćiwali Romni*, 233; Polish Roma, 230–34; religious ceremonies, 231; Roma groups, 210; sharing advice, 16; tools for surveillance, 235; using for trade, 233; virtual tools and platforms, 99; women, 233–34; and young people, 234, 235. *See also* Internet
social mobility, 36
social networks, 130
social norms, 63
social transformation, 4
social workers, 48–50
socioeconomic impacts, 252
Somatosphere website, 38
South Region of Brazil (*Região Sul do Brasil*), 104, 121
Souza, Edilma do Nascimento, 12, 13, 22, 98, 99, 128–133
Spain: anti-mask protesters, 86; austerity policies, 12, 36–37; conservative political actors, 86; COVID-19 deniers, 86; divided and unequal society, 37; education, 19–20; Minimum Income for Integration (RMI), 48, 49, 50, 82; Minimum Life Income, 286; Romani communities pre-pandemic, 35–38; scapegoating discourses, 84–85; segregated schools, 54; social services,

48–50; state approaches to Gitanos, 36–38, 40; state of emergency, 38, 46; storm Filomena, 34. *See also* Cañada Real; Gitanos
Spanish media, 47, 85
SPD (*Svoboda a přímá demokracie*), 264
"special schools," 252
Special Secretariat for Policies Promoting Racial Equality and Human Rights (SEPPIR, Brazil), 117–18
Spišské Vlachy, Slovakia, 160
spontaneous information campaigns, 177–78
SSG (Singular Specific Group), 54. *See also* Gitano children
Stará Drozd'árna, 261
Stará L'ubovňa, 167–171
State of the Roma Minority Report 2019 (Czech Republic), 251–52
#stayhome campaign, 236
stigmatization, 94, 187–88
storm Filomena, 34
street-based economic activities, 38
structural-health perspectives, 139
structural inequalities, 9
structural violence, 4, 13, 18, 34
Styrkacz, Sonia, 220, 221, 225
subalternity, 132–33
super-spreader events, 177
surveys, 187
symbolic power asymmetries, 180
syndemics, syndemic, 13, 250
systemic racism. *See* racism
Szandor (Polish Roma), 217–19
Szewczyk, Monika, 14, 234, 238

Tala, 216, 217–220, 222, 225
targeted testing, 163n5
temporary migrants, 224
tents, 111, 112
Teplice, Slovakia, 259–261, 264–65, 268
testing, 163, 187–88
Tomáš, Stanislav, 22–23, 260–61, 265, 267
trachoma eye disease, 93–94
"traditional behaviors," 8
"traditional peoples and communities" (Brazil), 94–95, 99, 118

transformed policy approaches, 286
translating information, 179
transnational circulation, 19. *See also* migration
"Transnational lives of Polish Roma" project, 197n12, 217n6
Trebišov, Slovakia, 165, 166
turma camps (family clusters), 112

UK, 13–14, 166, 206, 216–17, 220–21. *See also* Brexit
"The Unbelievable Invisibility Shrouding Cigano Peoples" (Flaeschen), 142
uncertainty of lives and society, 286–87
unequal power distribution, 177
Unified Health System, Brazil. *See Sistema Único de Saúde* (SUS, Brazil)
United Nations Office of the High Commissioner for Human Rights (OHCHR), 33
United States, 272–73
university-based research, 4
urgency, lack of, 12

vaccination passes, 21
vaccinations: Brazil, 99, 112–13; Czechia, 274–75
Valencian Community. *See* Comunidad Valenciana
Vallecas, Madrid, 40
Vaňová, Jarmila, 175
videos, 236–37
vilification of non-hegemonic modes of relating and being, 94
Villaverde Alto, Madrid, 40
Villaverde, Madrid, 37, 82
virtual discussions, 118
virtual relationships, 281–83
virtual tools and platforms, 99. *See also* Internet; social media
Visegrád Four countries, 248–49
Vitória da Conquista, Brazil, 99n21
Volný, Lubomír, 266

water supplies, 148n5
Weintraub, Abraham, 94–95
WhatsApp groups, 72

"White" hegemony, 180. *See also* racism
Wi-Fi, 20, 39. *See also* Internet; social media
witness, witnessing, i, 2, 4, 25n1, 287
women, 15–16, 99–100, 233–34
Workers' Party (Brazil), 141
"working empirically," 193
working in lockdowns, 223–24. *See also* informal economies
"working inclusively," 195

"working openly," 193–95
writing styles, 3

Zdravé regióny (Healthy Regions). *See* Healthy Regions (Zdravé regióny, Slovakia)
Žehra, Slovakia, 153, 159–164
ZOR—Asociación por los derechos del pueblo Gitano/Romani, 122–23

www.ingramcontent.com/pod-product-compliance
Lightning Source LLC
Chambersburg PA
CBHW070910030426
42336CB00014BA/2355